Atomic Friends

Atomic Friends

How America Deals with Nuclear-Armed Allies

Zachary Keck

ROWMAN & LITTLEFIELD
Lanham • Boulder • New York • London

Published by Rowman & Littlefield
An imprint of The Rowman & Littlefield Publishing Group, Inc.
4501 Forbes Boulevard, Suite 200, Lanham, Maryland 20706
www.rowman.com

86-90 Paul Street, London EC2A 4NE

Copyright © 2022 by The Rowman & Littlefield Publishing Group, Inc.

All rights reserved. No part of this book may be reproduced in any form or by any electronic or mechanical means, including information storage and retrieval systems, without written permission from the publisher, except by a reviewer who may quote passages in a review.

British Library Cataloguing in Publication Information Available

Library of Congress Cataloging-in-Publication Data

Names: Keck, Zachary, author.
Title: Atomic friends: how America deals with nuclear-armed allies / Zachary Keck.
Other titles: How America deals with nuclear-armed allies
Description: Lanham: Rowman & Littlefield Publishers, [2022] | Includes bibliographical references and index.
Identifiers: LCCN 2022025381 (print) | LCCN 2022025382 (ebook) | ISBN 9781538169704 (cloth) | ISBN 9781538169711 (paperback) | ISBN 9781538169728 (epub)
Subjects: LCSH: Nuclear weapons—Government policy—United States. |Nuclear arms control—Government policy—United States. | Nuclear nonproliferation—Government policy—United States. | Nuclear weapons—Political aspects. | Nuclear weapons—GreatBritain—History—20th century—Case studies. | Nuclear weapons—France—History—20th century—Case studies. | Nuclear weapons—Israel—History—20th century—Case studies. | Nuclear weapons—Pakistan—History—20th century—Case studies. | Security, International. | United States—Military relations—20th century.
Classification: LCC UA23 .K38465 2022 (print) | LCC UA23 (ebook) | DDC 341.7/34—dc23/eng/20220603
LC record available at https://lccn.loc.gov/2022025381
LC ebook record available at https://lccn.loc.gov/2022025382

Contents

Foreword *Graham T. Allison*	vii
Acknowledgments	ix
Chapter 1: Introduction	1
PART I: ALLIES	**35**
Chapter 2: The Ultimate Betrayal (Britain, 1939–1946)	35
Chapter 3: Stuck in the Mud (Britain, 1947–1955)	55
Chapter 4: Full Cooperation at Last (Britain, 1956–1962)	69
Chapter 5: A Bomb Is Born (France, 1945–1960)	83
Chapter 6: The General's Bomb (France, 1961–1975)	101
PART II: PARTNERS	**131**
Chapter 7: A Nuclear Cat and Mouse (Israel, 1950s–1963)	131
Chapter 8: The Bomb Which Shall Not Be Named (Israel, 1963–1979)	153
Chapter 9: The Bomb from Hell (Pakistan, 1973–1990)	181
Chapter 10: Pandora's Box (Pakistan, 1990–Present)	205
Chapter 11: Conclusion	235

Bibliography 255
Index 269
About the Author 285

Foreword

Graham T. Allison

It is sometimes said that most Americans live in "the United States of Amnesia." Less widely recognized is how many American policymakers live there too. Over the course of my career, I have come to recognize the crucial importance in American foreign policy of what my colleague Niall Ferguson has called the history deficit: the fact that key decision makers know alarmingly little, not just of other countries' pasts but also of their own.

In 2016, Ferguson and I sought to call attention to this deficit by launching the Applied History Project. Mainstream historians begin with a past event or era and attempt to provide an account of what happened and why. Applied historians begin with a current choice or predicament and attempt to analyze the historical record to provide perspective, stimulate imagination, find clues about what is likely to happen, suggest possible policy interventions, and assess probable consequences.

Ferguson and I offer the 2003 US invasion of Iraq as a case in point. As veteran US diplomat Dennis Ross notes in his *Doomed to Succeed* about the US-Israel relationship from Truman to Obama: "[A]lmost no administration's leading figures know the history of what we have done in the Middle East." In 2003, when President George W. Bush chose to topple Saddam Hussein and replace his regime with an elected government that represented the majority of Iraqis, he did not appreciate the difference between Sunni and Shiite Muslims, or the significance of the fact that Saddam's regime was led by a Sunni minority that had suppressed the Shiite majority.

Zach Keck's *Atomic Friends* applies history to clarify one of the most complex and important fields: nuclear statecraft. Keck challenges the conventional wisdom regarding the consequences of "letting allies go nuclear" through case studies of Washington's response to the nuclear ambitions of the United Kingdom, France, Israel, and Pakistan.

Consider the claim made by many analysts that if Japan and South Korea acquired nuclear weapons, this would allow the US to limit its security commitments and risks. However logical in theory that appears, Keck finds that the historical record suggests otherwise: US commitments to defend Britain, France, and other NATO members did not diminish after Britain and France developed nuclear arsenals. Indeed, quite the opposite: the US became even more entangled with its European allies, providing assistance to their nuclear programs. Moreover, after acquiring nuclear weapons, London and Paris contributed less to NATO's conventional military forces—with the result that the risk to the US that a conventional conflict could escalate into a nuclear war has increased. In South Asia, after Pakistan developed a nuclear arsenal, rather than withdrawing from this arena, the US became more involved in the India-Pakistan rivalry because Washington worried incidents and the limited wars the two have fought over decades could lead to a nuclear conflict.

This is just one of many insights from Keck's analysis of historical cases that provides clues to policymakers as they consider the possibility of Seoul, Ankara, Riyadh, Tokyo, or Canberra going nuclear.

As Thucydides famously reflected: "The present, while never repeating the past exactly, must inevitably resemble it. Hence, so must the future." By helping us better understand that past, Keck's analysis offers policymakers valuable guidance for the future.

Acknowledgments

Having lived a blessed life, I want to properly acknowledge everyone for whom I owe a debt of gratitude, but it would double the length of this book. I apologize for anyone I forgot to give proper credit.

I wouldn't be the person I am today without the love and support of my entire family. In particular, I want to thank my parents, Jack and Wendy, to whom this book is dedicated, as well as my sister, brother-in-law, and niece, Lindsey, Adam, and Avery Chalom.

It is no exaggeration to say this book wouldn't have been conceived or written without Henry Sokolski. No single individual outside of the author has had more influence on this book. I continue to be amazed and eternally grateful for your and Amanda's mentorship, support, and friendship. I wrote most of this book while working at the Nonproliferation Policy Education Center, and I received tremendous support from colleagues there, including Bianca Zhang, Leon Whyte, Maya Hardimon, Bailey Martin, and John Spacapan.

I've also benefited greatly from colleagues and bosses I've had throughout my career. These include James Pach, Harry Kazianis, Ankit Panda, Shannon Tiezzi, and Catherine Putz from *The Diplomat*, as well as Rebecca Miller, Robert Cantelmo, Jacob Heilbrunn, Rob Golan-Vilella, Laura Bate, and John Allen Gay from *The National Interest*. At the Belfer Center, I was privileged to work with so many incredible individuals, including Graham Allison, Gary Samore, Adam Siegel, Nathan Levine, Leore Ben-Chorin, Arjun Kapur, Eleanor Freund, Henry Rome, Will Ossoff, Wesley Morgan, Andrew Facini, John Masko, Josh Burek, and Sharon Wilke.

The people I had the pleasure of working with in Congress are too numerous to name but include Brad Sherman, Joaquin Castro, Don MacDonald, Sid Ravishankar, Leah Nodvin, Michelle Schein, Maggie Pillis, Lauren Wolman, Johan Propst, Shervin Taheran, Jaya Khetarpal, Dylan Jones, Patricia Gaviria, Jaya Khetarpal, Svetlana Shkolnivkoa, Matthew McLaughlin, Theresa Lou, Alex Bowe, David Dorfman, Corey Jacobson, Jennifer Rizzoli, Jessica Valdes, John Brodtke, Chas Morrison, Troy Dougall, Mark Erste, Sophie

Mirviss, Sophie Jones, Brandon Mendoza, Paul Kerr, Mary Beth Nikitin, Emma Chanlett-Avery, Drake Long, Brieanna Marticorena, Jessie Durret, Ben Thomas, Arya Ansari, Peter Mattis, Nargiza Salidjanova, Bryan Burack, Chris Farrar, Kate Gould, Zachary Hosford, Erica Fein, Colin Timmerman, Antonio De Loera-Brust, Kaitlyn Montán, Robert Zarate, Grant Schneider, Blake Narendra, Ryan Morgan, Rob Robilliard, Nandini Narayan, Ben Chao, Jessica Carter, Rachel Sorsensen, Ryan Uyehara, Clay Huddleston, Taylor Redick, and Meaghan Byrne.

There are countless others who deserve a shout-out, some of whom include Andrew Erickson, Ali Wyne, James Holmes, Shehzad Qazi, Alex Ward, Jack Detsch, Sameer Lalwani, April Arnold, Tim McDonnell, Elsa Kania, Frank Rose, Jacob Stokes, Mira Rapp-Hooper, Elbridge Colby, Andrew May, James Baker, Sharon Squassoni, Tom Mahnken, Abby Grace, Francis Bencosme, Gary Timmins, Nancy Kassop, Colin Dueck, Toshi Yoshihara, Dimon Liu, Bob Suettinger, Daniel Straub, Evan Braden Montgomery, Joey Siu, Brian Chow, Julia Famularo, Victor Gilinsky, Will Tobey, Harvey Rishikof, Ariel Higuchi, Benjamin Rhode, Shamila Chaudhary, Thomas Graham, Gary Schmitt, Van Jackson, Steven Aftergood, John Lauder, Alia Awadallah, Jeffrey Lewis, Michael Gordon, Adam Mount, Eric Brewer, Robert Einhorn, Bethany Allen-Ebrahimian, Nina Zimdahl, Samuel Rines, Timothy Gardner, Kirstina Biyad, David Stilwell, Patrick Malone, Matt Korda, Alexander Lanoszka, Robert Kelly, John Hudson, Richard Fontaine, Kate Beale, Peter Martin, Rachel Oswald, Rachel Paik, Taneer Greer, Laura Rozen, Jamie Metzl, Tom Nichols, Mark Hibbs, Eric Sayers, Kingston Reif, Ngoc Nguyen, and Ashley Wood.

I also need to thank everyone who allowed me to interview them for this book, some of whom are cited throughout. Others provided incredible insights but spoke with me on background.

This book would not have been possible without the support of the Smith Richardson Foundation, and I especially want to thank Allan Song and Kathy Lavery for their insights and patience. The same goes to my unbelievable editors at Rowman & Littlefield, Michael Kerns and Elizabeth Von Buhr. Thank you for taking a chance on me and for making this book far better than the product I originally submitted.

Finally, I want to thank Caroline Goodson. You make my life far better, and I appreciate you putting up with me while I was finishing up this book.

These and numerous other people have helped shape me and this book, and the product you are reading would be far worse without them. That said, all mistakes and shortcomings are mine alone.

Chapter 1

Introduction

How does allied proliferation impact US national security? This question preoccupied US officials during the Cold War when numerous allies and partners considered acquiring the bomb. In the immediate post–Cold War era, its importance has diminished. Most friendly countries that once considered nuclear weapons abandoned these ambitions. The few that hadn't, such as Israel and Pakistan, already acquired the bomb by 1991. Thus, America's post–Cold War proliferation concerns have revolved around small, hostile nations like North Korea, Iran, and Libya.

This has begun to change.[1] President Kennedy was consumed by fears the Federal Republic of Germany (FRG) would acquire nuclear weapons, and preventing that outcome was one of America's greatest nonproliferation successes. German elites are now debating the nuclear question.[2] Periodic polls out of South Korea show strong public support for acquiring nuclear weapons. Although most South Korean political leaders haven't endorsed this position, there have been calls for Washington to redeploy tactical nuclear weapons to the Peninsula. Moreover, Seoul has shown an enduring interest in producing its own fissile material (enriched uranium or separated plutonium)—the hardest obstacle for a nuclear aspirant to overcome.

Although many claim Japan has a nuclear allergy owing to the attacks on Hiroshima and Nagasaki, a rapidly deteriorating security situation has seen Tokyo revisit its pacifist constitution and boost defense spending. It's hardly unthinkable that Japan may eventually decide its rearmament should include a nuclear element, especially if China seizes the Senkaku Islands or Taiwan. Moreover, while discussing nuclear weapons used to be completely taboo, it is now spoken about openly among a small but seemingly growing number of Japanese elites.[3] If Tokyo did make this decision, no country is better prepared to rapidly build nuclear weapons, since Japan has both enrichment and reprocessing capabilities.

Saudi Arabia is perhaps the most troubling case of all. Saudi leaders have long threatened to acquire nuclear weapons if Iran is allowed to do so. In recent years, Riyadh has begun to take actions to put itself in a position to do so. Along with an ambitious nuclear energy program that makes no economic sense, Saudi Arabia has refused to sign strong international safeguards. According to media reports, the Kingdom—with assistance from China—has also acquired the ability to process uranium into yellowcake, an early step in the enrichment process. Similarly, Beijing has reportedly built Saudi Arabia a factory to produce ballistic missiles, the most common way to deliver nuclear weapons. Turkey and Egypt are also increasingly flirting with nuclear energy programs that make no economic sense. In 2019, Turkish President Recep Tayyip Erdogan bemoaned, "Some countries have missiles with nuclear warheads. . . . But (they tell us) we can't have them. This, I cannot accept."[4] In Brazil, the president's son, a member of Congress himself, has advocated for building nuclear weapons. Like Japan, Brazil's existing nuclear infrastructure would make this a relatively simple undertaking.[5]

If US policymakers are going to properly deal with allies' nuclear ambitions, they need to understand how allied proliferation impacts US security. Pundits, scholars, and policymakers have debated this issue for decades. While this debate has generated endless theoretical claims, these have not been tested against the historical record. This book seeks to correct this by examining how the four cases of allies and partners acquiring nuclear weapons actually impacted the United States. Detailed studies of the cases cast doubt on many of the claims made by all sides of the debate while also highlighting the importance of issues that aren't currently discussed.

This chapter begins by reviewing the current literature on the topic. This debate can be broken into three separate camps: optimists, relativists, and pessimists.[6] The optimists argue that allied proliferation will allow America to reduce its overseas commitments and avoid getting entangled in unnecessary wars. Although this optimistic camp receives a lot of attention in the literature, it isn't a widely held position, especially outside of academia and certain think tank analysts. The relativists don't support allied proliferation but ultimately believe other geopolitical issues should receive priority. This position is more likely to be held by policymakers and mainstream analysts, even if it isn't always expressed publicly. The pessimists strongly oppose nuclear proliferation, arguing it will lead to nuclear dominos and allies becoming more autonomous. Their concern is that allies acting too interdependently will entangle the United States into wars it doesn't want to fight. Publicly, most policymakers and members of the foreign policy establishment fall into the pessimist debate.

After reviewing the current debate, the second section discusses how a greater historical perspective can better inform policymakers grappling with these issues. The third section outlines the major conclusions from the four case studies in the book. Specifically, the case studies make clear that allied proliferation doesn't allow the United States to reduce its overseas commitments. In some cases, the opposite occurs. At the same time, friendly states acquiring the bomb makes it more difficult for America to achieve its objectives overseas. The relativists' argument that America should prioritize geopolitics over nonproliferation is also, at best, incomplete. In many cases, nuclear proliferation and geopolitics are far too interwoven to be compartmentalized. There is no evidence from the case studies that allied proliferation causes nuclear dominos to fall, but it does contribute to the spread of nuclear weapons in other ways. On the other hand, there is some evidence to support the pessimists' concerns that acquiring nuclear weapons leads allies to act more independently of the United States.

The fourth section discusses how the lessons from previous cases could apply to future ones. Finally, this chapter outlines how the rest of the book is organized.

LITERATURE REVIEW

Bombs for Peace?

The debate over the spread of nuclear weapons can really be divided into two separate questions. The first is whether nuclear proliferation enhances global peace. Building off the arguments made by the French and US Navy finite deterrence proponents, the eminent international relations scholar, Kenneth Waltz, popularized the argument that the spread of nuclear weapons reduces the chances of war.[7] Since the costs of attacking a state with a secure, second-strike nuclear capability overwhelmingly outweigh any prospective gains, and retaliation is so certain, no nuclear-armed country would start a total war with a nuclear-armed peer. Many other scholars concur with Waltz's proliferation optimism, while others—whom Peter Lavoy labels "proliferation relativists"—are more circumspect in their arguments. For instance, Bruce Bueno de Mesquita and William H. Riker argue that, in certain cases, the spread of nuclear weapons enhances peace, but—unlike Waltz—don't claim more is always better.[8]

Stanford University's Scott Sagan provided the most thorough challenge to Waltz. Just as Albert Wohlstetter countered the arguments of the finite deterrence proponents, Sagan put forth a number of reasons why Waltz's arguments would not translate to the real world. In particular, he used organizational theory to demonstrate that military organizations, like other bureaucracies, would not act as coolly rational as Waltz's arguments required. For instance, military organizations might not build large enough arsenals to deter surprise first strikes or invest in the safety features necessary to prevent unauthorized launches.[9]

Allied Proliferation

The more relevant debate for this book is how allies and partners acquiring nuclear weapons impacts the United States and the alliance. As noted in the next section, there has been almost no serious scholarly treatment of the issue. This hasn't stopped it from being debated in policy forums. This debate divides on similar lines as the previous question, with proliferation optimists, relativists, and pessimists.

At certain moments, especially during the 1950s, some parts of the US government favored allies and partners getting nuclear weapons.[10] By the mid- to late 1960s, however, Washington decided to prevent the spread of nuclear weapons to both friends and foes, although other interests sometimes took precedence. Still, the arguments first made in the earliest decades of the nuclear era never went away and have been heard more frequently as of late. For the most part, the proliferation optimists make two arguments. First, if allies acquire nuclear weapons, they will be able to protect themselves, allowing the US to reduce its defense spending and overseas commitments.[11] As a presidential candidate in 2016, Donald Trump expressed this view when stating, among other things, "We're better off if Japan protects itself against this maniac in North Korea, we're better off, frankly, if South Korea is going to start to protect itself."[12] A second optimist argument, which is related to the first, is that if allies can protect themselves, America won't risk getting entangled in unnecessary wars.[13] For instance, Stephen Walt argues that the United States shouldn't provide extended deterrence to allies—i.e., offer to use nuclear weapons to defend its allies—even if that means countries such as Germany and Japan acquire their own nuclear arsenals.[14]

While there are few policymakers who publicly endorse the optimists' arguments, many in the halls of power at least privately fall into the relativists' camp. Unlike the optimists who argue that allied proliferation benefits the United States, the relativists argue that Washington should accept it versus other bad outcomes. For example, former Department of Defense official Elbridge Colby argues it would be better if South Korea and Japan remained non-nuclear. At the same time, Colby believes that if Seoul or Tokyo are determined to go nuclear, Washington should acquiesce in order to preserve its alliances. Or, as he puts it, geopolitics must trump nonproliferation.[15] Jennifer Lind and Daryl Press have argued that the US should offer "political support" to South Korea if Seoul decides to seek nuclear weapons. For Lind and Press, a South Korean nuclear arsenal is the best way to deal with the credibility problem posed by North Korea being able to conduct nuclear attacks on the US homeland.[16] In conversations with this author, other Defense Department officials have wondered if stable, large allies like Australia getting nuclear weapons would matter one way or the other to the United States. Then-Secretary of State Rex Tillerson suggested that if North Korea failed to disarm, Japan might get nuclear weapons, which other conservative commentators also supported.[17] Others are merely fatalistic. The Center for Strategic and International Studies recently conducted a "thought experiment" that assumes that Japan, South Korea, Iran, Poland, Saudi Arabia, and Turkey will have nuclear weapons by 2030. This "inevitability" belief is something Trump also posited, telling CNN, "It's only a question of time" before more countries get the bomb.[18]

Still, most members of the foreign policy community fall into the pessimist camp. When Trump suggested America should encourage allies to get nuclear weapons, one commentator—herself a relativist—compared it to a presidential candidate declaring: "Hey, maybe we should think about communism. With one blasé comment, this entire foundation of US grand strategy is just blasted away."[19] The pessimists' most common argument is that nuclear proliferation, including by allies, will lead to a domino effect. According to this view, if one country gets the bomb, its enemies will get the bomb, and then their enemies will get the bomb. President John F. Kennedy expressed this fear when he admitted to being "haunted by the feeling" that the number of nuclear-armed countries would increase exponentially in the years ahead. Four decades later, CIA Director George Tenet had the same fears.[20] The pessimists are also concerned that nuclear-armed allies will act more independently of the United States. As President Kennedy warned, "If the French and other European powers acquire a nuclear capability they would be in a position to be entirely independent and we might be on the outside looking in."[21] In the most extreme cases, nuclear-armed allies could take risky actions that entangle the United States in unnecessary wars—the exact opposite effect the optimists anticipate.[22]

Finally, the pessimists contend the more countries that have nuclear weapons, the more likely their use becomes. This danger goes beyond mere arithmetic and probability. Paul Bracken has argued that deterrence and strategic stability is much more difficult in a multipolar world compared to a bipolar one. This is especially true because many recent and potentially future nuclear powers have stronger historical grievances and more zealous forms of nationalism.[23] Andrew Krepinevich and Jacob Cohn note that many new nuclear weapon states have fewer resources. This increases the chances of a nuclear exchange because they won't be able to afford secure second-strike capabilities. Fearing counterforce and decapitation strikes, many will adopt risky doctrines, like launch on warning and decentralized command and control, creating a greater risk of miscalculation or unauthorized launches.[24] And, of course, the more countries that have the bomb, the more likely it is that terrorists or nefarious actors will acquire it.

Determining which arguments are correct is important for numerous reasons. Many of these are obvious, but others are less so. For instance, it is easy to oppose allied proliferation in the abstract, but as Colby underscores, the question does not take place within a vacuum. In the real world, policymakers face resource constraints and competing interests. When faced with an ally who is determined to acquire nuclear weapons, policymakers have to make hard choices about how strongly to oppose them. A more robust understanding of how allied proliferation impacts Washington is required to make these assessments. Moreover, even if the United States is determined to prevent an ally or partner from acquiring nuclear weapons, there's no guarantee it will be successful. Therefore, US policymakers must understand how allied proliferation will impact the relationship and larger geopolitical dynamics.

THE ROLE OF HISTORY

A major shortcoming of the current debate over allied proliferation is all sides fail to incorporate history into their analysis. This non-historic approach was understandable decades ago when there were only a few cases of allied proliferation and nearly all information about them was classified. Now, however, nine nations have acquired nuclear arms, and a wealth of documents have been declassified, helping spark a nuclear studies' renaissance.[25] This has included fantastic histories of most nuclear-armed countries' quests to build their bombs, as well as a growing body of literature about America's attempts to stop their spread.[26] These latter histories tend to end when the countries acquire the bomb, instead of examining the consequences of America's failure to stop them. Other scholars have examined how acquiring nuclear weapons changes states' foreign policies, as well as the different nuclear doctrines adopted by second-tier nuclear powers. But this renaissance has not extended to allied proliferation. Instead, when discussing allied proliferation, participants on all sides at best make a passing reference to history, largely relying on conceptual arguments.

This book tries to correct that by doing in-depth case studies of the four cases of allied proliferation—the United Kingdom, France, Israel, and Pakistan. By peering into the past, this book gleans lessons for the future. In doing so, it employs the emerging framework that Graham Allison and Niall Ferguson have labeled *applied history*. Building off the foundational work of Richard E. Neustadt and Ernest R. May,[27] Allison and Ferguson define applied history as "the explicit attempt to illuminate current challenges and choices by analyzing historical precedents and analogues." They elaborate:

Mainstream historians begin with a past event or era and attempt to provide an account of what happened and why. Applied historians begin with a current choice or predicament and attempt to analyze the historical record to provide perspective, stimulate imagination, find clues about what is likely to happen, suggest possible policy interventions, and assess probable consequences.[28]

History is a powerful tool, but it is not a silver bullet. No two situations or countries are going to be exactly alike. No future case of allied proliferation will be identical to the cases in this book. As Henry Kissinger wrote in his memoirs, "history is not . . . a cookbook offering pretested recipes." Instead, Kissinger contended, "[history] teaches by analogy, not by maxims. It can illuminate the consequences of actions in comparable situations, yet each generation must discover for itself what situations are in fact comparable."[29]

There are other potential limitations of the current study, although I've tried to mitigate them. For instance, qualitative case studies can suffer from selection bias and choosing on the dependent variable. But the four case studies in this book are the only instances of a US treaty ally or a partner nation—defined as a major non-NATO ally—acquiring nuclear weapons. There are no other examples. Studying the entire universe of cases helps alleviate some of the shortcomings of qualitative research. As two political methodologists note: "Insofar as comparative-historical researchers select what can be considered the entire universe of cases . . . standard issues of selection bias do not arise, regardless of whether the cases were chosen for their values on the dependent variable."[30]

Despite comprising the entire universe of cases, this study still has important limitations. First, it's difficult to draw definitive conclusions from just four cases, even if they are the only cases that exist. Indeed, as noted elsewhere, policymakers shouldn't assume that a future case will be identical to any past case, or even the historical cases collectively. Examining past cases can still be incredibly beneficial to help policymakers anticipate some of the challenges that can arise from allied proliferation. Another obvious shortcoming is that the Non-Proliferation Treaty (NPT) will play a larger role in any future cases. The UK, France, and Israel acquired nuclear weapons before the NPT came into existence, while Pakistan never joined the NPT. Any future US ally or partner who acquires nuclear weapons will have to do so by withdrawing from the NPT or violating it. In outlining the best methods for learning from history, Neustadt and May recommend policymakers make a list of the similarities and differences between any historical cases and the current problem at hand. For allied proliferation, the NPT is at the top of the difference column.

There are two other challenges not directly related to case selection that deserve mention. First, it is difficult to assess how events would have been different had the allies and partners not acquired nuclear weapons. Some of these cases cover decades, and the world is not static. Even if these countries remained non-nuclear, the relationship and geopolitical situation would have changed. US policymakers wouldn't have faced the same situation as they did before nuclearization, even if they had prevented one of these countries from obtaining the bomb. For instance, if the UK hadn't acquired nuclear weapons, it wouldn't have kept its troop levels as high as they were in 1952, when the Korean War was still going on. But, as I try to show below, there is significant evidence nuclear weapons encouraged the UK and France to more drastically reduce defense spending, especially on conventional forces. Relatedly, as discussed below, the nuclearization of the Indo-Pakistani dispute made US policymakers treat every crisis with much greater urgency than they had previously. At the same time, the presence of nuclear weapons has almost certainly prevented some of the Indo-Pakistani crises from turning into full-blown wars, as happened quite frequently before the two countries acquired nuclear weapons.

Isolating nuclear weapons' impact is another major challenge. Social scientists like to point to a single variable to explain events and decisions, but government officials operate in a three-dimensional world. For most major events, they carefully weigh numerous factors, many of which will point in the same direction. Isolating the importance of each factor is ultimately impossible, often even by the participant himself or herself. Parsing out the influence of nuclear weapons is especially difficult, because they have such a ubiquitous presence that this factor often isn't discussed. When asked about the role that the nuclear shadow played in various Indo-Pakistani crises, one former senior US official told this author: "It plays a role in everyone's calculations every day without having it mentioned." He added: "That is on people's minds all the time, even if it's not spoken about."[31] Other policymakers interviewed for this book agreed. This makes it even more difficult to parse out the impact that allies' nuclear arsenals played, even when a researcher has access to primary documents.

Still, to understand the past, we must attempt to sort through these competing influences. Doing so will necessarily be subjective and imprecise. Interviews with the policymakers involved can help shed light on the relative importance of the motivations, but these are still necessarily inexact. This book makes judicious use of interviews with former policymakers in the Pakistani and, to a much lesser extent, Israeli cases. For the British, French, and for most of the Israeli case, the study is forced to rely on primary documents supplemented by memoirs and other people's interviews of former officials, along with secondary sources.

Introduction

THE LESSONS OF HISTORY

Despite these shortcomings, the four case studies in this book help illuminate the impact of allied proliferation far better than the abstract discussions that dominate the current literature. In some ways, it highlights factors that are currently absent from the discussion. For instance, the case studies demonstrate that formal treaty allies acquiring nuclear weapons impacts the United States very differently than partners building the bomb. Therefore, at times, it's necessary to treat the British and French cases differently from the Pakistani and Israeli ones.

Other factors cut across the cases. For both allies and partners, nuclear proliferation has not allowed the United States to reduce its overseas commitments; in some cases, it has had the opposite effect. Besides not reducing America's overseas commitments, allied proliferation has made it harder for Washington to achieve its objectives. How this occurs has depended on a number of factors—such as the nature of the bilateral relationship and the proliferator—but especially on whether the country is a formal treaty ally or simply a strategic partner.

There is little evidence that allied proliferation creates a nuclear domino effect, but it can contribute to the spread of nuclear weapons through the transfer of technology to friendly states. The relativists' argument that geopolitics should trump proliferation is also problematic, although not without any merit. The case studies repeatedly show that proliferation is often so interwoven with larger geopolitical questions that one cannot treat them separately. Still, the United States certainly has maintained productive relationships with at least Britain, France, and Israel, despite them acquiring nuclear weapons. Although less definitive, allies and partners appear to operate more independently of the United States after acquiring nuclear weapons. It is also abundantly clear that allied proliferation puts immense strain on the bilateral alliance in the near and medium term, although that is partly because the United States has strongly opposed it. This section goes through each of these points in greater detail.

Reducing US Commitments

Europe

Allied proliferation has not allowed the United States to reduce its overseas commitments. In the cases of Britain and France, this is best seen by examining US troop levels in Europe. Figure 1.1 shows how many US troop were stationed in Europe at various points in the Cold War. US troop levels in the region peaked around the mid-1955s, at about the time Britain acquired an operational nuclear arsenal. These levels dipped slightly by 1960, where they stabilized through the middle of the decade. US troops levels declined again, starting in the late 1960s and into the 1970s before rising substantially again in the 1980s.

Allied proliferation didn't cause these troop levels; the UK and France's arsenals were mostly irrelevant to how many US troops were deployed in Europe.[32] The key point is that despite two allies having nuclear weapons, the United States had to maintain a large number of troops in the region. Moreover, the fluctuations that did occur were caused by other factors. The peak in the mid-1950s was the result of fears after the Korean War began, whereas the decline in the late 1960s and 1970s is attributable to the Vietnam War. Ronald Reagan's muscular policy toward the Soviet Union led to the spike in the 1980s. All of this would have occurred regardless of whether London and Paris acquired nuclear weapons.

Israel

The United States has had a larger military presence in the Middle East and South Asia after Israel and Pakistan acquired the bomb. However, a better measurement of US commitment for major non-NATO allies like Israel and Pakistan is military assistance. If acquiring nuclear weapons allows partners to protect themselves, they shouldn't need substantial amounts of military aid. But in both the Israeli and Pakistani cases, military assistance was much larger after the countries acquired nuclear weapons. And, in Israel's case, this military assistance was directly related to its acquisition of nuclear weapons.

As seen in Figure 1.2, the United States first provided military aid to Israel in 1959. Between that time and the nine years until Israel built the bomb, US annual military aid averaged $91.9 million a year (in constant 2017 dollars). In the nine years after Israel became a nuclear state, American military assistance averaged around $2.5 billion, a more than 2,700% increase. Some of this increase can be explained by the need to replenish Israel's military

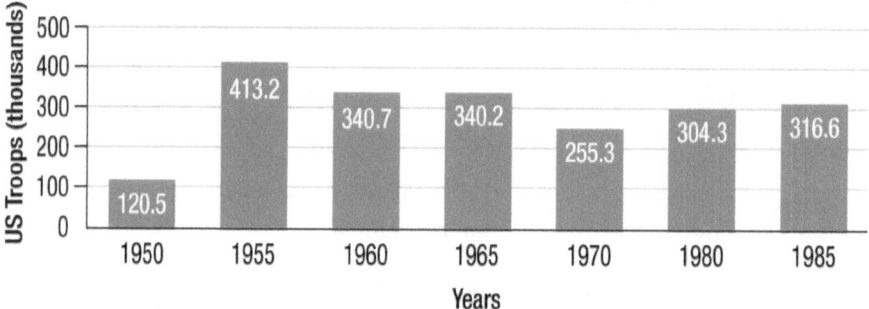

Figure 1.1. US Troops in Europe (thousands), Tim Kane/Heritage Foundation

stockpiles after the 1967 and 1973 wars. Yet this cannot account for all of it; US military assistance to Israel after this time has never been lower than $1 billion (in constant dollars), and usually, it's been much larger. Unlike with troop levels in Europe, there is causation here—what is now called Israel's qualitative military edge (QME) has its origins in Israel's nuclear program. In the 1950s and early 1960s, US policymakers did not want to sell Israel arms because they feared alienating Arab states. Their perspective changed as Israel's nuclear intentions became clearer. At first, US policymakers hoped that selling Israel conventional weapons would persuade its leaders that they didn't need nuclear ones. After Israel acquired the bomb, the rationale for providing military assistance to Israel shifted. Now, America needed to provide Israel with substantial amounts of military aid so it could defend itself without the use of nuclear weapons. In the 1990s, Robert Gallucci ran the US-Israel Joint Political Military Group, which helps coordinate the partnership. He told this author that QME was a "code word" for "keeping Israel capable of mounting a successful conventional defense against any combination of Arab states. . . . [They] were very intent on making sure that Israel was not put in a position where it would have to fall back on nuclear weapons when conventional weapons would do." Of course, a number of factors explain why America supports Israel's QME today. But for many US officials, especially early on, the primary factor was to prevent a situation where Israel would use nuclear weapons.

Pakistan

Nor did nuclear proliferation allow the United States to decrease its commitment levels in Pakistan. Washington first gave Islamabad military assistance in 1955. From then until the time the US became concerned about Pakistan's nuclear aspirations, annual military assistance averaged $198 million (in constant 2009 dollars). In the late 1970s, Washington periodically cut off all

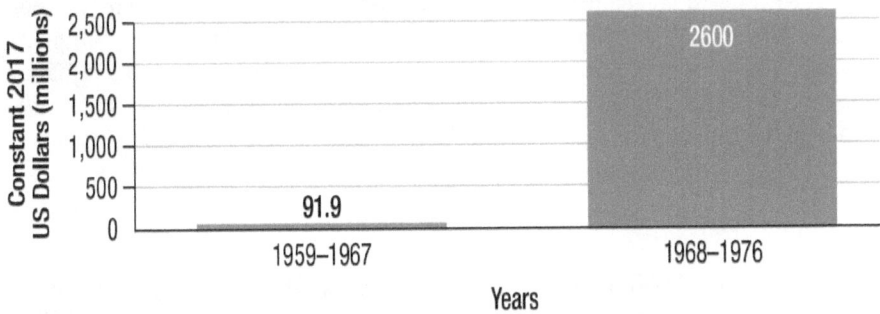

Figure 1.2. Annual Military Aid to Israel (millions), USAID, US Foreign Assistance, FY 1946–2017 (Greenbook)

assistance to Pakistan over the latter's refusal to limit its nuclear program. Despite these interruptions, average annual military assistance from 1977 to 1990 increased to $272 million. In October 1990, President George H. W. Bush was unable to certify Pakistan didn't possess a nuclear weapon, and US law forced his administration to cut off all military assistance. At first glance, this is consistent with the optimists' claim that allied proliferation will reduce America's overseas commitments. That is not how US policymakers saw it at the time. Teresita Schaffer, at the time the State Department's top South Asia expert, was sent to Capitol Hill to try to get a waiver from Congress to allow aid to continue. The administration's argument was that continuing assistance would give the US leverage to persuade Pakistan to roll back its nuclear program. Lawmakers were unpersuaded by this argument, and aid was suspended. Nonetheless, by the late 1990s, legislation was passed to allow a resumption of assistance to Pakistan, and from 2002 to 2010, military assistance averaged $1.641 billion a year. Thus, in the three and a half decades between 1955 and when it acquired the bomb, Pakistan received around $8 billion total in US military assistance. But in the nine years between 2002 and 2010, Pakistan received over $13 billion (all in constant 2009 dollars). Like the European cases, Pakistan's nuclear arsenal had a minimal impact on the levels of aid it received. Instead, Pakistan received large amounts of military assistance in the 1980s and after 2001 because of events in Afghanistan. Nonetheless, the point remains: allied proliferation hasn't allowed the United States to reduce its overseas commitments. Other geopolitical factors took precedence.

Achieving Overseas Objectives: Allies

Besides not allowing the US to reduce its overseas commitments, allied proliferation often made it more difficult for America to achieve its foreign policy objectives. The exact nature of these difficulties depended on a number of factors, including the nature of the bilateral relationship, ally or partner, and even individual leaders. Still, a clear distinction can be drawn between treaty allies and partner nations. Although it may not be immediately obvious, having to integrate separate nuclear arsenals into a formal military alliance presents different kinds of challenges than those found in partner states like Israel and Pakistan. This subsection deals with allies before the next one examines the two partners.

Launch Control

For the UK and France cases, allied proliferation created three major challenges: launch control, conventional military spending, and US basing. While the basing question is dealt with in a different subsection—and could apply

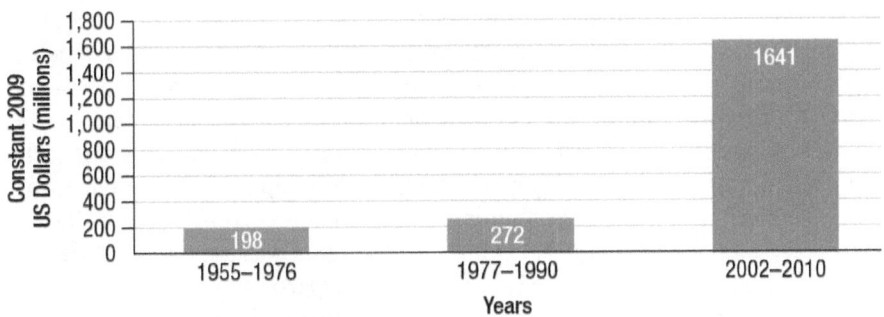

Figure 1.3. Average Annual Military Aid to Pakistan (millions), Wren Elhai/Center for Global Development

to partner nations—this one examines launch control and conventional military spending.

Launch control refers to the operational challenges posed by nuclear weapons within the context of a military alliance. In particular, which country(s) gets to decide when to use nuclear weapons. These have been a constant challenge in America's alliances with Britain, France, and all NATO countries. In many ways, they've never been fully resolved.

During World War II, the United States and Britain agreed that neither side would use nuclear weapons without the other's consent. Once the war was over, London agreed to drop this condition under heavy pressure from Washington. Launch control quickly became an issue.

From the allies' perspective—not only the UK and France, but also other NATO members—the issue cut both ways: they feared being both entrapped in a war and abandoned in a conflict. During the Berlin blockade in 1949, London agreed to have US bombers (without nuclear warheads) be forward deployed to UK territory. Once the crisis died down, however, British leaders were incredulous to learn the Americans believed they could use these bombers to launch atomic attacks on the Soviet Union without British input. Merely hosting the bombers made Britain a target for the Soviet Union once Moscow had intermediate-range ballistic missiles. But the Soviet Union would also retaliate against Britain if its territory was used to attack the USSR. As the British foreign secretary argued, it was unacceptable "that Britain should risk annihilating retaliation without being first informed or consulted."[33] Around the same time, UK Prime Minister Clement Attlee flew to Washington to pressure President Truman not to use atomic weapons in the Korean War.

The entrapment issue never completely abated—for instance, during the Euromissile crisis in the 1980s. But it became eclipsed by fears of abandonment. During the 1950s, NATO defense became entirely dependent on America using nuclear weapons to offset the Soviet Union's quantitative superiority in material and personnel. But as the Soviet Union acquired the ability to launch nuclear strikes on the US homeland, and later reached nuclear parity with the United States, European leaders naturally questioned whether America would pull the nuclear trigger. As French leader Charles de Gaulle put it, would Washington really trade New York for Paris? The Kennedy administration's rhetorical efforts to build up NATO's conventional forces as well as policies of bargaining during a nuclear conflict only added to Europe's fears. As we shall see, calming these fears was a major undertaking for American leaders and their European counterparts.

Although the United States did worry at times that allies acquiring nuclear weapons might lead them to seek neutrality with the Soviet Union, its bigger concern with launch control was entrapment.[34] Even with entrapment, the level of concern fluctuated. It was rarely present during the Eisenhower administration because of the president's overarching goal: building a Europe that could defend itself without US troops. Eisenhower was entirely willing to allow the Europeans to have their own nuclear forces—ideally, a singular nuclear force as part of a unified European command—to accomplish that. Similarly, after the Soviet Union reached nuclear parity, President Richard Nixon and Secretary of State Henry Kissinger came to view the independent arsenals in Paris and London as helping to bolster deterrence. Moscow might doubt America's willingness to use nuclear forces to defend Europe, but it would be harder to doubt France's willingness to protect itself or, perhaps, Germany.

America was most concerned about being entrapped by independent arsenals during the 1960s. The problem was President John F. Kennedy's (and later Lyndon B. Johnson's) Flexible Response policy. Flexible Response is best remembered as the JFK administration's attempts to build up NATO's conventional forces in order to meet Soviet aggression at different levels of intensity. This part of the doctrine was nothing new, as the Eisenhower administration had pushing for a similar buildup since the mid-1950s (although it's not clear President Eisenhower always agreed). As with its predecessor, the JFK and LBJ administration's conventional buildup never happened, at least in Europe.

A new component of the JFK administration's Flexible Response doctrine was an effort to find a way to use nuclear weapons in a conflict without immediately escalating to total war. What Secretary of Defense Robert McNamara came up with was a policy that today would be called Escalate to De-Escalate. In the event of war, McNamara envisioned using a few nuclear weapons against military targets while avoiding cities and keeping the bulk of the arsenal in reserve. The hope was that even after the Americans and Soviets exchanged a few nuclear weapons, they could continue to negotiate and terminate the conflict before a full-scale nuclear exchange. To be workable at all, this doctrine would require centralized nuclear decision making; if the British or French responded to limited Soviet nuclear attacks by unleashing their full arsenals or targeting cities, any hope of avoiding nuclear Armageddon would be lost. McNamara and the JFK administration ultimately concluded the gradual escalation policy was unworkable for a host of reasons.[35]

Before then, and indeed possibly after it, gradual escalation led the JFK administration to ponder trying to put the British "out of the nuclear business" and taking a hard line on the French nuclear program. Washington also set its sights on placing the British and French arsenals under NATO command, which really meant Washington's control. This produced mixed results. In exchange for US-made, submarine-launched ballistic missiles, London nominally agreed to place its entire nuclear force under NATO's command with the signing of the Nassau Agreement. In reality, the agreement stipulated that only the British prime minister could authorize the use of British nuclear weapons, and he or she could do so outside of NATO under extraordinary circumstances. The French were even less accommodating. Charles de Gaulle flatly refused to even nominally place the *force de frappe* under NATO's auspices, even when the US offered significant nuclear assistance to sweeten the deal. The nuclear sharing arrangements for NATO as a whole were even more tortured, and to this day the issues posed by launch control aren't entirely resolved.

Conventional Military Spending

Perhaps more importantly for the United States, the UK and France reduced their conventional military spending after they acquired nuclear weapons. As a regional hegemon with interests across Eurasia, US allies would ideally provide the bulk of the manpower within the alliance, with America's contribution primarily coming in the form of air and naval power. Indeed, nearly every post–WWII administration has pushed allies to increase their conventional military spending, usually with disappointing results.

The United Kingdom and France both decreased conventional military spending once they acquired nuclear weapons, much to the dismay of US officials. "We do not really see much point in the separate British nuclear deterrent," National Security Advisor McGeorge Bundy wrote to Kennedy. "We would much rather have British efforts go into conventional weapons."[36] Indeed, when US officials advocated for nuclear assistance to the UK and France, one of their principal arguments was it would free more funds for the allies to spend on conventional weapons.[37]

Although the United States eventually provided this assistance to London, both the UK and France pursued a "nuclear substitution" policy, whereas the acquisition of nuclear weapons made London and Paris secure enough to reduce their defense spending and especially the size of their armed forces. The UK first outlined this logic in a defense white paper in 1952, the same year it tested a nuclear bomb. London didn't acquire an operational nuclear deterrent until around 1955, however, and the cuts promised in 1952 didn't materialize until after the 1957 defense white paper.

After that, the cuts were drastic. In 1952, Britain's active personnel totaled 878,700, and remained at 703,900 in 1957. By 1960, that number had declined to 521,000. A decade later, London's active force was down to 373,000, a nearly 60% decline from 1952. Air force squadrons deployed on the frontlines in West Germany were reduced from thirty-six in 1957 to just twelve squadrons four years later. After 1956, British forces in Germany declined from about 77,000 to 55,000 (28% decline), and UK forces across Europe dropped from 94,500 to 63,000 (33% decline).[38] In the 1950s, UK defense spending peaked at 11% of its GDP in 1953; by 1960, the figure was 7.1%. A decade after that, it was only spending 5.2% of its GDP on the military. In discussions with US officials in 1956–1957, British officials primarily defended the cuts on the grounds of economic necessity. But they also repeatedly argued that some of the cuts in manpower were offset by the fact that those troops would be armed with nuclear weapons.[39] In addition, similar to US Air Force officials at that time, they argued conventional forces were of minimal importance in a thermonuclear era.[40]

Table 1.1.

Year	UK Active Military Personnel
1952	878,700
1957	703,900
1960	521,100
1970	373,000

Source: UK Ministry of Defence, data compiled by *The Guardian*. Available from: https://www.theguardian.com/news/datablog/2011/sep/01/military-service-personnel-total.

Table 1.2.

Year	UK Defense Spending (% of GDP)
1953	11
1957	8
1960	7.1
1970	5.2

Source: SIPRI Military Expenditure Database.

France's nuclear weapons also greatly reduced its conventional military spending. Once again, there was an explicit, underlying logic to these cuts. One of the early advocates of a French nuclear bomb was then-Colonel Charles Ailleret. Ailleret, who would go on to serve as chairman of the French Chiefs of Staff under de Gaulle, argued in 1954 that nuclear bombs are "inexpensive weapons in contrast to classic weapons [and] constitute the criterion of a modern army."[41] France first tested a nuclear weapon in 1960, and it acquired a crude operational capability in 1966. Accordingly, from 1961 to 1966, the size of the France's armed forces declined by 50%, from 1,000,000 to 522,000.[42] Roughly 90% of this decline came from the army, which didn't have a role in the nuclear arsenal.[43] French military spending also dropped substantially. France was spending 5.4% of its GDP on the military in 1960. Eight years later, only 4.1% of France's GDP was going to defense, and this declined to 3.1% by 1973.[44] The spending that did remain increasingly went to nuclear weapons instead of areas US policymakers preferred, such as the army. The French Army's share of the defense budget was 73% in 1949; two decades later, it was just 40%. By that time, 41% of France's defense spending was going to nuclear weapons.[45]

Of course, the UK and France would have reduced military spending regardless of their nuclear status as they wound down their empires and Cold War tensions abated. Still, these cuts were deeper than they otherwise would have been because of the security their nuclear arsenals afforded them, as well as their deterrence-by-punishment military doctrines. Table 1.3 shows how much the major European countries changed their military spending as a percentage of GDP between 1960 and 1980. Every country except Turkey saw their defense budget decrease during this time, but the French and British reductions were by far the largest.[46] Had France or Britain not acquired nuclear weapons, they wouldn't have reduced military spending as drastically, and defense dollars would have gone to areas US officials prioritized.

Table 1.3

Country	Change in defense spending (as % of GDP) 1960–1980
France	-2.7%
UK	-1.6%
Italy	-1.1%
Germany	-0.9%
Greece	-0.2%
Turkey	0.4%

Source: Todd Sandler and Justin George, "Military Expenditure Trends for 1960–2014 and What They Reveal," *Global Policy* 7, no. 2 (May 2016): 182.

Achieving Overseas Objectives: Partners

Partner nations acquiring nuclear weapons also made it more difficult for the United States to achieve its objectives, although in different ways from the allies. In fact, the complications posed by the proliferation appeared more unique to Israel and Pakistan and America's relationship with them than was the case with the allies. Of the two, Pakistan was the more devastating.

Israel

As discussed more in the relevant chapters, Israel is the hardest of the four cases to draw definitive conclusions about or glean lessons for future cases. This is due to the unique and peculiar nature of the US-Israeli relationship and the fact that Israel doesn't acknowledge its nuclear status. Interestingly, despite Jerusalem's opaque nuclear status, it has been a constant irritant for America's global nonproliferation agenda.

The one major nonproliferation regime that Israel signed onto was the Partial Test Ban Treaty, which prohibits testing nuclear weapons in the atmosphere. US officials were pleased when Israel signed the PTBT just days after it opened for signatures. But sixteen years later, Israel placed the treaty in jeopardy when it covertly tested a nuclear device off the coast of South Africa. Although a US satellite picked up the test, there was enough uncertainty that the Carter administration could deny a test had occurred.

In the eyes of US officials, Israel has also been an impediment to the Nuclear Nonproliferation Treaty (NPT). Washington put tremendous pressure on Israel to sign the NPT when it was first agreed to in 1968 because the LBJ administration feared that Israel's refusal to join would make it much more difficult to get countries like West Germany and Japan to join. Unlike with the PTBT, Israel remained steadfast in its refusal to join the NPT. In the end, the NPT went into effect in 1970 and, eventually, most major countries joined it—but not Israel. The text of the treaty called for the parties to decide whether to extend it twenty-five years after it went into force. In 1995, the Clinton administration made an indefinite extension of the NPT a major priority. Once again, Israel proved to be a major complication. A coalition of Arab states used the extension negotiations to pressure Israel to sign the NPT or, at least, to close its nuclear reactor. For Israel, this was a non-starter. The Clinton administration launched an extensive lobbying campaign to convince Egypt and other Arab states to agree to an indefinite extension without singling out Israel. Although progress was uneven, Washington succeeded in the end, although it required a major undertaking.

Another major Clinton administration nonproliferation priority was securing a fissile material cut-off treaty (FMCT). This would have stopped all countries from producing more fissile material—the enriched uranium or reprocessed plutonium that forms the core of nuclear weapons. By 1998, the momentum behind an FMCT was growing, but Israel remained staunchly opposed. Israeli leaders viewed an FMCT as the first step on a slippery slope that ended with a non-nuclear Israel. Then-Prime Minister Benjamin Netanyahu went so far as to reportedly warn President Clinton, "We will never sign the treaty, and do not delude yourselves—no pressure will help. We will not sign the treaty because we will not commit suicide." Fearing that Israeli opposition could derail political support for the negotiations, President Clinton offered an extraordinary concession: a written statement promising that America's nonproliferation policies would never threaten Israel's nuclear arsenal. Since then, every successive US president has made a similar written pledge to his Israeli counterpart upon taking office.[47]

Pakistan

Pakistan's nuclear arsenal has been far more detrimental to the United States. Some of the drawbacks are well known, such as the fear that terrorists would steal nuclear bombs or materials from Pakistan. Other ways are less appreciated by casual observers. One of example of this is Afghanistan in both the 1980s and after 9/11. When the Soviet Union invaded Afghanistan on Christmas Day, 1979, US officials quickly pledged to turn the conflict into Moscow's Vietnam. The US effort to arm the Afghan mujahedeen was funneled through Pakistan. Islamabad's nuclear aspirations made this much more difficult, especially because existing legislation and Congressional opposition limited assistance to countries seeking nuclear weapons. As the Reagan administration repeatedly argued to their Pakistani counterparts, Pakistan's nuclear program was the one factor that could prevent continued cooperation. The Reagan and George H. W. Bush administrations were able to successfully navigate maintaining assistance in the face of Pakistan's nuclear advances, but it was often quite difficult.

Pakistan's nuclear program was also a top concern when the George W. Bush administration debated its response to the 9/11 attacks. One of the main "downside risks" of the invasion plan that the administration discussed was the possibility of destabilizing Pakistan and its nuclear arsenal. The administration referred to this as the "nightmare scenario," and it greatly worried President Bush, Vice President Dick Cheney, National Security Advisor Condoleezza Rice, and the Pentagon. Similarly, as President Bush admits in his memoirs, his administration, at times, opted not to attack al-Qaeda operatives in Pakistan out of concern that it would destabilize the government and its nuclear arsenal.

The nuclearization of the Indo-Pakistani conflict also fundamentally changed how the United States approached it. India and Pakistan fought three conventional wars before they got nuclear weapons. While Washington was hardly a disinterested party in these, the US government didn't treat them as a major national security threat. That changed once the two countries were armed with nuclear weapons. Since the first nuclear crisis in 1990, successive US governments have had to treat every India-Pakistan crisis as a potentially existential matter because of the potential for nuclear use. Thus, US presidents began sending high-level emissaries to mediate the situation and personally intervening to prevent escalation.

More generally, and in direct contrast to what the optimists expect, Pakistan's nuclear arsenal has made it a far bigger priority to the United States. The Pakistani chapters are based in part on interviews with twenty-five to thirty US policymakers who worked on Pakistan for every administration from Jimmy Carter to Barack Obama. The author asked nearly every person whether Pakistan's nuclear arsenal makes it more important for the United States than it otherwise would be because of its geography, population size, or economy. Nearly every former official agreed that it did. As one former official said: "100 percent." After a slight pause, she added, "1,000 percent. There's no way around it."[48] Not unlike adversaries such as North Korea, the mere fact that Pakistan is armed with nuclear weapons has given it greater importance in the minds of US officials. In essence, it has become too big to fail.

In short, not only did allied proliferation not allow the United States to reduce its overseas commitments, it also complicated America's ability to achieve its foreign policy objectives.

Does Proliferation Beget Proliferation?

As noted above, one of the pessimists' greatest fears is that allied proliferation will cause a nuclear domino effect. In this scenario, one country acquiring nuclear weapons causes its enemies to acquire nuclear weapons, followed by those countries' enemies doing the same. The four cases of allied proliferation provide little evidence that this will occur. There's not a single rival that acquired nuclear weapons as a result of Britain, France, Israel, or Pakistan doing so. This is quite remarkable, especially in the case of Israel, which has long-standing rivalries with many of its Arab neighbors. At the same time, social scientists have repeatedly demonstrated that this nuclear domino effect has no empirical basis.[49] Some attribute the lack of a nuclear tipping point to far-sighted US interventions, while others doubt countries' interest in building the bomb.[50] Regardless of the reason, the four cases in this book didn't produce the domino effect.

Many of the countries in this book did contribute to the spread of nuclear weapons in another way. In three of the four cases, the new nuclear country helped friendly countries' nuclear efforts, thereby contributing to proliferation. France selling Israel almost everything it needed to build a nuclear weapon was the most prominent example of this phenomenon. Paris also tried to sell Pakistan and South Korea reprocessing plants, but Washington successfully intervened. France has helped Japan get reprocessing capabilities, but these have thus far not been used to build nuclear weapons. France has provided lesser forms of nuclear assistance to other countries as well.

While French nuclear assistance mostly went to countries that were friendly to the United States, Pakistan adopted the mantra that "the enemy of my friend is my friend." After acquiring nuclear weapons, Pakistan provided North Korea, Iran, and Libya with enrichment capabilities. These significantly advanced the former two countries' nuclear program. As Gary Samore, who tracked this assistance in the Clinton administration and later as the WMD czar under President Obama, put it: "Without that infusion of Pakistani technology, Iran's nuclear program would be nowhere near as advanced as it is now."[51] There is also evidence Pakistan tried to arm Saddam Hussein with nuclear weapons after he invaded Kuwait, but the deal didn't go through before the start of the First Gulf War.

Compared to France or Pakistan, Israel has been much more restrained in spreading nuclear technology. The one exception is apartheid South Africa. As two countries that believed they were being ostracized by the international community, Israel and South Africa cooperated extensively in the 1970s and 1980s. This extended to the strategic realm. In fact, declassified South African documents strongly suggest that Israel offered South Africa Jericho missiles with nuclear warheads. This deal never went through, but Israel later helped South Africa build ballistic missiles. It also supplied Pretoria with tritium, which is used to increase the yield and reliability of atomic weapons.

In short, while the pessimists are wrong about the mechanism, allied proliferation does contribute to the spread of nuclear weapons.

Can Geopolitics Trump Nonproliferation?

Some relativists argue that even though allied proliferation shouldn't be welcomed, ultimately, it might have to take a backseat to other geopolitical considerations. For instance, Elbridge Colby notes that "while nonproliferation is certainly a (quite substantial) good, it is not *the* good." America has other objectives, such as alliance cohesion, and these "may in certain circumstances be more important to the service of that higher aim than unyielding adherence to nonproliferation goals." Put more succinctly, "geopolitics should trump nonproliferation."[52]

In the article, Colby is specifically arguing that if Japan or South Korea acquired nuclear weapons, America shouldn't automatically terminate its alliances with them.[53] The cases in this book substantiate this argument—certainly the United States has benefited from maintaining its alliances with Britain and France after they got nuclear weapons. But just because America shouldn't terminate its alliances if Japan or South Korea gets nuclear weapons, this doesn't mean nonproliferation strengthens other geopolitics objectives. In fact, it often weakens them. For instance, Colby is rightly concerned with the strength of America's alliances with Japan and South Korea. But all four cases of allied proliferation put tremendous strain on America's relationships with the country, and in the NPT era, that is likely to be doubly true. Even if America were to take a permissive stance on nonproliferation, the British and French cases underscore that operational military issues are unavoidable. Moreover, nuclear weapons usually come at the expense of conventional military spending, which causes its own frustrations for the United States.[54]

More generally, the four case studies demonstrate that proliferation issues are intertwined with larger geopolitical issues, and thus cannot be easily compartmentalized. This was evident before the first atomic bomb was ever built. In 1941, the British demonstrated on the paper that an atomic bomb was possible for the first time. With London in the lead, the Americans proposed a joint program to build the ultimate weapon. The British stonewalled this request, instead preferring to build the bomb in England despite the country being under constant attack by Nazi Germany. British officials offered the Americans a number of excuses, but in internal deliberations, they spoke more candidly. As Winston Churchill's top science advisor explained, the atomic weapons program should be a national effort because "whoever possesses such a plant should be able to dictate terms to the rest of the world."[55] By mid-1942, UK leaders realized the American program had surpassed their own and therefore approached the United States about a joint program. Now it was America's turn to obfuscate, for nearly the exact same reasons. After the war, geopolitical issues would continue to dictate US-UK atomic relations.

Larger geopolitical issues were also front and center in the French case. Charles de Gaulle had long-standing views on issues like alliances, France's place in the world, and the dangers of dependency on foreign powers. All of these predated America acquiring nuclear weapons, much less France doing so. Yet, de Gaulle saw a French nuclear arsenal as the linchpin in being able to act on his viewpoints. And, as described more in the context of freedom of action, he used the *force de frappe* to implement his vision. Similarly, the policies Eisenhower, Kennedy, and Nixon adopted toward France's nuclear program were all dictated by larger geopolitical questions. Eisenhower's overriding interest was in empowering Europe to protect itself so America could drawdown its commitment to the region. This led him to take a permissive view toward France's nuclear program. Richard Nixon, who was Eisenhower's vice president, took a similar view when he became president. Both Nixon and Kissinger believed a more independent Europe was essential, partly because the Soviet Union had reached nuclear parity but also because they didn't believe Americans wouldn't support as active a foreign policy after the Vietnam War. For President Nixon, France was the only European power that could lead a more independent Europe, and supporting the French nuclear program was part of that.

President Kennedy saw reining in West Germany's nuclear aspirations as essential to stabilizing the US-Soviet relationship and maintaining NATO cohesion. He viewed France's nuclear program almost solely through these lenses. This view was correct, as the Soviet Union was able to tolerate West Germany if it were dependent on the United States for its security, but not a nuclear-armed Federal Republic of Germany (FRG) that could act independently. Ensuring the FRG accepted its non-nuclear status was difficult but essential to easing tensions in the Cold War. This is relevant to Walt's argument that the United States is better off with a nuclear-armed Japan and Germany than continuing to extend its nuclear umbrella. This may be true from America's point of view, but not necessarily from adversaries' perspectives. What would China and South Korea's reactions be to a nuclear-armed Japan compared with America extending nuclear deterrence to Tokyo?

The point that nuclear proliferation is deeply interwoven with geopolitics cuts both ways, however. Britain, France, Israel, and Pakistan have, thus far at least, not proven intolerable to the United States, despite acquiring nuclear weapons. And there are real costs in trying to prevent allies and partners from building the bomb. This book highlights many of the challenges allied proliferation causes, but that doesn't mean these issues outweigh the harm in trying to prevent proliferation.

In any case, even strong nonproliferation policies don't guarantee success. The United States was successful in preventing Pakistan from acquiring a plant to reprocess plutonium, but Pakistan's determination to acquire the bomb led it to acquire enrichment facilities to produce fissile material. Many people believe the United States didn't adopt strong enough nonproliferation policies against Pakistan because Washington needed Islamabad's support to fight the Soviet Union. As we shall see, however, even before Moscow invaded Afghanistan, US officials didn't see a viable path to stopping Pakistan's enrichment program. The lesson for the future is US policymakers will have to weigh all the different costs when faced with potential cases of allied proliferation.

Freedom of Action

Another concern that pessimists have is proliferation will allow allies and partners to act with more autonomy and freedom of action. Proving whether this is the case is difficult. For one thing, it's impossible to discern with certainty whether a country would've taken a specific action if it hadn't had nuclear weapons. Moreover, it is difficult to assess the relative importance of various factors in a country's decision making. This is especially true if multiple factors all motivate a country to act in a certain way. Despite these difficulties, there is circumstantial evidence from all the cases that freedom of action is a valid concern.

In his study on how Britain's acquisition of nuclear weapons impacted its foreign policy, Mark Bell examines how independently the UK was willing to act in the Middle East before and after 1955, the year Bell argues London had an operational nuclear arsenal. Since the only major variable to change during this time was nuclear acquisition, Bell argues he can isolate the influence nuclear weapons had on Britain's willingness to act independently.[56]

To make the case, Bell examines how the UK responded to six distinct challenges to its position in the Middle East. Three of these happened before 1955: Iran's oil nationalization in 1951; the Saudi Occupation of Buraimi in 1952; and Egyptian leader Gamal Nasser's efforts to eject Britain from Suez in 1952–1954. He then examines the Suez Crisis in 1956 and subsequent crises in Oman and Jordan. For the instances before 1955, Bell finds "Britain was extremely wary of responding to challenges with force without the support of the United States, and British responses were characterized by compromise and deference to US preferences." This changed once Britain acquired an operational nuclear deterrent. According to Bell, "[A]fter 1955, Britain became more willing to use force unilaterally and paid less attention to American preferences."[57]

Of course, other factors might have played a role in the events Bell describes. Even if nuclear weapons didn't make London more independent, US policymakers felt that they did. In a conversation with the British Foreign Minister in 1962, Secretary of State Dean Rusk stated that "the more the UK stressed its independence the more it tended to move in on [US] independence." More generally, Rusk lamented that nuclear weapons are not "a path to freedom but a path to slavery," and the "US has never had less independence than it has today in the areas affected by these weapons."[58]

Compared to Britain, France under Charles de Gaulle was always more willing to act independently from the United States. De Gaulle was not a fan of alliances or American power and made restoring France's place in the world his life's work. He also increasingly saw NATO and US influence in Europe as infringing on French sovereignty (as he defined it). But even de Gaulle was far more willing to assert independence from NATO and the United States once he had an operational nuclear deterrent. De Gaulle began chafing at NATO the moment he returned to power in 1958. Despite these objections, France continued to participate in NATO's integrated military command and hosted large numbers of NATO (and American) troops. Then, shortly after the first leg of France's nuclear arsenal became operational—the Mirage planes—de Gaulle announced France was withdrawing from NATO's military command and removing all NATO troops and bases from its territory. Around the same time, de Gaulle also began a charm offensive toward the Soviet Union, including a landmark visit to Moscow in June 1966.

Since they were not in formal treaty alliances with the United States, Israel and Pakistan were never as dependent on the United States. Still, Pakistan began acting more aggressively in ways that were detrimental to US interests after it acquired the bomb. After its lopsided defeat in the 1971 war, Pakistan didn't directly challenge India over the next two decades. This started to change once it had built all of the components for nuclear weapons. Thus, Pakistan precipitated a border crisis over Kashmir in the spring of 1990, during which time it assembled its first nuclear bomb. After India and Pakistan tested nuclear weapons in 1998, Pakistani forces infiltrated the border region over the winter of 1998–1999, sparking the Kargil War. This plan had been drawn up years earlier but wasn't acted upon until after the nuclear tests. Pakistani proxy groups like LeT and JeM also provoked the most serious Indo-Pakistani crisis of the nuclear era in the fall of 2001 and spring of 2002. It is also worth noting that, as mentioned above, America's freedom of action toward Pakistan is more limited because of the latter's nuclear arsenal. So, at least in the case of Pakistan, the nuclear partner's freedom of action increased while America's freedom of action decreased.

LESSONS FOR FUTURE CASES

A number of lessons can be derived from these past cases for how future allied proliferation could impact the United States. For the most part, these are best discussed in the context of concrete examples.

Allies

For instance, in trying to foresee how a nuclear-armed Japan or South Korea would impact the United States, the lessons from the British and French cases are probably more relevant. First off, we would almost certainly see tensions over launch control issues. To some extent, these are already apparent, especially in the case of the US–Republic of Korea alliance.[59] During his first year in office, President Donald Trump regularly threatened to attack North Korea. This led South Korea President Moon Jae-in to publicly rebuke Trump, arguing that the United States could not do so without Seoul's permission.[60]

At the same time, the South Korean military has been acquiring the capabilities to implement its so-called Kill Chain doctrine. Under this controversial strategy, Seoul is acquiring the capabilities to conduct preemptive military strikes on North Korea's nuclear and missile sites, as well as target Kim Jong-Un and his inner circle, independently of the United States. As a sovereign nation, South Korea has a right to defend itself. At the same time, the United States has over twenty-eight thousand troops in South Korea. All of them would be prime targets of North Korea's retaliation, as would US forces in Japan and, possibly, even the US homeland. Given that America would be targeted in response, future US leaders are likely to demand a say in launching these preemptive strikes. As thorny as these issues are in a conventional context, they would only become more troublesome if nuclear weapons were involved.[61]

More generally, as discussed above, Britain's and France's nuclear arsenals inhibited America's ability to pursue the Flexible Response strategy developed during the Kennedy and Johnson administrations. One doesn't have to support the escalate to de-escalate doctrine McNamara put forth—which seemed to ignore the fog of war and primordial violence part of Clausewitz's trinity—to see the dangers of this for the future. As already noted, McNamara and the rest of the administration determined it was unworkable. Still, the key point is that US leaders were unable to adopt the strategy they felt was best suited to protect America's interests in part because of allied proliferation. Even if Flexible Response was wrongheaded, there is no guarantee that future allied proliferation won't prevent the US from adopting more sound strategies for urgent national security challenges.

Beyond launch control issues, the case studies indicate that acquiring nuclear weapons would lead Japan and South Korea to reduce their military spending and the size of their armed forces. Some would contend that this wouldn't matter, since Japan and South Korea could protect themselves. This ignores how vital Japan (in particular) is to Washington's ability to check China's growing regional ambitions. The Japanese Self-Defense Forces (SDF) are easily the largest regional counterweight to China, especially in terms of air and naval power. South Korea is less likely to be a counterweight to China, but ROK forces provide the bulk of the manpower on the Korean Peninsula. Compared to 28,000 US troops deployed in Korea, the ROK has 464,000 people under arms. Were either of these countries, but especially Japan, to drastically reduce conventional military spending or the size of its armed forces, it would be a devastating blow to the US position in the region.

An even more alarming possibility is that South Korea or Japan could order US forces off of their territory as de Gaulle did during the Cold War. France's nuclear arsenal didn't cause de Gaulle to leave NATO's military command. He made this decision based on his views on alliances and France's role in the world, which long predated France's acquisition of nuclear weapons. But an operational nuclear deterrent gave de Gaulle the security to act on his views in a way he did not beforehand.

In some ways, that de Gaulle's withdrawal was based on his own peculiar views is reassuring. After all, the French general will not be running a nuclear-armed Japan or South Korea. This largely misses the point, however. France's nuclear program was initiated by Fourth Republic leaders when de Gaulle was out of power. By the time he returned, France's nuclear program was already on autopilot. This is important because Fourth Republic leaders viewed nuclear weapons in ways similar to their British counterparts—they believed a nuclear arsenal would enhance France's position within the Western alliance but, ultimately, be a part of it. Then de Gaulle returned and used the bomb in ways antithetical to their beliefs. The clear lesson is that America cannot control who runs allied countries. Even if a strongly pro-American leader like the late Shinzo Abe were to initiate a nuclear weapons program, there is no guarantee a hostile future leader won't use his creation to undermine the alliance.

It is also worth emphasizing that losing access to Japan or South Korea would be far more devastating to the United States than losing France was during the Cold War. Although de Gaulle's actions created an immediate crisis for US policymakers, its impact was mitigated by NATO's multilateral nature. This allowed Washington to relocate its forces to other NATO countries. The same is not true in Asia, where the United States maintains a "hub and spoke" system of bilateral alliances. If Seoul or Tokyo demanded America's withdrawal, these forces could not easily be relocated somewhere else in the region. Already, Japan hosts the largest contingent of US troops anywhere in the world, and the US home stations an aircraft carrier in the country. Moreover, as US military leaders have long emphasized, American forces in the Indo-Pacific need to be more dispersed to counter China's precision-guided missiles.[62]

Partners

From the Israel case, the most important lesson that is not unique to Israel is the impact allied proliferation can have on America's arms control and nonproliferation agendas. As already mentioned, the NPT's absence is a major shortcoming of the case studies. None of the case studies in this book signed the NPT as non-nuclear weapon states, but any future ally or partner that acquires nuclear weapons will have been a signatory of the NPT. This would create a whole set of complications that were not present in the UK, France, Israel, or Pakistan cases. That being said, it is certain that an NPT country going nuclear would have major implications for America's general arms control and nonproliferation policies. The same was true of Israel, although almost certainly to a lesser extent. Depending on the circumstances, it's possible the US might urge the country to adopt an opaque nuclear posture in a similar vein as the Israelis. Even if the partner nation withdrew from the NPT, not formally acknowledging its nuclear arsenal could perhaps limit the damage to America's global nonproliferation goals. Of course, a country's willingness to be an opaque nuclear power would depend on details that cannot be foreseen. In final analysis, a future case of allied proliferation would impact America's nonproliferation goals as Israel did, but the specific details are likely to be quite different.

Beyond this example, the lessons most salient for future partner cases will probably depend heavily on which partner acquires nuclear weapons. At the time of this writing, the US partner that is most interested in nuclear weapons is Saudi Arabia. That case has interesting parallels to Pakistan. Saudi Arabia is not the terrorist safe haven that Pakistan is (no country is), but Riyadh also has strong radical Islamist elements within its society. For this reason, US officials would be rightly concerned about an insider threat to the Saudis' nuclear arsenal. It would hardly be unthinkable that radical Islamist scientists might infiltrate Saudi Arabia's nuclear establishment. Once there, they might provide stolen nuclear materials or, perhaps, even warheads to terrorist groups with similar ideologies. The radicalization of military officers involved in the nuclear program would also be a major concern.

In addition, the stability of the current monarchy would become a more pressing matter for Washington if Saudi Arabia acquires nuclear weapons. There are plenty of worrying trends in the country—beyond the fact that it is a strict conservative monarchy in an increasingly modernized world—that suggest the Saudi regime might not be secure internally over the long term.[63] It is always possible that the downfall of the Saudi government could pave the way for a more secular, democratic one. It is much more likely that a more radical regime would come to power, just as occurred in Iran in 1979 and in Egypt initially after the Arab Spring. Even if the Saudi regime survived an internal uprising, a prolonged civil war along the lines of Syria would be deeply troubling if the country had nuclear weapons.

Another similarity between Saudi Arabia and Pakistan is that both are locked in an eternal struggle with an archenemy. As already discussed, the nuclearization of the Indo-Pakistani dispute made it a far graver concern to US policymakers, even though the countries fought three conventional wars before acquiring nuclear weapons. Washington is already deeply concerned about the growing Saudi-Iranian proxy war. But if the nuclear shadow hung over the proxy wars between Saudi Arabia and Iran, it would significantly elevate the dispute's importance in Washington. Complicating matters further is that the nuclearized dispute would really be trilateral, given Israel's involvement. Managing this standoff to prevent nuclear use would require significant US attention and resources, which would come at the expense of priorities like China's rise and Russia's resurgence. Moreover, there is no guarantee that greater attention would guarantee success. The Middle East has bedeviled US administrations for decades, and it would be a challenge to maintain the already low success rate in the region if nuclear weapons were introduced into the equation.

ROADMAP

The bulk of the rest of this book is devoted to detailed case studies of the four allied and partner nations. Chapters 2 through 4 examine the British case from the World War II era until the Nassau Agreement in 1962. The chapters show that American-British nuclear collaboration was plagued by tensions from the beginning. London's belief that cooperation would continue after the end of WWII created a situation where the UK felt betrayed when the US ended this collaboration. This threatened a relationship that was otherwise growing rapidly in the earlier years of the Cold War. Chapters 5 and 6 examine France's nuclear program from the 1950s until the 1970s. These chapters show that France's nuclear program was initiated by Fourth Republic leaders when de Gaulle was out of power. These leaders believed a nuclear arsenal would elevate France's position within NATO. But then de Gaulle returned to power and used their creation in ways that they would have abhorred. The French case is also notable in that the United States approached the issue through the broader lens of geopolitics in Europe, and especially about how it would impact West Germany.

Chapters 7 through 10 deal with the partner nations. The first two chapters look at the Israeli case from the 1950s until the early 1970s—with some attention paid to certain events afterward. The Israeli case is less generalizable than the other chapters. Like the British case, the nuclear program created tensions in a bilateral relationship that was otherwise growing closer. Similar to the French case, US policymakers worried about the impact Israel's nuclear program would have on geopolitics in the Middle East and even Europe. One interesting takeaway from the Israeli case study is that what is now called the qualitative military edge had its origins in the nuclear program. Chapters 9 and 10 examine the Pakistan case from the 1970s until the present time. Chapter 9 disputes the common narrative that the United States could have stopped Pakistan from acquiring nuclear weapons if Washington hadn't prioritized thwarting the Soviet Union in Afghanistan. As the chapter makes clear, US policymakers could not see a viable way to prevent Pakistan from acquiring nuclear weapons even before the Soviets invaded Afghanistan on Christmas Day 1979. Chapter 10 then examines all the major Indo-Pakistani crises since 1990, the role of the Pakistani nuclear arsenal in America's war on terrorism, and the AQ Khan network. At the end of each case study, I pause to examine some of the specific lessons the case has for potential future cases. As I did in the previous section, I try to apply these lessons to concrete potential future examples like South Korea or Saudi Arabia. The concluding chapter then examines the collective lessons for future cases in much greater detail.

NOTES

1. For similar arguments, see Chuck Hagel, Malcolm Rifkind, Kevin Rudd, and Ivo Daalder, "When Allies Go Nuclear," *Foreign Affairs*, February 12, 2021; and Eric Brewer, "The Nuclear Proliferation Landscape: Is Past Prologue?" *Washington Quarterly* 44 no. 2 (2021).

2. Christian Hacke, "Why Germany Should Get the Bomb," *National Interest*, August 12, 2018; Tristan Volpe & Ulrich Kühn, "Germany's Nuclear Education: Why a Few Elites Are Testing a Taboo," *Washington Quarterly* 40, no. 3 (2017); and Hagel et al., "When Allies Go Nuclear."

3. Eric Heginbotham & Richard J. Samuels, "Vulnerable US Alliances in Northeast Asia: The Nuclear Implications," *Washington Quarterly* 44, no. 1, (2021): 162–63.

4. "Erdogan Says It's Unacceptable That Turkey Can't Have Nuclear Weapons," *Reuters*, September 4, 2019.

5. Richard Mann, "Eduardo Bolsonaro Defends Possession of Nuclear Weapons," *Rio Times*, May 15, 2019.

6. The terms optimists and pessimists are features of the current literature. See, for example, Peter Feaver, "Optimists, Pessimists, and Theories of Nuclear Proliferation Management: A Debate," *Security Studies* 4 (1995).

7. The fullest expression of Waltz's arguments can be found in Scott D. Sagan and Kenneth N. Waltz, *The Spread of Nuclear Weapons: A Debate Renewed* (New York: Norton, 2003), Chapters 1, 3, and 4. On the navy's finite deterrence argument, see Edward Kaplan, *To Kill Nations: American Strategy in the Air-Atomic Age and the Rise of Mutually Assured Destruction* (Ithaca, NY: Cornell University Press, 2015), Chapter 6; and William Burr, "'How Much is Enough?': The U.S. Navy and 'Finite Deterrence,'" *National Security Archive*, Briefing Book no. 779, October 14, 2021. The French arguments are cited in the relevant chapters.

8. Bruce Bueno de Mesquita and William H. Riker, "An Assessment of the Merits of Selective Nuclear Proliferation," *Journal of Conflict Resolution* 26, no. 2 (June 1982); and Peter R. Lavoy, "The Strategic Consequences of Nuclear Proliferation:

A Review Essay," *Security Studies* 4, no. 4 (1995). Also see John J. Mearsheimer, "The Case for a Ukrainian Nuclear Deterrent," *Foreign Affairs* (Summer 1993); and Stephen Van Evera, "Primed for Peace: Europe after the Cold War," *International Security* 15, no. 3 (Winter 1990/91).

9. Scott D. Sagan, "More Will Be Worse," in *The Spread of Nuclear Weapons: A Debate Renewed* (New York: Norton, 2003), 46–87. Also see Feaver, "Optimists, Pessimists, and Theories of Nuclear Proliferation Management"; Stephen R. David, "Risky Business: Let Us Not Take a Chance on Proliferation," *Security Studies* 4, no. 4 (Summer 1995); and Bruce G. Blair, *The Logic of Accidental Nuclear War* (Washington, DC: Brookings, 1993), among many others. Wohlstetter's arguments are captured in Albert Wohlstetter, "Nuclear Sharing: NATO and the N+1 Country," *Foreign Affairs* (April 1961).

10. Masakatsu Ota, "U.S. Weighed Giving Japan Nuclear Weapons in 1950s," *Kyodo*, January 23, 2015. Also see President Eisenhower's policies throughout the book.

11. See Doug Bandow, "Let Them Make Nukes," *Foreign Affairs*, July 26, 2016; Andres Corrs, "Japan: Go Nuclear Now," *Forbes*, January 31, 2017; and Harvey M. Sapolsky and Christine Leah, "Let Asia Go Nuclear," *National Interest*, April 14, 2014; John J. Mearsheimer, "Back to the Future: Instability in Europe After the Cold War," *International Security* 15, no. 1 (Summer 1990).

12. "Full Rush Transcript: Donald Trump, CNN Milwaukee Republican Presidential Town Hall," *CNN*, March 29, 2016. Also see Maggie Haberman and David Sanger, "Transcript: Donald Trump Expounds on His Foreign Policy Views," *New York Times*, March 26, 2016.

13. Christopher Layne, "Hillary Clinton and Nuclear Weapons: More Dangerous Than Trump?" *National Interest*, October 31, 2016; Sapolsky and Leah, "Let Asia Go Nuclear"; Charles Krauthammer, "Cold War Relic, Present Day Threat," *Washington Post,* January 5, 2017; James Van de Velde, "Go Ahead. Let Japan and South Korea Go Nuclear," *National Interest*, October 1, 2016.

14. Indeed, he argues "it is not obvious that acquisition by Japan or Germany would be a terrible outcome from a purely US perspective." See Stephen Walt, "It's Time to Fold America's Nuclear Umbrella," *Foreign Policy*, March 23, 2021. Robert W. Tucker has similarly argued that if America ending its security alliances results in more proliferation, and this leads to nuclear conflict, America can still stay out of those wars. See "What This Country Needs Is a Touch of New Isolationism," *New York Times*, June 21, 1972.

15. Elbridge Colby, "Choose Geopolitics Over Nonproliferation," *National Interest*, February 28, 2014.

16. Jennifer Lind and Daryl G. Press, "Should South Korea Build its Own Nuclear Bomb?" *Washington Post*, October 7, 2021.

17. Jeremy Ludi, "The Rising American Chorus for a Nuclear Japan," *Asia Times*, August 29, 2017.

18. Clark Murdock and Thomas Karako, *Thinking about the Unthinkable in a Highly Proliferated World* (Washington, DC: Center for Strategic and International Studies) July 2016; and "Full Rush Transcript: Donald Trump."

19. Zack Beauchamp, "Trump's Comments on Japanese Nukes Are Worrisome—Even By Trump Standards," *Vox*, March 31, 2016.

20. John F. Kennedy, "The President's News Conference," March 21, 1963, http://www.presidency.ucsb.edu/ws/?pid=9124; and Michael R. Gordon with Felicity Barringer, "Nuclear Standoff: North Korea Wants Arms and More Aid from U.S," *New York Times*, February 13, 2003.

21. "Record of the 508th Meeting of the National Security Council," January 22, 1963, *Foreign Relations of the United States (FRUS)*, 1961–1963, vol. VIII, doc. 125.

22. Albert Wohlstetter, *Swords from Plowshares: The Military Potential of Civilian Nuclear Energy* (Chicago: University of Chicago Press, 1979), 146; and Gene Gerzhoy and Nick Miller, "Donald Trump Thinks More Countries Should Have Nuclear Weapons. Here's What the Research Says," *Washington Post*, April 6, 2016.

23. Paul Bracken, *The Second Nuclear Age: Strategy, Danger, and the New Power Politics* (New York: Times Books, 2012). Also see Henry Kissinger, "Henry Kissinger on Nuclear Proliferation," *Newsweek*, February 6, 2009.

24. Andrew Krepinevich and Jacob Cohn, "Rethinking the Apocalypse: Time for Bold Thinking About the Second Nuclear Age," *War on the Rocks*, March 1, 2016. Also see Wohlstetter, "Nuclear Sharing"; Wohlstetter, *Swords from Plowshares;* and Peter D. Feaver, "Command and Control in Emerging Nuclear Nations," *International Security* 17, no. 3 (Winter 1992/93).

25. Scott D. Sagan, "Two Renaissances in Nuclear Security Studies," H-Diplo/ISSF Forum, no. 2 (2014), https://issforum.org/ISSF/PDF/ISSF-Forum-2.pdf. South Africa also built a small nuclear arsenal but later voluntarily dismantled it during the transition away from apartheid. Ukraine, Kazakhstan, and Belarus inherited nuclear weapons from the former Soviet Union but surrendered them.

26. Francis J. Gavin, "Strategies of Inhibition: U.S. Grand Strategy, the Nuclear Revolution, and Nonproliferation," *International Security* 40, no. 1 (Summer 2015); Gene Gerzhoy, "Coercive Nonproliferation: Security, Leverage, and Nuclear Reversals" (PhD diss., University of Chicago, 2014); Philipp C. Bleek and Eric Lorber, "Security Guarantees and Allied Proliferation," *Journal of Conflict Resolution* 58, no. 3 (2014); and Jeffrey W. Knopf, ed., *Security Assurances and Nuclear Proliferation* (Stanford, CA: Stanford University Press, 2012).

27. Richard E. Neustadt and Ernest R. May, *Thinking in Time: The Uses of History for Decision Makers* (New York: Free Press, 1986).

28. Graham Allison and Niall Ferguson, "Applied History Manifesto," October 2016, http://www.belfercenter.org/project/applied-history-project#!our-manifesto.

29. Henry Kissinger, *White House Years* (Boston: Little, Brown, 1979), 54.

30. James Mahoney and P. Larkin Terrie, "Comparative-historical Analysis in Contemporary Political Science," in *Oxford Handbook of Political Methodology*, eds. Janet M. Box-Steffensmeier, Henry E. Brady, and David Collier (New York: Oxford University Press, 2008), 743.

31. Marc Grossman, interview with author Zachary Keck, Washington, DC, July 18, 2018.

32. As discussed below, US officials did believe the UK and France cutting their troop levels and general contributions to NATO did force the United States to

shoulder a larger burden of the defense of NATO than they otherwise would have. The Eisenhower administration did appear to hold off or obscure its own drawdown of forces in Europe in 1957, when the British were announcing their cuts.

33. Quoted in John Baylis, *Ambiguity and Deterrence: British Nuclear Strategy, 1945–1964* (Oxford: Clarendon Press, 1996), 120.

34. Both concerns were raised by Members of Congress before the first UK atomic test. See "Meeting of the Joint Congressional Committee on Atomic Energy," July 20, 1949, *FRUS*, vol. I, 1949, doc. 177.

35. Besides the logical flaws, it seems clear that US command and control technology wasn't close to being sufficient for implementing such a policy. On this point see Kaplan, *To Kill Nations*, 199. On Flexible Response more generally, see Francis J. Gavin, *Nuclear Statecraft: History and Strategy in America's Atomic Age* (Ithaca, NY: Cornell University Press, 2012), chapter 2.

36. "Memo from Bundy to President Kennedy," 1961–1963, *FRUS*, vol. XIII, doc. 392.

37. "Record of Meeting," December 28, 1962, 1961–1963, *FRUS*, vol. 13, doc. 410; "Memorandum of Conference with the President on Sharing Nuclear Information with the United Kingdom," October 25, 1957, *Digital National Security Archive (DSNA)*. Also see Eisenhower's and McNamara's comments in Marc Trachtenberg, *A Constructed Peace: The Making of the European Settlement, 1945–1963* (Princeton, NJ: Princeton University Press, 1999), 178 and 365. Interestingly, NATO Secretary-General Paul-Henri Speak made this exact point to Dulles as well. See "Discussion with Mr. Spaak of NATO Political and Military Subjects," October 24, 1957, 1955–1957, *FRUS*, vol. 4, doc. 58.

38. G. Wyn Rees, *Anglo-American Approaches to Alliance Security, 1955–60*, 55 and Mark Bell, *Nuclear Weapons and Foreign Policy*, 113.

39. "Wilson and Sandys Discussion," January 28, 1957, 1955–1957, *FRUS*, vol. 27, doc. 253; "Dulles and Sandys Discussion," January 29, 1957, ibid., doc. 254; and "Eisenhower and Macmillian Discussion," March 22, 1957, ibid., doc. 257.

40. "Eden Letter to Eisenhower," July 18, 1956, 1955–1957, *FRUS*, vol. IV, doc. 34.

41. Quoted in Lawrence Scheinman, *Atomic Energy Policy in France Under the Fourth Republic* (Princeton, NJ: Princeton University Press, 1983), 109.

42. IISS Military Balances 1961 and 1967. Some of this decline would've happened anyway because of the end of the Algiers War.

43. Jurgen Brauer and Hubert van Tuyll, *Castles, Battles, and Bombs: How Economics Explains Military History* (Chicago: University of Chicago Press, 2008), 268.

44. SIPRI Military Expenditure Database.

45. Brauer and van Tuyll, *Castles, Battles, and Bombs*, 261.

46. The UK figure is distorted by the fact that major cuts were made before 1960. If you date it from 1956, UK defense spending as a percentage of GDP declined by 2.81 percent according to UK public spending data.

47. Quoted in Zia Mian and A. H. Nayyar, "Playing the Nuclear Game: Pakistan and the Fissile Material Cutoff Treaty," *Arms Control Today* (April 2010), 19. Also

see Adam Entous, "How Trump and Three Other U.S. Presidents Protected Israel's Worst Kept Secret: Its Nuclear Arsenal," *New Yorker*, June 18, 2018.

48. Shamila Chaudhary, interview by phone with author Zachary Keck, July 25, 2018.

49. Philipp C. Bleek, "Does Proliferation Beget Proliferation? Why Nuclear Dominos Rarely Fall" (PhD diss., Georgetown University, 2010).

50. Nicholas L. Miller, "Nuclear Dominoes: A Self-Defeating Prophecy?" *Security Studies* 23, no. 1 (2014), pp. 33–73.

51. Gary Samore, interview by phone with author Zachary Keck, July 13, 2018.

52. Colby, "Choose Geopolitics Over Nonproliferation."

53. Colby was responding to an article by David Santoro, which argued that America should immediately terminate its alliance with Japan or South Korea if they acquire nuclear weapons. See David Santoro, "Will America's Asian Allies Go Nuclear?" *National Interest*, January 30, 2014.

54. Robert Zarate made some similar points in response to Colby's article. See Robert Zarate, "America's Allies and Nuclear Arms: Assessing the Geopolitics of Nonproliferation in Asia," *Project 2049 Institute*, May 6, 2014.

55. Quoted in Richard Rhodes, *The Making of the Atomic Bomb, 25th Anniversary Edition* (New York: Simon & Shuster, 2012).

56. Mark Bell, "Nuclear Weapons and Foreign Policy" (MIT Doctoral diss., September 2016), 73. It is generally believed the United Kingdom had an operational deterrent when the V bomber entered into service in 1956. Bell cites the Royal Air Force's (RAF's) secret internal history of the program, written by Humphrey Wynn and later released publicly, that says the RAF could deliver a nuclear weapon in 1955. Other studies have come to the same conclusion. See ibid., 96.

57. Bell, "Nuclear Weapons and Foreign Policy," 116.

58. MemCon, Secretary's European Trip (18–28 1962), "Role of the UK Nuclear Deterrent," June 25, 1962, NSA at George Washington University, Washington, DC.

59. Turkey's refusal to allow US troops to use its territory to invade Iraq is an imperfect but still relevant example.

60. See Alex Ward, "The President of South Korea Has a Strong Message for Trump," *Vox*, August 17, 2017.

61. This paragraph draws from Zachary Keck and Henry Sokolski, "How to Handle South Korea's Missile Ambitions," *Foreign Affairs,* November 6, 2017.

62. "America's Top Brass Responds to the Threat of China in the Pacific," *The Economist*, March 13, 2021.

63. Karen Elliot House, *On Saudi Arabia: Its People, Past, Religion, Fault Lines—and Future* (New York: Vintage, 2012).

PART I
Allies

Chapter 2

The Ultimate Betrayal (Britain, 1939–1946)

The British case is often held up as the gold standard of allied proliferation. According to this narrative, US-British atomic collaboration is a prototypical example of how allies and partners getting nuclear weapons can be done without negatively impacting US national interests. Indeed, some observers go so far as to claim that the United States helped England build the bomb.

In social science parlance, Britain's nuclear weapons would be considered a "most-likely" test case.[1] That means that even if the British case is found to be favorable to US interests, it doesn't necessarily follow that this would be true of other cases. If, however, it turns out that Britain's acquisition of nuclear weapons presented serious challenges for the United States, this makes it especially likely that allied proliferation is harmful to US foreign policy. After all, there are few countries in the world closer than the US and the UK.

A closer look at the history reveals that the British case was not as seamless as is commonly believed. Although the United States and England were growing closer on nearly every front in the immediate post–WWII years, nuclear cooperation was a stark anomaly. Britain's pursuit of nuclear weapons put tremendous stress on the alliance that, at times at least, hurt the broader relationship.

The origins of these tensions can be traced back to their cooperation in World War II. Specifically, while Franklin D. Roosevelt (FDR) decided to bring the British into the Manhattan Project, most of his advisors opposed the idea. More importantly, President Roosevelt hid from his advisors a secret agreement to continue this cooperation after the war. They only found out about it from the British after Roosevelt's death. This created a toxic dynamic where the British expected atomic cooperation to continue after the war, while the American side insisted that it ended with Japan's surrender. This ultimate betrayal soured bilateral relations until at least 1958, and lingering issues continue to this very day.[2]

The UK is nonetheless a best-case scenario for allied proliferation. Without question, England's acquisition of nuclear weapons hurt US interests less than future cases. Still, that is not saying much. It is preferable to lose a finger over a hand, but people don't normally cut off their fingers. Even if Britain's nuclear program was not as damaging as France's, there is little doubt that Truman and Eisenhower administration officials found it extremely difficult to manage Britain's quest for atomic weapons. Some of these issues, particularly over launch control, continued to frustrate the Kennedy and future administrations.

To tell this story, one must start with the peculiar nature of Britain and America's cooperation during World War II. The level of intimacy on atomic issues between the United States, Britain, and Canada during the war has not been replicated by any countries since. Nonetheless, even then a healthy amount of distrust existed. When Britain's program was more advanced, London rebuffed Washington's efforts to combine their programs. It was only after the United States surpassed England that British officials had a change of heart. But US officials also had a change of heart by then—they now opposed a joint program on many of the same grounds London had once cited. Above all, their concerns were centered on the geopolitical influence a country would derive from having sole possession of the most powerful weapon. This was just the first example of the difficulties of separating allied proliferation from geopolitics.

Many of the same issues led Washington to break off atomic cooperation with the British after the war, despite the secret wartime agreements. Although the Truman administration flirted with restoring nuclear ties at various points, little progress was made during its time in office. British officials hoped that would change with the election of Dwight Eisenhower in 1952, given that the former army general had always favored cooperating closely with the British. Although Eisenhower remained in favor of restoring nuclear ties as president, he rarely risked any political capital to make it happen during his first years in office. It was only after the Suez Crisis in 1956 and the Sputnik moment the following year that the political environment in Washington became amenable to atomic cooperation. President Eisenhower acted on this opening and amended the Atomic Energy Act to allow for nuclear cooperation with the British. As is evident from the wording of that legislation, however, it was Britain's unilateral progress in exploding atomic and hydrogen devices that was ultimately most important in persuading Congress to restore nuclear cooperation. Still, launch control issues continued to plague the alliance, as did London's decision to slash conventional spending after acquiring the bomb.

The next three chapters tell this story. This one examines how the US went from being nuclear rivals to nuclear partners during the war and the ultimate betrayal that followed the fighting. The next two chapters detail the long road back to partnership, and the challenges that remained afterward.

WORLD WAR II

In June 1942, Michael Perrin, the secretary-general of Tube Alloys (the code name given to the British atomic weapons program) arrived in the United States. He was there to view the progress of his American counterparts. What he found shocked him: the United States was pouring seemingly unlimited resources into acquiring an atomic bomb, including four different methods for extracting fissile material: gaseous diffusion, centrifuges, electromagnetic enrichment, and a graphite pile dedicated to the newly discovered element of plutonium.[3] Within days of arriving in the United States, Perrin sent an urgent message to his superiors across the pond: The Americans were quickly overtaking the British in atomic weapons, and will soon "completely outstrip us in ideas, research, and application of nuclear energy." Once that happens, Perrin warned, the Americans will "quite rightly . . . see no reason for our butting in."[4]

British Lead

It was a dramatic turnabout from less than a year before when it was the Americans that tried to combine efforts with the British—only to rebuffed. England had taken an early lead in the pursuit of atomic weapons, thanks to a March 1940 memo written by Otto Frisch and Rudolf Peierls, two expatriate physicists then working at the University of Birmingham under Mark Oliphant. The Frisch-Peierls memo provided technical calculations proving for the first time that a nuclear chain reaction could be created with a small enough amount of uranium to fit inside an air-delivered bomb. The "super-bomb" that would result, Frisch and Peierls wrote, would produce an explosion equal to one thousand tons of dynamite and a "temperature comparable to that in the interior of the sun." The explosion would also release radiation that would spread its destruction to people outside the immediate blast area.[5]

The Frisch-Peierls memorandum piqued the interest of the British scientific and political communities. In response, London formed the MAUD Committee to substantiate the theoretical work done by Frisch and Peierls. Work was divided among four universities and a private company, Imperial Chemical Industries (ICI). The MAUD Committee's groundbreaking report was finished in July 1941. "We have now reached the conclusion that it will be possible to make an effective uranium bomb which, containing some 25 lbs of active material, would be equivalent as regards destructive effect to 1,800 tons of TNT and would also release large quantities of radioactive substances," it stated. The report further concluded that enough fissile material for a bomb could be obtained by 1943. The scientists implored their political leaders to pursue the bomb as quickly as possible because, "except in the unlikely event of complete disarmament . . . no nation would care to risk being caught without a weapon of such destructive capabilities."[6]

The MAUD report would have an enormous impact on both the British and the American atomic efforts. At the time it was completed, the United States had already been investigating the potential military applications of the atom for a number of years, but not as vigorously as the British. Only a few months before the MAUD Committee's report, the National Academy of Sciences had produced a similar report with much more timid conclusions about the feasibility and timeline of an atomic weapon.[7] Mark Oliphant, the Australian-born physicist who supervised Frisch and Peierls at Birmingham University, made it his mission to shake the Americans of their complacency. Oliphant, a member of the MAUD Committee, was in America in the summer of 1941 to work on radar systems. He spent most of his time trying to impress upon the top American scientists the importance of the MAUD Committee's findings and promote greater collaboration between London and Washington. This included lobbying Vannevar Bush, who led the Office of Scientific Research and Development, which oversaw the military's scientific research program, and one of his key deputies, James Conant. Oliphant found a more sympathetic audience with Ernest Lawrence and Robert Oppenheimer in California. Lawrence, in particular, helped convince Conant of the merits of a serious atomic weapons program; Conant, in turn, persuaded Bush. In September 1941, Conant and Bush approached Charles Darwin, Britain's scientific liaison in Washington, about establishing a joint program between England and the United States.[8]

Conant and Bush's efforts accelerated after they finally received a copy of the full MAUD Committee report in October 1941. Bush briefed FDR about the findings of the report on October 9, six days after he received it. As late as July 1941, Bush downplayed the possibility of an atomic bomb in conversations with the president. Now, he warned FDR that America risked falling behind and urged him to write to Churchill immediately to propose combining programs, which Roosevelt did on October 11. To emphasize the content's importance, FDR had the letter hand-delivered to Churchill in London.[9]

Churchill's leisurely response indicated his disinterest in the proposal. Whereas Churchill often responded to FDR within days, the prime minister kept the president waiting for two months to this proposal.[10] The substance was also not encouraging—Churchill only vaguely offered to have their scientific advisors look into the matter, something that had already been occurring. The initial meetings did not leave the Americans with much confidence. Bush and Contant stressed to Sir John Anderson, the cabinet official in charge of atomic matters in England, and Frederick Lindemann (Lord Cherwell), Churchill's trusted science advisor, that the US was "anxious" to cooperate. The British officials said this wouldn't be possible until the Americans strengthened their standards for screening personnel and protecting confidential information.[11] In other meetings, the British charged the Americans with only being interested in collaborating in order to gain advantages in the industrial uses of atomic energy after the war.[12] Ironically, the United States would repeatedly cite the same two concerns in opposing collaboration in the years ahead.

In reality, Britain's disinterest ran deeper. In internal deliberations, Anderson, Lindemann, and the British chiefs of staff all pushed Churchill for a national program, despite the fact that the UK was under constant aerial bombardment from Nazi Germany. Lindemann (Lord Cherwell) was particularly influential, having maintained a close relationship with the prime minister for over two decades. He argued London had little to gain from collaborating with the Americans, given their country's technological lead. But Lindemann's primary concern was the geopolitical influence the British empire would derive from having sole possession of the bomb. In making his case for a national program, Lord Cherwell wrote to Churchill: "[A]bove all the fact that whoever possesses such a plant should be able to dictate terms to the rest of the world."[13]

Tables Turned

In late August 1941, Churchill became the first world leader to initiate a nuclear weapons program. Then the program stalled, marred by weak leadership and organization. The opposite was true of the United States. It wasn't until January 1942, a month after Pearl Harbor, that FDR greenlit a pilot project to explore an atomic bomb. Immediately, the United States began pouring more resources and manpower into this task than Britain could possibly muster, which led to Michael Perrin's warning in June 1942.

A month later, Anderson "reluctantly" warned Churchill that Britain was falling behind and recommended a complete merger of the British and American programs. Churchill agreed. London had every reason to believe the Americans would enthusiastically accept the offer—at a summit meeting in June 1942, FDR had reiterated his interest in combining their atomic programs. By this time, the US commander in chief was preoccupied with running the war, leaving Bush and Conant temporarily in charge of the atomic weapons program. They were supplanted by General Leslie Groves in September 1942, when FDR transferred control over the atomic program to the military. General Groves was a hardened Anglophobe and would serve as a leading opponent of cooperating with the British through the post–WWII era. But even normally pro-British officials like Secretary of War Henry Stimson believed America should strictly limit cooperation with London on atomic matters. Bush and Conant lost their early support for combining programs once they realized the United States was in the lead. They downplayed this in meetings with UK officials, instead citing security concerns and the military's opposition to explain the delay in cooperation.

Behind the scenes, they expressed mostly the same concerns as Groves did. First, the US officials doubted Britain could really contribute much to building the bomb. Moreover, US officials were highly suspicious that Britain's interest in cooperation was aimed at securing a commercial advantage in the atomic energy industry after the war. It didn't help that many leading British atomic energy officials, including Akers and Perrin, came from Imperial Chemical Industries, a private company.[14] Ultimately, though, maximizing America's postwar geopolitical power was the primary reason they opposed combining programs. As Conant stated in one memo, "knowledge of the design, construction and operation of these plants is a military secret which is in a totally different class from anything the world has ever seen." As such, "the major consideration [on atomic cooperation] must be that of national security and post-war strategic significance."[15] Thus, just like the British, the Americans saw the nuclear issue as indistinguishable from geopolitics.

The plan the US officials involved in the atomic program arrived at was to devise a draconian security system to keep everything as compartmentalized as possible in the name of security. This would enable the British to help advance America's program in areas where they were ahead, like heavy water, while cutting them out of entire areas, like the construction and operation of nuclear plants and everything to do with plutonium.[16] This would limit London's ability to build a bomb or atomic energy program independently of the United States after the war. A committee forwarded this proposal to FDR near the end of 1942, and he approved it without apparently giving it much thought.

Britain was stunned when it received the report in January 1943. "This development has come as a bombshell, and is quite intolerable," John Anderson, the British cabinet official in charge of Tube Alloys, complained to Churchill.[17] Churchill grew so desperate that in April 1943, he ordered a feasibility study to determine how difficult and expensive it would be to build a British bomb without the Americans, perhaps in collaboration with Canada.[18] The response was that the costs would be astronomical. Many of his science advisors believed it was nearly an impossible undertaking, at least in the short term. As late as June 1942, the British were trying to keep the Americans away from their atomic program without harming the larger relationship. Only months later, London faced being frozen out of the entire atomic enterprise. There was only one person who could throw them a lifeline: FDR.

FDR Intervenes

Franklin Delano Roosevelt was one of America's greatest leaders, but he hated confrontation. As such, he had a well-deserved reputation for leaving everyone with the impression he agreed with them. This was certainly on display in the first half of 1943. FDR and Churchill were scheduled to hold a summit in Washington in May 1943, and the prime minister spent the first four months of the year sending increasingly desperate pleas to Harry Hopkins, FDR's closest advisor.[19] Although there is no record of the relevant talk at the Washington Summit, the British believed FDR had decided to restore full cooperation.[20] But the mercurial president continued to consult his advisors on the matter afterward, and Bush and Conant also believed he was in agreement with their views.

Finally, on July 20, FDR handed down his verdict. "While I am mindful of the vital necessity for security in regard to this, I feel that our understanding with the British encompasses the complete exchange of all information," Roosevelt wrote to Bush. "I wish, therefore, that you would renew, in an inclusive manner, the full exchange of information with the British Government regarding Tube Alloys."[21] Bush was stunned, and his deputy, Conant, urged him to protest to the president and convince him to reverse course.[22]

While Bush and Conant were focused on the narrow issue of the atomic program, FDR's decision was likely based on a more holistic view of the relationship. By mid-July, the president was looking ahead to the upcoming Quebec Conference with Churchill the following month. At the top of the agenda was planning the Atlantic allies' final assault on Nazi Germany. The British insisted the allies continue to focus their efforts on fighting in Italy and the Mediterranean as a way to tie down as many German troops as possible.[23] The United States, on the other hand, was determined to launch a cross-channel invasion of France as soon as possible. FDR also wanted an American commander to run the cross-channel invasion. Getting London's acquiescence on these points was Roosevelt's overriding priority for the Quebec Conference, and his decision about nuclear cooperation was likely influenced by these considerations. It was the first but certainly not the last time American leaders sacrificed nonproliferation for other geopolitical ends.

Developments moved quickly after FDR handed down his directive. In fact, the Quebec Agreement on atomic cooperation parroted a proposal

Churchill had made to visiting US officials two days after FDR's decision. The major components were:

- A full exchange of information between Britain and the United States.
- Both sides agree not to use the bomb against each other.
- Both sides agree not to share any information with a third party without each other's consent.
- Both sides agree not to use the bomb against other countries without each other's consent.

Churchill also made an extraordinary proposal to alleviate America's concerns about Britain's industrial interests after the war. Specifically, he proposed "that the commercial or industrial uses of Great Britain should be limited in such manner as the President might consider fair and equitable in view of the large additional expense incurred by the US."[24] That the proud British leader would accept such a restriction—much less propose it himself—underscored London's desperation. Regardless, the Quebec Agreement would go even further, stating "The Prime Minister expressly disclaims any interest in these industrial and commercial aspects beyond what may be considered by the President of the United States to be fair and just and in harmony with the economic welfare of the world."[25] It also established the Combined Policy Committee (CPC) to implement the agreement, consisting of Stimson, Conant, Bush, two Britons, and a Canadian.

Churchill was ecstatic with the agreement, but it was an illusory victory.[26] The exact terms of the cooperation were left vague but generally adhered to Groves's preferences. It allowed for a "full and effective" cooperation in areas where both sides were already working. On the other hand, cooperation in the "design, construction and operation of large-scale plants" would take place through "*ad hoc* arrangements." These *ad hoc* arrangements would be created for the sole purpose of accelerating the bomb's completion. Given that the Manhattan Project was being run by the Anglophobe General Groves, and the Combined Policy Committee was stacked with three Americans who were skeptical of cooperation, these terms were not strong enough to prevent British scientists from being boxed out of much of the program. In particular, the British scientists were not heavily involved in the production and manufacturing processes, leaving them unable to quickly build the bomb after the war.

Before then, two other important wartime agreements were signed. The first, signed in June 1944, was the Agreement and Declaration of Trust, which created the six-member Combined Development Trust, designed to secure as much of the world's uranium and thorium supplies as possible.[27] The agreement left it to the Combined Policy Committee to distribute the stockpiles acquired. This became a frequent irritant to the relationship after the war, although it was also the sole area of cooperation that remained at certain points. Finally, in September 1944, Roosevelt and Churchill inked the Hyde Park Aide Memoire. This document committed the United States to "full collaboration" on atomic matters after the war "until terminated by joint agreement."[28] Like the Quebec Agreement and Declaration of Trust, the Hyde Park Aide Memoire was an executive wartime agreement, and might not hold up to Congressional scrutiny after the war. This was something the British understood.[29] Unlike the two earlier agreements, President Roosevelt kept the existence of the Hyde Park agreement hidden from nearly all his advisors. While Churchill informed his own team gleefully of the agreement, top US officials only learned of its existence from the British after FDR passed away. In fact, the United States was not even able to locate FDR's copy of the agreement until 1957, twelve years after the war ended.[30]

It is not entirely clear how seriously Roosevelt took the Hyde Park Aide Memoire. Churchill appears to have been the one who broached the subject, and it is possible that FDR acquiesced simply to avoid creating tensions at a critical time in the war. Regardless of his actual intentions, the aide memoire created a dynamic after the war whereby the British assumed atomic cooperation would continue, while the Americans insisted wartime agreements ended with Japan's surrender. These differing expectations poisoned ties for over a decade.

THE ULTIMATE BETRAYAL

Japan announced its surrender on August 15, 1945, following the atomic bomb attacks on Hiroshima and Nagasaki. Although only a year had passed since the signing of the Hyde Park Aide Memoire, much had changed in the United States and Great Britain. In April 1945, FDR passed away and was succeeded by his vice president, Harry Truman. In July of the same year, the Labor Party in England defeated the Conservative Party, and Churchill was succeeded by Clement Attlee. Like Truman, Attlee had served as Churchill's deputy during the war. Also like Truman, Attlee was not read into the Manhattan Project until taking power. As one historian accurately puts it: "Fate could not have selected a more uninformed pair of world leaders to address the critical issues surrounding the atomic bomb in the waning year of the war and the immediate postwar period."[31]

Truman's ignorance was quickly put on display. In the months after the war, Truman repeatedly said that Britain and Canada had as much information about making atomic bombs as the United States. This was patently untrue, but the president appeared to believe it. Fortunately for Great Britain, Truman initially supported continuing atomic cooperation. In November, Attlee and Truman signed a document with Canadian Prime Minister Mackenzie King that stated: "We desire that there should be full and effective cooperation in the field of atomic energy between the United States, the United Kingdom, and Canada."[32] The same document directed their subordinates to discuss proper revisions to the Combined Policy Committee and Combined Development Trust in light of the new peacetime conditions.

Unfortunately for the British, neither Truman nor his secretary of state, James Cyrnes, took a strong interest in managing atomic cooperation.[33] This left operationalizing the leadership's directive to people like Bush and especially Groves. On the same day of the trilateral statement, Groves and Sir John Anderson worked out a Memorandum of Intention that outlined possible revisions to their wartime collaboration. The British side came away from these talks thinking they had secured America's help in building their own bomb.[34] In reality, the memorandum strongly favored the American side. This document did agree to eliminate the fourth clause of the Quebec Agreement that gave the US president veto power over a British atomic energy program. Besides that, it heavily favored the United States. For instance, it agreed to "full and effective" cooperation but only in "the field of basic scientific research." In the more important area of "development, design, construction, and operation of plants," the memorandum only said it would be desired "in principle."

More important was what the Memorandum of Intention said about the distribution of raw materials. For the better part of a decade after the war, America's need for uranium would nearly outstrip global supplies. US officials therefore constantly worried about securing enough raw materials to feed their ever-expanding nuclear buildup. No one worried more than Groves, who had eyed monopolizing the entire world's supply of uranium since the beginning of the Manhattan Project.[35] According to the terms of the 1944 agreement, supply was distributed through the Combined Development Trust, which the British had an equal stake in. To achieve his goal of an expansive US arsenal, then Groves would need London's help. With the Memorandum of Intention, Groves got Anderson to agree to state that all raw materials would be distributed on the basis of need. Since only the United States actually had nuclear plants, this effectively meant it would be given all supplies.

Coming off the spectacular win of the Memorandum of Intention, Groves made a peculiar move. On December 4, the Combined Policy Committee asked a small group of officials (including Groves but not Anderson) to write up a new agreement to supersede the wartime ones based on the recommendations that Groves and Anderson had drawn up the month before.[36] This document was submitted to the CPC on February 15, 1946. It closely mirrored the document Groves and Anderson drew up except for one crucial difference—the full cooperation clause would be applied to both basic scientific research and the production and manufacture processes. The new proposal simply stated, "There shall be full and effective cooperation between the three Governments in regard to the exchange of information concerning atomic energy required for their respective programmes of atomic energy development."[37]

It is not clear why this change was made. But it is notable that Groves—who was one of three members of the sub-committee that drew up the new document—began secretly campaigning against it before it was even presented to the CPC. Two days before that meeting, Groves sent an urgent memo to the secretary of state warning against adopting the document he himself had helped write. "The scope of the new arrangements extends far beyond that ever contemplated by the Quebec Agreement and in effect will constitute an outright alliance." Groves then detailed all the reasons it should be rejected. First, the United States did not owe Britain anything, since the burden of building the atomic bomb had fallen nearly entirely on Washington. Second, Article 102 of the new UN charter mandated that all new international agreements be made public. If the three parties made this proposed agreement public, it would destroy efforts at international control, which Truman and Secretary Byrnes were currently spearheading (but Groves wasn't optimistic about). Third, Groves warned that the British believed full cooperation would entail the Americans helping London build production plants in the British Isles. At this point, the general said that he had consulted with Dwight Eisenhower who "feels very strongly" that no large scale production plant should be built in Britain because it would be vulnerable to Soviet attacks or even seizure in the event of an invasion. Instead, Groves recommended all British facilities be built in Canada. The US would press this position repeatedly in the years ahead.[38]

Although the documentary evidence is unclear, it is not unreasonable to assume Groves agreed to this more expansive cooperation language in order to sour his superiors about cooperating with the British at all. If so, he was widely successful. At CPC meetings, the US side especially emphasized any new agreement would violate Article 102 of the UN charter.[39] The British shared this concern but devised an ingenious work around—instead of creating a new agreement, London proposed amending the Quebec Agreement. Since this latter agreement predated the UN charter, it would not be necessary to register the updated agreement with the UN.[40] The US officials, joined by the Canadians, rejected Britain's legal reasoning, creating a paralysis within the CPC. Eventually, the body decided the decision would have to be made at the head of state level.[41]

In an indication of how seriously London viewed the problem, Attlee shot off a long memo to Truman the day after this decision was made. Attlee told Truman he was "gravely disturbed" that the CPC's discussions seemingly nullified their November 1945 understanding. He continued that the three heads of states had agreed to full cooperation in the November statement, and "this cannot mean less than full interchange of information and a fair division of the material." Attlee ended by "strongly urging" Truman to direct the US members of the CPC to find a work around that would allow for the British to receive all of America's atomic secrets.[42]

By this time, President Truman's views on atomic cooperation, undoubtedly influenced by Groves, had changed. In responding to Attlee, Truman said that the intention behind the November agreement did not extend to the manufacture and operation of atomic facilities. Had that been the intention of the statement, he never would've signed it, Truman claimed. To bolster his claim, he pointed to the Memorandum of Intention signed by Groves and Anderson. While Truman admitted that "I was not aware of the existence of this paper," he nonetheless insisted that it "shows conclusively" that the words "full and effective cooperation" only related to "the field of basic scientific information."[43] Behind the scenes, Secretary of State Byrnes, who also admitted to previously being unaware of the Memorandum of Intention, was using it in conversations with the British to limit atomic cooperation.[44]

Attlee took his time responding to Truman's April 20 letter, finally sending a long missive on June 7. He spent most of the letter laying out a history of atomic relations that, if not outright false, certainly framed events in a light most favorable to Britain. But near the end of the letter, Attlee highlighted two important issues that hung over the partnership for years to come. The first was what Attlee referred to as the "McMahon bill" that had just passed the Senate the day before. This was the legislation that ultimately became the Atomic Energy Act of 1946 or the McMahon Act, named after its first sponsor, Senator Brien McMahon. In the United States, the main issue in the bill related to whether there was to be military or civilian control over atomic weapons. London's concern was that the McMahon Act also prohibited the transfer of "restricted data" to other countries. The legislation defined restricted data as "all data concerning the manufacture or utilization of atomic weapons, the production of fissionable material, or the use of fissionable material in the production of power."

In effect, this made it illegal for the Truman administration to engage in the kind of atomic cooperation that the British were seeking. Curiously, the British did not blame President Truman himself for allowing the legislation to pass. As Attlee put it, "It wasn't Truman's fault. Congress was to blame."[45] But in reality, the Truman administration kept Congress almost entirely in the dark about the extent of England's involvement in the Manhattan Project. The British had earlier urged President Truman to disclose more information about wartime collaboration, and even possibly publish the Quebec Agreement. The president refused, leaving Congress ignorant on the subject.

Years later, Senator McMahon would confess that if Congress "had seen this [Quebec] agreement, there would have been no McMahon Act."[46] In this sense, Truman was absolutely to blame.

The other important issue that Attlee's June letter raised was allocation of raw materials. As noted earlier, the Americans needed British assistance in securing enough uranium to fuel its nuclear buildup. Up until the early part of 1946, all the uranium that could be mined in the Belgian Congo (which made up most of the supplies then) had gone to the United States, even though it was jointly financed. That made sense since neither Britain nor Canada had much use for it. That changed, however, during the February 15 CPC meeting when the British announced that they were initiating an atomic research program with an eye to establishing industrial and military programs.[47] In anticipation of constructing a pilot plant, London wanted to begin building up a uranium stockpile. Toward that end, they proposed dividing all the uranium obtained between the end of the war through the end of 1946 on a fifty-fifty basis between the United States and England.[48]

This alarmed the US side, which would have to drastically reduce the size of its planned nuclear buildup. Unsurprisingly, Groves was irate. He wrote to Bush and Under Secretary of State Dean Acheson on April 29, complaining that "such a plan completely disregards the principle of need; it would permit the British to build up stockpiles of material for which they have no immediate requirement." He also vented that a fifty-fifty division was unfair because Britain had only made a small contribution to the atomic program. Furthermore, in any future war, Great Britain and the United States would be allies. As such, they both had an interest in the uranium available being used in the most efficient manner. Of course, this meant it should go to the United States. Finally, as was usually the case, Groves suspected London had ulterior motives, in this case "a stock of materials to take advantage of potential commercial uses."[49] On the same day, Groves sent a separate memo to Acheson to warn that based on the available supplies of uranium, the British plan "cannot be carried out without effecting a shut-down of our own plants in about two years." He also reiterated his concern that a production plant in England would be destroyed or seized by the Soviets in a future war.[50]

While Groves wanted to take a hardline approach toward the British, he was overruled by more senior individuals. These officials feared that pushing London too hard might lead it to cut off all raw material collaboration, gravely threatening America's nuclear buildup. Attlee had made a veiled threat to that effect in his June 7 letter to Truman, noting that while the United States was cutting off the exchange of information, "we have not thought it necessary" to abandon the joint control of raw materials. The British ultimately decided not to use this leverage to the fullest extent possible, probably because it needed US support on other issues unrelated to atomic matters. This allowed the two sides to reach a compromise where each would get half of the uranium received from April 1946 through the end of the year, but the United States kept all the raw materials acquired before then. The agreement also included another concession for the United States—namely, the new deal was "made without prejudice to establishing a different basis of allocation for subsequent years." This allowed Washington to continue to insist on raw materials being divided based on the principle of need once the year was over.

Still, by mid-1946, US-UK atomic collaboration was severed in all areas besides raw materials—the one area where Washington needed London more than vice versa. This was consistent with Anglo-American atomic relations since the MAUD Committee report, where the party in the lead sought to maintain its advantage to the greatest extent possible. That was because both parties saw atomic weapons as inseparable from larger geopolitical issues such as the postwar order and influence. Strong tensions characterized atomic cooperation from the beginning, and this proved true in the years ahead.

NOTES

1. Harry Eckstein, "Case Studies and Theory in Political Science," in *Handbook of Political Science*, vol. 7, eds. Fred Greenstein and Nelson Polsby (Reading, MA: Addison-Wesley, 1975), 119–20.

2. As discussed below, one of the most contentious issues after the war related to launch control—who could order the use of what weapons and when. The question of whether America has veto power over Britain's use of nuclear weapons continues to be an issue in British defense circles. See Jake Wallis Simons, "How Washington Owns the UK's Nukes," *Politico*, April 30, 2015.

3. Fissile material is the highly enriched uranium or plutonium used to spark a chain reaction in nuclear bombs.

4. Septimus H. Paul, *Nuclear Rivals: Anglo-American Atomic Relations, 1941–1942* (Columbus, OH: Ohio State University Press, 2000), 28.

5. Otto Frisch and Rudolf Peierls, "The Frisch-Peierls Memorandum," March 1940, https://web.stanford.edu/class/history5n/FPmemo.pdf.

6. M.A.U.D. Committee, *Report by M.A.U.D. Committee on the Use of Uranium for a Bomb* (London: Ministry of Aircraft Production, July 1941).

7. Paul, *Nuclear Rivals*, 20–21.

8. See Graham Farmelo, *Churchill's Bomb: How the United States Overtook Britain in the First Nuclear Arms Race* (New York: Basic Books, 2013), 197–198; Richard G. Hewlett and Oscar E. Anderson, Jr., *vol. I: A History of the United States Atomic Energy Commission, The New World, 1939/1946* (University Park, PA: The Pennsylvania State University Press, 1962), 43–44; and Paul, *Nuclear Rivals*, 23.

9. Paul, *Nuclear Rivals*, 22–24; and Farmelo, *Churchill's Bomb*, 194.

10. Farmelo, *Churchill's Bomb*, 203.

11. Farmelo, *Churchill's Bomb*, 204; and Paul, *Nuclear Rivals*, 26.

12. Paul, *Nuclear Rivals*, 26.

13. Quoted in Richard Rhodes, *The Making of the Atomic Bomb, 25th Anniversary Edition* (New York: Simon & Shuster, 2012), 372. The Joint Chiefs of Staff also told Churchill they were "strongly in favor of its development," as quoted in Paul, *Nuclear Rivals*, 23. Also see Farmelo, *Churchill's Bomb*, 190.

14. Hewlett and Anderson, *The New World*, 271–73; "The Director of the Office of Scientific Research and Development (Bush) to the President's Special Assistant (Hopkins)," March 31, 1943, in *Foreign Relations of the United States* (hereafter *FRUS*), Conferences at Washington and Quebec, 1943, doc. 7. (Note: the conferences are under the 1941 section of *FRUS*.) See also, James G. Hershberg, *James B. Conant: Harvard to Hiroshima and the Making of the Nuclear Age* (Stanford, CA: Stanford University Press, 1995), 179–82.

15. Quoted in Hershberg, *James B. Conant*, 172. In their defense, Lord Cherwell freely admitted to wanting manufacturing information in order to build a bomb for Britain after the war. See Hewlett and Anderson, *The New World*, 273.

16. The areas the British were to be excluded from included "all manufacturing and bomb design data, details of the electromagnetic method, the production of heavy water, and fast neutron reactions." They would be included in the areas of the diffusion process and the heavy-water research where the British were ahead. Hershberg, *James B. Conant*, 184.

17. Martin J. Sherwin, *A World Destroyed: Hiroshima and Its Legacies*, 3rd ed. (Stanford, CA: Stanford University Press, 2003), 76.

18. When approached, however, the Canadians informed the British that if they were forced to choose, they would side with the Americans. See Paul, *Nuclear Rivals*, 46.

19. See for example, "Prime Minister Churchill to the President's Special Assistant (Hopkins)," March 20, 1943, *FRUS*, Conferences at Washington and Quebec, 1943, doc. 5.

20. "Roosevelt–Churchill meeting, evening," May 25, 1943, *FRUS*, Conferences at Washington and Quebec, 1943, doc. 84; and "Cherwell letter to Hopkins," May 30, 1943. Referenced in "Roosevelt–Churchill luncheon meeting, 1 p.m.," May 24, 1943, *FRUS*, Conferences at Washington and Quebec, 1943, doc. 74.

21. "The President to the Director of the Office of Scientific Research and Development (Bush)," July 20, 1943, *FRUS*, Conferences at Washington and Quebec, 1943, doc. 325.

22. "The Acting Chairman of the Military Policy Committee (Conant) to the Director of the Office of Scientific Research and Development (Bush)," July 30, 1943, *FRUS*, Conferences at Washington and Quebec, 1943, doc. 330.

23. Churchill almost certainly preferred this option as a way to limit Soviet influence after the war. John T. Correll, "Churchill's Southern Strategy," *Air Force Magazine*, January 2013, 74.

24. "Memorandum by the Secretary of War's Special Assistant (Bundy)," July 22, 1943, *FRUS*, Conferences at Washington and Quebec, 1943, doc. 326.

25. "Quebec Agreement," August 19, 1943.

26. Churchill's advisors, especially Lord Cherwell, realized this immediately, and it was a point of contention between them through the end of the war. See, Farmelo, *Churchill's Bomb,* pp. 243, 250, and 266.

27. "Agreement Between the United States and the United Kingdom for the Establishment of the Combined Development Trust," June 13, 1944, *FRUS,* Diplomatic Papers, 1944, General: Economic and Social Matters, vol. II, doc. 885.

28. "Aide-Mémoire Initialed by President Roosevelt and Prime Minister Churchill," September 19, 1944, *FRUS,* Conference at Quebec, 1944, doc. 299.

29. Timothy J. Botti, *The Long Wait: The Forging of the Anglo-American Nuclear Alliance, 1945–1948* (New York: Greenwood Press, 1987), 5.

30. Paul, *Nuclear Rivals,* 68.

31. Paul, *Nuclear Rivals,* 72.

32. "Memorandum by President Truman, the British Prime Minister (Attlee), and the Canadian Prime Minister (King)," November 16, 1945, *FRUS,* 1945, vol. II, doc. 28.

33. Truman initially did not take must interest in US nuclear strategy or oversight of the nascent US arsenal. See, David Alan Rosenberg, "The Origins of Overkill: Nuclear Weapons and American Strategy, 1945–1960," *International Security,* vol. 7, no. 4 (Spring 1983), 11–12.

34. Botti, *Long Wait,* 13.

35. Rhodes, *The Making of the Atomic Bomb,* 500.

36. The full committee was Groves, the Canadian ambassador to the United States, L. B. Pearson, and a British minister in the United States, Roger Makins.

37. "Draft Report to the Combined Policy Committee by a Sub-Committee," February 15, 1936, *FRUS,* 1946, vol. 1, doc. 604.

38. "Memorandum by the Commanding General, Manhattan Engineer District (Groves), to the Secretary of State," February 13, 1946, *FRUS,* 1946, vol. 1, doc. 603.

39. "Minutes of the Meeting of the Combined Policy Committee at the Department of State," February 15, 1946, *FRUS,* 1946, vol. 1, doc. 605.

40. "Proposal by the British Members of the Combined Policy Committee," Undated, *FRUS,* 1946, vol. 1, doc. 609.

41. "Minutes of the Meeting of the Combined Policy Committee at the Department of State," April 15, 1946, *FRUS,* 1946, vol. 1, doc. 614.

42. "The British Prime Minister (Attlee) to President Truman," April 16, 1946, *FRUS* 1946, vol. 1, doc. 615.

43. "President Truman to the British Prime Minister (Attlee)," April 20, 1946, *FRUS,* 1946, vol. 1, doc. 619.

44. "Memorandum of Conversation, by the Secretary of State," April 18, 1946, *FRUS,* 1946, vol. 1, doc. 618.

45. Quoted in Paul, *Nuclear Rivals,* 103.

46. Quoted in Ferenc Morton Szasz, *British Scientists and the Manhattan Project: The Los Alamos Years* (New York: Macmillan, 1992), 50.

47. "Statement by the British Ambassador (Halifax)," February 15, 1946, *FRUS,* 1946, vol. 1, Doc. 606.

48. "Memorandum on Allocation by the British Members of the Combined Policy Committee," Undated, *FRUS*, 1946, vol. 1, doc. 612.

49. "Memorandum by the Commanding General, Manhattan Engineer District (Groves), to the Under Secretary of State (Acheson) and the Director of the Office of Scientific Research and Development (Bush)," April 29, 1946, *FRUS*, 1946, vol. 1, doc. 621.

50. "Memorandum by the Commanding General, Manhattan Engineer District (Groves), to the Under Secretary of State (Acheson)," April 29, 1946, *FRUS*, 1946, vol. 1, doc. 622.

Chapter 3

Stuck in the Mud (Britain, 1947–1955)

The McMahon Act represented a terrible betrayal, but Great Britain remained determined to revive nuclear cooperation. For the next decade, this would mostly result in disappointment. The Truman administration periodically sought greater cooperation with the British when it needed a larger share of the limited uranium reserves. Even then, it only offered the bare minimum amount of cooperation necessary to secure British concessions. While a new, modest cooperation agreement was signed in 1948, a series of spy scandals beginning in 1950 derailed any further cooperation for the rest of Truman's time in office. Eisenhower winning the presidency in the 1952 election gave London renewed hope that America would agree to full cooperation in the nuclear sphere. Not only did Eisenhower personally favor atomic cooperation, but in October 1952, the United Kingdom conducted its first nuclear test. This, British leaders believed, would force the Americans to revive atomic cooperation. Alas, London was largely disappointed during Eisenhower's first term, as the NATO commander proved reluctant to use much political capital on greater atomic cooperation. This would only begin to change in Eisenhower's second term as a result of a series of external events.

MODUS VIVENDI

The first example of the United States using nuclear cooperation to gain a greater share of the uranium reserves was the Modus Vivendi signed in January 1948. London began pushing for a revival of cooperation in early 1947 after Atlee initiated a formal nuclear weapons program.[1] The United States initially responded coldly to these overtures. The Joint Chiefs of Staff worried that any secrets shared with Britain would be leaked to the Soviets. They also worried that any atomic facilities built in the UK would be vulnerable to being attacked or even seized by the Soviet Union. Their main objection, however, was that all raw materials should be used to build up US nuclear forces.[2] These three issues would be raised repeatedly by opponents of nuclear cooperation in the years to come.

A number of factors caused the Americans to reconsider their position as 1947 progressed. In the spring of that year, David Lilienthal, a former director of the Tennessee Valley Authority, became the first chairman of the newly formed Atomic Energy Commission (AEC). Immediately upon taking over the AEC, Lilienthal raised concerns about hiding the wartime agreements from the Joint Committee on Atomic Energy (JCAE), the congressional body created to oversee the AEC and atomic affairs. Lilienthal wasn't actually privy to the Quebec Agreement, and Truman initially denied an agreement existed.[3] Undeterred, Lilienthal raised the issue with the JCAE.[4] Intrigued, the congressmen demanded a full briefing, which Under Secretary of State Dean Acheson delivered on May 12. Rusk's briefing was comprehensive and included the Hyde Park Aide Memoire (of which the United States still couldn't locate its own copy) and developments since the war.[5] The JCAE was shocked and particularly angry that the Quebec Agreement gave London veto power over America using atomic weapons. As one State Department official characterized the reaction: "The hearing room erupted in indignation and anger. Several members walked out at the very thought that we'd have to ask anybody's permission to use these weapons."[6] The administration therefore faced pressure to nullify that clause of the Quebec Agreement.

The scarcity of uranium supplies was the main reason Washington wanted to renew cooperation. When Lilienthal took over the AEC in 1947, he was appalled to find that the United States only had a dozen atomic bombs, far too few to carry out the military's war plans.[7] There was simply not enough uranium to bring the stockpiles up to acceptable levels. Aside from a small mine in Canada, almost all the available uranium came from a single mine in the Belgian Congo.[8] This produced two thousand tons a year, only half of which the United States received because of the fifty-fifty allocation agreement with Britain. Meanwhile, Britain was stockpiling uranium it wouldn't need for years. By the fall of 1947, the US government was determined to get its hands on this stockpile.

The only question, then, was the best way to go about this. Members of Congress, and some in the administration, wanted to use economic coercion. In 1946, the United States had agreed to loan the British $3.75 billion (roughly $50 billion today) to stave off bankruptcy. Many argued further assistance should be suspended until Great Britain agreed to surrender its uranium stockpiles and nullify the veto clause of the Quebec Agreement.[9] Cooler heads in the administration opposed linking the two issues and persuaded

Congress to keep this option in their back pocket while allowing negotiations to proceed.[10]

Although some administration officials wanted to offer extensive cooperation, they were overruled. Going into the talks, then, Washington's goal was to offer the minimum amount of cooperation necessary for London to agree to annul the mutual consent clause of the Quebec Agreement and transfer some of its uranium stockpile to the United States. Negotiations proceeded briskly, and the United States was widely successful in achieving its objectives. At first, the British insisted on keeping its entire stockpile but agreed that the United States could have all the Belgian uranium for the next two years. The American side was unsatisfied with this offer. After further pressure from the US, London agreed that it would use its own stockpile to meet America's requirements if the Belgian supply was insufficient. Since the requirement was set at 2,547 tons each year, and the Belgium plant was only pumping out 2,000 tons, this effectively meant the British would transfer around 550 tons a year to the Americans.[11] However, if political problems in the Congo cut off supplies, London would have been on the hook for much more.[12] London also agreed to nullify all parts of the wartime agreements except those related to raw material allocation.

In return, the Americans agreed to restart cooperation in nine areas, most of which were of little interest to the British. Three areas had already been declassified, and in two other areas—extraction of low-grade ore and the design of natural uranium reactors—England was equal to or more advanced than the United States.[13] One area was cooperation with South Africa and other dominions, where the British were essentially helping the Americans secure raw materials. The three remaining areas were on minor issues that London didn't particularly care about, such as research on the uses of radioactive isotopes and stable isotopes, detection of a distant nuclear explosion, and survey methods for source materials. London almost certainly agreed to these limited exchanges because the American negotiators continued to maintain that the areas of cooperation would be expanded in the future. They therefore viewed the modus as signifying a new era and were less concerned about the minute details at the moment. The British likely also viewed the agreement as America implicitly accepting London's decision to build production plants in the British Isles. Other issues outside of atomic matters, such as the growing Soviet menace, also influenced London's accommodation. Still, it's undeniable that the United States—as was the case time and time again—came out with the better end of the bargain. As Under Secretary of State Robert A. Lovett bragged to the JCAE: "We have achieved more than we might have expected before the talks were begun."[14]

STUCK IN THE MUD (1948–1952)

The Modus Vivendi arguably represented the high point of US-British atomic collaboration for the remainder of the Truman administration. That is not saying much. While the agreement was faithfully implemented, a number of developments caused the United States to resist further expanding cooperation as had been promised during the negotiations. The first of these was the Attlee government's decision to publicly disclose in May 1948 that the prime minister had initiated a nuclear weapons program. The British gave the Truman administration prior notice, and US officials within the administration had long known about the program anyway.[15] Members of Congress were less informed but initially did not react much to the announcement. This changed the following month when a group of US scientists visited the UK and discovered that Britain was building a plutonium production plant. They informed Lilienthal of this fact, who raised it with others in the administration. Most US officials were nonplussed, pointing out that the modus did not prohibit London from this course of action. One administration official who was alarmed was Lewis Strauss, one of five commissioners on the AEC. As will be seen, Strauss would spend the next decade trying to undermine the British nuclear program and US-UK atomic cooperation. In this instance, Strauss took his concerns directly to two senators serving on the JCAE, Arthur Vandenberg and Bourke Hickenlooper.[16] This hardened the JCAE's position against cooperating with London.

Congressional opposition further increased later that summer when it was discovered that Cyril Smith, an American metallurgist, was headed to England to discuss the "basic metallurgy of plutonium." Once again, it was Strauss who relayed the information to Senators Hickenlooper and Vandenburg. The senators then raised it directly with Secretary of Defense James Forrestal, arguing that this area was not covered under the modus agreement.[17] Forrestal agreed and stopped Smith from exchanging any information. At the same time, Forrestal told the two senators that the United States could not break up cooperation with the British, because of the need for raw materials.

It was in this context of increasing congressional hostility that the British officially requested that atomic cooperation be expanded beyond the nine areas contained in the modus. The US side had actually tried to preempt this issue by quietly telling London it was not the right time to seek expanded cooperation.[18] England ignored this advice and formally sent a request on September 1, 1948. This request asked for an "exchange of information on atomic weapons" including on the "metallurgy and methods of fabrication of plutonium with particular reference to its use in bombs."[19] The United States did not immediately reject this, although it reiterated that Britain's nuclear program should be relocated to Canada and that London needed to strengthen its security system to prevent leaks to the Soviet Union. The United States also floated the possibility that America could "earmark" some nuclear weapons for England if London agreed not to build its own arsenal.[20] Mostly, the United States pressed the British to delay the issue until after America's elections in the fall.[21]

Confounding all political prognosticators, Truman stunningly won reelection in 1948. Moreover, Democrats took power in both houses of Congress. Truman also made a number of personnel changes that boded well for atomic cooperation. Dean Acheson, an Anglophile who long favored greater support for Britain, replaced Marshall as secretary of state. William Webster, another proponent of cooperation, was named chairman of the Military Liaison Committee, the military advisory body to the AEC. America's need for raw materials also fueled renewed interest in cooperation. The allocation arrangement worked out in the modus would expire in 1949. More urgently, the Belgian Congo mines were set to undergo reinventions that would temporarily reduce output. US officials estimated they'd need between six hundred and one thousand tons of uranium from England's stockpile in 1949 to replace this loss.[22]

With this in mind, in January 1949, members of the AEC, State Department, and the Department of Defense (DOD), convened a conference at Princeton University to develop a new proposal for expanded cooperation with the British. The recommendations from this conference were later incorporated into a specially appointed subcommittee of the NSC and approved by President Truman on March 31. The plan was more favorable toward atomic cooperation than earlier ones, but that was a low bar to meet. It recognized the legitimacy of the UK's interest in atomic weapons and proposed full and effective cooperation, but only on America's terms. Thus, it called for all major atomic facilities and fissile material to be located in the United States and Canada, and that the facilities in Canada should not consume more than 10 percent of all raw materials over the next five years.[23] As one historian puts it, the plan basically called for a "virtual absorption of the British program by the American [one], similar to what happened in the war."[24]

The British didn't immediately reject the proposal out of hand, but negotiations dragged on for the rest of 1949. Then, in January 1950, a bombshell upended them. That month, Klaus Fuchs, a German scientist who had been nationalized in Britain and worked on the Manhattan Project, confessed to being a Soviet spy. This was followed by Bruno Pontecorvo, another nationalized British scientist (originally from Italy), defecting to the Soviet Union in October 1950. Then, in June of the following year, Donald Maclean, a British diplomat and former member of the CPC, followed Pontecorvo to the Soviet Union. These leaks and defections had a devastating impact on US-UK atomic cooperation. As Secretary of State Acheson acutely observed: "The talks with the British and Canadians returned to square one, where there was a deeper freezer [sic] from which they did emerge in my time."[25] In other words, they did not emerge until the Eisenhower administration.

LAUNCH CONTROL

With nuclear cooperation stalled, the issue of launch control became increasingly prominent in Truman's final years in office. It was an issue that would plague the alliance for years. Launch control goes to the heart of how to operationalize nuclear weapons in the context of alliance—specifically, who gets to decide when to use what weapons. Of course, this issue wasn't entirely new. The Quebec Agreement had given both countries veto power over the bomb, a requirement the Americans pressured the UK into annulling during the Modus Vivendi talks. England soon regretted making this concession when President Truman vaguely alluded to using nuclear weapons in Korea in November 1950. Nearly immediately, Prime Minister Attlee flew to Washington to raise the issue with the president directly.[26] To assuage Attlee's concerns, Truman agreed to "consult" with Attlee before using nuclear weapons.[27] Consultation was a far cry from the veto power British leaders previously enjoyed. Nonetheless, at Acheson's suggestion, even the consultation language was left out of the final communique to avoid angering Congress.[28]

The bigger launch control disagreements were over issues closer to home. Initially, they revolved around the use of American bombers stationed in England. During the Berlin Crisis of 1948, Washington asked London if it could forward deploy bombers in the British Isles. England immediately accepted this request, and ninety B29 "Superfortress" bombers were in East Anglia by September 1948 (without nuclear warheads).[29] To even the Truman administration's surprise, England accepted these bombers without any formal understandings. Undoubtedly, the British were initially thrilled by America's offer, with strong fears persisting that Washington would return to its isolationist roots. Later, London began reflecting on the implications of this arrangement. In particular, British officials asked whether they would have to approve any decision to use these bases to attack the Soviet Union. The mere presence of the bombers made their territory a target once the Soviet Union had the means to reach them. But surely, British leaders insisted, the United States couldn't commit their country to war without their consent. In their excitement over America's enduring commitment to European security, they hadn't bothered to ask. Although it meant "life and death for the country and for Western Europe," Sir John Slessor, the chief of the British air staff, admitted to his colleagues in the summer of 1950, "we know little about the United States Strategic Air Plans with reference to the part to be played by aircraft based in this country."[30] British Foreign Secretary Herbert Morrison was more blunt in conversations with Acheson, stating that it was unacceptable "that Britain should risk annihilating retaliation without being first informed or consulted."[31]

The Americans resisted any firm commitment, regularly falling back on the excuse that constitutional requirements tied their hands. US officials were especially fearful of congressional reaction, given the anger from Capitol Hill when the Quebec Agreement had been made public. But Atlee's government also had domestic opinion to consider.[32] The two sides agreed to negotiate over the issue. Throughout these discussions, London wanted assurances that the United States would at least consult, and preferably get its consent, before either using British bases to launch attacks or using the atomic bomb in general. Truman and Atlee reached an understanding in a December 1950 meeting, convened after the president's vague threat to use nuclear weapons to end the Korean War. Truman agreed to try to consult with the United Kingdom before using nuclear weapons, but he refused to put that in writing.[33] An agreement on the bases in Great Britain was reached by Truman and Churchill in 1952. This read: "The use of these bases in an emergency would be a matter for joint decision by His Majesty's Government and the United States Government *in the light of the circumstances prevailing at the time*[34] [emphasis added]." Obstinately, this gave the British the assurances they sought. In reality, this gave the Americans the ability to use these bases without British consent.[35]

Unlike the UK, some US officials anticipated that British nuclear weapons would pose launch control issues before London first tested the bomb. This is seen clearly from a congressional briefing the administration held when it was seeking more expansive cooperation in 1949. At the meeting, members of Congress raised questions about how England acquiring nuclear weapons would impact the alliance. For instance, Senator Hickenlooper worried that a nuclear-armed Great Britain might seek to stay neutral in a US-Soviet war. Other members wondered if a nuclear-armed UK might entrap the United States in a conflict with the Soviet Union.[36] Despite foreseeing these potential complications, the Truman administration did not address them. This was left to future administrations—particularly, John F. Kennedy's.

HOPE SPRINGS ETERNAL

After years of stalemate, the British believed Dwight Eisenhower's accession to the presidency in January 1953 would bring the atomic cooperation they had long sought. They had every reason to be optimistic, but they would end up being disappointed. As a general, including the first Supreme Allied Commander Europe (SACEUR), Eisenhower was a strong advocate for closer relations with the United Kingdom, including on atomic issues. Indeed, as discussed throughout this book, Eisenhower's overarching goal was to build Europe up as a "third force" that could defend itself against the Soviet Union without permanently stationing US troops on the continent. Faced with a nuclear-armed adversary in the Soviet Union, this would only be possible if Europe had a nuclear deterrent under its control.

The British had other reasons for optimism. Winston Churchill had returned to power in London in October 1951. Whereas Washington had always been weary of Attlee and his Labour Party's socialist economic agenda, Churchill was a hero among the American people and admired by their leaders. Moreover, in October 1952, England tested its first atomic bomb. This was crucial because both the Attlee and Churchill governments had concluded that once England had demonstrated it had the bomb, the United States would no longer withhold its nuclear secrets.[37] President Eisenhower would publicly say the same thing in the years ahead. Another factor promoting greater cooperation was the Soviet Union's growing nuclear capabilities. After testing an atomic device in 1949, Moscow detonated a thermonuclear bomb in August 1953. For many in London, this undermined the argument that America couldn't share secrets with Great Britain because the information would leak to Moscow. After all, the Soviet Union already possessed these secrets.

Another important development was the discovery of large amounts of uranium in the United States. The raw material situation had grown even more dire when the Truman administration decided to launch a hydrogen bomb program in 1950. But in November 1953, the United States determined it would soon be self-sufficient in uranium because of these discoveries. To some extent, though, this was a double-edged sword for atomic cooperation. On the one hand, the United States was less concerned a British atomic program would consume raw materials that America needed. At the same time, the US had less reason to expand atomic cooperation with England now that it didn't need uranium from London.[38]

Nonetheless, early signs out of the Eisenhower administration were encouraging. In a press conference in July 1953, the president called the McMahon Act "really outmoded." Now that the Soviet Union had nuclear weapons, Eisenhower didn't understand the logic of withholding information from America's allies.[39] As the president later complained privately about the law, "it was as if we had been fighting wars with bows and arrows and then acquired pistols. Then we refused to give pistols to the people who were our allies even though the common enemy already had them."[40] In December 1953, Eisenhower told reporters he would be seeking changes to the McMahon Act, although not on information dealing with the "scientific processes of nuclear fission or building of weapons."⁴¹ This suggested he wanted to share external characteristics of US atomic weapons to allow NATO allies to carry US atomic bombs on their own weapon systems.

This was consistent with the administration's "New Look" strategy that sought to use tactical nuclear weapons to offset the Soviet Union's conventional superiority. The internal document detailing New Look, NSC 162/1, stated a greater reliance on nuclear weapons was only possible if the United States got buy-in from its allies.⁴² In general, the Eisenhower administration put greater emphasis on alliances. NSC 162/1 also concluded that America could not "meet its defense needs, even at exorbitant cost, without the support of allies." The United States needed the ability to discuss nuclear weapons with these allies to gain their support, and the allies needed certain information to help America implement its preferred strategy. But it was also tied to Eisenhower's long-term goal of making Europe a third force. This was a theme he returned to time after time. At one National Security Council meeting in October 1953, Eisenhower complained that "the stationing of US divisions in Europe had been at the outset an emergency measure not intended to last indefinitely. Unhappily, however, the European nations have been slow in building up their own military forces and had now come to expect our forces to remain in Europe indefinitely."⁴³ During the first term, this manifested itself in Eisenhower and Secretary of State John Dulles insisting on rearming West Germany over the objections of allies like France. But President Eisenhower would also come to favor a European independent nuclear deterrent. Ideally, this would be under the control of an integrated European military force. Still, Eisenhower favored assisting national nuclear forces, such as the UK, as an interim step.

Initially, though, the Eisenhower administration focused on being more forthcoming with America's allies on nuclear weapons. Accordingly, the president approached Congress about loosening some of the restrictions in the McMahon Act. In officially making the request in February 1954, Eisenhower wrote: "Under present law, we cannot give them tactical information essential to their effective participation with us in combined military operations and planning, and to their own defense against atomic attack."⁴⁴ America's own security required a greater exchange of information. By this time, the JCAE generally favored some nuclear exchanges with allies and on August 30, 1954, Congress passed the Atomic Energy Act of 1954. While still forbidding the transfer of information related to the design or manufacture of nuclear weapons, the legislation gave the administration more leeway in revealing the external characteristics of America's atomic bombs. Congress did retain the right to vote down any bilateral agreement the administration concluded, forcing US officials to keep congressional attitudes in mind when negotiating a new agreement with the British.

Negotiations began in October 1954, and a bilateral agreement was signed in June the following year by Eisenhower and Anthony Eden, Churchill's foreign secretary who succeeded him as prime minister in April 1955. The agreement allowed for the transfer of information about military plans and training personnel in the use and defense against atomic weapons.[45] In an effort to win congressional support, the administration insisted on the principle of reciprocity on civil nuclear matters. British leaders saw the new pact as a half measure. It didn't help London reduce the time or costs associated with strengthening its nuclear arsenal. Consequently, around this time, England accelerated its own efforts, including initiating a hydrogen bomb program.[46] Once again, the prevailing view in London was that America's cooperation hinged on demonstrating unilateral progress. As the UK's ambassador in Washington, Harold Caccia, explained, Britain needed to show it had "megaton as well as kiloton weapons."[47]

The next few years were full of disappointment for the British. This was largely because, despite his own views on nuclear sharing, Eisenhower was constrained by Congress, which was controlled by the Democratic Party. Even so, the president rarely was willing to invest much political capital on the issue. One example of this was the implementation of the 1955 accord. The agreement allowed for the transmission of the external characteristics of America's atomic bombs, but Washington was slow to provide it. This was largely due to the influence of Lewis Strauss, whom Eisenhower had made chairman of the AEC despite the fact that they held widely different views about cooperation with allies. In late 1955, the Department of Defense officially requested permission to transfer information relating to the weight, size, and attachment systems of US nuclear bombs to Great Britain. The AEC under Strauss objected on the grounds that this would violate US law by exposing design and fabrication information.[48]

Strauss and his allies in Congress also slowed progress on transferring nuclear propulsion technology for submarines. The US Navy commissioned its first nuclear-powered submarine in the fall of 1954, and some in the administration wanted to include sharing nuclear propulsion technology with the British as part of the 1955 agreement. The DOD was in favor of this option, and Attorney General Herbert Brownell said the 1954 Atomic Energy Act permitted such an exchange. As a practical matter, however, Brownell advised that the administration get congressional approval before entering into an agreement on the matter.[49] The Eisenhower administration decided to not include it in the 1955 accord to avoid irking Capitol Hill. When the administration did raise it with Congress later on, the JCAE opposed it on the grounds that the British could use submarine propulsion technology to advance their civil nuclear program. If America was to provide this technology to the British, the JCAE wanted London to hand over the technology it used for its gas-cooled, graphite-moderated Calder Hall reactor. This was one area where the UK was ahead of the United States, and some in Washington believed the reactor held great promise for commercial purposes. The British refused to share this technology, which they insisted was a military plant. The administration appeared to defy Congress by signing an amended agreement with the British that allowed for the exchange of submarine propulsion technology in June 1956.[50] Although outraged, Congress failed to block the new agreement. But then President Eisenhower agreed to a JCAE request to delay transferring the technology.[51] Once again, despite being in favor of greater cooperation, Eisenhower refused to use political capital to make it happen. London felt betrayed—again. Thus, despite the early promise, nuclear cooperation was largely unsatisfactory to the British by the time Eisenhower's first term wrapped up.

NOTES

1. John Baylis, "Exchanging Nuclear Secrets: Laying the Foundations of the Anglo-American Nuclear Relationship," *Diplomatic History* 25, no. 1 (January 2001), 35.

2. Quoted in James F. Schnabel, *History of the Joint Chiefs of Staff, Volume 1: The Joint Chiefs of Staff and National Policy, 1945–1947* (Washington, DC: Office of Joint History, 1996), 136–37; and Timothy J. Botti, *The Long Wait: The Forging of the Anglo-American Nuclear Alliance, 1945–1948* (New York: Greenwood Press, 1987), 27–28.

3. "Memorandum by the Chairman of the United States Atomic Energy Commission (Lilienthal) to the Commissioners," April 23, 1947, *FRUS*, 1947, vol. 1, doc. 411.

4. Septimus H. Paul, *Nuclear Rivals: Anglo-American Atomic Relations, 1945–1942* (Columbus: Ohio State University Press, 2000), 117.

5. "Statement by the Under Secretary of State (Acheson) to an Executive Session of the Joint Congressional Committee on Atomic Energy," May 12, 1947, *FRUS*, 1947, vol. 1, doc. 412.

6. Quoted in Paul, *Nuclear Rivals*, 117.

7. Botti, *Long Wait*, 26.

8. There was another source in South Africa, but that wasn't expected to come online until 1950. See Paul, *Nuclear Rivals*, 120.

9. "The Chairman of the Joint Congressional Committee on Atomic Energy (Hickenlooper) to the Secretary of State," August 29, 1947, *FRUS*, 1947, vol. 1, doc. 427; and Botti, *Long Wait*, 30.

10. "Minutes of a Meeting of the Secretaries of State, War, and Navy, Washington, September 11, 1947, 10:30 a.m.," September 11, 1947, *FRUS*, 1947, vol. 1, doc. 429.

11. As it turned out, America was able to meet its entire needs from the Belgian Congo mine in 1948. See "Report by the Policy Planning Staff, Annex 1," February 7, 1949, *FRUS*, 1949, vol. 1, doc. 158.

12. Botti, *Long Wait*, 34.

13. Paul, *Nuclear Rivals*, 125.
14. Quoted in Paul, *Nuclear Rivals*, 129.
15. Paul, *Nuclear Rivals*, 132.
16. Paul, *Nuclear Rivals*, 134.
17. Paul, *Nuclear Rivals*, 134; and Botti, *Long Wait*, 42.
18. Botti, *Long Wait*, 43; and "Memorandum of Conversation, by Mr. Donald F. Carpenter, Deputy to the Secretary of Defense (Forrestal) on Atomic Energy Matters," September 16, 1948, *FRUS*, 1948, vol. 1, part 2, doc. 100.
19. "The Head of the British Naval Mission in the United States (Moore) to the Secretary of Defense (Forrestal)," September 1, 1948, *FRUS*, 1948, vol. 1, part 2, doc. 98.
20. "The Head of the British Naval Mission in the United States (Moore) to the Secretary of Defense (Forrestal)," September 1, 1948, *FRUS*, 1948, vol. 1, part 2, doc. 98.
21. "Memorandum by Mr. R. Gordon Arneson to the Acting Secretary of State," September 27, 1948, *FRUS*, 1948, vol. 1, part 2, doc. 103; and "Memorandum for the File by Mr. R. Gordon Arneson, Special Assistant to the Under Secretary of State (Lovett)," September 22, 1948, *FRUS*, 1948, vol. 1, part 2, doc. 102.
22. Paul, *Nuclear Rivals*, 144–45.
23. "A Report to the President by the Special Committee of the National Security Council on Atomic Energy Policy With Respect to the United Kingdom and Canada," March 2, 1949, in "Memorandum by the Executive Secretary of the National Security Council (Souers) to President Truman," March 2, 1949, *FRUS*, 1949, vol. 1, doc. 164.
24. Botti, *Long Wait*, 51.
25. Quoted in Paul, *Nuclear Rivals*, 169.
26. N. J. Wheeler, "British Nuclear Weapons and Anglo-American Relations 1945–54," *International Affairs* 62, no. 1 (Winter, 1985–1986), 73–74.
27. "Jessup Memorandum for the Record," December 7, 1950, *FRUS*, 1950, vol. 7, doc. 1003.
28. Paul, *Nuclear Rivals*, 177–78. It seems the JCAE might have gotten word of this agreement because in March 1951, its chairman, Senator McMahon, asked Acheson whether Truman had made any agreement that would restrict the president's freedom of action in using nuclear weapons. Acheson assured the senator Truman had not. "Acheson to McMahon," March 14, 1951, *FRUS*, 1951, vol. 1, doc. 287.
29. John Baylis, "American Bases in Britain: The 'Truman-Attlee Understandings,'" *World Today* 42, no. 8/9 (August–September, 1986), 155.
30. Quoted in Baylis, "American Bases in Britain," 155.
31. Quoted in John Baylis, *Ambiguity and Deterrence: British Nuclear Strategy, 1945–1964* (Oxford: Clarendon Press, 1996), 120.
32. "Memorandum of Conversation," September 11, 1951, *FRUS*, 1951, vol. I, doc. 308.
33. Phillip C. Jessup, "Memorandum for the Record," December 7, 1950, in "Memorandum for the Record by Special Assistant to the Secretary of State R. Gordon Arneson," "Truman-Atlee Conversations of December 1950: Use of Atomic Weapons," January 16, 1953, *NSA*.

34. "The Text of the Truman-Churchill Announcement," *Associated Press*, January 9, 1952.

35. Baylis, "Exchanging Nuclear Secrets," 36. When the British and US revisited this after Suez, it appears the United States gave London more control. See "Murphy to Dulles, Joint Report to the President and Prime Minister on Procedures for Launching Nuclear Retaliation from the United Kingdom," June 7, 1958, NSA.

36. "Meeting with the Joint Congressional Committee on Atomic Energy, Washington," July 20, 1949, *FRUS*, 1949, vol. 1, doc. 177.

37. Baylis, "Exchanging Nuclear Secrets," 35; Botti, *Long Wait*, 93–94; and Andrew J. Pierre, *Nuclear Politics: British Experience with an Independent Strategic Force, 1939–1970* (Oxford, UK: Oxford University Press, 1972), 74–78.

38. Botti, *Long Wait*, 123–24.

39. Dwight D. Eisenhower, "The President's News Conference," July 8, 1953, The American Presidency Project, http://www.presidency.ucsb.edu/ws/index.php?pid=9632.

40. "NSC meeting," August 18, 1959, *FRUS*, 1958–1960, vol. 12 (Part 2), doc. 128.

41. Dwight D. Eisenhower, "The President's News Conference," December 16, 1953, *The American Presidency Project*, http://www.presidency.ucsb.edu/ws/index.php?pid=9784.

42. "Lay Report to the NSC," October 30, 1953, *FRUS*, 1952–1954, vol. 2, part 1, doc. 101.

43. "NSC meeting," October 7, 1953, *FRUS*, 1952–1954, vol. 2, part 1, doc. 94.

44. Dwight D. Eisenhower, "Special Message to the Congress Recommending Amendments to the Atomic Energy Act," February 17, 1954, *The American Presidency Project*, https://www.presidency.ucsb.edu/documents/special-message-the-congress-recommending-amendments-the-atomic-energy-act.

45. "Agreement Between the Government of the United States of America and the Government of the United Kingdom of Great Britain and Northern Ireland for Cooperation Regarding Atomic Information for Mutual Defense," June 15, 1955.

46. Botti, *Long Wait*, 144.

47. Quoted in John Baylis, "The 1958 Anglo-American Mutual Defence Agreement: The Search for Nuclear Interdependence," *Journal of Strategic Studies 41*, no. 3 (June 2008), 433.

48. Botti, *Long Wait*, 154–55.

49. Botti, *Long Wait*, 148, 153, 158.

50. "Amendment to the UK-US Agreement Government for Cooperation on the Civil Uses of Atomic Energy of June 15, 1955," Washington, June 13, 1956, http://treaties.fco.gov.uk/docs/fullnames/pdf/1956/TS0035%20(1956)%20CMD-9847%201956%2013%20JUN,%20WASHINGTON%3B%20AMENDMENT%20TO%20AGREEMENT%20BETWEEN%20GOV%20OF%20UK,%20NI%20&%20USA%20FOR%20CO-OPERATION%20ON%20CIVIL%20USES%20OF%20ATOMIC%20ENERGY.pdf.

51. Botti, *The Long Wait*, 163; and Baylis, "Exchanging Nuclear Secrets," 38.

Chapter 4

Full Cooperation at Last (Britain, 1956–1962)

Just when it seemed like full nuclear cooperation was unattainable, two events led President Eisenhower to finally expend the political capital necessary to achieve it. The first was the fallout caused by the Suez Crisis—after humiliating the British on the world stage, Eisenhower was determined to repair the alliance. He saw offering full nuclear cooperation as an expedient way to do so. Despite early progress, negotiations became bogged down until the shock of the Soviet Union's Sputnik satellite test in October 1957. While the Suez Crisis and the Sputnik Moment created momentum, congressional support was only forthcoming because the British successfully tested thermonuclear weapons on their own. This validated the British leaders who had argued that the country must demonstrate its own nuclear capabilities before America would agree to cooperate.

Full cooperation did not fix all the problems caused by the UK nuclear arsenal. What changed was that, after Washington had dictated the terms on nuclear issues since 1943, London suddenly began to prevail. Since 1952, British defense strategies had proposed using nuclear weapons to reduce the size and costs of its conventional forces. As the UK's nuclear deterrent became operational in the mid- to late 1950s, London announced plans to drastically reduce the size of its armed forces. Despite fierce opposition from the Eisenhower administration, London went through with this plan. Full nuclear cooperation still left the issue of launch control unresolved. In fact, these concerns returned with a vengeance during the JFK administration. As was the case with the conventional cuts, this time the British prevailed over the Americans.

Chapter 4

THE SUEZ OPPORTUNITY

Two prominent international events intervened to break the gridlock and pave the way for the 1958 US–UK Mutual Defense Agreement, which finally provided for full cooperation. Surprisingly enough, the first event was the Suez Crisis. In July 1956, Egyptian leader Gamal Abdel Nasser announced the nationalization of the Suez Canal, the main maritime artery connecting Europe to Asia. London was furious at the move, and Eden faced tremendous pressure at home to reverse the nationalization. In secret negotiations, the British government agreed to a French-devised plan to restore control over the canal. The plan called for Israeli forces to invade Egypt in late October 1956, and for the British and French to use this as a pretext to seize the canal. The plot began in late October, and the international outrage was immediate. The Soviet Union issued nuclear threats against London, Paris, and Jerusalem. The US reaction was more problematic for the British. After Nasser's nationalization, the Eisenhower administration had made its opposition to any military intervention clear to London. The US feared that any intervention would invoke memories of colonization and strengthen the Soviet Union's position in the Middle East. Making matters worse, the invasion was launched only days before the 1956 presidential election. Eisenhower saw this as a personal betrayal. The United States supported a UN resolution calling for a complete withdrawal and threatened to tank the British currency if London didn't comply.

As described in the relevant case studies, the Suez Crisis had a major impact on the nuclear aspirations of France and Israel, especially the latter. But it also led to greater US-UK atomic cooperation because, after forcing the British to back down, President Eisenhower decided to take drastic action to repair the alliance. Nuclear cooperation offered a perfect means. The Suez Crisis forced Eden from power, and he was succeeded by Harold Macmillan in January 1957. President Eisenhower quickly invited Harold Macmillan to a leadership summit in Bermuda in March. A month before the Bermuda Conference, Eisenhower ordered the AEC, State, and DOD to begin implementing the 1956 agreement he had previously delayed under congressional pressure.[1] The president also finally ordered Strauss to begin sharing the external characteristics of US atomic weapons so Britain's bombers could be built to carry them.[2]

The Bermuda Conference was an enormous success. Eisenhower wrote in his diary that it was "by far the most successful meeting I have attended since the close of World War II."[3] Among other things, the United States agreed to give Britain some of the uranium supplies that had been earmarked for Washington, which London badly needed to ramp up nuclear weapons production.⁴ Although this concession was relatively easy for Washington, it signaled America's acceptance of a British nuclear arsenal. The most important nuclear issue discussed at the Bermuda Conference was America's desire to forward deploy intermediate-range Thor ballistic missiles in Britain.⁵ London was initially favorable to this request, seeing it as enhancing US-UK nuclear cooperation. Before the conference at Bermuda, the two sides reached a preliminary agreement to deploy sixty Thor missiles (four squadrons) to the British Isles. The warheads would theoretically remain under US custody, and their use would require a joint decision. This was better terms than the United States had offered for the forward deployed bombers.⁶ But as negotiations continued after the conference, the talks became bogged down over a number of issues. The two sides disagreed on everything from cost sharing and Britain's ability to replace the Thors with its own future intermediate-range ballistic missiles (IRBMs), to targeting and decision making on usage. Some of these disputes were caused by continued British resentment over the bomber launch control issues.

THE SPUTNIK MOMENT

Just as it looked as if cooperation might once again stall, another international crisis breathed new life into the initiative. On October 4, 1957, the Soviet Union shocked the world with the launch of the Sputnik satellite. This set off panic in the United States and the Western world that Moscow was winning the technology arms race. Some British officials immediately recognized the opportunity. Three days after Sputnik, Harold Caccia, London's ambassador in Washington, urged Macmillan to use America's alarm to push for the McMahon Act's repeal.⁷ On October 10, Macmillan wrote to Eisenhower that Sputnik proved that no country could defeat the Soviet menace on its own. "Has not the time come when we could go further towards pooling our efforts and decide how best to use them for our common good," Macmillan asked. The best place to start pooling resources, the prime minister argued, was "nuclear weapons, ballistic missiles, anti-missile defenses, and anti-submarine weapons."⁸

Eisenhower indeed believed that the moment had arrived. After not risking political capital on nuclear cooperation for nearly five years, Eisenhower was now ready to tackle the issue. As one historian puts it: "Frightened by the Soviet Sputnik successes, the Eisenhower administration accomplished more in Anglo-American nuclear relations in two months than American officials had in twelve previous years."⁹ This began with another leadership summit in Washington in late October. According to Macmillan, at the summit Eisenhower "shocked some of his people" by calling the McMahon Act "one of the most deplorable incidents in American history."[10] In the summit's joint declaration, Eisenhower committed to amending the McMahon Act "to permit of close and fruitful collaboration of scientists and engineers of Great Britain, the United States, and other friendly countries."[11]

CROSSING THE FINISH LINE

Two working groups were created to hash out the details. For the most part, these talks were relatively easy. One issue that did cause some consternation was the impact US-UK atomic cooperation would have on other allies, especially in NATO. Eisenhower himself told the British that much of the cooperation would have to be on a "confidential basis" to avoid alienating other members of NATO.[12] The concern about NATO's reaction also became embroiled in the simultaneous negotiations over the deployment of IRBMs elsewhere in Europe. The United States viewed the Britain-based missiles as strengthening America's nuclear umbrella over Western Europe and therefore under SACEUR (and NATO's) command, at least in theory. Although Eisenhower wasn't concerned about the warheads truly being under British control, he did want them to be used as part of NATO's general war plan. London viewed the Thors through a national lens, seeing them as a stopgap measure until British IRBMs were built. In a sign of the alliance's changing dynamics, England prevailed on the issue. The final agreement, signed in February 1958, said that the missiles would be launched after a joint decision by England and the United States. Only a vague mention of Article 5 was included in the agreement.[13]

As negotiations progressed, the Eisenhower administration turned its focus to winning congressional support for the amendments. This was no easy task—although Sputnik had softened congressional attitudes, there was still intense opposition to anything that could be perceived as promoting nuclear proliferation. What really carried the day in Congress was that the British already demonstrated both an atomic and thermonuclear weapon capability when they successfully tested hydrogen bombs in the fall of 1957.[14] This allowed Congress to amend the Atomic Energy Act in a way that carved out an exception for Great Britain. Specifically, it allowed nuclear assistance only if an allied country had already demonstrated "substantial progress in the development of atomic weapons."[15] Although not included in the legislation, administration officials privately promised Congress that this clause only applied to countries that had made substantial progress at the time the law went into effect.[16] The British were grandfathered in, but countries like France would not gain the same benefits once they had acquired the bomb.

The amendments to the Atomic Energy Act passed on June 30, 1958. Fittingly, this was Strauss's last day as chairman of the AEC. Eisenhower signed the bill into law on July 2, 1958. On the same day, the United States and England signed a new bilateral agreement governing their atomic cooperation. At last, the great betrayal had been rectified.

A NEW TYPE OF MILITARY

The passage of the 1958 legislation finally gave Great Britain the full partnership it had craved since 1943. But that did not put an end to tensions over nuclear issues. Indeed, in the case of Skybolt, nuclear cooperation actually created new tensions. But two issues plagued the alliance more than any other: British conventional military cuts and launch control issues. These would persist throughout the early 1960s.

British conventional military reductions began before the signing of the 1958 agreement. London had first hinted at a nuclear substitution strategy in a Global Strategy Paper in 1952. Written by the British Joint Chiefs of Staff, the Global Strategy Paper was, in many ways, a precursor to the future New Look strategy under Eisenhower. The joint chiefs argued that nuclear weapons would be sufficient to deter the Soviet Union from attacking Western Europe and would therefore constitute the main thrust of NATO's deterrence posture in the future. Even if deterrence failed, the 1952 paper argued that there wouldn't be a protracted conflict in the mold of the two world wars. Instead, events would quickly escalate into a nuclear fight, the outcome of which would be decisive. Thus, the Western world should reduce its conventional forces, which were not only strategically nonessential but also a financial burden. Like the Eisenhower administration, the 1952 paper believed that relying heavily on atomic weapons would strengthen the West economically, allowing it to outlast the Soviet Union over the course of a long competition. Conventional forces were still needed as a "complementary deterrent," but only at levels that were affordable.[17]

The 1952 Global Strategy Paper was aspirational in nature. London wouldn't conduct its first nuclear test until later that year and wouldn't have an operational nuclear deterrent until its V bombers came into force in 1955 or 1956.[18] As noted above, its first hydrogen bomb tests took place in fall 1957. Before those tests, however, Britain began preparing for the implementation of a defense posture built on the logic of the 1952 paper. It would be codified in a defense white paper published by Minister of Defense Duncan Sandys in early 1957.

British leaders began preparing their American counterparts for it the year before. In July 1956, Prime Minister Eden sent Eisenhower a long letter that explained the logic that would now guide British defense planning. Eden argued that thermonuclear weapons on both sides created a condition that would later be referred to as mutually assured destruction. This made war unlikely and made democratic countries unwilling to "accept the social and human sacrifices" of large conventional forces. Nuclear weapons, Eden argued, would be used to both deter a Soviet attack and respond to one if deterrence failed. Conventional forces had a role as a "shield" but would "no longer [be] our principal military protection."[19] Along with the strategic logic, British officials also emphasized that financial considerations were driving this shift. According to the UK government's estimates, defense spending was taking up 10 percent of GDP, as well as over 50 percent of "technical manpower." Moreover, forward deployments in Europe were creating severe balance of payments issues, much as they did for the United States.[20]

As President Eisenhower acknowledged, the new British strategy sounded a lot like America's New Look. But, by this time, the United States was trying to move away from a reliance on massive retaliation—although President Eisenhower himself still seemed to support it at various times.[21] At the beginning of the Eisenhower administration, the United States enjoyed an overwhelming nuclear superiority over the Soviet Union. By 1956, Washington was preparing for eventual nuclear parity. In light of this, even before the JFK administration, many US officials were agitating for the Western alliance to build stronger conventional forces. Building up NATO's "shield forces" was necessary to give Western leaders choices beyond surrender and nuclear war. As Dulles wrote in 1956, "we find unacceptable any proposal which implies the adoption of a NATO strategy of total reliance on nuclear retaliation."[22] From Washington's perspective, though, European NATO members should shoulder most of the conventional buildup's burden. Since 1954, the Eisenhower administration had called for a "fair burden." The US insisted that the costs of America's nuclear arsenal and powerful naval forces must be included when calculating a "fair burden.". As Dulles kept pointing out in the fall of 1956 and 1957, the costs of the US nuclear deterrent and navy were growing exponentially. Therefore, Dulles complained, European allies should "increasingly assume a greater share" of the conventional forces in Europe.[23]

The biggest fear was that British conventional cuts, and especially reductions in its troop presence in Europe, would make it less likely that Germany and France would contribute more to the alliance. Berlin and Paris had already failed to fulfill the troop commitments made in 1954, when Germany had been allowed to rearm. At that time, France had pledged fourteen divisions to the defense of the continent and Germany had pledged twelve divisions. But now, Germany was only expected to have five divisions by the end of 1957. France would only contribute four. Therefore, America's relative contributions to the alliance had increased rather than decreased. As Dulles complained to the secretary general of NATO, "If the other NATO nations want the US to lead the Soviets in the missile race, then they should do more in other fields. Perhaps the Soviets got ahead because the US was spending too much on its ground forces in Europe."[24]

All of this fell on deaf ears in London. In March 1957, Defense Ministry Sandys published the defense white paper. In somewhat hyperbolic terms, Sandys claimed that this was "the biggest change in military policy ever made in normal times." Substantively, the white paper made many of the same points Eden had to Eisenhower about how thermonuclear weapons had changed the strategic situation. The most dramatic change was the end to national service and the reduction of military personnel from 690,000 men in 1957 to 375,000 men by 1962. With regards to Europe, the white paper was more vague, probably because of intense US lobbying. It declared that London would no longer make a "disproportionately large contribution" to NATO ground forces. But in concrete terms, it said British forces in Germany would only be reduced from 77,000 to 64,000 over the next year. After that, further reductions would be made but only after consultations with allies. The reduction in air power was more dramatic, with the UK cutting in half the number of aircraft it deployed in Germany by March 1958. Once again drawing a direct connection between these cuts and Great Britain's nuclear arsenal, the white paper stated the quantitative reductions in men and aircraft would be offset by arming the remaining soldiers and planes with nuclear weapons. For months, British leaders had made this point privately to their American counterparts.[25]

With the benefit of hindsight, London's defense cuts were substantial but not quite as dramatic as British leaders were hoping. Although Eden and Sandys claimed their country was spending 10% of GDP on defense in 1957, the actual figure was a little over 7%. This would be reduced to under 4% by 1980. While the UK government hoped to reduce the size of armed forces to 375,000 men in five years, it wouldn't reach that level until 1970.[26] British forces deployed in Germany would decrease by nearly 29% to 55,000 men by 1960.[27] The number of aircraft in Germany was cut more drastically than envisioned in the white paper, with strength falling from thirty-six squadrons in 1956 to twelve squadrons by 1961.[28]

While it was inevitable that Great Britain would reduce its defense spending and military strength, the scale of the reductions was larger because of nuclear weapons. This is quite explicit in the logic underpinning the white paper. Moreover, as noted above, British leaders argued that equipping the remaining forces with atomic weapons would offset the quantitative reductions. This was cold comfort to the United States, and especially to a president like Eisenhower who was determined to reduce US forces in Europe. A month after Sandys's white paper came out, Secretary of State Dulles told a NATO meeting that "to reassure the Allies in light of the British Government's decision to reduce their forces on the continent . . . the President had no plans to withdraw United States forces from Europe."[29] And when Eisenhower left office, there were 340,650 US troops in Europe, compared to the 250,601 the year he was elected.[30]

SOLVING LAUNCH CONTROL

As we have seen, launch control had been a major issue since before the first atomic bombs were dropped. At the Quebec Conference, FDR and Churchill agreed that neither country would use the bomb without the consent of the other. This agreement sparked outrage when Congress learned of it after the war, forcing the Truman administration to pressure the British into nullifying it as part of the Modus Vivendi in 1948. America's decision to forward deploy bombers to the British Isles later the same year created strong resentment in London when Washington insisted on using these unilaterally. The Eisenhower administration managed the issue of launch control slightly better when it worked out an agreement to deploy intermediate-range ballistic missiles in the United Kingdom. Still, the underlying tension over launch control remained unresolved.

These tensions came to the fore during the John F. Kennedy administration, becoming embroiled in the Skybolt air-launched ballistic missile program. In March 1960, Eisenhower agreed to sell London Skybolt air-launched ballistic missiles to extend the life of the British V bombers. This had become a necessity when the UK canceled its own Blue Streak IRBMs because of cost overruns and their vulnerability to Soviet first strikes. The March 1960 Skybolt agreement was contingent on America deciding to go forward with developing the missile. Even before the deal was reached, many British leaders were casting doubt that the missile would ever come into existence. These doubts multiplied in the months and years ahead.[31]

Nonetheless, when the British learned that the JFK administration was canceling the Skybolt missile in November 1962, London was furious.[32] In the words of one historian, "The ensuing crisis was, after Suez, the most serious postwar rift in Anglo-American foreign relations."[33] It's possible some British leaders reacted harshly because they feared America's actual motivation was denuclearizing the United Kingdom. This fear was not unreasonable. As discussed more during the French chapters, the JFK administration was far more skeptical about allied proliferation than Eisenhower had been. Unlike the former NATO commander, JFK wanted the United States to play a much more active leadership role in the transatlantic alliance. This included centralizing nuclear decision making to carry out a graduated response/no cities nuclear strategy. Moreover, the Kennedy administration worried that the special nuclear relationship with Britain was imperiling its relations with other NATO countries, like France and Germany.[34] For these reasons, an early JFK administration planning document noted, "over the long run it would be desirable if the British decided to phase out of the nuclear deterrent business."[35]

The Kennedy administration certainly believed British anger over Skybolt was animated by its fears over America wanting to eliminate its nuclear arsenal altogether. Defense Secretary Robert McNamara remarked that London wanted a "categorical assurance" that Washington was in favor of an independent British nuclear arsenal, which he had refused to give.[36] In reality, this wasn't the case. Prime Minister Harold MacMillan confided in his diary that the decision to scrap Skybolt was made "on good general grounds—not merely to annoy us or drive G. Britain out of the nuclear business."[37] Rather, as Ken Young has argued, British leaders probably exaggerated their outrage in order to extract concessions from the United States.[38] By the early 1960s, London had calculated that the only way its small nuclear arsenal could survive in the missile era was by placing much of it on hard-to-detect submarines. America tested the first submarine-launched ballistic missile, the Polaris, in 1960, and Britain hoped to purchase these in lieu of Skybolt.

As discussed more in the French chapters, the Skybolt crisis and resulting Nassau Agreement was part of a much larger initiative President Kennedy launched after the Cuban Missile Crisis. This initiative was designed to stabilize relations with the Soviet Union by ensuring West Germany remained non-nuclear. Earlier in his time in office, President Kennedy had accepted the arguments of people like Dean Acheson and State Department official George Ball that the Federal Republic of Germany (FRG) couldn't be asked to foreswear nuclear weapons if Britain and France were allowed to have their own. As he grew more confident about these matters, President Kennedy took a different tack whereby the United States would accommodate France's and Britain's nuclear arsenal while still demanding nuclear abstinence from Germany.

This created space for a grand bargain between the two allies. Instead of eliminating the UK's nuclear arsenal, the Kennedy administration ultimately set its sights on placing the British arsenal under NATO command. Since an American general led the alliance's military command, and the US was the strongest force within the alliance, this arrangement would accomplish many of the Kennedy administration's goals. Namely, it would allow for centralized nuclear decision making while also making it easier for West Germany to accept its non-nuclear status. After all, if British and French nuclear forces were part of NATO, they weren't really national deterrents.

Therefore, at the Nassau Conference in December 1962, JFK offered MacMillan Polaris missiles if London agreed to place its nuclear arsenal under NATO command. As we have seen, since 1943 America had dictated the terms of nuclear cooperation with the British. On this issue, Washington failed to get its way.[39] The two sides agreed to a compromise that was, at least on paper, little more than a face-saving measure for the United States. Under the deal, Kennedy agreed to sell the UK Polaris missiles. In return, MacMillan agreed that "such forces would be assigned as part of a NATO nuclear force and targeted in accordance with NATO plans." There was one important caveat, however: MacMillan said that the British arsenal would be used for the defense of the Western alliance "except where her Majesty's Government may decide that supreme national interests are at stake." Thus, Britain still retained the right to use its weapons unilaterally. Moreover, as British Defense Secretary Denis Healey underlined in 1967, only the British prime minister could order the firing of Polaris missiles.[40] This agreement was not dissimilar to the one Truman had made when he agreed to consult the British before using America's forward deployed bombers when circumstances allowed. Except, with the Nassau Agreement, it was the UK that was in control. The Nassau Agreement settled that the British arsenal, for all intents and purposes, remained under national control.

CONCLUSION

What are the major takeaways from the British case, and what lessons does it hold for potential future cases of allied proliferation, like Japan, South Korea, or Turkey? Undoubtedly, the first lesson is that even under the best of circumstances, allies acquiring nuclear weapons creates severe tensions in the alliance. It's hard to imagine circumstances as favorable to allied proliferation as this one. Not only were Anglo-American ties strong, but there were no strong norms against proliferation. In the NPT era, the environment would be much less favorable.

The British case also makes clear that proliferation cannot be neatly compartmentalized from larger geopolitical issues. During WWII, first the British and later the United States opposed combining programs, because each country saw the geopolitical benefits of being in sole possession of nuclear weapons. This struggle continued after the war in Groves's and others' dogged pursuit of all global uranium supplies. While these were needed to achieve the massive nuclear buildup, which ultimately protected British and European security, it also conveniently ensured the United States maintained a monopoly on the bomb. When the United States considered expanding atomic cooperation with the British, it was usually in service of acquiring more uranium.

Eisenhower's New Look strategy was more conducive to allied proliferation, but the opposite was true of the John F. Kennedy administration's Flexible Response. Furthermore, even Eisenhower was sensitive to how nuclear cooperation with the British would impact alliance cohesion with NATO.

Military operational issues also plagued the alliance. The most notable of these was launch control issues, which were a factor from 1943 until at least the early 1960s. As noted in the introduction, launch control issues are already evident in the case of the US-ROK relationship. To some degree, they are inherent in any military alliance because they go to the foundational issues of abandonment and entrapment.[41] But when nuclear weapons are involved, the stakes are existential. How would the United States ensure that South Korea and Japan didn't turn a conflict with North Korea or China into a nuclear Armageddon? US tactical nuclear weapons in Turkey currently require a joint decision to be used. Would Turkey put its own nuclear weapons under a similar arrangement?

After World War II, one of the strongest US objections to an independent British nuclear program is that its location made it vulnerable to a Soviet Union attack or even seizure in a conflict. The British themselves came to appreciate this danger in canceling its IRBM missile program and pushing for Polaris submarine-launched ballistic missiles. In 1991, the George H. W. Bush administration removed tactical nuclear weapons from the Korean Peninsula, in part because of the difficulty of protecting them.[42] The proliferation of precision-guided missiles only dramatically increases this vulnerability. China has the largest and most diverse missile forces in the world, and North Korea has tested increasingly accurate missiles with maneuverable reentry vehicles.[43] Once again, America's Asia allies already present a similar danger in the form of South Korea's and Japan's nuclear reactors, which could easily be targeted in a war. But this danger would grow if Seoul or Tokyo feared their likely modest-sized arsenals were vulnerable in a time of heightened tensions or war.

Finally, the United Kingdom used its nuclear arsenal to reduce the size of its conventional forces. From America's perspective, the British nuclear arsenal contributed almost nothing to the strength of the Western alliance's strategic deterrent. After all, the US nuclear arsenal dwarfed it in size. But the UK conventional reductions did force America to shoulder a larger share of the burden when it came to ground forces.[44] Today, Turkey maintains the largest military of any European NATO power, and Ankara reducing the size of its forces would weaken the strength of NATO. Similarly, South Korea provides the bulk of the ground forces on the southern half of the Korean Peninsula, although Seoul's acquisition of nuclear weapons would probably reduce the need for US forces to defend against the North Korean threat. And Japan provides the main regional counterweight to the Chinese military, and it is especially proficient in certain areas like submarines and anti-submarine warfare (ASW). Despite the rapid growth of China's nuclear arsenal, US nuclear forces are already more than sufficient to counter China's nuclear weapons. From the perspective of the United States, a Japanese arsenal would not change the strategic balance in any appreciable way. But Tokyo reducing its conventional forces to pay for nuclear weapons would reduce the overall balance of power in Asia in China's favor. Given the current power trajectory, this is something the United States and its allies cannot afford.

Of course, despite all the issues presented by nuclear weapons, the US-UK relationship remains one of the most productive and fruitful in the world today. Allied proliferation comes with a cost. In the case of the UK, the alliance's value has far outweighed these costs.

NOTES

1. Timothy J. Botti, *The Long Wait: The Forging of the Anglo-American Nuclear Alliance, 1945–1948* (New York: Greenwood Press, 1987), 178; and John Baylis, "Exchanging Nuclear Secrets: Laying the Foundations of the Anglo-American Nuclear Relationship," *Diplomatic History 25*, no. 1 (January 2001), 40.

2. John Baylis, "The 1958 Anglo-American Mutual Defence Agreement: The Search for Nuclear Interdependence," *Journal of Strategic Studies* 41, no. 3 (June 2008), 435.

3. Quoted in Tore T. Petersen, *The Middle East Between the Great Powers: Anglo-American Conflict and Cooperation, 1952–7* (New York: Palgrave Macmillan, 2000), 111.

4. Botti, *Long Wait*, 179–80.

5. At the same time, the US was proposing to forward deploy different ballistic missiles (Jupiters) to other NATO allies like Italy and Turkey. See Baylis, "The 1958 Anglo-American Mutual Defence Agreement," 434.

6. Baylis, "The 1958 Anglo-American Mutual Defence Agreement," 434. The British were left with the impression that they'd actually have full control over the warheads, which later events mostly proved true. See Marc Trachtenberg, *A Constructed Peace: The Making of the European Settlement, 1945–1963* (Princeton, NJ: Princeton University Press, 1999), 198.

7. Baylis, "The 1958 Anglo-American Mutual Defence Agreement," 437.

8. "Letter From Prime Minister Macmillan to President Eisenhower," October 10, 1957, *FRUS*, 1955–1957, vol. XXVII, doc. 304.

9. Botti, *Long Wait*, 210.

10. Harold Macmillan, *Riding the Storm, 1956–1959* (London: Macmillan, 1971), 324.

11. "Declaration of Common Purpose by the President and the Prime Minister of the United Kingdom," October 25, 1957, *The American Presidency Project*, https:

//www.presidency.ucsb.edu/documents/declaration-common-purpose-the-president-and-the-prime-minister-the-united-kingdom.

12. Memorandum of Conversation, "Free World Cooperation; Meeting Presided over by the President and Prime Minister, Macmillan," October 24, 1957, https://www.eisenhower.archives.gov/research/online_documents/declassified/fy_2014/089_005.pdf.

13. "Letter From Prime Minister Macmillan to President Eisenhower," February 16, 1958, *FRUS*, 1958–1960, vol. VII, part 2, doc. 338; Botti, *Long Wait*, 220; Baylis, "Exchanging Nuclear Secrets," FN 48; and Ian Clark, *Nuclear Diplomacy and the Special Relationship* (New York: Clarendon Press, 1994), 73–74.

14. Some observers later questioned whether these were merely boosted fission tests that achieved significantly less yield than Britain pretended. Regardless, at the time of the 1958 hearings, Britain was believed to have tested a hydrogen bomb. See Norman Dombey and Eric Grove, "Britain's Thermonuclear Bluff," *London Review of Books* 14, no. 20 (October 1992).

15. Amendments to the Atomic Energy Act, 1958, available from: https://www.govtrack.us/congress/bills/85/hr12716/text.

16. Botti, *The Long Wait*, 230, and 235–36.

17. John Baylis, *Ambiguity and Deterrence: British Nuclear Strategy, 1945–1964* (New York: Oxford University Press, 1995), chap. 4.

18. See Ministry of Defence, "The History of the UK's Nuclear Weapons Programme," Fact Sheet 5, *Foreign & Commonwealth Office*, Undated, https://assets.publishing.service.gov.uk/government/uploads/system/uploads/attachment_data/file/27383/Cm6994_Factsheet5.pdf

19. "Letter From Prime Minister Eden to President Eisenhower," July 18, 1956, *FRUS* 1955–1957, vol. IV, doc. 34.

20. "Eisenhower and Macmillian Discussion," March 22, 1957, *FRUS*, 1955–1957, vol. 27, doc. 277.

21. See Eisenhower's comments in ibid.; and "Telegram From the United States Delegation at the North Atlantic Council Ministerial Meeting to the Department of State," December 11, 1956, *FRUS*, 1955–1957, vol. 4, doc. 42.

22. "Dulles memo to President," October 1, 1956, *FRUS*, 1955–1957, vol. 5, doc. 37.

23. Ibid.

24. "Dulles and Spaak Meeting, NATO Political and Military Subjects," October 24, 1957, in *FRUS*, 1955–1957, vol. 4, doc. 58

25. See, for example, "Dulles and Sandys Discussion," January 29, 1957, *FRUS*, 1955–1957, vol. 27, doc. 254; and "Eisenhower and Macmillian Meeting," March 22, 1957, *FRUS*, 1955–1957, vol. 27, doc. 277.

26. "Army cuts: How have UK armed forces personnel numbers changed over time?" *Guardian*, September 1, 2011.

27. Peter Speiser, *The British Army of the Rhine: Turning Nazi Enemies into Cold War Partners* (Champaign, IL: University of Illinois Press, 2016), 21.

28. Royal Air Force Historical Society, *Royal Air Force in Germany, 1945–1993* (Brighton, UK: Royal Air Force Historical Society, 1999), 14.

29. "Editorial Note," *FRUS*, 1955–1957, vol. IV, doc. 56.

30. Tim Kane, "Global U.S. Troop Deployment, 1950–2003," Heritage Foundation, October 27, 2004.

31. Ken Young, "The Skybolt Crisis of 1962: Muddle or Mischief?" *Journal of Strategic Studies* 27, no. 4 (2004), 617–19.

32. McNamara discussed the decision with the UK Ambassador in Washington and the British Defense Minister. "Notes of Conversations Relating To Skybolt," November 9, 1962, *FRUS*, 1961–1963, vol. 13, doc. 399.

33. Young, "Skybolt Crisis," 614.

34. "Letter From Secretary of State Rusk to Secretary of Defense McNamara," September 8, 1962, *FRUS*, 1961–1963, vol. 13, doc. 396.

35. "Policy Directive," April 20, 1961, in *FRUS*, 1961–1963, vol. XIII, doc. 100. This was on policymakers' minds during the Skybolt crisis. See "Rusk Letter to McNamar," September 8, 1962, *FRUS*, 1961–1963, vol. XIII, doc. 396.

36. "Memorandum of Conversation," December 16, 1962, *FRUS*, 1961–1963, vol. XIII, doc. 401. This was at least what he told other US officials. He may have told the British that he would support it. See Marc Trachtenberg, *A Constructed Peace: The Making of the European Settlement, 1945–1963* (Princeton, NJ: Princeton University Press, 1999), 364.

37. Quoted in Matthew Jones, *The Official History of the UK Strategic Nuclear Deterrent, Volume I: From the V-Bomber Era to the Arrival of Polaris, 1945–1964* (New York: Routledge, 2017), 392.

38. This is also essentially Marc Trachtenberg's interpretation, although he notes that Macmillan had other reasons for exaggerating the affair. See Trachtenberg, *Constructed Peace*, 360–63.

39. The negotiations took place in person. See "Memorandum of Conversation," December 19, 1962, *FRUS*, 1961–1963, vol. XIII, doc. 403; and "Memorandum of Conversation," December 20, 1962, ibid., doc. 406.

40. Ian Davis, *The British Bomb and NATO: Six Decades of Contributing to NATO's Strategic Nuclear Deterrent* (Solna, Sweden: Stockholm International Peace Research Institute, November 2015), 12.

41. Glenn H. Snyder, "The Security Dilemma in Alliance Politics," *World Politics* 36, no. 4 (July 1984), 461–95.

42. Zachary Keck, "4 Reasons America Shouldn't Send Nuclear Weapons to South Korea or Japan," *National Interest*, September 15, 2017.

43. Henry Sokolski and Zachary Keck, "Kim Jong Un Is Going Ballistic In More Ways Than One," *Wall Street Journal*, July 30, 2017; and Michael Elleman, "North Korea's Newest Ballistic Missile: A Preliminary Assessment," *38 North*, May 8, 2019.

44. See, Dulles comments in "Editorial Note," *FRUS*, 1955–1957, vol. IV, doc. 56; "Discussion with Mr. Spaak of NATO Political and Military Subjects," October 24, 1957, ibid., doc. 58; and especially "Dulles and Sandys Discussion," January 29, 1957, *FRUS*, 1955–1957, vol. 27, doc. 254.

Chapter 5

A Bomb Is Born
(France, 1945–1960)

In his seminal book on France's nuclear diplomacy, Wilfred L. Kohl observes, "[Charles] de Gaulle's nuclear policy undoubtedly had a greater impact on France's allies than on her enemies."[1] Indeed, the so-called *force de frappe* didn't alter the East-West strategic balance, given America's massive nuclear forces. It didn't even create the first European nuclear force, which theoretically could reduce concerns about the credibility of extended deterrence. On the other hand, France's atomic weapons poisoned US-French relations for decades and allowed de Gaulle to pursue a more autonomous foreign policy. This most notably included de Gaulle withdrawing from NATO command and ordering all alliance forces off French territory.

None of this was inevitable. In fact, when France first launched its nuclear program, it was scarcely conceivable. Although de Gaulle is usually considered the father of the French bomb, he inherited a full-fledged nuclear program. The Fourth Republic leaders who initiated France's nuclear program had wildly different views than de Gaulle about the value of alliances and the bomb. They viewed a French bomb in a similar manner as their British counterparts. That is, they thought having the bomb would increase their country's influence with Washington and NATO. But ultimately, Fourth Republic leaders thought the *force de frappe* would have a role within the Western alliance.[2]

These plans were upended when de Gaulle returned to power in 1958, just two years before France exploded its first device. The bomb did not change de Gaulle. His views were well established by World War II. As President Dwight Eisenhower, who had worked with de Gaulle during the war, once complained, there is "no single soul who can influence de Gaulle. . . . He knows all the answers, and thinks only in terms of 'Glory, Honor, France.'"[3] Nuclear weapons, however, allowed de Gaulle to act on his ambitions. Without the bomb, de Gaulle would have still chafed at the restrictions NATO placed on France, but he ultimately would have accepted them. Armed with nuclear weapons, de Gaulle could pursue the policies he had long dreamed of, to the detriment of NATO and the United States. In the 1960s, US diplomacy skillfully minimized the harm de Gaulle caused, but it wasn't easy or entirely successful.

This creates something of a paradox. Proliferation optimists argue that nuclear-armed allies will be able to protect themselves, allowing America to reduce its overseas commitments. In one sense, France validates their argument as Paris expelled US forces from its territory. But this didn't eliminate America's commitment to defend Europe, and US policymakers realized they couldn't protect the rest of Europe without defending France itself. At the same time, the loss of French territory complicated America's ability to honor US commitments to Europe and weakened NATO by removing one of its largest members from the military command. The impact of all this shouldn't be overstated; it was more of a nuisance than a catastrophic event. As discussed below, in some ways, de Gaulle's withdrawal from NATO's military command strengthened the alliance by making it more cohesive.

The same cannot be said for France's conventional forces. As in the British case, a nuclear-armed France significantly reduced its defense spending and the size of its military. Throughout the 1960s, France cut the size of its armed forces from one million men to five hundred thousand men. Some 90 percent of this decline came from the Army, which had no role in France's atomic arsenal. Overall, this left the United States with a larger proportional commitment.

One of Washington's greatest concerns was that a French bomb made it impossible for the FRG to remain non-nuclear. Although President Eisenhower was sympathetic to Germany eventually acquiring nuclear weapons, the Soviet Union sparked the Berlin Crisis that lasted from 1958–1962, in large part because of fears over Bonn acquiring nuclear weapons. The Kennedy administration and its successor understood this and sought to increase US leadership within NATO to forestall an independent German nuclear capability (among other reasons). This was not always skillfully done. The multinational nuclear force (MLF) that JFK and later Lyndon B. Johnson pushed was ill received by both the Soviet Union and America's NATO allies. Although the MLF was ultimately scrapped, the entire episode raised serious questions about Washington's judgement in the minds of its closest allies.

The French case also demonstrates the close intersection between nuclear weapons and the geopolitical issues of the day. This was certainly the case for Charles de Gaulle, who—as already noted—viewed a French nuclear arsenal as an instrument for achieving his larger geopolitical ambitions. But nuclear weapons were completely intertwined with the larger issues in US policy as well. A good example of this is President Eisenhower and

Kennedy's differing views on French and German nuclear weapons. Lord Hastings Lionel Ismay, NATO's first secretary general, famously said the alliance's purpose was to keep the Soviet Union out, the United States in, and the Germans down. Eisenhower and Kennedy were in complete agreement on the need to keep the Soviets out but prioritized the other two goals differently. Eisenhower's ultimate objective was building up Europe as a third force able to defend itself from Moscow without a large US military footprint. He recognized Europe needed nuclear weapons to protect itself from a country that possessed its own nuclear forces. As a frontline member, this European arsenal would have to include the FRG in some form. Thus, Eisenhower took a rather lax view of allied proliferation, although he ultimately preferred a multilateral deterrent over competing national ones. By contrast, Kennedy believed that keeping Germany down was the most important goal after keeping the Soviets out, and he indeed felt that keeping Bonn down might be necessary to keep Moscow out. He therefore sought more active US leadership in the alliance, especially with regards to nuclear weapons. This included going so far as to try to put England and France out of the "nuclear business" to prevent a West German bomb. Later, Richard Nixon and Henry Kissinger sought nuclear cooperation with France to achieve their larger goal of a more active Europe led by France.

The next couple of chapters tell the story of this development.

A BOMB IS BORN

On December 26, 1954, Prime Minister Pierre Mendès France convened a meeting of his top political, military, and scientific advisors. Once the esteemed men had been seated, Mendès France handed down a draft decision. The first sentence read, very simply: "The making of the bomb is decided."[4]

This decision, more than any other, marked the start of France's nuclear weapons program. A lot had transpired beforehand. In October 1945, shortly after the end of World War II, Paris had established the Commissariat a l'Energie Atomique (CEA), France's atomic energy agency. This was a purely civilian body, at least at first, although the military possibilities weren't completely lost on French leaders. In December 1948, France's first nuclear reactor, Chatillon, EL-1 (Zoe) went critical. This was a primitive, pool-type, heavy water reactor, with fuel coming from a facility built at CEA's Saclay Nuclear Research Center at Le Bouchet.[5] In 1951, Saint-Gobain Nuclear Company, one of France's premier nuclear firms, was given permission to build a pilot reprocessing plant at Fontenay-aux-Roses. This plant was completed in 1954.[6]

1952 was an important year for France's nuclear development. In January, the French Army created the Special Weapons Command, which was supposed to coordinate protection against nuclear, biological, and chemical weapons. But Colonel Charles Ailleret was put in charge of the command. Ailleret was one of the major proponents of a French national deterrent, and under his leadership, the Special Weapons Command effectively served as a "nuclear think tank" within the army. This included ordering feasibility studies into building a bomb.[7] In July 1952, the National Assembly (France's Parliament) approved the country's first five-year nuclear plan. This called for constructing two plutonium-producing nuclear reactors and a reprocessing plant at Marcoule. The first of these reactors, G-1, was small (40 MW thermal) and went critical in 1956. Two larger, 250 MW reactors (G-2 and G-3) were built at the same site. Together, these three reactors produced about half of France's military plutonium.[8]

Nineteen fifty-four was an even more pivotal year for France's nuclear development, culminating in Mendès France's decision that December. The proximate cause of this decision was NATO's decision to rearm West Germany. The United States had been pushing for the FRG to rearm for years because its large economic resources and manpower reserves were necessary to build up NATO conventional forces. France had opposed Bonn raising a national army, but that outcome became inevitable when the National Assembly rejected the European Defense Community (EDC) in August 1954.[9] Knowing that Paris couldn't stop Washington from rearming West Germany, Mendès France managed to secure a pledge from German Chancellor Konrad Adenauer that his country would unilaterally renounce its right to build atomic, biological, or chemical weapons. That pledge at the London and Paris Conferences in the fall of 1954 paved the way for a NATO agreement that Bonn would raise military forces, although these would ultimately be under NATO command. This changed Mendès France's calculation about a French nuclear arsenal. As Jacques Hymans explains his thinking: "French military power must remain at least one order of magnitude superior to Germany's; thus, the fewer the restrictions on German conventional weapons, the greater the need for a French atomic force."[10] Having not received sufficient assurances about West German rearmament, Mendès France ordered studies into the cost and difficulty of building a French nuclear bomb. On December 26, 1954, the prime minister approved a plan to spend 80 billion francs (the equivalent of roughly $2.1 billion USD today) to build a bomb in five to six years. Another 45 billion francs was believed to be necessary for nuclear submarines.[11]

PREPARING THE GROUNDWORK

Three days later, the Bureau of General Studies was established within the CEA. This organization, later renamed Military Applications Directorate, began exploring places around Paris to set up the necessary research facilities. Mendès France's government fell in February 1955, but this did not interrupt progress on the nuclear program. In May, the Ministry of Defense (MOD) and CEA signed a secret memorandum that explicitly gave the latter organization the primary responsibility for building the bomb.[12] Under this accord, the MOD began funding the Bureau of General Studies, including the construction of a third nuclear reactor, G-3.[13]

The biggest potential impediment to a French nuclear bomb was the political instability of the Fourth Republic. Indeed, many histories of France's nuclear program depict the effort as being driven entirely by bureaucrats without any political leadership. While there were undoubtedly strong bureaucratic influences, this view understates the importance that political leaders like Mendès France played in creating and sustaining the program. Still, the first political threat to the program came when Guy Mollet became prime minister in January 1956. A member of the Socialist Party, Mollet entered office as a fierce opponent of a French nuclear arsenal. In his inauguration speech, Mollet endorsed a proposal that every member of the European Atomic Energy Community (EURATOM)—a proposed multilateral atomic agency—renounce the right to build nuclear weapons, and all fissile material be centrally controlled.[14]

US officials doubted that Mollet had the political capital to bring this proposal to fruition, and their skepticism proved well founded.[15] Nearly immediately, Mollet came under intense pressure from French nationalists who threatened to derail the entire EURATOM treaty. Mollet quickly abandoned the prohibition proposal and announced France's nuclear weapons program publicly for the first time.[16] Despite this, the influential French diplomat Jean Monnet downplayed France's nuclear ambitions to US officials, calling the French nuclear weapons program "a myth."[17] A few months later, Mollet signed a "long-term directive" to prepare a nuclear weapon, including the production of highly enriched uranium, weapons-grade plutonium, and preparation for an eventual nuclear test.[18] Around this time, Paris initiated a long-range missile program and began building the first Mirage IV aircraft prototype. The latter would serve as the air leg of its nuclear triad.[19]

This spur of activity was likely prompted by the Suez Crisis described in the last chapter. There was another, more subtle issue that had been building for some time as well: namely, the "nuclearization" of the NATO alliance. As the Eisenhower administration pushed NATO to use nuclear weapons to offset the Soviet Union's numerically superior forces, Paris found itself losing influence within the alliance. As General Jean Etienne Valluy, France's permanent representative to NATO's Standing Group, explained to Mendès France, France's manpower had given it considerable influence when NATO strategy had centered around a conventional defense. But a NATO built around nuclear weapons would render a non-nuclear France to second-class status.[20]

The acceleration of France's nuclear program in the second half of 1956 did not receive much attention within the Eisenhower administration. In February 1957, the administration invited Premier Mollet to visit Washington in an effort to normalize relations following the Suez Crisis. France's nuclear program barely factored into the discussion. Dulles did report to the president that he asked Mollet about "French intentions with respect to nuclear weapons." According to Dulles, the premier responded that "he would never approve of France" building nuclear weapons but "that France should reserve the right to do so."[21] The first part wasn't true, as Mollet had already disclosed publicly. Furthermore, the British informed Washington that Paris had asked London for assistance in building nuclear weapons.[22] Even if Mollet had been telling the truth, this wouldn't be reassuring as Washington expected Mollet's government to soon fall.[23]

Sure enough, Mollet's government fell in June 1957. He was succeeded by Maurice Bourgès-Maunoury, previously the defense minister. Immediately, the US intelligence community began forecasting France would now move toward a more overt nuclear weapons program. A June 1957 National Intelligence Estimate (NIE) stated that "France is on the verge of a decision to develop nuclear weapons."[24] A different NIE in August said it was "probable" that "funds and efforts will be diverted [from conventional forces] to an independent nuclear weapons program."[25] France provided ample reason for concern. In July 1957, General Paul Ely, the French equivalent of the chairman of the Joint Chiefs of Staff, asked his American counterpart Admiral Radford if Paris could purchase IRBMs from the United States. Besides wanting to save money, Ely explained that France acquiring these missiles was necessary because "the risk of limited war in Europe is greater as long as modem weapons are in the hands of the US alone." More generally, General Ely said that "disassociation of atomic weapons from conventional weapons is becoming more and more theoretical."[26] The changing rhetoric was matched by continued progress in France's nuclear program. Although unbeknownst to the Americans at the time, in July 1957, France selected the Sahara Desert in Algeria as the best site for its first nuclear test.[27]

The Eisenhower administration was not alarmed by any of these developments. This is evident from a meeting Dulles had with Foreign Minister Christian Pineau in Washington in September 1957. A week or so earlier, the Soviet Union had alluded to its intercontinental ballistic program. Noting this, Pineau proposed that the West pool its scientific resources together in an effort to maintain its technological edge. Dulles said that both he and the president agreed with the sentiment in principle but were constrained by the Atomic Energy Act. Still, Dulles assured Pineau that "[they] would look into the possibilities of further cooperation in the missile field except for the warhead."[28] This is not surprising given Eisenhower's overarching goal of building up Europe as a third force capable of defending itself against the Soviet Union. President Eisenhower was quite clear he would give NATO allies nuclear weapons if only Congress hadn't tied his hands.

By the beginning of October, the Bourgès-Maunoury government had fallen and Félix Gaillard would soon replace him as prime minister. Before Gaillard could take office, the Soviet Union shocked the world with the Sputnik launch. As described in the last chapter, this sparked panic in the West that the Soviet Union was quickly surpassing the West technologically. It also created uncertainty in Europe about the credibility of America's extended deterrence. Once the Soviet Union could retaliate against American cities, would the US really use nuclear weapons to defend Europe from the Soviet Union? After all, in line with Eisenhower's strategic direction, NATO had adopted MC 48, a strategy that relied heavily on US nuclear weapons.

Although President Eisenhower was not personally alarmed by Sputnik, he knew that the United States had to take action to calm allies' nerves. Moreover, he saw a political opportunity to get Congress to loosen the restrictions in the Atomic Energy Act, as he had long favored. The first move was to accelerate plans to allow for greater nuclear sharing within NATO, and to deploy intermediate range ballistic missiles (IRBMs) to Europe. The Eisenhower administration didn't initiate this policy because of the Sputnik surprise.[29] But Sputnik did provide a new sense of urgency.

In December 1957, NATO held its first heads of state summit since the creation of the alliance a decade earlier. It was at this meeting that Eisenhower officially secured support for NATO's nuclear stockpile plan. As the communique read, "NATO has decided to establish stocks of nuclear warheads, which will be readily available for the defense of the Alliance in case of need."[30] Technically, the nuclear warheads would remain in US custody and only be released to the allies in the event of a war—in a "dual key" arrangement—with the allied nations manning the delivery systems. In reality, as a congressional committee that toured US nuclear installations in 1960 quickly realized, America's control over the weapons was essentially "fictional." This was intentional on the part of President Eisenhower.[31] The dual-use system was a convenient fiction to circumvent the Atomic Energy Act, which Eisenhower detested. In addition, the December 1957 summit "also decided that intermediate range ballistic missiles will have to be put at the disposal of the Supreme Allied Commander Europe [SACEUR]."[32] Behind closed doors,

Eisenhower even raised the possibility that America would provide NATO allies with blueprints to build their own IRBMs, although nominally to be used only in accordance with SACEUR's plans.[33] France initially seemed intrigued by the offer but had lingering concerns. First among these was that any IRBMs stationed on French soil could not be used without Paris's consent. As noted in the Chapter 4, this was a huge concern for the United States, who believed that NATO's supreme commander needed to be able to use them to destroy Soviet forces on the ground.[34]

As these alliance-wide matters were being debated, France's nuclear program continued to advance, and Paris made little effort to hide this from the United States. In a meeting with US officials in February 1958, General Buchalet of CEA "spoke as if it were a foregone conclusion that a French atomic bomb would be set-off soon." He also confirmed that the first French test would take place in the Sahara Desert.[35] US officials thus were not surprised when Prime Minister Gaillard issued a directive in April that a French atomic bomb be tested within the first three months of 1960.[36] At this point, France's nuclear weapons program was on autopilot.

THE GENERAL RETURNS

Soon after the April directive, political instability once again gripped France, and Gaillard's government fell. In the ensuing chaos, Charles de Gaulle took the reins of power in what some French officials considered a last-ditch effort to save the country from the domestic Communist Party.[37] While allowing that "US relations with de Gaulle will be admittedly difficult," US officials and their French allies were initially cautiously optimistic that de Gaulle would not severely disrupt the Western alliance. They did know de Gaulle would demand a much greater say in Western affairs, and the United States considered creating a "Big Three" of the United States, the UK, and France to appease him.[38] Regarding nuclear weapons, French officials confirmed to their American counterparts what the latter already believed: de Gaulle was intent on acquiring nuclear weapons. He also viewed US-USSR efforts to halt all atmospheric nuclear tests as an attempt to keep Paris out of the nuclear club. Still, two senior French officials told Washington that "while France wants at least a few bombs under her exclusive control, she does not regard this as a substitute for integrated defense. France does not aspire to autonomy in the field of nuclear weapons."[39] This, like the notion that de Gaulle would remain committed to NATO, turned out to be false.

In early July 1958, Dulles traveled to Paris to meet with de Gaulle. By this time, Washington was already bracing for the possibility that nuclear issues would be an irritant in the relationship. A State Department memo prepping

Dulles for the trip warned that "the primary difficulty you should expect to encounter in your talks centers on de Gaulle's determination to have France become the fourth nuclear power." Foggy Bottom particularly believed that de Gaulle would take umbrage with Washington's unwillingness to provide France with the same atomic assistance it was going to provide Britain under the amended Atomic Energy Act. This proved prescient as nuclear issues would torpedo bilateral relations for the next decade.[40]

As expected, nuclear weapons were discussed at length during the meeting in Paris. Dulles began by stressing that the Eisenhower administration was committed to finding arrangements whereby NATO could use nuclear weapons "without having to depend on a United States political decision." He also said Washington wanted a workable NATO concept "so that each member state would not feel compelled to develop an independent nuclear potential." That said, Dulles assured de Gaulle that this didn't extend to a French nuclear arsenal; Washington merely didn't want all NATO countries devoting scarce resources to atomic weapons. De Gaulle responded by stating he was "certain that France would [soon] have atomic bombs." He agreed with Dulles that it was inefficient for the alliance to duplicate efforts in this field. Thus, France was open to acquiring nuclear weapons from the United States or through information given by Washington, but only if Paris retained sole discretion about their use. If the American proposal was that the US president or NATO Supreme Commander would decide when to use them, Paris was not interested. In fact, any missiles or nuclear weapons located in France would have to fall under France's custody. "The weapons could be utilized in accordance with NATO plans," de Gaulle said, but only if France had the same plans.[41] The fact that Secretary of State Dulles felt the meeting was successful underscored the Eisenhower administration's support for European control over nuclear weapons.[42]

Any hope that de Gaulle's return would not derail Franco-American relations was crushed in September 1958. At that time, de Gaulle sent President Eisenhower a letter proposing a tripartite body comprised of the United States, France, and Britain. This tripartite organization would be responsible for setting political and military policy not only in Europe but also in Africa, the Middle East, and the Indo-Pacific region. In fact, French officials would tell their American counterparts, de Gaulle was most interested in coordinating policy outside of Europe. "It would be up to this organization," de Gaulle wrote in the letter, "on the one hand, to take joint decisions on political questions affecting world security and on the other, to establish and if necessary, to put into effect strategic plans of action, notably with regard to the employment of nuclear weapons."[43] The Americans and the British didn't know what to make of de Gaulle's proposal—it wasn't even entirely clear what he was proposing. Did he want a formal decision making organization or just regular informal consultations? Even French officials seemed confused on many points. For instance, they initially assured US and UK officials that de Gaulle didn't want veto power over any decision to use atomic weapons. But de Gaulle himself soon made clear that this was indeed what he wanted.[44] To avoid completely alienating the French president, London and Washington indulged him by holding various sub-cabinet- level meetings to discuss the proposal. Neither country had any intention of accepting the tripartite organization, not least because it would offend the rest of NATO. Although de Gaulle would raise this proposal again and again over the years, it never gained serious traction.

It's fair to question de Gaulle's sincerity in proposing the tripartite body as it was completely at odds with everything he believed. To be sure, de Gaulle resented what he saw as America's dominant role in Western policy both in Europe and around the world. Getting a coequal say in those policies was something that would appeal to him. In addition, he saw France as a great power and therefore believed it should be in an exclusive club that didn't include lesser allies, like Germany and Italy. At the same time, de Gaulle had a visceral hatred of integration. He longed for the days of complete sovereignty and regularly complained that French troops would have to take orders from foreign commanders and fight as part of a multilateral force. Yet here he was proposing that French foreign and military policy all around the world be held hostage to British and American wishes. Some scholars have argued that de Gaulle was setting the stage for his later moves to reduce France's participation in NATO. That is, he was making a proposal that he knew would be rejected in order to later justify breaking away from the alliance. As Kohl points out, in de Gaulle's memoirs "the general confirmed that he had not expected a favorable response to his tripartite demarche, and that it was the key to his plan for a step-by-step French disengagement from NATO."[45]

But it also highlighted a key point about de Gaulle; namely, his completely contradictory policies, which made it impossible to please him. If one studies any person closely enough, he or she is certain to find a host of contradictions. After all, no one engages in intense self-study throughout their lives to ensure complete consistency on every point. That is the work of biographers. Still, de Gaulle's contradictory policies are so glaring they are impossible to ignore. Trachtenberg correctly identifies three distinct strands of thought de Gaulle maintained and altered between at will.[46] The first is the nationalistic one that he is best known for. Then there was a "Western" strand best exemplified with the tripartite proposal. This stood in direct contradiction to the third "European" strand of thought. In this perspective, de Gaulle sought a continental approach that excluded what de Gaulle termed "Anglo-Americans" and instead featured close German-French cooperation. But this European approach was also contradicted by de Gaulle's inherent fears of a stronger

Germany. Not surprisingly, de Gaulle's policies were almost always incoherent. When he first took office in 1958, he canceled all nuclear cooperation with Germany because he feared it could lead to a nuclear-armed, militaristic Germany. He often called this a "red line." Later, around 1962, he spoke about the need for French-German nuclear cooperation.[47] He often feared that the US wasn't committed enough to risk the security of its cities to help defend Europe once the Soviet Union had intercontinental ballistic missiles (ICBMs). Yet, he openly resented US involvement in European affairs and his policies seemed designed to push America out. In one particularly egregious case, de Gaulle told the US Ambassador in Paris, "that US should not be mixed up in Western European difficulties and should keep itself apart only bringing its weight to bear in case of necessity."[48]

These contradictions were apparent shortly after making the tripartite proposals. The US and UK had agreed to explore de Gaulle's proposal, and soon informal discussions were getting under way. Against this backdrop, de Gaulle began disengaging militarily in NATO, starting with an announcement that France wouldn't integrate its fighter jets in an alliance-wide air defense network at the December 1958 NATO meeting.[49] The following spring, de Gaulle announced France would not participate in NATO's IRBM plan unless all warheads and missiles were under the exclusive control of Paris.[50] In March, de Gaulle declared he was withdrawing French naval ships from NATO's Mediterranean command.[51] Two months later, he established a national naval command for the Mediterranean Sea and North Africa.[52] To make matters worse, these moves came during a severe East-West crisis over Soviet Premier Nikita Khrushchev's November 1958 demand that France, Britain, and the United States pull their forces out of West Berlin within six months. As discussed below, this began the Berlin Crisis that would continue—in an on-again, off-again fashion—until the Cuban Missile Crisis in October 1962.

FRANCE GOES NUCLEAR

The growing crisis in France's relations with the United States did not impact its nuclear weapons development, which continued to progress on schedule. Shortly after returning to power in July 1958, de Gaulle reaffirmed his predecessor's decision to test a bomb in early 1960.[53] The following spring, France launched a ballistic missile program, creating a quasi-private consortium called SEREB to coordinate all work on missiles. SEREB initially signed an agreement with the US firm Boeing for assistance in missile development, but this was quickly voided by the State Department.[54] The G-3 reactor mentioned above went critical in June 1959, before reaching full power the following year.⁵⁵ That same month, the Mirage IV strategic bomber took its maiden test flight. In August, France selected the plane to serve as the air leg of its future triad, despite the fact that it would require in-flight refueling to attack the Soviet Union and Paris did not have any tanker planes or plans to acquire them.⁵⁶ Nonetheless, the next defense budget provided funding to build fifty bombers.⁵⁷ In November, de Gaulle gave a major speech to military officials, in which he stated, "What we must achieve during the coming years is a [nuclear] force capable of acting exclusively on our behalf."⁵⁸

On February 13, 1960, France tested its first nuclear bomb in the Sahara. It was a plutonium device that produced a yield of sixty to seventy kilotons. This was followed by another test in April and two more over the following year.⁵⁹ Unsurprisingly, the Eisenhower administration was not overly alarmed and continued ongoing bilateral negotiations over increased atomic energy and military cooperation after the test.⁶⁰ Indeed, two weeks before the first French test, Eisenhower again publicly advocated for loosening the Atomic Energy Act to allow for greater atomic sharing with allies.⁶¹ When asked about the French test at a press conference a few days later, the president said "it's only natural that first Britain and then France" acquired nuclear weapons.⁶² As noted, Eisenhower and Dulles (who passed away in May 1959) truly sought a nuclear deterrent controlled multilaterally by the European NATO members, but they were willing to live with national deterrents as a starting point.

If he had his way, Eisenhower would've gladly supplied a Western European multilateral force with American warheads and delivery systems that weren't subject to a US veto. At one point, he even told de Gaulle that "I would like to be able to give it to you," in reference to nuclear weapons.⁶³ However, the Atomic Energy Act and congressional attitudes made this impossible. The administration tried to find work-arounds like the dual key system where, as noted above, America's control over the warheads was illusory. Along with Congress, the president's vision faced strong opposition from State Department officials and others. Still, everyone recognized that the Europeans in general—and Germany in particular—were going to need to at least feel they had a greater say over the use of nuclear weapons. Solving this problem was a constant source of tension for multiple US administrations. The latest attempt to do so came in the waning days of the Eisenhower administration, when US officials proposed a multilateral force (MLF) based on American ships armed with nuclear-tipped Polaris missiles. As discussed more below, these ships would feature a mixed-manned crew of sailors from different NATO nations. Eisenhower himself was skeptical of this approach, but his next two successors would both advocate it (before later turning against it).

The most immediate change from the French nuclear test is that Paris began asking for atomic assistance. For all of de Gaulle's talk about independence, French officials expected US atomic assistance once they tested the bomb, just as Britain had. These expectations grew after the 1958 amendments to the Atomic Energy Act, which allowed for assistance to countries that had demonstrated "substantial progress." A few months after the 1958 amendments had passed, the senior French diplomat Francois de Rose declared: "It is certain that our effort will soon place us in a position to lay claim to this cooperation."[64] US officials had encouraged this view at times.[65] After his country's second nuclear test, France's ambassador in Washington, Hervé Alphand, along with other officials, approached US officials to inquire about whether France now qualified for assistance.[66] Washington shot down these requests, citing congressional opposition. This angered Paris, with Secretary of State Herter reporting, "the French are suspicious that we are trying to avoid this spread of atomic knowledge. They feel we could stretch our current law to permit sharing of atomic secrets with them."[67]

The Eisenhower administration left office with most of the French issues unresolved. De Gaulle continued to insist on a trilateral directorate and was unhappy with the level of cooperation Washington and London offered. Above all, the United States and Britain were not willing to abide by de Gaulle's demands on strategic questions, like the use of nuclear weapons.[68] Unhappy on this front, de Gaulle was doing his best to "wreck" NATO, as Eisenhower put it in July 1960.[69] The irony is that no US president was more sympathetic to de Gaulle's vision than Eisenhower. Eisenhower and Dulles had gone as far as they could in providing France with nuclear weapons within (and beyond) the limitations of the Atomic Energy Act, and even French officials were surprised de Gaulle didn't accept it.[70] As the French leader would soon learn, he missed a key opportunity by shunning the Republican president—although this wouldn't be the last time he'd turn down a strong offer of US assistance.

NOTES

1. Wilfred L. Kohl, *French Nuclear Diplomacy* (Princeton, NJ: Princeton University Press, 1971), 207.

2. That Fourth Republic leaders opposed the way de Gaulle used nuclear weapons, see Antoine Pinay's comments in "Foy D. Kohler Letter to James Gavin," February 2, 1962, John F. Kennedy Presidential Library (hereafter JFKL), National Security Files (NSF): Countries, Box 71; and Henry Kissinger to Carl Kaysen, "Notes on Lunch with General Sthlin in Paris, February 5, 1962," February 9, 1962, in ibid. The author thanks Timothy P. McDonnell for all documents from JFKL.

3. Quoted in Nicholas L. Miller, *Stopping the Bomb: The Sources and Effectiveness of U.S. Nonproliferation Policy* (Ithaca, NY: Cornell University Press, 2018), 163.

4. Quoted in Jacques Hymans, *The Psychology of Nuclear Proliferation: Identity, Emotions and Foreign Policy* (Cambridge, UK: Cambridge University Press, 2006), 105.

5. Jeffrey T. Richelson, *Spying on the Bomb: American Nuclear Intelligence from Nazi Germany to Iran and North Korea* (New York: Norton, 2006), 197–98.

6. United States of America, Central Intelligence Agency, 1964 report, 6.

7. Bruno Tertrais, "Destruction Assurėe: The Origins and Development of French Nuclear Strategy, 1945–81," in *Getting MAD: Nuclear Mutual Assured Destruction, Its Origins and Practice,* ed. Henry D. Sokolski (Washington, DC: Strategic Studies Institute, 2004), 53.

8. "France's Nuclear Weapons: French Nuclear Facilities," *Nuclear Weapons Archive*, May 1, 2001.

9. The EDC was a supranational European military force that was supposed to be a compromise between the United States—which wanted to harness West German power to defend Europe—and France and other countries that were terrified about German rearmament. Instead of raising a national West Germany army that would become a NATO member, the EDC integrated West German forces into a supranational military.

10. Hymans, *Psychology of Nuclear Proliferation*, 102.

11. Hymans, *Psychology of Nuclear Proliferation*, 105.

12. Pierre Billaud and Venance Journe, "The Real Story Behind the Making of the French Hydrogen Bomb: Chaotic, Unsupported, but Successful," *Nonproliferation Review* 15, no. 2, 354.

13. Kohl, *French Nuclear Diplomacy*, 24.

14. Guy Mollet, "Inaugural Speech," January 31, 1956, *L'ours*. http://www.lours.org/archives/defaulte903.html?pid=334.

15. "Dillon telegram to DOS," February 3, 1956, *FRUS*, 1955–1957, vol. 4, doc. 152.

16. Hymans, *Psychology of Nuclear Proliferation*, 112.

17. "Memcon," July 14, 1956, *FRUS*, 1955–1957, vol. 4, doc. 181.

18. Tertrais, "Destruction Assurėe," 55; and Kohl, *French Nuclear Diplomacy,* 22.

19. Kohl, *French Nuclear Diplomacy*, 46.

20. Hymans, *Psychology of Nuclear Proliferation*, 95; and Paul M. Pitman, "'A General Named Eisenhower': Atlantic Crisis and the Origins of the European Economic Community," in *Between Empire and Alliance: America and Europe During the Cold War*, ed. Marc Trachtenberg (Oxford, UK: Rowman & Littlefield Publishers, 2003), 45.

21. "Memorandum of a Conversation Between Prime Minister Mollet and Secretary of State Dulles, Washington, February 26, 1957," *FRUS*, 1955–1957, vol. 27, doc. 41.

22. "Dulles and Lloyd Memcon on (1) French Request (2) Test Limitations," March 23, 1957, *Wilson Center Digital Archive* (hereafter *WCDA*), https://digitalarchive.wilsoncenter.org/document/110063.pdf?v=49f39311e9986af7a247aace2d845a44.

23. "Elbrick Memo to Dulles," December 31, 1956, *FRUS*, 1955–1957, vol. 27, doc. 31.

24. "NIE 100–6–57, 'Nuclear Weapons Production in Fourth Countries—Likelihood and Consequences,'" June 18, 1957, *NSA*, https://nsarchive2.gwu.edu/NSAEBB/NSAEBB155/prolif-2.pdf. Also see CIA, "French Position on Disarmament May Be Shifting," May 29, 1957, *NSA*, https://nsarchive2.gwu.edu/NSAEBB/NSAEBB184/index.htm.

25. "National Intelligence Estimate 22–57, The Outlook For France," August 13, 1957, *FRUS*, 1955–1957, vol. 27, doc. 50.

26. "Draft Memorandum for the Record of a Meeting," July 11, 1957, *FRUS*, 1955–1957, vol. 27, doc. 49. Only months earlier, Mollet had criticized Eisenhower for trying to replace conventional forces with nuclear weapons. See "Memorandum of a Conversation, Cabinet Room, White House, Washington," February 26, 1957, ibid., doc. 40. It is worth noting, however, that French military officials had long believed that nuclear weapons had to play a prominent role in the defense of Western Europe. In this regard, Mollet's view might have been an outlier. See Marc Trachtenberg, *A Constructed Peace: The Making of the European Settlement, 1945–1963*, 175.

27. Richelson, *Spying on the Bomb*, 200.

28. "Memcon," September 7, 1957, *FRUS*, 1955–1957, vol. XXVII, doc. 52.

29. Trachtenberg, *Constructed Peace*, 176–77.

30. Mr. P.H. Spaak, "Final Communiqué," December 19, 1957, *NATO*. https://www.nato.int/docu/comm/49-95/c571219a.htm.

31. The congressional report, which was based on a tour of over a dozen nuclear installations in Europe, is referred to as the Holifield Report. It called America's control over the forward deployed nuclear weapons fictional. For the report, see Document 5 in William Burr, "The U.S. Nuclear Presence in Western Europe, 1954–1962, Part II," *National Security Archive*, Briefing Book 722, September 16, 2020. Eisenhower saw the dual key arrangement as a way to circumvent the Atomic Energy Act. In a meeting with Macmillian and de Gaulle in 1958, Eisenhower offered France the same dual key arrangement as the UK had. But, the president noted, this dual key arrangement was an "illusory precaution." "In fact it would not be too difficult to obtain a key in a real emergency," Eisenhower argued, noting a host country could "always arrange to seize control of the key." See Trachtenberg, *Constructed Peace*, 209. This was before the advent of permissive action links.

32. Spaak, "Final Communiqué," December 19, 1957.

33. Quoted in Trachtenberg, *Constructed Peace*, 207.

34. "Embassy in France to DOS," December 20, 1957, *FRUS*, 1955–1957, vol. 27, doc. 59.

35. "MEMCON," February 21, 1958, *FRUS*, 1958–1960, vol. VII, part 2, doc. 3.

36. Richelson, *Spying on the Bomb*, 200; and Tertrais, "Destruction Assurée," 55.

37. "Embassy in France to DOS," June 10, 1958, *FRUS*, 1958–1960, vol. VII, part 2, doc. 19.

38. "Elbrick to Herter," May 27, 1958, *FRUS*, 1958–1960, vol. VII, part 2, doc. 12; and "Elbrick to Dulles," June 5, 1958, *FRUS*, 1958–1960, ibid., doc. 18.

39. "Embassy in France to DOS," June 11, 1958, *FRUS*, 1958–1960, vol. VII, part 2, doc. 20.

40. "Elbrick to Dulles," June 26, 1958, *FRUS*, 1958–1960, vol. VII, part 2, doc. 27. Also see Paul Nitze memo to McGeorge Bundy, "The French Nuclear Problem," February 27, 1962, JFKL, National Security Files, Regional Security, Box 225A.

41. "Memorandum of Conversation," July 5, 1958, *FRUS*, 1958–1960, vol. VII, part 2, doc. 34.

42. "Telegram From Secretary of State Dulles to the Department of State," July 5, 1958, *FRUS*, 1958–1960, vol. VII, part 2, doc. 37.

43. "Letter From President de Gaulle to President Eisenhower," September 17, 1958, *FRUS*, 1958–1960, vol. VII, part 2, doc. 45.

44. "Memorandum of Conversation," December 4, 1958, *FRUS*, 1958–1960, vol. VII, part 2, doc. 77; and Kohl, *French Nuclear Diplomacy*, 111.

45. Kohl, *French Nuclear Diplomacy*, 77.

46. Trachtenberg, *Constructed Peace*, 335.

47. Ibid., 336–37.

48. "Embassy in France to DOS," March 16, 1962, *FRUS*, 1961–1963, vol. XIII, doc. 250.

49. Kohl, *French Nuclear Diplomacy*, 86.

50. "Letter From President de Gaulle to President Eisenhower," May 25, 1959, *FRUS*, 1958–1960, vol. VII, part 2, doc. 117.

51. Kohl, *French Nuclear Diplomacy*, 86–87.

52. "Letter From President de Gaulle to President Eisenhower," March 25, 1959, *FRUS*, 1958–1960, vol. VII, part 2, doc. 117.

53. *Spying on the Bomb*, 200; and Kohl, *French Nuclear Diplomacy*, 63.

54. Kohl, *French Nuclear Diplomacy*, 102.

55. Kohl, *French Nuclear Diplomacy*, 84.

56. It would purchase 11 KC-135s from the United States in 1962.

57. Kohl, *French Nuclear Diplomacy*, 101–02.

58. Quoted in Michael Karpin, *The Bomb in the Basement: How Israel Went Nuclear and What That Means for the World* (New York: Simon & Schuster, 2007), 369, FN 3.

59. Richelson, *Spying on the Bomb*, 200–01.

60. "DOS to the Embassy in France," January 15, 1960, *FRUS*, 1958–1960, vol. VII, part 2, doc. 155; and "Embassy in France to DOS," April 14, 1960, *FRUS*, 1958–1960, vol. VII, part 2, doc. 163.

61. Dwight D. Eisenhower, "The President's News Conference," February 3, 1960.

62. Dwight D. Eisenhower, "The President's News Conference," February 17, 1960.

63. Quoted in Trachtenberg, *Constructed Peace*, 228–29.

64. Quoted in Kohl, *French Nuclear Diplomacy*, 81.

65. "Herter and Major Eisenhower's discussion with President Eisenhower," May 2, 1959, *FRUS*, 1958–1960, vol. VII, part 2, doc. 110.

66. "Memorandum of Conversation," April 15, 1960, *FRUS*, 1958–1960, vol. VII, part 2, doc. 164; and "Despatch From the Embassy in France to the Department of State," April 14, 1960, *FRUS*, 1958–1960, vol. VII, part 2, doc. 163.

67. "Memorandum of Conference With President Eisenhower," April 22, 1960, *FRUS*, 1958–1960, vol. VII, part 2, doc. 166.

68. "Telegram From the Department of State to the Embassy in the United Kingdom," June 30, 1960, *FRUS*, 1958–1960, vol. VII, part 2, doc. 187.

69. "Memorandum of Telephone Conversation Between President Eisenhower and Secretary of State Herter," July 1, 1960, *FRUS*, 1958–1960, vol. VII, part 2, doc. 188.

70. Trachtenberg notes the French Ambassador to the US "thought that de Gaulle had not understood" what the administration was proposing when he rejected a Dulles proposal of a system where nuclear weapons could be used without US approval. See *Constructed Peace*, 226.

Chapter 6

The General's Bomb (France, 1961–1975)

Unlike other cases, France's nuclear program created more bilateral tensions after Paris tested nuclear weapons than when it was pursuing them. This can be explained in part by John F. Kennedy and his advisors' greater hostility toward France's proliferation. This animosity was largely driven by the belief that France's nuclear arsenal made it more difficult to rein in West Germany's nuclear aspirations. In turn, preventing a West German bomb was seen as critical to stabilizing the US-Soviet competition. President de Gaulle also strained Franco-American Relations in the 1960s. The French leader used his country's nuclear arsenal to pursue a more assertive foreign policy, and one that diminished America's influence in Europe. This chapter explores the deep freeze France's nuclear program caused in bilateral relations with the United States throughout the 1960s. It also explores how France's nuclear arsenal weakened its conventional forces, and how Paris proliferated nuclear technology to other countries. Finally, the chapter closes by examining why, starting with Richard Nixon, the United States accepted France's nuclear program and even began assisting it.

THE LONG FREEZE

Any complaints de Gaulle had with US policy under President Eisenhower were magnified tenfold under John F. Kennedy. This was especially true with regards to nuclear weapons. Eisenhower and Kennedy were, in many ways, a study in contrasts. At the time of the transition, Eisenhower was the oldest president in US history; Kennedy was the youngest. Eisenhower had grown up in a family of modest means in Kansas and Texas. His successor was born into a wealthy and politically influential family. Eisenhower had risen through the military—graduating from West Point, serving as supreme allied commander in Europe during World War II, and later as supreme commander of NATO. He only reluctantly decided to run for president when the presumptive Republican nominee refused to support America's participation in NATO. By contrast, Kennedy seemed destined for greatness at a young age. After attending the best boarding schools as a child, he enrolled in Harvard for college. After serving in the navy during World War II, JFK became a congressman and later senator. Eisenhower ran his administration as a well-oiled machine, with a highly organized interagency process befitting the president's military background. Kennedy relied on a more *ad hoc* process.

The two also had diametrically opposing views on the issue of nuclear proliferation. Where Eisenhower was sympathetic to allied proliferation, JFK viewed it in almost apocalyptic terms. He confessed to being "haunted by the feeling" that there would be ten nuclear weapon states by 1970, and as many as twenty by 1975.[1] This kind of viewpoint was not absent in the Eisenhower administration. While the president himself didn't subscribe to it, other officials in the administration—particularly in the State Department—were opposed to proliferation, even among allies and friends.[2] What changed with the Kennedy administration is this concern now percolated through the entire administration, up to the president himself. As Secretary of State Dean Rusk explained early in the administration, the United States opposed further nuclear proliferation because it "will increase [the] risk of war by accident or miscalculation, diminish [the] possibility [of] controlled nuclear response in [the] event of hostilities, raise new obstacles [to] arms control, and pose [a] very grave threat to allied political cohesion."[3]

The views of advisors were especially influential early on in the JFK administration. Perhaps because of his relative inexperience, Kennedy relied heavily on his advisors for the first year and a half or so of his administration. Many times, notably the Bay of Pigs fiasco, this got the president in trouble. Kennedy also brought in many Democratic foreign policy heavyweights to advise him. This included naming Dean Rusk, who had served as an assistant secretary of state during the Truman administration, as his secretary of state. But it was best exemplified by Kennedy's decision to bring in Dean Acheson, a hardliner who served as Truman's secretary of state, to advise him from the State Department on a number of issues, including the Berlin Crisis.

Although the JFK administration opposed all proliferation, it was first and foremost concerned with the prospect of a nuclear-armed West Germany. In fact, the French nuclear program was viewed almost entirely through the lens of how it would impact Bonn's nuclear decision making. As Kennedy put it, "the chief argument against the French having nuclear information has been the effect it would have on the Germans."[4] And Germany acquiring nuclear weapons, JFK wrote to British Prime Minister MacMillan in May 1961, would "shake NATO to its foundations."[5] At least some of the fears about

West Germany getting nuclear weapons centered on how this would impact the ongoing Berlin Crisis with Moscow. To understand how JFK initially dealt with the French nuclear program, it's essential to understand some of the Berlin Crisis.

BERLIN CRISIS

Between 1958 and 1962, superpower relations were kept in near-constant crisis over Soviet moves in Berlin and later Cuba. The crisis was rooted in the postwar settlement, which gave the British, French, and Americans control over the western part of Berlin, which was located deep inside the territory of what became the German Democratic Republic (GDR), or East Germany. The Soviet Union facilitated access to West Berlin for the Western powers, who maintained a troop presence in the city. In November 1958, Soviet Premier Nikita Khrushchev announced that Moscow was signing a peace treaty with the East German government, which would include ending Western military access to Berlin. He gave the United States, France, and Great Britain six months to also sign a treaty with the GDR to establish Berlin as a "free city." By this time, West Berlin had become a flourishing, economically vibrant democracy. Any agreement would consign West Berliners to living under the Soviet Union's iron curtain. Allowing this to happen would undermine US credibility and potentially shatter relations with the FRG. If the US was willing to sell out West Berlin, what would stop Washington from doing so elsewhere, especially as the Soviet Union gained nuclear parity?

There was a number of factors that played a role in Khrushchev making this risky gambit. At the time, the Soviets and Chinese Communist Party were vying for supremacy over the international communist movement, and Beijing constantly accused Moscow of being too soft with the West. Additionally, as West Berlin became more prosperous and East Berlin became less free, East Germans were fleeing to the West through West Berlin, creating a massive brain drain for the GDR. These factors, however, were—at best—secondary concerns. For instance, the brain drain problem could've been solved by erecting a wall, which Walter Ulbricht, the East German leader, had been pushing Moscow to do for eight years before the Berlin Wall was erected.[6] If Khrushchev was motivated by the refugees fleeing the GDR, he could've taken this less risky action in 1958.

Instead, as Trachtenberg has demonstrated, Soviet probes in Berlin were strongly motivated by its concerns over West German rearmament, especially Bonn getting nuclear weapons.[7] Khrushchev didn't hide this fact. Before announcing the ultimatum, the Soviet premier spent the speech discussing Moscow's growing concerns over West German military power, especially nuclear weapons. With regards to the latter, he mentioned "speeches by Chancellor Adenauer and Defense Minister Strauss, [and] the atomic arming" of the West German military. This was not completely unwarranted. There were two separate components to this issue—although the Soviets didn't always see it that way—and both were pointing in the wrong direction for Moscow. The first had to do with NATO, which had become increasingly reliant on nuclear weapons. Accordingly, NATO and Washington were seeking to place US nuclear weapons in Germany under dual key arrangements. At the time of Khrushchev's speech, the United States was training German pilots to fly planes loaded with nuclear weapons, and NATO was setting up a nuclear storage facility in the FRG. NATO was also strongly in favor of putting medium-range ballistic missiles in Germany under a dual key arrangement.

The second issue was an independent German nuclear capability. Chancellor Adenauer and especially Defense Minister Strauss had made public and private comments indicating West Germany eventually needed a nuclear arsenal. This hadn't been missed by the United States. In May 1957, Dulles told Eisenhower that the Adenauer administration "has refused to foreclose the possibility of eventual German possession of tactical nuclear weapons if an agreement on disarmament is not reached in the next several years." US intelligence estimates at the time believed the same. Furthermore, France, Italy, and Germany were undertaking joint atomic research that even some French officials feared would ultimately result in a German nuclear bomb.[8]

The Soviet Union saw matters the same way, but to them, it was an existential issue. Moscow could tolerate the United States extending its nuclear umbrella over the FRG, but it could not live with an FRG with an independent nuclear arsenal. Because Berlin was militarily indefensible for the United States and NATO, it was one area where the Soviets had considerable leverage to pressure the West. As Khrushchev famously said, "Berlin is the testicles of the West. Every time I want to make the West scream, I squeeze on Berlin."[9] From the outset, US leaders understood the Berlin gambit was motivated in large part by concerns over keeping West Germany non-nuclear. Only days after Khrushev's speech, a State Department intelligence report said the Soviets' "ultimate objectives" were to "separate Germany from the West, to prevent German acquisition of nuclear weapons, and to obtain withdrawal of US forces from Germany, thus weakening and dividing the NATO alliance."[10] Soviet leaders often brought this up to both US and other European officials.[11] Although Khrushchev allowed his initial deadline to pass on Berlin without taking any action, the general expectation was that he would force the issue again under a new president in 1961. President Kennedy understood that solving this dilemma would ultimately require addressing Soviet concerns about FRG rearmament, and especially nuclear acquisition. This colored how he viewed France's nuclear program, at least through the middle of 1962.

LAUNCH CONTROL AND FLEXIBLE RESPONSE

Although West Germany was the most important issue for the Kennedy administration, Washington had other concerns with France's nuclear program. Most notably, Washington viewed allied arsenals as inhibiting its emerging Flexible Response doctrine. Flexible Response is often thought of as an effort to build up conventional forces to have more options for dealing with Soviet intrusions in Europe and elsewhere around the world. This never really occurred in Europe, where US forces actually declined during the 1960s.[12] The other aspect of Flexible Response was developing a nuclear doctrine that took into account the Soviet Union's growing nuclear parity, including the ability to survive a first strike and cause intolerable damage to the US homeland. During the Eisenhower administration and into the early part of the JFK administration, US officials were confident they could pursue a successful nuclear first strike. This was especially true with regards to taking out the Soviet Union's intercontinental delivery systems. The Soviet Union had only a limited ability to launch nuclear attacks against the United States. Therefore, Washington could credibly base NATO's military strategy on massive retaliation and the use of tactical nuclear weapons, although the Eisenhower administration repeatedly pressured European allies to strengthen their conventional forces. As Moscow acquired a second-strike capability—one that could survive a US first strike and still retaliate against American cities—Washington sought ways to enhance the credibility of its extended deterrence in Europe. In the nuclear realm, Secretary of Defense Robert McNamara initially decided on a gradual, controlled escalation that could force the Soviets to back down before reaching a total nuclear war. This was what Secretary of Defense McNamara meant by a city-avoidance nuclear doctrine. The hope was that if the United States only targeted Soviet military installations—principally, its nuclear forces—bargaining could continue, and a general war could be avoided. By contrast, if the United States began by launching massive nuclear attacks on the Soviet population, there would be nothing left to hold hostage.[13]

All of this was highly theoretical and seemed to ignore what Carl von Clausewitz termed the fog of war as well as the primordial violence component of his trinity.[14] It's unclear if the Kennedy administration itself believed that cool, rational calculation could continue to take place once nuclear weapons began flying. In any case, McNamara would soon determine the policy was unworkable, in part because the US lacked the command and control capabilities to conduct this nuclear bargaining.[15] There was also a more immediate concern about execution: gradual, controlled escalation required centralized nuclear decision making by both sides. The Soviet Union had centralized decision making, but NATO had three distinct nuclear decision makers in the United States, Great Britain, and France. Even if Washington was pursuing a limited nuclear strike against Soviet military installations, it couldn't stop France or Britain from launching their own nuclear attacks against Soviet cities. In fact, the allies' small nuclear forces almost mandated attacks against Soviet cities. Moscow certainly wouldn't abide by a city avoidance exchange if America's allies were targeting Russian cities.

The United States first confronted its allies about this in a speech McNamara gave to a NATO meeting in Athens, Greece in May 1962. "There must not be competing and conflicting strategies in the conduct of nuclear war," McNamara told the alliance. "We are convinced that a general nuclear war target system is indivisible and if nuclear war should occur, our best hope lies in conducting a centrally controlled campaign against all of the enemy's vital nuclear capabilities." McNamara painted a picture of nuclear-armed allies creating an unlimited nuclear war right as Washington and Moscow had agreed to a ceasefire. "Such a failure in coordination," he warned, "might lead to the destruction of our hostages—the Soviet cities—just at a time at which our strategy of coercing the Soviets into stopping their aggression was on the verge of success."[16] This theme of the indivisibility of nuclear decision making was one the administration would return to repeatedly.[17] Its implication was that competing allied arsenals in London and Paris inhibited NATO strategy, a criticism that was sometimes made rather overtly.[18] Privately, the claims were even more startling. One internal document stated, "It is vital that the major part of US nuclear power not be subject to veto. . . . It is, however, most important to the US that use of nuclear weapons by the forces of other powers in Europe should be subject to US veto and control."[19] Thus, Washington wanted to use nuclear weapons unilaterally while exercising a veto over British or French nuclear use. This is why, as discussed in the British case, the JFK administration talked about putting London out of the "nuclear business."

ATOMIC ASSISTANCE

This was the antithesis of what de Gaulle believed, creating immense tension between Washington and Paris. When JFK first came to power, France was pushing for the same kind of atomic assistance that Britain received from the United States. Some US officials, including members of the Joint Chiefs of Staff, DOD officials like Paul Nitze, CIA Director John McCone, and Ambassador to France James Gavin, favored granting more assistance for various reasons, including saving France money so it could use it on conventional forces.[20] But the president, strongly influenced by key officials like Rusk and Acheson, opposed any assistance to France's nuclear weapons or ballistic missile programs.[21] Even minimal gestures were rejected out of a concern that it would lead to more requests from Paris. The administration did this knowing full well, as Dean Rusk put it, "that our position on this subject may hamper development of closer relations with France."[22] Indeed, France grew increasingly harsh in its criticism of the United States, with France's premier declaring in 1962 "that relations between France and the United States would remain unsettled as long as Washington opposed France's ambitions to become an independent nuclear power and a major European military force."[23] But at least until late 1962, John F. Kennedy refused to accede to nuclear cooperation with France. Under Secretary of State George Ball went so far as to direct the US ambassador in Paris to not discuss nuclear issues at all.[24]

Bilateral tensions expanded beyond the nuclear realm, as de Gaulle became increasingly forceful in pushing for French leadership in Europe at the same time Kennedy attempted to assert greater control over the alliance. This included de Gaulle's efforts to create a separate bilateral relationship with West Germany, which Washington feared would extend to the nuclear realm. France also blocked Great Britain from joining the European Economic Community. Some in the administration believed that these moves were de Gaulle's way of retaliating against the United States for its refusal to offer atomic assistance. Regardless of France's motives, Kennedy's frustration at times boiled over into anger. In one meeting with a French cabinet official in May 1962, Kennedy accused de Gaulle of trying to kick the United States and the United Kingdom out of Europe.[25] This was not a transient thought. Most administration officials were convinced—because of the policies he pursued as part of his European strand of thought—that de Gaulle wanted a Western Europe free of the United States, and they weren't completely wrong.[26] President Kennedy was especially worried that once France had an operational nuclear deterrent, de Gaulle would cut a deal with the Soviets to "break up NATO, and push the US out of Europe."[27] This proved prophetic and demonstrated that it was often difficult to disentangle nuclear matters from larger geopolitical issues.

THE MULTILATERAL FORCE

In an attempt to deal with all these issues—worries about West Germany's nuclear ambitions and the Soviet Union's response, the need to centralize nuclear decision making, and thwarting France's efforts to assert leadership in Europe—the Kennedy administration revived the multilateral force (MLF) concept that had originated in the late Eisenhower administration.[28] In reality, it solved none of these things, instead alienating all parties. Eventually JFK realized this and abandoned the concept, but his death provided an opportunity for the MLF supporters in the administration to revive it under LBJ.

At its height, the MLF envisioned having twenty-five surface ships with mixed-manned crews and eight Polaris missiles on each vessel.[29] Unlike with Eisenhower, Kennedy insisted that the US president exercise complete control over using nuclear weapons.[30] In fact, President Kennedy placed permissive action links on America's warheads in Europe to prevent unauthorized use by allies or rogue US troops. Essentially, Washington was asking the allies to help finance Polaris missiles without receiving any control over their use. Despite years of lobbying by the United States, no European ally had any lasting interest in the MLF.[31] For its part, the Soviet Union strongly opposed the MLF. In Moscow's eyes, the MLF was the first step toward a nuclear West Germany. As the influential Soviet Ambassador in Washington, Anatoly Dobrynin, put it, "MLF is only a first step toward full proliferation."[32]

JFK'S NEW TUNE

President Kennedy first embraced the MLF at the urging of State Department officials, just as he initially accepted that the only way to prevent West Germany from building the bomb was to reverse France and the UK's nuclear programs. As he became more confident in himself, however, Kennedy began questioning both premises.[33] While he expressed doubts earlier, as evident from a memorandum he sent to Ball in June 1962, the Cuban Missile Crisis was a clear turning point. In the middle of one intense National Security Council meeting, "the President asked Secretary Rusk to reconsider present policy of refusing to give nuclear weapons assistance to France."[34] Kennedy's new thinking, as Trachtenberg explains, was that "even if Britain and France were helped, the Germans could still be told that they could not have their own nuclear weapons. They would not like it, but . . . they could be made to swallow the pill."[35]

In the months following the Cuban Missile Crisis, JFK pursued new avenues for reassuring NATO allies while also reducing tensions with the Soviet Union by reining in FRG nuclear aspirations. When the United States and Britain reached the Nassau Agreement described in the British case, the president offered France the same deal. Indeed, as Kennedy put it, "a sizeable part of the Nassau arrangements was designed to please the French."[36] Under this proposal, the United States would sell France Polaris missiles, thereby saving Paris substantial amounts of money. This went against everything Secretary of State Rusk and his deputy, George Ball, believed. There is significant evidence that Rusk and Ball tried to sabotage the initiative behind the president's back.[37] President Kennedy seemed to anticipate this by providing instructions to the US negotiation team directly, without Rusk or Ball present.[38] In the end, de Gaulle rejected America's offer, and publicly dismissed it as "useless" in a press conference a few days later. This effectively ended any appetite within the United States to offer atomic assistance to France until the Nixon administration.[39] But it also unburdened President Kennedy from the MLF.

STABILIZING THE GERMAN QUESTION[40]

This freed up President Kennedy to stabilize US-Soviet ties by making real progress on solving the German nuclear question. His first year in office was dominated by Berlin after Premier Khrushchev announced that he would turn over control of the city to the East German regime unless the United States accepted a deal.

The extreme dangers made evident by the Cuban Missile Crisis brought both sides back to the negotiation table. And, after some back and forth, an informal and imperfect understanding began to take shape. This involved complex dynamics between the United States, Soviet Union, and West Germany. What America wanted most was the acceptance of the status quo in central Europe. Moscow sought a guarantee that West Germany would remain non-nuclear, while Bonn needed assurances that Washington could protect it. By this time, Kennedy had basically abandoned the MLF concept, which the Soviet Union considered a covert way to arm Germany with nuclear weapons. This paved the way for a compromise with the Soviet Union. The informal compromise was that if the Soviet Union would stop challenging the status of Berlin, the United States would ensure that West Germany wouldn't build nuclear weapons. This informal arrangement was codified by the two superpowers in the Limited Test Ban Treaty (LTBT), which prohibited countries from testing nuclear weapons in the atmosphere. This allowed the United States to deal with the West German nuclear question without singling out Bonn. FRG signing the LTBT under US pressure assured Moscow of its sincerity. Moscow, in turn, was tied to the arrangement by the implicit understanding that if it continued to challenge the status of Berlin, it might end up with a German nuclear bomb—the exact outcome it sought to avoid.[41] In addition, to get Bonn to sign the LTBT, Washington pledged to maintain a sizable US military presence in West Germany on a basically permanent basis. This was done by Rusk during a speech in Frankfurt a month before Kennedy was assassinated.[42] Although German Chancellor Adenauer was still opposed to signing the LTBT, he was no longer powerful enough to defy the United States. Thus, West Germany signed the LTBT. Although Bonn's nuclear ambitions were not fully extinguished until the Non-Proliferation Treaty, this complex, informal arrangement stabilized the situation.

DE GAULLE'S WORLD

As the United States dealt with these weighty issues, France continued to make advances on the nuclear front, and de Gaulle's ambitions grew in tandem with his country's arsenal. In June 1962, France launched a program to develop nuclear-powered, ballistic missile submarines (SSBNs). The first of these entered into service in 1972, and four more followed. Each boat carried sixteen submarine-launched ballistic missiles with increasingly larger yields.[43] Also in June 1962, the United States agreed to sell France the KC-135 tankers it needed to refuel its future Mirage bombers in flight. Those were delivered two years later.[44] Then, in July 1962, the National Assembly increased funding for the nuclear program.[45] The following year, France decided to focus its missile program on intermediate-range ballistic missiles (IRBMs).[46] The resulting S-2 IRBM was first flight tested in 1968 before being deployed in 1971. It ultimately procured sixteen of these ground-based missiles, which had a single 150-kiloton warhead and a range of 2,750 kilometers (1,708 miles).[47] Most significantly, in October 1964, the first of what would ultimately be thirty-six Mirage IV planes entered into service. Each plane carried a 60-kiloton fission gravity bomb.[48] These provided France with the first leg of its nuclear triad. For the first time, France had an operational nuclear deterrent.

This set the stage for de Gaulle's most brazen policy: withdrawing from NATO command in March 1966. This had been a long time coming. As already noted, de Gaulle withdrew French forces from NATO's Mediterranean Command in 1959 and set up a competing command. Then, in June 1963, he informed NATO that France was withdrawing all its naval forces from the alliance. More generally, de Gaulle had been challenging NATO's structure since returning to power, including through his tripartite proposal. Additionally, de Gaulle regularly decried the need to have a unified military command, instead of a traditional military alliance. After JFK's death, US-France relations continued to nosedive. In January 1964, de Gaulle reestablished relations with Mao Zedong's People's Republic of China, becoming the first Western country to do so. In the years that followed, de Gaulle became an increasingly outspoken critic of the US war in Vietnam, much to Washington's dismay.

None of these compared to de Gaulle's decision to withdraw France from NATO command and remove all NATO personnel and bases from French territory. The United States was not taken completely off guard when the French president informed LBJ of his decision in March 1966. In September 1965, a "high level foreign office source" told the US ambassador in Paris, Charles Bohlen, that de Gaulle was planning to withdraw from the North Atlantic Treaty itself. Bohlen told Secretary of State Rusk that the source had "proved to be reliable in the past," although his information this time wasn't exactly correct.[49] Then, in February 1966, de Gaulle alluded to the coming decision in a press conference.[50] A few days after that, Bohlen told Washington that the French president had asked his foreign minister to draft papers "(1) denouncing all multilateral agreements connected with NATO except the North Atlantic Treaty itself, and (2) all military bilateral agreements with US."[51] This was actually what de Gaulle did: he was keeping France in the alliance but not within its military command structure.

These warnings gave US policymakers time to decide how to respond to de Gaulle's move. While some in the State Department leadership advocated for taking a hard line, President Johnson decided on a more accommodating stance.[52] Before de Gaulle had even sent his letter, Rusk—despite his personal opposition—cabled instructions to America's NATO missions. "Backbiting, recriminations, attempts to downgrade the importance of France as a nation" should be avoided, he said. If de Gaulle insists on removing US troops from France, Rusk directed US representatives to "accede gracefully" and "move promptly" to find other locations. If Paris further withdraws from NATO and other international bodies, "it should be made very clear to French public opinion that there is an empty chair always ready and waiting for France." One reason the president had decided on this policy, according to Rusk, was that de Gaulle's "messianic" views on the "glory and importance of France" couldn't be changed by reasoned argument. In any case, French public opinion was largely opposed to de Gaulle on these matters. America should therefore keep the door open to a future French regime more favorable to the United States.[53] Behind the scenes, Rusk didn't heed LBJ's directive. After de Gaulle made his announcement, Rusk told journalists "on deep background" that "de Gaulle wants to bring about [a] return of 18th-century type alliance in which there are no integrated command arrangements or common strategy. . . . French objective in promoting such alliance designed to advance the hegemony of French state in Europe."[54] In reality, administration officials couldn't explain de Gaulle's motives.

On March 7, de Gaulle informed LBJ of his decision to remove France from NATO command and evict all NATO forces and bases from French territory (including NATO's headquarters), while still remaining a party to the Atlantic Treaty. The French president did say that he may allow NATO to use French territory during war time, but only if Paris itself joined the conflict. Over the next few days, France sent its decision to the rest of NATO. The notice repeated much of what de Gaulle had been saying for years—namely, that NATO's structure made sense when America enjoyed a nuclear monopoly, but it no longer corresponded to the realities on the ground. Notably, de Gaulle made absolutely clear that France's nuclear arsenal had been central to the decision. "France, in particular, is equipping herself with atomic weapons, the very nature of which preclude her being integrated."[55] This was confirmed by other French officials. The "heart of the matter," Jean Daniel Jurgensen, the director of Western Affairs at the Ministry of Foreign Affairs, said in January 1966, "was [the] nuclear problem. Nothing else really mattered." "After [France's] 1966 tests in Pacific," he warned, "[the] situation would change."[56] Indeed, it did.

Before responding in great detail, LBJ consulted with other NATO allies. When he finally did write back to de Gaulle, the US president told his French counterpart that he believed NATO's integration demonstrated the unity of purpose necessary to deter Moscow. France's removal could create doubts in the minds of Soviet leaders about the West's unity, thereby undermining deterrence.[57] Still, he ended the letter on a conciliatory note, stating "As our old friend and ally her place will await France whenever she decides to resume her leading role."[58]

Behind the scenes, the administration focused its efforts on ensuring the unity of the remaining NATO members. Naturally, some feared France's defection would spur other allies to follow suit.[59] This was one of the reasons the State Department wanted LBJ to take a stronger stance against France. Instead, the administration tried to find ways to improve cohesion among the rest of NATO. This was largely successful. In December 1966, they built on JFK's previous efforts in resolving the German nuclear question by establishing NATO's Nuclear Planning Group with the FRG serving as a permanent member. The Nuclear Planning Group helped institutionalize nuclear planning in the alliance, giving non-nuclear allies influence over the ultimate weapon. This signaled the end of the MLF, paving the way for the negotiation of the Nonproliferation Treaty (NPT) with the Soviets, which formally ended the German nuclear issue when Bonn signed onto the treaty in 1969.[60] France's withdrawal also led the Johnson administration to back the Harmel Doctrine, named after the Belgium Foreign Minister Pierre Harmel. In a report to NATO, Harmel argued that the alliance must reaffirm its collective defense purpose while also pursuing more stable relations with the Warsaw Pact members.[61] This gave NATO a more political function and was in line with the thinking of many of the European members at the time.[62] Moreover, with de Gaulle's France no longer playing the spoiler role, there was more agreement among the remaining NATO members. For instance, in late 1967, the alliance finally approved the Flexible Response doctrine.

There are two main questions that must be answered: first, what was the impact of de Gaulle's withdrawal, and second, could it have been avoided?

With regards to the former, there was undoubtedly a major impact in the short term. Although there were a host of complicated issues surrounding the post-withdrawal relationship with France—for example, overflight rights—of most immediate concern were the enormous logistical challenges involved in vacating the country. As France's foreign minister told US officials in April 1966, de Gaulle "was adamant on US departure as rapidly as physically possible."[63] France demanded that all NATO bases be transferred over to French control by April 1, 1967, and military personnel be out of the country at the same time. This bordered on impossible—by some estimates, the US alone had thirty military bases and 26,000 military personnel in the country.[64] The alliance failed to meet the deadline but still pulled off minor miracles. An entire new headquarters for the Supreme Headquarters Allied Powers Europe (SHAPE) was built and inaugurated in Belgium in time for the deadline. The entire relocation effort was completed in October 1967.[65]

France's withdrawal also provided a short-term boom for the Soviet Union. This went beyond the propaganda win; shortly after announcing his withdrawal, de Gaulle visited the Soviet Union and began trying to negotiate a detente with Moscow. This was exactly what JFK had feared half a decade earlier. Soviet leaders recognized the benefits the French president was providing them. As Leonid Brezhnev told Polish leaders "while he [de Gaulle] was an enemy, his policies had the advantage of weakening US positions in Western Europe."[66]

The long-term impact of France's withdrawal was more muted.[67] Part of this had to do with the fact that NATO was a multilateral alliance. Although extremely disruptive, bases could be relocated to other NATO countries. This wouldn't be possible in other regions like Asia, where America maintains a hub-and-spoke alliance system. The lasting impact of de Gaulle's decision was also muted by LBJ's deft handling of the situation, including strengthening the unity of the remaining NATO members. Another factor that helped was that de Gaulle's withdrawal was nearly universally opposed by the French elite, including the military. As Bruno Tertrais has explained, "When the military realized that getting the bomb and leaving the NATO integrated military structure—an unthinkable option for any self-respecting French officer at that time—were part of the same deal, their hostility would be even more acute."[68] This meant that although France was technically not part of the NATO command, its military leaders continued to cooperate closely with the alliance. In fact, French forces were kept in Germany, just not under NATO's purview.[69]

The other question is whether de Gaulle's withdrawal could have been avoided. The answer to this is probably not, unless France had remained non-nuclear. In announcing its withdrawal, Paris claimed it had repeatedly tried to reorganize the alliance to conform with the new geopolitical realities, only to be rebuffed by the other members. But as the United States pointed out, Article 12 of the NATO Treaty explicitly allowed for amendments to be made to the alliance, and Washington had encouraged Paris to make use of this mechanism. It never had.[70] Moreover, the United States and Britain at least entertained de Gaulle's tripartite directorate, but it was unclear what the former general really wanted. The reality was, as the French diplomat François de Rose later conceded, de Gaulle was determined to pull out of NATO no matter what flexibility the United States and other members showed. "Pulling out was the decision he wanted, the rest was pretext," de Rose said.[71] Without nuclear weapons, de Gaulle may have been forced to accept the military alliance, even if he despised it. With them, there was no stopping him.

CONVENTIONAL MILITARY CUTS

If the impact of de Gaulle's withdrawal from NATO's military command was relatively short-lived, the *force de frappe* had a more enduring impact on France's conventional military power. In truth, France had not made a large military contribution to NATO for some time. In 1959, France had only two divisions under NATO command in Germany, the same number as Belgium and the Netherlands. Even these two divisions were not seen as combat troops. By way of comparison, West Germany had seven divisions, the US had five, and Great Britain had three. But this was because so much of the French army was tied down in Algeria; in 1960, the French Army had 418,000 troops fighting in North Africa compared to just 253,000 soldiers in France and West Germany.[72]

France had long promised NATO that its military contribution would increase once the Algerian war was wound down, with returning French units put under SACEUR. This never occurred, primarily because of de Gaulle's hostility to military integration. Still, the costs of France's nuclear arsenal were exploding, cutting into conventional forces and capabilities. By the middle of the 1960s, the *force de frappe* accounted for 25% of France's military budget.[73] The nuclear arsenal consumed over 50% of France's spending on military equipment.[74] These percentages not only reflected the costs of the arsenal but also the decline in French military spending. In 1960, the year France first tested a nuclear weapon, Paris spent 5.4% of its GDP on the military, down from 7.6% in 1953. By the early 1970s, France was only devoting 3.1% of its GDP to defense, a 43% decline from 1960.[75]

This was by design. One of the earliest advocates of a French nuclear arsenal was the military officer Charles Ailleret. Ailleret, who would go on to serve as chairman of the French Chiefs of Staff under de Gaulle, argued in 1954 that nuclear bombs are "inexpensive weapons in contrast to classic weapons [and] constitute the criterion of a modern army."[76] Indeed, as Phillip Gordon has explained, a nuclear-armed France's military doctrine mandated that Paris keep only token conventional forces.[77] This is reflected in the budgetary figures. The army, which didn't have a role in the nuclear arsenal, saw its share of the defense budget decline from 73% in 1946 and 52% in 1958, to 40% by 1969.[78] Meanwhile, the size of France's armed forces declined from over a million in the early 1960s, to 500,000 by the end of the decade.[79]

Again, strategic logic, not only economic considerations, was behind the drastic reduction in the size of France's standing force. French officials had long complained that JFK's Flexible Response undermined the credibility of America's willingness to use nuclear weapons. Thus, after it acquired its own nuclear weapons, Paris cut the size of its armed forces drastically to make clear to Moscow it would have to use nuclear weapons if a conflict arose. In other words, France's nuclear arsenal drained resources from its conventional forces and provided the strategic logic for allowing France's army to atrophy. None of this was much comfort for US leaders who spent decades pushing European allies to shoulder more of the burden in Europe.

NUCLEAR OFFSPRING

Like conventional military power, France's nuclear offspring also had a lasting effect. As noted in the introduction to this book, Britain, France, Israel, and Pakistan's nuclear acquisition did not lead to a nuclear domino effect in the way the term is usually used. That is, rivals and neighbors did not acquire nuclear weapons in response to them doing so. On the other hand, starting with France, the new nuclear powers did help proliferate nuclear weapons to other countries through technology transfers.

France is perhaps the best example of this, at least in terms of the quantity of countries involved. The political scientist Matthew Kroenig defines sensitive nuclear assistance as the "state-sponsored transfer of the key materials and technologies necessary for the construction of a nuclear weapons arsenal to a non-nuclear weapon state." There are three kinds of sensitive nuclear assistance, according to Kroenig: assisting in the design of nuclear weapons, transferring significant quantities of weapons grade fissile material; and helping build reprocessing or enrichment facilities that can be used to produce fissile material.[80] Of the fourteen cases of sensitive nuclear assistance Kroenig identifies, France was the seller in five cases: Israel (reprocessing plant, 1956–1965); Japan (pilot-scale processing plant, 1971–1974), Pakistan (reprocessing plants, 1974–1982), Taiwan (reprocessing plant, 1975), and

Egypt (hot cells, 1980–1982). Paris also agreed to sell South Korea a reprocessing plant, but Seoul backed out of the deal under US pressure.

France's most extensive assistance went to Israel. As discussed in more detail in the following chapter, partly in return for Israel's help in what became the Suez Crisis, Paris provided Israel with a plutonium-producing reactor and a reprocessing plant; basically, an entire bomb-making kit. No other country has provided this level of nuclear assistance to a non-nuclear power. Paris might have done the same with Pakistan, Taiwan, and South Korea, but US intervention prevented these deals from coming to fruition. By the time America convinced France to abandon the deal with Pakistan, however, many of the blueprints for the reprocessing plant had already been transferred, allowing Islamabad to build the plant itself, albeit at a much slower rate.

France also played a role in helping other nuclear aspirants, although the assistance was more limited. In the late 1970s, France agreed to sell Iraq a forty-megawatt research reactor based on the French Osiris design. It did this despite Saddam Hussein declaring publicly that the deal represented "the first Arab attempt at nuclear arming."[81] Iraq probably intended to use this reactor—which Israel destroyed in an air strike in 1981—to either produce plutonium or gain expertise to build a parallel unsafeguarded program. Nonetheless, the Osiris reactors used highly enriched uranium (HEU), and Paris provided Iraq with roughly twelve and a half kilograms of this weapons-grade material as part of the agreement.[82] After Iraq invaded Kuwait in 1990, Saddam Hussein tried to use this HEU (as well as Russian-supplied material) in a crash program to build crude nuclear devices in hopes of deterring the eventual US-led military coalition.[83]

France's nuclear assistance resulted in at least one country acquiring nuclear weapons (Israel)—and arguably one and a half if one includes Pakistan.[84] It could have been much, much worse. The United States expended significant diplomatic capital persuading France to cancel nuclear sales and other allies like Taiwan and South Korea to terminate their purchasing agreements. Israel's air strikes against Iraq's reactor in 1981 along with Saddam Hussein's decision to invade Kuwait might have been all that prevented Baghdad from getting the bomb. Moreover, Iraq's nuclear program convinced the Islamic Republic of Iran to restart the Shah's dormant nuclear program. Although plenty of other factors were at play, Iran's program is something the United States is still grappling with today. In short, France's nuclear offspring have been detrimental to US interests.

COMING IN FROM THE COLD

As was the case with Great Britain, the United States eventually accepted France's nuclear arsenal. It also assisted France's nuclear development, although not to the same degree as it had with London. The change was spearheaded by President Richard Nixon and Henry Kissinger and began nearly immediately after they took office. Just weeks into his presidency, Nixon explained to de Gaulle that "he took a different view of the French nuclear deterrent [than his predecessors]. He thought it was good for the US to have another power like France with a nuclear capability."[85] The following month, Nixon commissioned a study on military cooperation with France and asked that it "include options in the area of nuclear weapons cooperation."[86] De Gaulle's sudden resignation in April 1969 temporarily put the initiative on hold, but Nixon approved cooperation after meeting with de Gaulle's successor, Georges Pompidou, in February 1970.

There were a number of different reasons that Nixon decided to end the policy of shunning France's nuclear program. One of these is that he and Kissinger generally believed that independent arsenals in the West enhanced deterrence against the Soviet Union. The Soviets truly achieved nuclear parity around the time that Nixon took office, a fact that the president and Kissinger often bemoaned. They regularly spoke nostalgically about the Cuban Missile Crisis, when the US enjoyed overwhelming strategic superiority. In private, they even doubted whether the US nuclear umbrella was workable in an era of strategic parity.[87] In this sense, they saw France's and Britain's nuclear arsenals as creating uncertainty for the Soviet Union. For instance, before joining the administration, Kissinger wrote, "the nuclear forces of our allies should not be viewed as an alternative to United States strategic power, but as a complement."[88] They also believed independent arsenals helped reassure America's European allies. In his memoirs, Kissinger argued that "the American attempt to monopolize the central nuclear decisions could be portrayed as ensuring for us the option . . . of 'de-coupling' our defense from that of our allies."[89] These were the exact arguments de Gaulle and French generals had always made.[90] Now that the United States was on board, NATO officially endorsed the value Britain's and France's nuclear forces played in deterring the Soviets.[91]

Another reason the Nixon administration could seek nuclear cooperation with France was that a West German bomb now seemed like a remote possibility. The president and Kissinger were far less worried about a German bomb compared with JFK and LBJ, and Nixon even directed his administration not to pressure West Germany to sign the NPT.[92] To some extent, this reflected the fact that they didn't view allied proliferation as problematic for

US interests as the Democratic presidents of the 1960s had. At the same time, it also reflected the reduced danger of a West German bomb. Despite not being pressured, Bonn signed the NPT in 1969, and its ambitions to build an independent nuclear force basically ended with it.[93] Still, the administration insisted that nuclear and missile cooperation with France be done covertly in large part so that allies wouldn't think Washington was awarding Paris for getting the bomb, as well as for its general intransigence.

As was the case with Eisenhower, JFK, and LBJ, Nixon's position on France's nuclear program was ultimately influenced most importantly by larger geopolitical questions. Nixon, like Eisenhower (with whom he served as vice president), wanted a strong, independent Europe. As he told French President Pompidou, "To be safe the world requires the five fingers on the hand, which are a strong Europe, a strong US, Russia, China, and for the future, Japan."[94] Nixon and Kissinger believed that France was best suited to play a leadership role in Europe. As Kissinger explained to Pompidou, "We have always believed that in a strong Europe . . . France would play a pivotal role."[95] For Nixon and Kissinger, Britain—besides not being a continental power—no longer sought a strong role on the global stage. They also distrusted the West German government under Willy Brandt, especially its Ostpolitik policy of seeking to strengthen ties to the Communist states.[96] So Nixon and Kissinger were intent on improving the overall character of Franco-American relations, and they recognized, as had Kennedy, that this could not be done without engaging France on nuclear matters. That geopolitics was the driving factor is evident from the fact that, despite considerable pressure from within the administration, Nixon and Kissinger repeatedly ruled out adopting a quid-pro-quo approach toward nuclear cooperation. Whereas many in the administration wanted to make missile and nuclear cooperation conditional on France reintegrating with NATO or adopting other policies America favored, the president and his national security advisor insisted it take place with no strings attached. The objective was not to get France to adopt specific policies the United States preferred. In fact, Nixon and Kissinger accepted, at least rhetorically, that Paris would at times pursue policies America opposed. Nonetheless, they wanted these disagreements to occur in a more favorable environment. "The real quid pro quo," Kissinger once explained "is the basic orientation of French policy."[97]

Nixon and Kissinger were less interested in the actual details of cooperation. The importance was the "political gesture to Paris."[98] Accordingly, the administration started slowly. For years, France had been trying to buy advanced computers that were of use to its nuclear program. While Nixon refused to remove all the restrictions on these exports, he agreed to loosen them. He also approved cooperation to improve the reliability and operability of France's existing missiles, but did not help it acquire new capabilities.

Finally, he approved talks about nuclear safety, such as ensuring that nuclear weapons weren't used inadvertently.[99]

The hope was this would "whet their [France's] appetites," and indeed it did.[100] The French were happy with the results of this cooperation, but quickly began pushing for it to be expanded. In March 1973, Nixon approved assistance to four new areas, including information on nuclear effects; exports of small simulators; technology to harden missiles, reentry vehicles, and silos; and intelligence on Soviet anti-ballistic missile systems.[101] At a meeting in Reykjavik in June 1973, Nixon and Pompidou discussed expanding cooperation into issues involving nuclear cores.[102] The issue here was the United States was still restricted by the Atomic Energy Act on what information it could provide France on actual nuclear warhead designs. To circumvent these restrictions, Paris and Washington devised a system called negative guidance whereas the French would inform the Americans what they were doing and the latter would let them know whether they were on the right track or not.[103]

Before this more expansive cooperation could commence, larger geopolitical issues intervened. Kissinger had proclaimed 1973 as the "Year of Europe." By this he meant the administration would focus on strengthening the NATO alliance. European nations viewed this as an attempt for America to reassert leadership and control over an increasingly vibrant Europe. Accordingly, the initiative quickly became a disaster as a result of European opposition. From the Nixon administration's perspective, the French were the worst offenders. Washington could not understand why Pompidou and his government suddenly took such an anti-American bent. Relations only got worse in October 1973 as a result of the Yom Kippur War between Israel and the Arab nations. France harshly criticized US support for Israel during the conflict. The ensuing oil embargo and energy crisis also strained American-Franco ties.

While most of Europe was opposed to America's Middle East policy at the time, Kissinger once again viewed France as the ringleader. He was incensed, venting that the French "are organically hostile to the US and now clearly constitute the greatest global opposition to US foreign policy."[104] Separately, he warned German Foreign Minister Walter Scheel (who was acting as the European Community's liaison) that because of European opposition, Nixon had "discussed seriously the possibility of unilateral US troop withdrawal [from Europe]."[105] In this context, America's defense attaché in Paris was directed to inform the French that their "policies were removing the political basis for the earlier understandings on military matters," including nuclear cooperation. This cooperation was essentially halted for the final months of 1973 and most of 1974.

Ultimately, this flare- up proved to be temporary. In April 1974, Georges Pompidou died of cancer. He was succeeded by Valéry Giscard d'Estaing. That August, Nixon resigned over Watergate and his vice president, Gerald

Ford, took office. Although Ford mostly kept Nixon's national security team in place, the leadership changes allowed the two countries to move past the bitterness. By June 1975, Ford agreed to expand the missile and nuclear assistance program.[106] By this time, the United States was concerned that France's nuclear arsenal was vulnerable to a Soviet first strike as a result of Moscow's arming its missiles with multiple independently targetable reentry vehicles (MIRVs). Washington sought to increase its cooperation with France to make the latter's arsenal more survivable.[107] As the president put it, the United States should provide "information which will assist the French in assessing the vulnerabilities of their strategic missile forces to Soviet attack."[108] Ford also approved assistance on underground testing.[109]

Through the end of the Ford administration, nuclear cooperation with France continued to be bitterly opposed by many parts of the government.[110] Surprisingly, then, the program was continued under Jimmy Carter. In fact, according to Richard H. Ullman, the Princeton University professor who exposed US-Franco nuclear cooperation in 1989, cooperation was "at its most intense" during the Carter administration.[111] Overall, the cooperation proved to be successful. As Ullman observed, "The result of these arrangements is impressive and significant. French nuclear forces would be considerably more effective in the event of war because of past American assistance. Yet at the same time, they would be far less likely to catalyze Armageddon."[112]

CONCLUSION

France's nuclear program was far more disruptive to the United States than Great Britain's, but the two shared many things in common. One example is the intersection between proliferation and geopolitics. The two were certainly related in de Gaulle's mind, who saw nuclear weapons as the best way to achieve his geopolitical objectives. But it was also true for the American leaders responding to the program. Eisenhower and Nixon tolerated France's nuclear ambitions because they wanted a strong Europe that didn't rely so heavily on the United States. For Kennedy, a French nuclear arsenal undermined his efforts to assert stronger US leadership in Europe. To the extent that it motivated a German nuclear weapon, France's nuclear program also contributed to crises with the Soviet Union in Berlin and Cuba.

As was the case with London, the French arsenal also created problems of launch control for the Western alliance. These thorny issues were even more difficult to solve with the uncompromising de Gaulle. For France, determining who got to authorize nuclear use was "the most delicate problem," and de Gaulle refused to host NATO nuclear weapons unless Paris controlled when they were used.[113] Launch control would be an equally difficult problem for future treaty allies that acquired nuclear weapons, like Japan, South Korea, or Turkey. In particular, which country would get to decide when to use nuclear weapons? How would the procedures work? Acquiring nuclear weapons also led France to reduce its conventional military forces, which were of far greater importance to the United States. This occurred because of vast sums of money Paris spent on its nuclear arsenal as well as the strategic logic of nuclear France's military doctrine. Not only did France pursue a "conventional substitution" policy but it believed strong conventional forces would reduce the credibility of its nuclear deterrence. Japan, South Korea, or Turkey reducing their conventional military forces after going nuclear would likely harm US national security. This is certainly true of Japan. Tokyo is the main regional counterweight to China, and its military forces will be increasingly critical to America's defense posture in Asia as China's own power grows. Turkey maintains the largest non-US army in NATO. South Korea provides the overwhelming majority of the ground forces on the Korean Peninsula, although it's possible a large conventional troop presence wouldn't be as necessary if Seoul had nuclear weapons. Still, as even the Eisenhower administration was forced to admit in the late 1950s, relying solely on nuclear weapons for defense is a dangerous business. Washington's interest is best served by these countries using their finite resources to build up their conventional military power, not nuclear weapons that add little to the alliance's overall strategic forces.

France also differed from Great Britain in interesting ways. Once France acquired an operational nuclear deterrent, de Gaulle removed France from NATO's military command. Nuclear weapons didn't cause de Gaulle to pursue this policy. Rather, he did so because of his own views about the nature of alliances and France's place in the world. This worldview long predated the *force de frappe*. Still, it would be a mistake to assume that a similar dynamic would not be present in future allied countries that acquire nuclear weapons. Although a future nuclear-armed Japan, South Korea, or Turkey will not be led by de Gaulle, the French leaders who initiated the nuclear program didn't hold de Gaulle's views either. Rather, they believed having nuclear weapons would strengthen France's position within NATO. Then de Gaulle returned to power and used the arsenal to pursue policies they found abhorrent. The clear lesson for US policymakers is Washington cannot control who leads allied countries in the future. Even if a pro-American leader begins a nuclear program, there's no guarantee a more hostile leader won't use it to undermine the alliance in the future. Moreover, de Gaulle's nationalism and desire for greater autonomy is hardly unique to him. Arguably, Recep Tayyip Erdoğan and Moon Jae-in in Turkey and South Korea respectively hold similar worldviews about their own country's alliances with America.

Although de Gaulle removing France from NATO command was not overly disruptive in the long term, the circumstances are very different for the United States in Asia. Unlike in Europe, where America has a multilateral alliance, in Asia the US has a hub-and-spoke alliance system. Thus, if a Japanese or South Korean leader evicted the US military, it would be much more difficult to relocate these forces elsewhere in the region. At a time of precision-guided missiles, the United States needs to disperse its forces more. Losing bases in South Korea or Japan would make that nearly impossible.

Finally, France also proliferated technology to other countries. Although many of these countries were friends of the United States, this policy still created headaches for policymakers in Washington. Two of France's nuclear offspring are Israel and Pakistan, the remaining two case studies in this book. It is to those cases we now turn.

NOTES

1. John F. Kennedy, "News Conference 52," March 21, 1963. He expressed the same feelings privately, telling Khrushchev in their first summit that if no test ban treaty is reached, "then in a few years there might be ten or even fifteen nuclear powers." See "Memorandum of Conversation," June 4, 1961, *FRUS*, 1961–1963, vol. VII, doc. 31.

2. As Charles Burke Elbrick, the assistant secretary of state for Europe, put it, "the basic issue was not merely opposition to a fourth country producing nuclear weapons but the fact that this might lead to fifth, sixth and seventh countries entering the field." Quoted in Jeffrey T. Richelson, *Spying on the Bomb: American Nuclear Intelligence from Nazi Germany to Iran and North Korea* (New York: Norton, 2006), 160.

3. "DOS to Embassy in France," May 5, 1961, *FRUS*, 1961–1963, vol. XIII, doc. 227.

4. Quoted in Marc Trachtenberg, *A Constructed Peace: The Making of the European Settlement, 1945–1963* (Princeton, NJ: Princeton University Press, 1999), 305.

5. "DOS to Embassy United Kingdom, Message from President Kennedy to Prime Minister Macmillan," May 08, 1961, *Wilson Center Digital Archive*. https://digitalarchive.wilsoncenter.org/document/111184.

6. Hope M. Harrison, "New Evidence on the Building of the Berlin Wall," Cold War International History Project, e-Dossier No. 23, *Wilson Center*. On the Sino-Soviet split, a CIA intelligence estimate about Khrushchev's motives noted that "[n]or does our considerable evidence on the Sino-Soviet dispute indicate that the Chinese Communists exert an important influence." CIA, "Soviet Short-Term Intentions Regarding Berlin and Germany," April 25, 1961, National Intelligence Estimate 11–7–61.

7. Trachtenberg, *Constructed Peace*, chaps. 7–9. Also see Jeffrey D. Sachs, *To Move the World: JFK's Quest for Peace* (New York: Random House, 2014), 47.

8. Trachtenberg, *Constructed Peace*, 233 and 252–54; "Dulles Memorandum to Eisenhower," May 24, 1957, *FRUS*, 1955–1957, vol. XXVI, doc. 111; Office

of Intelligence Research, "West German Attitudes Toward Nuclear Arms," July 2, 1957, U.S. Declassified Documents Online, CK2349407657; National Security Council, "U.S. policy toward Germany (NSC 5803)," February 7, 1958, U.S. Declassified Documents Online, CK2349018025; "U.S. Embassy Paris to DOS, Telegram 3600," February 1, 1958, *NSA*; "Murphy to Eisenhower: NATO Atomic Stockpile in Germany," December 24, 1958, *Digital National Security Archive (DSNA)*; and "Linebaugh to Schaetzel: West German Nuclear Weapons Program," March 29, 1957, *DSNA*.

9. Quoted in Nicholas Thompson, *The Hawk and the Dove: Paul Nitze, George Kennan, and the History of the Cold War* (New York: Henry Holt & Company, 2009), 175.

10. Bureau of Intelligence and Research, "Berlin in the Communist Scheme for a Political Offensive in Germany, No. 7874," November 19, 1958, U.S. Declassified Documents Online, CK2349414285. Also see "DOS to Embassy in Germany," November 17, 1958, *FRUS*, 1958–1960, vol. VIII, doc. 45; "Embassy in Germany to DOS," February 16, 1959, ibid., doc. 174; Central Intelligence Agency, "Soviet Objectives in the Berlin Crisis: SNIE 100–18–58," December 23, 1958, *DSNA*; and Herter's meeting with the French Foreign Ministry, cited in Trachtenberg, *Constructed Peace*, 254.

11. "Dulles-Mikoyan Meeting," January 16, 1959, *FRUS*, 1958–1960, vol. VIII, doc. 135; "Nitze-Menshikov Meeting," July 15, 1961, *FRUS*, 1961–1963, vol. XIV, doc. 70; and Trachtenberg, *Constructed Peace*, 253. That the issue was unsettled after the Berlin Wall went up was also clear. See "Dobrynin and Rusk Discussion," August 8, 1962, 1961–1963, vol. VII, doc. 216.

12. As noted in the introduction, increasing NATO's conventional forces was not unique to the JFK administration; it had been a major point of emphasis for the Eisenhower administration as well.

13. On the city avoidance and nuclear bargaining, see Lawrence Freedman, *The Evolution of Nuclear Strategy*, 3rd ed. (New York: Palgrave Macmillan, 2003), chaps. 14–15.

14. von Clausewitz never used the term *fog of war* but did write "War is the realm of uncertainty; three quarters of the factors on which action in war is based are wrapped in a fog of greater or lesser uncertainty."

15. Even McNamara admitted that the limited strikes he envisioned would kill around 25 million Soviet citizens. "Speech to the NATO Ministerial Meeting in Athens," May 5, 1962, *NSA*. On command and control, see Edward Kaplan, *To Kill Nations: American Strategy in the Air-Atomic Age and the Rise of Mutually Assured Destruction* (Ithaca, NY: Cornell University Press, 2015), 171.

16. Robert McNamara, Athens Speech, May 5, 1962.

17. See, for instance, "Memorandum of Conversation," May 31, 1962, *FRUS*, 1961–1963, vol. XIII, doc. 254; "Rusk Telegram Rusk to DOS," June 20, 1962, *FRUS*, 1961–1963, vol. XIII, doc. 255; and McBundy Memorandum for Secretary of McNamara, "Untitled," April 26, 1962, JFKL, National Security Files (NSF), Departments & Agencies, Box 274. The author thanks Tim McDonnell for the latter file and others from the JFKL.

18. Robert McNamara, "Commencement Address, University of Michigan, Ann Arbor," June 16, 1962. https://robertmcnamara.org/wp-content/uploads/2017/04/mcnamara-1967-22no-cities22-speech-p.pdf.

19. "Policy Directive: NATO and the Atlantic Nations," April 20, 1961, *FRUS*, 1961–1963, vol. XIII, doc.100. Also see "Rostow memo to Rusk on European Unity," March 22, 1962, JFKL, NSF, Regional Security, Box 212.

20. On the members within the administration in each camp, see, Winifred L. Kohl, *French Nuclear Diplomacy* (Princeton, NJ: Princeton University Press, 1971), 219. Also see Ambassador Gavin Memo to President Kennedy, "Balance Sheet of U.S. and French Requests in Military," March 5, 1962, JFKL, National Security Files: Countries, Box 71. The author thanks Timothy P. McDonnell for all documents from JFKL.

21. "DOS Telegram to the Embassy in France," May 5, 1961, *FRUS*, 1961–1963, vol. XIII, doc. 227; "DOS Telegram to the Embassy in France," November 29, 1961, *FRUS*, 1961–1963, vol. XIII, doc. 237; and "Memorandum of Telephone Message from Foy D. Kohler to 'Paul H. Nitze and Roswell L. Gilpatric,'" March 9, 1962, History and Public Policy Program Digital Archive. Obtained and contributed by William Burr and included in NPIHP Research Update #2.

22. "DOS Telegram to the Embassy in France," November 29, 1961, *FRUS*, 1961–1963, vol. XIII, doc. 237.

23. Robert C. Doty, "U.S.-French Strain Laid to Paris Plan for Nuclear Force," *New York Times*, February 27, 1962. Although the comments were made off the record, US officials knew it was Michel Jean-Pierre Debré. Debré confirmed this when confronted. "Embassy in France Telegram to DOS," March 9, 1962, *FRUS*, 1961–1963, vol. XIII, doc. 241.

24. "DOS to the Embassy in France," March 14, 1962, *FRUS*, 1961–1963, vol. XIII, doc. 243.

25. "Memorandum of Meeting," May 11, 1962, *FRUS*, 1961–1963, vol. XIII, doc. 249.

26. See Theodore Sorensen's comments in Kohl, *French Nuclear Diplomacy*, 220.

27. "Summary Record of NSC Executive Committee Meeting No. 38 (Part II)," January 25, 1963, *FRUS*, 1961–1963, vol. XIII, doc. 169.

28. "Ball Memorandum to Kennedy, Answer to Eight Questions," June 17, 1962, *United States National Archive (Hereafter USNA)*, RG 59, Records of Undersecretary of State, George W. Ball, 1961–1966, Box 21.

29. Lawrence Kaplan, *NATO Divided, NATO United: The Evolution of an Alliance* (Westport, CT: Praeger, 2004), 39.

30. Also, the Eisenhower administration had proposed the MLF as supplementing the medium-range ballistic missiles it proposed deploying to Europe. The Kennedy administration proposed the MLF as an alternative to the MRBMs. See ibid.

31. See Hal Brands, "Non-Proliferation and the Dynamics of the Middle Cold War: The Superpowers, the MLF, and the NPT," *Cold War History* 7, no. 3 (2007), 389–423. West Germany at first embraced the concept but soon turned against it.

32. Quoted in Brands, "Non-Proliferation and the Dynamics of the Middle Cold War," 397. In fact, Soviet opposition to the MLF was what held up the superpowers completing a nuclear nonproliferation treaty. See ibid.

33. In May 1962, JFK said of the MLF: "Is it not a fact that the NATO nuclear concept is still-born?" Around the same time, he asked, "Are we certain that [nuclear] cooperation with the French" will encourage the FRG to demand their own nuclear weapons? See "Ball Memorandum to Kennedy: Answer to Eight Questions," June 17, 1962, *USNA*, RG 59, Records of Undersecretary of State, George W. Ball, 1961–1966, Box 21.

34. "NSC meeting," October 20, 1962, *FRUS*, 1961–1963, vol. XI, doc. 34. Also see "Minutes of the 506th Meeting of the National Security Council," October 21, 1962, *FRUS*, 1961–1963, vol. XI, doc. 38.

35. Trachtenberg, *Constructed Peace*, 356.

36. "NSC Meeting," January 31, 1963, *FRUS*, 1961–1963, vol. XIII, doc. 64.

37. In a secret telegram, Rusk told the lead US negotiator, Ambassador Charles Bohlen, to make the offer contingent on France integrating its nuclear forces into NATO, a condition that de Gaulle was sure to reject and that went against JFK's wishes. See "DOS Telegram to the Embassy in France," January 1, 1963, *FRUS*, 1961–1963, vol. XIII, doc. 262. Only a few days before de Gaulle's press conference, George Ball visited France and insisted on the multilateral component. See Richard E. Neustadt, *Report to JFK: The Skybolt Crisis in Perspective* (Ithaca, NY: Cornell University Press, 1999), 104–05.

38. President Kennedy went around Rusk in giving instructions to Ambassador Bohlen directly, where he insisted that integrating France's nuclear arsenal was negotiable. In presenting the plan to de Gaulle, Bohlen described the multilateral concept "as a matter for further discussion." See Trachtenberg, *Constructed Peace*, 367; and "Embassy in France Telegram to DOS," January 4, 1963, *FRUS*, 1961–1963, vol. XIII, doc. 263.

39. There was a brief proposal after the signing of the Partial Test Ban Treaty. See Trachtenberg, *Constructed Peace*, 388–91. The US also sold France the K-135 tanker, which was needed to refuel Mirage planes in-flight. See Kohl, *French Nuclear Diplomacy*, 222–24.

40. This section draws heavily on Trachtenberg, *Constructed Peace*, chap. 9.

41. Trachtenberg, *Constructed Peace*, 390.

42. Dean Rusk, "Toward a New Dimension in the Atlantic Partnership," October 27, 1963, in *The Department of State Bulletin* 39, no. 1271 (November 11, 1963), 726–31.

43. Avery Goldstein, *Deterrence and Security in the 21st Century: China, Britain, France, and the Enduring Legacy of the Nuclear Revolution* (Stanford, CA: Stanford University Press, 2000), 208; and "France's Nuclear Weapons: Origin of the Force de Frappe," *Nuclear Weapons Archive*, December 24, 2001.

44. Kohl, *French Nuclear Diplomacy*, 222–24.

45. Kohl, *French Nuclear Diplomacy*, 214.

46. Goldstein, *Deterrence and Security in the 21st Century*, 205.

47. Fredrik Wetterqvist, *French Security and Defence Policy: Current Developments and Future Prospects* (Stockholm: National Defence Research Institute, 1990), 89; and "France's Nuclear Weapons: Origin of the Force de Frappe," *Nuclear Weapons Archive*, December 24, 2001.

48. Goldstein, *Deterrence and Security in the 21st Century,* 204–05.

49. "Embassy in France to DOS: EMBTEL 1433," September 17, 1965, *USNA,* RG 59, Central Foreign Policy Files, 1964–1966, Pol 1, FR-US, Box 2186; and "Embassy in France to DOS: EMBTEL 1438," September 17, 1965, ibid.

50. Document IV-1, "Reply Made by the President of the French Republic (General de Gaulle) to a Question asked at a News Conference, February 21, 1966 (Excerpt)," in *American Foreign Policy Current Documents: 1966* (Washington, DC: Historical Division, Bureau of Public Affairs, 1969), 316.

51. "Telegram From the Embassy in France to the Department of State," February 25, 1966, *FRUS,* 1964–1968, vol. XII, doc. 54. Also see "Embassy in France to DOS: EMBTEL 5247," February 25, 1966, *USNA,* RG 59, Subject Numeric Files, 1964–1966, DEF 4, NATO, Box 1596.

52. On the State Department wanting to take a harder line, see John M. Leddy's comments in "Moments in U.S. Diplomatic History: France has de Gaulle to Withdraw from NATO," June 2014, Association for Diplomatic Studies & Training and Sylvia Ellis, "A Foreign Policy Success? LBJ and Transatlantic Relations," *Journal of Transatlantic Studies* 8, no. 3 (2010): 251. White House aides were more in line with the president. See "Komer to Johnson," March 16, 1966, FRUS, 1964–1968, Volume XIII, Document 143.

53. "DOS Circular Telegram to All NATO Missions," March 2, 1966, *FRUS,* 1964–1968, vol. XIII, doc. 55.

54. "DOS to Embassy in France, REF: Embtels 5621 and 5699," March 11, 1966, *USNA,* RG 59, Subject-Numeric Files, 1964–1966, DEF 4, NATO, Box 1596.

55. Document IV-4, "French Memorandum to the 14 Representatives of the NATO Governments, March 8 and 10, 1966," in *American Foreign Policy Current Documents: 1966* (Washington, DC: Historical Division, Bureau of Public Affairs, 1969), 318–21. Premier Pompidou made the same point in explaining the decision to the French National Assembly in April. See "Speech by Georges Pompidou to the French National Assembly," April 13, 1966. https://www.cvce.eu/content/publication/2002/3/12/1cc55b75-80af-4fe5-9e5d-8960923c55f4/publishable_en.pdf. The connection between the Mirage planes becoming operational and de Gaulle's pulling out is one many experts make. See, for instance, Bruno Tertrais, "*Destruction Assurée*: The Origins and Development of French Nuclear Strategy, 1945—81," in *Getting MAD: Nuclear Mutual Assured Destruction, Its Origins and Practice,* ed. Henry D. Sokolski (Washington, DC: Strategic Studies Institute, 2004), 59.

56. "Embassy in France to DOS: EMBTEL 4401, Subject: U.S.-French Relations," January 27, 1966, *USNA,* RG 59, Central Foreign Policy Files, 1964–1966, Pol 1, FR-US, Box 2186.

57. On the other hand, France justified its decision in part on the argument that Flexible Response, with its focus on a conventional response first, undermined deterrence. "Speech by Georges Pompidou to the French National Assembly," April 13, 1966.

58. Document IV-6, "Letter From the President of the United States (Johnson) to the President of the French Republic (General de Gaulle)," March 22, 1966, in

American Foreign Policy Current Documents: 1966 (Washington, DC: Historical Division, Bureau of Public Affairs, 1969), 323.

59. "Memorandum by the Acheson Group," Undated, *FRUS*, 1964–1968, vol. XIII, doc. 173.

60. Brands, "Non-Proliferation and the Dynamics of the Middle Cold War," 389–423; and Gene Gerzhoy, "Alliance Coercion and Nuclear Restraint: How the United States Thwarted West Germany's Nuclear Ambitions," *International Security* 39, no. 4 (Spring 2015), 91–129.

61. "The Future Tasks of the Alliance," December 13–14, 1967, *NATO*, https://www.nato.int/cps/ua/natohq/official_texts_26700.htm.

62. See for example, "Embassy in Belgium to DOS, Subj: NATO," March 10, 1966, *USNA*, RG 59, Records of the Department of State, Subject-Numeric Files, 1964–1966, DEF 4, NATO, Box 1596.

63. "Embassy in France to DOS: EMBTEL 6964," April 20, 1966, *USNA*, RG 59, Central Foreign Policy Files, 1964–1966, Pol 1, FR-US, Box 2185.

64. Frank Costigliola, *France and the United States: The Cold Alliance Since World War II* (New York: Twayne Publishers, 1992), 144–45.

65. See https://www.nato.int/docu/review/2007/issue2/english/history.html.

66. Quoted in Henrik Bering, "The Audacity of de Gaulle," February 1, 2013, *Hoover Institution*, https://www.hoover.org/research/audacity-de-gaulle.

67. Jamie Shea, "1967: De Gaulle pulls France out of NATO's integrated military structure," March 03, 2009, *NATO*, https://www.nato.int/cps/en/natohq/opinions_139272.htm.

68. Tertrais, *"Destruction Assurée,"* 63. Also see "Embassy in France to DOS: EMBTEL 5725," March 11, 1966, *USNA*, RG 59, Subject-Numeric Files, 1964–1966, DEF 4, NATO, Box 1596.

69. As Lawrence Kaplan notes, "France continued to be represented in every NATO military headquarters, although its representatives were identified as 'missions' not 'delegations.'" Kaplan, *NATO Divided, NATO United*, 34.

70. "Aide-Mémoire From the U.S. Government to the French Government," April 12, 1966, *FRUS*, 1964–1968, doc. 154.

71. Quoted in Shea, "1967: De Gaulle pulls France out of NATO's integrated military structure," March 3, 2009, *NATO*.

72. Arthur J. Olsenspecial, "NATO Shield Units Lag in Building Up," *New York Times*, January 2, 1960; and Phillip H. Gordon, *A Certain Idea of France: French Security Policy and Gaullist Legacy* (Princeton, NJ: Princeton University Press, 1993), 56.

73. Erin Mahan, *Kennedy, De Gaulle, and Western Europe* (New York: Palgrave Macmillian, 2002), 69.

74. Gordon, *Certain Idea of France*, 65.

75. SIPRI Military Expenditure Database.

76. Quoted in Lawrence Scheinman, *Atomic Energy Policy in France Under the Fourth Republic* (Princeton, NJ: Princeton University Press, 1983), 109.

77. Gordon, *Certain Idea of France*, 67–68.

78. Jurgen Brauer and Hubert van Tuyll, *Castles, Battles, and Bombs: How Economics Explains Military History* (Chicago: University of Chicago Press, 2008), 261.

79. The Military Balance, "Part III, Table I: Mobilized Manpower," (London: The International Institute for Strategic Studies, 1961); The Military Balance, "Tables," (London: The International Institute for Strategic Studies, 1970), 112; and Robert J. Lieber, "The French Nuclear Force: A Strategic and Political Evaluation," *International Affairs* 42, no. 3 (July 1966), 422.

80. Matthew Kroenig, "Exporting the Bomb: Why States Provide Sensitive Nuclear Assistance," *American Political Science Review* 103, no. 1, 117–18. Also see Matthew Kroenig, *Exporting the Bomb: Technology Transfer and the Spread of Nuclear Weapons* (Ithaca, NY: Cornell University Press, 2010), 10–11.

81. Quoted in Nuclear Threat Initiative, "Iraq," July 2015. https://www.nti.org/area/nuclear/.

82. Louis Rene Beres, "Nuclear Weapons and the War Between Iran and Iraq," *Chicago Tribune*, October 14, 1987.

83. International Atomic Energy Agency, "Iraq Nuclear File: Key Findings," Undated.

84. After France abandoned its nuclear deal, Pakistan set up an enrichment program that enabled it to get highly enriched uranium.

85. "Memorandum of Conversation," March 1, 1969, *FRUS*, 1969–1976, vol. XLI, doc. 118.

86. "National Security Study Memorandum 47," April 21, 1969, *FRUS*, 1969–1976, vol. XLI, doc. 123.

87. Francis J. Gavin, *Nuclear Statecraft: History and Strategy in America's Atomic Age* (Ithaca, NY: Cornell University Press, 2012), 111–13.

88. Henry Kissinger, *The Troubled Partnership: A Re-Appraisal of the Atlantic Alliance* (New York: McGraw-Hill, 1965), 166.

89. Henry Kissinger, *White House Years* (Boston: Little, Brown, 1979), 84.

90. This point was not lost on Nixon and Kissinger. As the latter told the French ambassador: "De Gaulle was basically right. . . . It is too dangerous to have one country as the repository of nuclear weapons. We would like France to be a possessor." See "Kissinger meeting with Ambassador Jacques Kosciusko-Morizet," April 13, 1973, *DNSA*, Kissinger Transcripts Collection, 9.

91. This was done in 1974 in the so-called Ottawa Declaration. See "Declaration on Atlantic Relations," June 19, 1974. Nixon and Kissinger also wanted a stronger Europe because of their fear that, in the wake of Vietnam, domestic support for an active US foreign policy was endangered.

92. "National Security Decision Memorandum 6," February 5, 1969, *FRUS*, 1969–1976, vol. E-2, doc. 8. Somewhat ironically, by this time, the French had become extremely concerned about West Germany building the bomb as a result of it forming an enrichment company with the Dutch and British. "Memorandum of Conversation," March 31, 1969, *FRUS*, 1969–1976, vol. XLI, doc. 120; and "Embassy in France to DOS," April 18, 1969, *FRUS*, 1969–1976, vol. XLI, doc. 121.

93. Gerzhoy, "Alliance Coercion and Nuclear Restraint."

94. "Nixon-Pompidou Meeting," May 31, 1973, *DNSA*, Kissinger Transcripts Collection, 4.

95. "Kissinger-Pompidou Meeting," May 18, 1973, *DNSA*, Kissinger Transcripts Collection, 7.

96. Marc Trachtenberg, "The French Factor in U.S. Foreign Policy during the Nixon-Pompidou Period, 1969–1974," *Journal of Cold War Studies* 13 (2011), 5.

97. "Memorandum of Conversation," September 5, 1973, Gerald R. Ford Presidential Library.

98. "Memorandum from Henry A. Kissinger to President Nixon, 'Military Cooperation with France,'" March 25, 1971, History and Public Policy Program Digital Archive, Obtained and contributed by William Burr and included in NPIHP Research Update #2.

99. "National Security Decision Memorandum 103," March 29, 1971, *FRUS*, 1969–1976, vol. XLI, doc. 153; "National Security Decision Memorandum 104," March 29, 1971, *FRUS*, 1969–1976, vol. XLI, doc. 154; and William Burr, "U.S. Secret Assistance to the French Nuclear Program, 1969–1975: From 'Fourth Country' to Strategic Partner," July 12, 2011, Nuclear Proliferation International History Project.

100. Quoted in Burr, "U.S. Secret Assistance to the French Nuclear Program."

101. "Kissinger Memo to Richardson," March 9, 1973, *FRUS*, 1969–1976, vol. E-15, part 2, doc. 305.

102. Trachtenberg, "The French Factor," 29.

103. "Memorandum of Conversation," August 17, 1973, *FRUS*, 1969–1976, vol. E-15, part 2, doc. 312; and "Memorandum of Conversation," August 31, 1973, *FRUS*, 1969–1976, vol. E-15, part 2, doc. 313.

104. Quoted in Trachtenberg, "The French Factor," 50.

105. Quoted in Trachtenberg, "The French Factor," 49.

106. "Memorandum From President Ford to Secretary of Defense Schlesinger," June 23, 1975, *FRUS*, 1969–1976, vol. E-15, part 2, doc. 331.

107. "Memorandum From President Ford to Secretary of Defense Schlesinger," June 23, 1975, *FRUS*, 1969–1976, vol. E-15, part 2, doc. 331. The US was actually concerned about the survivability of France's nuclear forces in light of Soviet MIRVs in 1973, before cooperation was more or less halted. "Memorandum of Conversation," August 31, 1973, *FRUS*, 1969–1976, vol. E-15, part 2, doc. 313.

108. "Memorandum From President Ford to Secretary of Defense Schlesinger," June 23, 1975, *FRUS*, 1969–1976, vol. E-15, part 2, doc. 331.

109. "National Security Decision Memorandum 299," June 23, 1975, *FRUS*, 1969–1976, vol. E-15, part 2, doc. 330.

110. See "Memorandum of Conversation," March 29, 1976, *FRUS*, 1969–1976, vol. E-15, part 2, doc. 335; and "Memorandum From Secretary of Defense Rumsfeld to President Ford," March 13, 1976, *FRUS*, 1969–1976, vol. E-15, part 2, doc. 336. Also see Giscard and Kissinger's comments in "Memorandum of Conversation, 'Economic Policy/Cyprus; French Nuclear Programs; Energy,'" August 01, 1975, History and Public Policy Program Digital Archive, *National Archives*, Record Group 59,

Office of the Counselor, 1955–77, box 4, France 1975. Obtained and contributed by William Burr and included in NPIHP Research Update #2.

111. Richard H. Ullman, "The Covert French Connection," *Foreign Policy,* no. 75 (Summer, 1989), 18.

112. Ullman, "Covert French Connection," 18.

113. Quoted in Trachtenberg, *Constructed Peace*, 67.

PART II

Partners

Chapter 7

A Nuclear Cat and Mouse
(Israel, 1950s–1963)

David Ben-Gurion knew it was a once-in-a-lifetime offer and one that could guarantee his country's survival.

Ben-Gurion obsessed over Israel's survival. Although he had been in Palestine during the Holocaust, Israel's founding father witnessed its gruesome aftermath in visits to the concentration camps following the war. He dedicated his life to preventing a sequel. That was easier said than done. Israel was a tiny, backward nation surrounded by much larger, more populous Arab countries bent on its destruction. Israel's only chance of survival was to maintain a technological edge over its enemies. And no technological edge was as formidable as a nuclear weapon. Ben-Gurion often professed his faith in "the Jewish brain" to produce cutting edge technology.[1] But even he knew that Israel in the 1950s was not capable of building the bomb itself. That is why Ben-Gurion could hardly believe his luck when, in return for Israel's participation in the Suez Crisis, France was offering to sell the Jewish state everything it needed to build the bomb. This was an opportunity that would never come again. There was just one problem: Israel didn't have the money to secretly fund what was estimated as an $80 million nuclear deal.[2] The solution? "Call Abe," Ben-Gurion told his advisors.

Abe referred to Abe Feinberg, a wealthy, politically connected Jewish-American businessman. Feinberg met many of Israel's future leaders after World War II, when he helped smuggle Holocaust survivors and weapons into Palestine for the War of Independence. He was also a member of the rich Jewish diaspora group, the Sonneborn Institute, which helped fund that war. Thus, it was only natural that Ben-Gurion would turn to Feinberg to raise money for the nuclear deal with France. Feinberg delivered, raising about $40 million for the Israeli nuclear program between 1958 and 1960. This was crucial; as Michael Karpin observes, "it is doubtful that [Ben-Gurion] would have undertaken the deal with France" without the money Feinberg raised.

In his home country, Feinberg had cultivated Democratic Party leaders by playing a crucial role in helping Harry Truman get elected in 1948. Democratic leaders knew of his deep ties in Israel. Accordingly, when America discovered Israel's nuclear plant in the desert on the eve of his inauguration, John F. Kennedy turned to Feinberg to get Ben-Gurion to allow American inspectors into the Dimona reactor. Time and again, Presidents Kennedy and Lyndon B. Johnson would use Abe as an interlocutor to Israeli leaders on the nuclear program. Therefore, the same man who funded Israel's nuclear program was being relied on by American presidents to help rein it in.[3]

Abe Feinberg's story helps illustrate the peculiar and unique nature of the Israeli nuclear program. Of all the case studies in this book, Israel is the most frustrating one to study. Israel's refusal to acknowledge its nuclear weapons, and the nature of the US-Israeli relationship, makes it difficult to come to definitive conclusions on many major points. It is even more difficult to draw lessons that might be applicable for future cases.

These caveats notwithstanding, there are some conclusions that can be taken away from the Israel case. The nuclear program undoubtedly put an enormous strain on bilateral ties during the JFK and LBJ administrations. In fact, US officials repeatedly stressed that the nuclear program was the one issue that could destroy Israel's relationship with the United States. As one National Security Council staffer told the Israelis, the nuclear program was the one issue where the "vital interests [of] over 190 million Americans would simply have to override those of 2 1/2 million Israelis."[4] Similarly, Secretary of State Dean Rusk warned the Israelis that building nuclear weapons would have a "disastrous effect" on bilateral ties and warned that America would be "utterly harsh on the matter of non-proliferation."[5] Israel also helped South Africa develop its missiles and nuclear weapons. At one point, Jerusalem likely even offered apartheid South Africa missiles with nuclear warheads.

Similar to the previous cases, Israel's nuclear program was often completely intertwined with larger geopolitical issues. While US officials were concerned that Israel's nuclear program would have a domino effect on the region, they were even more worried that Israel going nuclear would enable the Soviet Union to increase its influence in the Middle East. In specific, Washington feared that the Arab countries would turn to the Soviet Union to protect them against an emboldened Israel. This might take the form of Moscow forward deploying troops or even nuclear weapons to Arab allies. Furthermore, Washington believed Israel getting the bomb would make it more difficult to restrain West Germany's nuclear ambitions. Repeatedly over the years, Israel's nuclear program also complicated America's efforts to forge larger arms control and nonproliferation treaties.

What became known as the qualitative military edge was initially rooted in Israel's nuclear arsenal. During the 1950s and early 1960s, Washington refused to sell Israel major military weapons for fear of alienating the Arab states. This reluctance began evaporating as Israel's nuclear program progressed. First, US officials hoped to use arms sales as leverage to extract nuclear concessions from Israel. When this didn't work, US officials hoped superior conventional weapons would persuade Israel that nuclear weapons were unnecessary. Once Israel had nuclear weapons, it became necessary to ensure Israel could defend itself with conventional weapons so it wouldn't turn to nuclear ones. Accordingly, US military assistance increased exponentially after Israel acquired the bomb. Undoubtedly, other factors influenced America's arms sales and military assistance to Israel. But Israel's nuclear arsenal played a major, underappreciated role.

Israel differs from the previous two cases in this book in a number of ways, many of which it shares in common with Pakistan. For starters, Israel is not a military treaty ally of the United States. The operational military challenges that were present in the British and French cases are not applicable to the Israeli and Pakistani cases. Jerusalem and Islamabad are also not recognized nuclear weapon states in the NPT. Israel is also the first case in the book where it feels like the story is still being written. England and France are accepted nuclear states without much controversy. Although it is impossible to predict the future, it is hard to imagine drastic changes in those countries' nuclear policies. It seems much more probable that major developments could occur in the Israeli and Pakistani nuclear stories. To state one obvious example, Israel could formally declare itself a nuclear weapons state, perhaps in response to another Middle Eastern country acquiring nuclear weapons.

Although certainly not unique to this case, one characteristic is more pronounced in the Israeli case than others. Namely, since the moment America discovered the Dimona reactor, US and Israeli officials have had to create and perpetuate alternative facts to deal with the program. In fact, these alternative facts—which have been told to other countries, the US Congress, the general public, and sometimes between Israel and the United States itself—are arguably the defining characteristic of the Israeli nuclear case. The most obvious fiction is that both countries refuse to acknowledge Israel's nuclear status. But there are other examples, such as the Carter administration's efforts to explain away a nuclear test in South Africa in 1979. These fictions were created for understandable reasons, and they have unquestionably advanced US and Israeli interests at various times. They nonetheless have a cost, albeit one that is hard to quantify.

This chapter traces Israel's nuclear development through the death of John F. Kennedy. It demonstrates that geopolitical concerns had a large influence on Israel's nuclear program. The chapter also highlights JFK's role in US policy. Although many accounts of Israel's nuclear program depict Kennedy as absolutely determined to stop Israel's nuclear program, the reality is that his interest in this program waxed and waned.[6] Early on in his administration, he pushed strongly for an inspection of Dimona. Once this was accomplished JFK turned his attention to other matters until the Cuban Missile Crisis motivated him to address proliferation issues around the world. His efforts to rein in Israel's program at this point were cut short by his assassination.

A BOMB IS BORN

Israel's dedication to using science to ensure its survival predates the state itself. In March 1948, a few months before it declared its independence, Israel's military created a science division called HEMED. Shortly thereafter, HEMED would conduct a geological survey of the Negev (desert) in an unsuccessful effort to find uranium. Four years later, David Ben-Gurion reorganized the Ministry of Defense. As part of this reorganization, he created a Division of Research and Infrastructure (EMET) and placed HEMED—renamed Machon 4—under EMET. Also in 1952, the Israel Atomic Energy Commission (IAEC) was created. David Bergmann, a professor close to Ben-Gurion, was put in charge of EMET, Machon 4, and the IAEC.[7] Along with Ben-Gurion and Shimon Peres, then a young, rising star in the Ministry of Defense, Bergmann would become one of the key figures in Israel's nuclear development.

Even at this early date, it was clear that Israel's primary decision makers were interested in acquiring nuclear weapons. For instance, in 1955 EMET recruited and funded promising science students' graduate studies abroad. The students were told the purpose of this program was to help Israel build a nuclear weapon, and the scholarship required them to work for EMET after they graduated.[8] The only disagreement among the three towering figures of Israel's nuclear program was the best way to acquire the bomb. Bergmann maintained a fanatical faith in Israel's indigenous capabilities, whereas Peres was far more skeptical. Thus, as Bergmann sponsored Israeli students' foreign studies, Peres went to Paris to establish a working relationship with French officials. At first, Peres sought conventional weapons, but the possibility of future nuclear cooperation wasn't lost on Peres and Ben-Gurion.[9] In France, Peres found natural allies among French officials like Interior Ministry official Abel Thomas, who had resisted Nazi Germany and lost family members to that struggle. Other officials felt indebted to Israel because of the role their country played in sending French Jews to concentration camps. But the strategic dimension of the relationship was more important. At the time, France was in a brutal struggle with the Algerian independence movement, and Egyptian President Gamal Abdel Nasser was one of the insurgency's main backers. Israel was in its own struggle with Nasser, and Paris turned to Israel for intelligence on Nasser and Algeria. Although Israel was part of America's Atoms for Peace program, this was for civilian purposes.[10] The French connection was more promising for a bomb program, and by early 1956, Peres was seeking to persuade French officials to expand their relationship into the nuclear realm.[11]

The French connection received a boost when Guy Mollet became prime minister in February 1956. One of his first orders of business was making the Interior Minister Maurice Bourges-Maunoury the defense minister. Abel Thomas was one of Bourges-Maunoury's top aides, and like his subordinate, Bourges-Maunoury felt a strong bond with Israel.[12] This immediately began paying dividends for Israel—Bourges-Maunoury sold Israel Mystère fighter jets over the objections of Foreign Ministry officials. Ties only expanded from there. At a joint bilateral defense meeting in June 1956, Peres asked for a $70 million arms deal that included 200 tanks, 72 Mystère fighters, 10,000 anti-tank rockets, and 40,000 artillery shells. Bourges-Maunoury agreed.[13]

The real turning point came in July 1956 when President Nasser announced the nationalization of the Suez Canal. The Suez Canal was a crucial choke point in trade between Europe, Asia, and the Middle East. Egyptian control would give Nasser significant leverage over European powers, including effectively cutting off the continent's oil supplies. Each day, 1.2 million barrels of oil—roughly two-thirds of Western Europe's entire oil supplies—passed through the Suez Canal on its way to Europe.[14] Before Nasser's nationalization, the canal was administered by a company jointly owned by Britain and France, which provided a major source of revenue for both countries. The day after Nasser's announcement, Bourges-Maunoury asked Peres to meet immediately. The French defense minister wanted to know how quickly the Israeli Defense Forces (IDF) could mobilize and invade the Sinai Peninsula as part of a tripartite operation with Britain. Peres said Israel would be interested under certain conditions, with a nuclear reactor in mind. Ben-Gurion remained skeptical of the proposal, but progress proceeded swiftly. In September, France, Britain, and Israel finalized the details during a summit at Sevres near Paris. Israel would invade the Sinai, and Britain and France would call for a ceasefire. When the fighting continued, London and Paris would intervene, ostensibly to separate the two warring parties. They would then argue that their control of the Suez Canal should be reinstated to ensure its stability. Following the tripartite meeting, France and Israel secretly consecrated the nuclear agreement—at least verbally.[15]

Although Israel's invasion was a tactical success, the operation was an unmitigated disaster, with the Soviets and Americans issuing strong threats to all parties involved, especially Israel. The Soviet Union warned Jerusalem that its actions placed "the very existence of Israel as a state in question."[16] Dwight Eisenhower was equally enraged, having been kept in the dark about the operation. A resolution calling on Israel to withdraw passed the United Nations overwhelmingly, with only Israel opposing it. Paris and London quickly lost their nerve and urged Israel to heed the international community's demands. Golda Meir, Israel's foreign minister, flew to Paris, where she was told France couldn't come to Israel's aid if Jerusalem refused. Before agreeing to withdraw, Israel extracted more concessions from Paris on the nuclear deal. First, it asked that the verbal agreement from Sevres be placed in writing. In addition, it asked for a larger, forty-megawatt reactor capable of producing roughly ten to fifteen kilograms of plutonium annually. Finally, it secured France's agreement to include a reprocessing plant in the deal.[17] With these conditions in hand, Israel withdrew its troops from the Sinai.

These assurances were almost derailed by the political instability of France's Fourth Republic. The Suez Crisis led to the downfall of Guy Mollet's government. Fortunately for Israel's sake, he was replaced by Bourges-Maunoury in June 1957. Before long, however, Bourges-Maunoury's government was teetering. With his government about to fall in September 1957, Israel worried that the nuclear deal (which Paris hadn't formally approved) would disappear with him. Peres rushed to Paris to try and salvage the agreement. Fortunately for Israel's sake, as his last act as prime minister, Bourges-Maunoury approved the agreement.[18] It is hard to overstate the significance of the agreement. As Michael Karpin observes, "These agreements had no precedent and are unique even to this day. No country has ever supplied another with a package of equipment and materials for the development of a nuclear option."[19] The agreements would continue to be implemented by bureaucrats through the remainder of the Fourth Republic. Charles de Gaulle tried to end the arrangement when he assumed power, but bureaucratic inertia meant the agreement basically went through as drawn up.[20]

US OUT OF THE DARK

The United States was not aware of any of this until the fall of 1960. The first time the US raised any concerns about Israel's nuclear ambitions was in January 1956, when the intelligence community (IC) placed Israel in the lowest category of interest.[21] The best chance for Washington to stop Israel's nuclear program came in early 1958. U-2 aerial reconnaissance planes were sent to the Negev (where the Dimona reactor is located) to observe Israeli military exercises. By happenchance, they saw early extractions of what would become the Dimona reactor. Even at this early juncture, the IC judged that this was a "probable" nuclear-related site. The information was presented to President Eisenhower, who didn't show much interest, according to the intelligence officers who briefed him. The IC asked the embassy in Israel to follow up, but, as the Joint Atomic Energy Intelligence Committee (JAEIC) later concluded, not enough was done.[22] It was a major missed opportunity but not the only one. In early 1959, London learned that Dan Tolkowsky, the chief of staff of the Israeli Air Force, had resigned over his opposition to a nuclear weapons program. The British passed this information to America's naval attaché in Israel, who in turn notified the Central Intelligence Agency (CIA). The CIA asked the embassy to try and confirm it. When they couldn't, the matter was dropped.[23]

Despite these warning signs, the United States did not take an active interest in the construction project in the desert until the summer of 1960. On August 2, the US embassy reported that a technician had informed it that French nationals were helping to construct a large reactor in the Negev.[24] Shortly thereafter, a secretary in the US embassy revealed that her Israeli boyfriend had told her about the reactor during a date they went on in Negev. The boyfriend had also confirmed the French connection.[25] Washington followed up by having embassy officials and reconnaissance satellites photograph Dimona.[26] The British were also photographing the site, and by November, the CIA had concluded it was "probably" a nuclear reactor.[27]

Israel apparently realized its secret was blown and decided to get in front of it by inviting Henry Gomberg—a nuclear scientist at the University of Michigan—to visit Israel. During his trip in late November, Israeli scientists brought Gomberg around the small research reactor that had been built by the United States as well as other facilities. Over the course of the conversation, his Israeli interlocutors let on that their country was building a much larger reactor with French assistance. While this was almost certainly an Israeli ploy to inform the Americans about their plans,[28] Gomberg believed he had scored an intelligence coup. On the advice of the US ambassador, he immediately left Israel for Paris, where he reported his discovery. "Israel, with French assistance, is building a powerful nuclear reactor in the Negev, with the intention of producing weapons-grade plutonium," Gomberg cabled Washington.[29]

At this point, the United States went into overdrive. On December 2, the JAEIC concluded that Israel was building a two-hundred-megawatt reactor, roughly five times the actual power output of Dimona.[30] The following day, Bergmann told the US ambassador, Ogden Reid, that Israel is building a reactor but only for peaceful purposes. The United States did not buy this for a minute. A special National Intelligence Estimate published a few days later concluded, "On the basis of all available evidence . . . we believe that plutonium production for weapons is at least one major purpose of this effort."[31] At a national security meeting on the same day, CIA Director Allen Dulles noted that "the Israeli nuclear complex cannot be solely for peaceful purposes."[32] Israel's ambassador in Washington, Avraham Harman, first claimed to have no knowledge of the reactor. But on December 20, he confirmed that Israel was building a reactor but said its output was only twenty-four megawatts and it was for peaceful purposes. While refusing to submit to international safeguards, the ambassador did say that "friendly countries" would be allowed to visit the reactor when it was complete. Harmon also said that Ben-Gurion would address the controversy publicly the following day.[33]

During parliamentary questions the next day, Ben-Gurion announced that Israel was building a twenty-four-megawatt "research reactor" and that it would be completed in three or four years. He added that the reactor would "be used only for peaceful purposes" and that it "will be open to trainees from other countries" once construction was finished.[34] This was far from the comprehensive disclosure the Americans sought, but US officials chose what would become a familiar tactic. In public, they sought to downplay concerns about Israel's burgeoning nuclear program. Behind the scenes, they pushed Israel for greater transparency. On New Year's Eve 1960, the State Department directed Ambassador Reid to press Ben-Gurion for "clear and complete answers" on five questions: (1) what would Israel do with the plutonium; (2) will it agree to "adequate" safeguards for the plutonium; (3) will it "permit qualified scientists from the IAEA or other friendly quarters" to visit the reactor, and if so, how soon; (4) will other reactors be built; and (5) "can Israel state categorically that it has no plans for producing nuclear weapons?"[35] The cable describing Ben-Gurion's responses remains classified, but a summary contained in a later document reveals he did say "categorical[ly]" that Israel had no plans to build nuclear weapons. He was evasive on how Israel would dispose of the plutonium, even though France had told Washington it would be sent back to Paris.[36] Ben-Gurion ruled out IAEA visits until all countries agreed to them, but reiterated that friendly countries could visit Dimona. Finally, he said no additional reactors were being built.

ENTER KENNEDY

In public, the Eisenhower administration continued to downplay concerns about Israel's nuclear program. Privately, the outgoing administration was suspicious, telling the Kennedy transition team that India and Israel were candidates to join the nuclear club. Secretary of State Herter stressed that Israel could produce about two hundred pounds of plutonium by 1963.[37] The secrecy surrounding the reactor alarmed both administrations as well as members of Congress. As Senator William Fulbright explained to Eisenhower officials, "if the Israelis had nothing to hide, as GOI [Government of Israel] statements indicated; why did they hide it?"[38] The Israelis claimed the secrecy was necessary so the French firms that were participating wouldn't be subject to Arab boycotts. Although the new administration felt there was "considerable justification" for this claim, it remained concerned about Israel's program.[39] As Secretary of State Dean Rusk told the president, if Israel acquired nuclear weapons, the United States could witness the "stationing of Soviet nuclear weapons on the soil of Israel's embittered Arab neighbors."[40] Even the appearance that Jerusalem was moving in that direction could increase Soviet influence in the region. The administration monitored high-level Soviet visits to the Middle East closely for evidence that this was happening.[41]

Kennedy's immediate goal was to be able to assure other countries that Israel's nuclear activities were completely peaceful. This required having US inspectors on the ground. The new administration exerted intense pressure on the Israelis to allow such a visit. In the month of February alone, Rusk, National Security Advisor McGeorge Bundy, and G. Lewis Jones, the assistant secretary of state for Near East Affairs, all separately pressed Ambassador Harmon to arrange an inspection.[42] President Kennedy received constant updates on these meetings. In what would become a pattern for the decade, Israel tried its best to delay the inspection, claiming a cabinet crisis in Israel prevented a visit in the near term.[43]

Frustrated by the lack of progress, in late March, JFK sent Abe Feinberg and Myers Feldman, his personal representative on many Middle Eastern issues, to appeal to Ben-Gurion directly. Like Feinberg, Feldman was extremely close to Israel. Together, they worked out a deal where Ben-Gurion agreed to an inspection in return for a personal meeting with JFK.[44] Israel did set a number of conditions. Some were minor, such as referring to the inspections as "visits." Others were more concerning, especially Israel's demand that the visits be kept secret. This mostly defeated the purpose of the inspections, since America wanted to reassure Israel's neighbors that its nuclear activities were peaceful. As Rusk pointed out, the "whole purpose" of the Dimona inspections was to enable the United States to "reassure [the] world as to [the] peaceful nature [of] Israel's nuclear activities."[45] For the time being, Washington accepted this demand.[46]

The visit was an enormous gamble for Israel. Although Ben-Gurion had acknowledged the reactor, he hadn't disclosed the reprocessing plant being built underground. If the Americans discovered this, Jerusalem's cover story—already flimsy—would be completely blown. To a large degree, the American visits were designed to try and find a reprocessing plant. One of the US scientists that conducted some of the inspections in later years was chosen for his expertise in reprocessing.[47] The two American inspectors for the first visit, Ulysses M. Staebler, the assistant director of the AEC Reactor Development Division, and Jesse Croach, a heavy-water expert, arrived in Israel on May 17. They visited Dimona on May 20, a Saturday when there would be fewer workers on site. The Israelis also set strict guidelines: no written materials or pictures.[48] In more ways than the Americans realized, the entire visit was carefully choreographed. According to an Israeli whistleblower, Mordechai Vanunu, Israel built a dummy control room to show the visiting Americans. The real one was underground where the reprocessing plant was being constructed.[49]

During the visit, the Israeli interlocutors explained the history of the project and some basic information, including that the reactor would be completed in 1964. Most revealing, the director of Dimona, Mannes Prat, said there would eventually be a "pilot plant" for plutonium separation on site.[50] Staebler and Croach bought the Israeli story hook, line, and sinker. In debriefing Washington, they reported being "satisfied that nothing was concealed from them and that the reactor is of . . . [a] peaceful character." Although the reactor would produce "small quantities" of plutonium, "there is no present evidence that the Israelis have weapon production in mind." Their one recommendation was that another visit be conducted within a year.[51] As Avner Cohen has observed, "Israel could not have hoped for a better report."[52]

This move stabilized the situation for the time being. Although JFK is often depicted as being extremely concerned with Israel's nuclear program during his presidency, the truth is more complicated. After securing the initial inspection, his attention turned to other matters. The only time Dimona was discussed at a high level in 1962 was in a December meeting between Kennedy and Israeli Foreign Minister Golda Meir. It wasn't until after the Cuban Missile Crisis that JFK again began to focus on Israel's nuclear program as part of a broader effort to reduce nuclear dangers around the world.

In the interim, bilateral relations improved, starting with Kennedy and Ben-Gurion's meeting in New York at the end of May 1961. Kennedy went into the meeting seeking two concessions from Israel about the nuclear program. His first objective was to convince Ben-Gurion to allow America to inform the Arab states that it had inspected Dimona and found nothing afoul. This was important, as Kennedy colorfully put it, because "a woman should not only be virtuous but also have the appearance of virtue." To that end, Kennedy also asked if the Israelis would permit scientists from "neutral" countries to visit the reactor since many Arab nations distrusted America. Surprisingly, Ben-Gurion immediately agreed to both requests (though the neutral visits didn't occur), but he also made a more concerning statement. After reaffirming Israel's nuclear program was peaceful, he added, "[but] we do not know what will happen in the future; in three or four years we might have [a] need for a plant to process plutonium."[53] Given that Israel claimed the reactor wouldn't even be running for three years, this was hardly reassuring. It was also inconsistent with the pledge that the plutonium produced in the Dimona reactor would be returned to France.[54] President Kennedy didn't press the issue, however, and the two leaders soon moved on to other issues.

Thus, just as America stopped focusing on the nuclear program, there were growing signs that Israel's intent was not entirely peaceful. Prat's comment about the pilot reprocessing plant and especially Ben-Gurion's warning in his meeting with JFK were only part of this growing body of evidence. A few days before the inspectors arrived in Israel, an Israeli embassy official in Washington, Mordechai Gazit, asked State Department official Philip J. Farley out to lunch. During the conversation about the inspections, Gazit repeatedly brought up the "grim security situation" Israel faced, and said that "in this situation Israel naturally looked to whatever means it could find for protecting itself."[55] With these comments, Gazit was directly tying Dimona to Israel's security, a linkage Ben-Gurion worked hard to avoid. Then, in July 1961, Israel tested what it claimed was a domestically built experimental rocket, the Shavitt II, followed by another in August. While primitive, the tests showed that Israel was pursuing technology that could be used to launch nuclear weapons. After dragging its feet, Jerusalem allowed a second inspection of Dimona in September 1962, but it limited this visit to forty-five minutes, precluding the scientists from doing a comprehensive review.

None of these was a "smoking gun." Taken together, however, they strongly suggested Israel was building a bomb. This isn't only apparent in hindsight—the intelligence community and Pentagon repeatedly forecast as much at the time.[56] The diminished attention America paid to Israel's nuclear activities in the second half of 1961 and almost all of 1962 was not because of Jerusalem's actions. Rather, it stemmed from a lack of political interest. That was about to change.

JFK'S LAND STAND

The Cuban Missile Crisis had a profound impact on President Kennedy. The confrontation was the closest the two superpowers had come (and would come) to nuclear war. During the standoff, Kennedy put the odds of a full-scale nuclear war at "between 1 in 3 and even."[57] After Moscow and Washington escaped the conflict, Kennedy dedicated the last year of his life to reducing the dangers posed by nuclear weapons. As discussed in the French case, this included assuaging Soviet concerns by reining in West Germany's nuclear aspirations with the Limited Test Ban Treaty. But more generally, the Cuban Missile Crisis gave President Kennedy a greater appreciation of the dangers of nuclear proliferation. It was in March 1963 that he famously admitted to being "haunted" by the prospect of nuclear proliferation.

Israel became embroiled in this during the spring of 1963, which led to perhaps the greatest confrontation between Israel and an American president outside of the Suez Crisis. One of the earliest indications of President Kennedy's renewed focus on the Israeli nuclear program was a national security action memorandum (NSAM) he issued on March 26, 1963. The NSAM, drafted by McGeorge Bundy, directed the IC to increase its surveillance of Israel's nuclear program, as well as Israel's and Egypt's (then called the United Arab Republic) missile programs. Kennedy also wanted America's "next informal inspection of the Israeli reactor complex to be undertaken promptly and to be as thorough as possible." Finally, he ordered the State Department to develop new proposals for how to restrain both programs.[58] Coincidentally, Shimon Peres was in Washington, DC, a week later for unrelated matters, but JFK used the meeting to grill Peres about Israel's nuclear program. Taken aback, Peres blurted out, "I can tell you most clearly that we will not introduce nuclear weapons to the region, and certainly we will not be the first."[59] This was the first formulation of Israel's opaque nuclear doctrine. This was not sufficient for President Kennedy. On the same day as the Peres meeting, America's ambassador to Israel, Walworth Barbour, pressed Ben-Gurion to begin allowing two inspections of Dimona each year, starting immediately.[60] Although Ben-Gurion "did not demur," he sought to use political developments in the region to once again delay. Instead, President Kennedy turned the tables on him.

The opportunity came on April 17, 1963, when Egypt, Syria, and Iraq signed the Arab Federation Proclamation, which called for a military union in order to liberate Palestine. This was par for the course of Arab rhetoric at the time, and most senior Israeli officials did not take it seriously. Ben-Gurion did. Besieged at home politically, and possibly failing mentally at the age of seventy-six, Ben-Gurion launched what his biographer called an "unprecedented diplomatic campaign."[61] This included reaching out to fifty world leaders, including the Soviet Union, United States, and France. In the seven-page letter Ben-Gurion sent to Kennedy, he compared the Arab Federation Proclamation to the Holocaust and asked to fly to Washington immediately to meet with JFK.[62] President Kennedy's response reaffirmed America's support for Israel but dismissed the importance of the Arab Federation Proclamation. Instead, JFK pivoted to the topic he did deem important—the development of nuclear and missile capabilities in the region. "The danger," Kennedy wrote, is not "an early Arab attack" but the "successful development of advanced offensive systems."[63] This hinted where the United States was going—namely, an initiative seeking to restrain Israel's nuclear activities.

By this time, the intelligence agencies were forecasting additional dangers of Israel acquiring a nuclear weapons arsenal beyond increasing Soviet influence in the region. For instance, one estimate said a nuclear-armed Israel would act with less restraint in the region. It also predicted a nuclear-armed Israel would try to co-opt the United States into supporting it more forcefully. The IC further believed that Israel building the bomb would cripple

America's influence in the Arab world. The Arab states would believe the United States was complicit in Israel's nuclear program, and "US influence with the Arabs, limited at best, would be drastically reduced." Interestingly, the IC downplayed the Arab states' ability to build their own nuclear weapons, even if Israel built them.[64] It was thus larger geopolitical issues that concerned US policymakers.

The group formed by Kennedy's NSAM ultimately decided on a joint approach to Israel and Egypt that was stillborn. Instead, President Kennedy took matters into his own hands, and focused solely on reining in Israel. This began with a letter to Ben-Gurion in May 1963 that asked for biannual inspections of Dimona, which was something the IC believed was necessary because the reactor would be refueled every six months if geared toward producing nuclear weapons.[65] Kennedy's note to Ben-Gurion conveys the immense importance he now placed on proliferation, with the president declaring "there is no more urgent business for the whole world than the control of nuclear weapons." Kennedy also presented Israeli nuclear restraint as essential for keeping "larger countries" (i.e., West Germany) from building their own arsenals. Notably, Kennedy informed Ben-Gurion that he opposed Israel developing a "nuclear weapons capability," rather than just the weapons themselves. And he warned the Israeli leader that America's support for Israel would be "seriously jeopardized" if Washington was unable to obtain reliable information on "Israel's efforts in the nuclear field."[66]

According to Avner Cohen, Kennedy's letter set off a "mini-crisis" among Ben-Gurion's closest advisors. Cohen notes that it was "perceived as 'harsh,' even 'brutal,' both in substance and form."[67] Kennedy intended as much, but he didn't get the results he wanted. In his response, Ben-Gurion only agreed to annual visits while ignoring Kennedy's request for two each year. Furthermore, whereas Kennedy had asked for the next one to take place that very month, Ben-Gurion said it could be held at the end of 1963 or early 1964, when the reactor started operating. He also again hinted that Israel might build nuclear weapons if the regional security situation deteriorated.[68]

This was wholly unacceptable to Kennedy, and some advisors considered it a "step backward" in terms of access to Dimona.[69] The scientific branches of the IC opined that Ben-Gurion's offer failed to meet their minimum requirements. At a bare minimum, the scientists assessed, they would need to visit the reactor in the summer of 1963 before it started operating. This was necessary to establish a baseline and access parts of the reactor that would be inaccessible once it was operating. The next visit would be needed in the summer of 1964, when the reactor had been running for six months, and at six-month intervals after that. These conditions formed the basis of Kennedy's response, which was forwarded to the embassy in Tel Aviv. Before Ambassador Barbour could deliver it, Ben-Gurion resigned suddenly on June

16, 1963. He never provided a full explanation for this decision, and personal issues (including deteriorating health) and domestic politics almost certainly played a role. Some people, including some Israeli cabinet officials, believe Kennedy's pressure contributed to the decision. In this view, Ben-Gurion believed resigning would buy some time with the Americans and put off the confrontation until after Dimona was operating.

If so, the gambit failed. On June 23, Levi Eshkol was selected as Ben-Gurion's successor. Barely a week later, Barbour delivered almost the same letter Kennedy had prepared for Ben-Gurion to the new Israeli prime minister. While apologizing for burdening Eshkol so soon after he took office, Kennedy once again threatened that America's commitment to Israel would be "seriously jeopardized" if it couldn't confirm Israel's nuclear activities were peaceful.[70] To gain confidence in Israel's peaceful intentions, Kennedy proposed a timeline of visits in very specific detail. He also stated that America's scientists must have access to any related part of Dimona, "such as fuel fabrication facilities or [a] plutonium separation plant."[71] According to Cohen, with the exception of the Suez Crisis, an American president had never been as blunt to an Israeli leader. Zvi Dinstein, an aide to the new Israeli leader, later reflected that "Kennedy was presenting him [Eshkol] with an ultimatum; it certainly was an ultimatum. It caused a great deal of anxiety, a great deal."[72]

Eshkol was unsure how to respond. He was aware of the Dimona project because he had served as the finance minister for the last decade, but he was not well versed in the subject. As Ben-Gurion's hand-chosen successor, Eshkol believed he had a responsibility to see Israel's founding father's pet project through to fruition. The question was how he could do so, especially without causing a break in relations with the United States? To buy himself more time, Eshkol first sent an interim reply and then tried to create some goodwill. On July 25, 1963, Britain, the United States, and the Soviet Union announced the Limited Test Ban Treaty (PTBT). Four days later, Eshkol announced Israel's support for the new treaty. True to his word, Eshkol signed the agreement on August 8, a few days after it officially opened for signature. This was a huge relief for the Kennedy administration.

Six weeks after receiving Kennedy's letter, Eshkol sent his full response. The content was a mixed bag from the US perspective. The new prime minister started by mostly reaffirming Ben-Gurion's peaceful intent and agreed to allow US inspectors to visit Dimona before it began operating. Eshkol also said that all spent fuel from the reactor would be returned to France, which wasn't true. On the other hand, Eshkol didn't agree to semi-annual visits once Dimona was operational, instead stating vaguely they could reach an agreement on this issue later. Eshkol also didn't commit to allowing unimpeded access to the entire complex.[73] In short, Eshkol sought to follow Ben-Gurion's approach on Dimona. That is, he tried avoiding an open break with the Americans while preserving Israel's nuclear option. There were a couple of subtle but important differences between their approaches. For the most part, Ben-Gurion treated the Dimona reactor as entirely separate from Israel's security situation. Eshkol quickly linked the two issues. Even in his interim reply, Eshkol noted, "We are the only state in the international community whose existence is challenged and, indeed, openly threatened by all its neighbors. This gives Israel's security problem a unique intensity and urgency."[74] Relatedly, Eshkol broke from Ben-Gurion in refusing to allow the US to share its findings from the inspections with Nasser.[75] As he would explain repeatedly in the years ahead, Eshkol saw it as "desirable" if Egypt was unsure of Israel's nuclear status, because "this could have [a] useful deterrent effect."[76] This terrified US officials, who were convinced that Nasser would go to war before allowing Israel to go nuclear, "no matter how suicidal" that conflict was for Cairo.[77] Moreover, as Rusk pointed out, Israel's efforts to create ambiguity in the Arab world "also created ambiguity in Washington."[78] Still, even when LBJ pressed Eshkol personally to relent on this issue, the Israeli leader refused.[79]

The Kennedy administration was disappointed with Eshkol's reply, but decided it was "the most we can hope to get at this time."[80] The president's reply implied that Eshkol had agreed to hold biannual inspections starting in 1964, despite the fact that the Israeli leader had not done so.[81] Kennedy thought he could deal with this problem when the time came. He would not get the chance to do so, however, because he was assassinated in November 1963.

NOTES

1. Quoted in Avner Cohen, *Israel and the Bomb* (New York: Columbia University, 1998), 10.

2. Shimon Peres, who was Israel's liaison with France for the nuclear deal, estimated it at $80 million, but it was likely much more. See Cohen, *Israel and the Bomb*, 70.

3. Michael Karpin, *The Bomb in the Basement: How Israel Went Nuclear and What That Means for the World* (New York: Simon & Schuster, 2006), 129.

4. "Embassy in Israel to DOS, EMBTEL, 1119" March 5, 1965, USNA, RG 59, Records of Under Secretary of State George W. Ball, 1961–1966, Box 21, Folder 17.

5. "Memorandum of Conversation, Nuclear Proliferation," February 9, 1966, USNA, RG 59, CFPF, 1964–1966, Box 2356, POL, ISR-US; and "DOS to Embassy in Israel, DEPTEL, 652," February 10, 1966, USNA, RG 59, CFPF, 1964–1966, Box 3068.

6. My findings on this are similar to Galen Jackson's. I depart from Jackson's views in that Kennedy and US officials weren't concerned with Israel acquiring a nuclear weapon. Although he is right, the US did not want to offer Israel a security guarantee; most US officials were determined to prevent an Israeli bomb, although, as detailed in the next chapter, they didn't enjoy LBJ's support. See Galen Jackson, "The United States, the Israeli Nuclear Program, and Nonproliferation, 1961–1969," *Security Studies* 28, no. 2 (2019).

7. Cohen, *Israel and the Bomb*, 11 and 30–31.
8. Cohen, *Israel and the Bomb*, 43; and Karpin, *Bomb in the Basement*, 102.
9. Karpin, *Bomb in the Basement*, 59–60.
10. Karpin, *Bomb in the Basement*, 53; and Cohen, *Israel and the Bomb*, 44.
11. Cohen, *Israel and the Bomb*, 52–53.
12. Karpin, *Bomb in the Basement*, 65.
13. Karpin, *Bomb in the Basement*, 67–69.
14. Rose McDermott, *Risk-Taking in International Politics: Prospect Theory in American Foreign Policy* (Ann Arbor: University of Michigan Press, 2001), 137.
15. Cohen, *Israel and the Bomb*, 55; and Karpin, *Bomb in the Basement*, 85–86.
16. Quoted in Karpin, *Bomb in the Basement*, 88.
17. Karpin, *Bomb in the Basement*, 89 and 109–110. Cohen suggests that this deal occurred in early 1957. Cohen, *Israel and the Bomb*, 58. While either timeline could be correct, it makes more sense that Paris would have agreed to it during the crisis rather than in the months following it.
18. Karpin, *Bomb in the Basement*, 90–91.
19. Karpin, *Bomb in the Basement*, 92.
20. Cohen, *Israel and the Bomb*, 73.
21. Cohen, *Israel and the Bomb*, 81.
22. Cohen, *Israel and the Bomb*, 82–84.
23. Karpin, *Bomb in the Basement*, 124–126, 247; and Jeffrey T. Richelson, *Spying on the Bomb: American Nuclear Intelligence from Nazi Germany to Iran and North Korea* (New York: Norton, 2006), 247.
24. "Embassy in Tel Aviv to DOS, Despatch 75," August 2, 1960, in Avner Cohen and William Burr, "The U.S. Discovery of Israel's Secret Nuclear Project," *National Security Archive*, Electronic Briefing Book No. 510 (April 15, 2015).
25. Karpin, *Bomb in the Basement*, 154; and Richelson, *Spying on the Bomb*, 250.
26. Karpin, *Bomb in the Basement*, 155; and Richelson, *Spying on the Bomb*, 250.
27. Richelson, *Spying on the Bomb*, 250.
28. This is the conclusion of Michael Karpin. See Karpin, *Bomb in the Basement*, 146–50. Also, Israeli officials including Bergmann told Gomberg that Ben-Gurion was planning on making a public statement about the reactor in three weeks' time. See "MEMCON," December 1, 1960, in Avner Cohen and William Burr, "The U.S. Discovery of Israel's Secret Nuclear Project," *National Security Archive*, Electronic Briefing Book No. 510.
29. Quoted in Karpin, *Bomb in the Basement*, 146.
30. Richelson, *Spying on the Bomb*, 252.

31. CIA, "Implications of the Acquisition by Israel of a Nuclear Weapons Capability," SNIE, 100–8–60, December 18, 1960, https://www.cia.gov/library/readingroom/docs/DOC_0005796843.pdf.

32. "NSC meeting," December 8, 1960. *FRUS*, 1958–1960, vol. XIII, doc. 177.

33. "DOS to Embassy in Israel," December 9, 1960, *FRUS*, 1958–1960, vol. XIII, doc. 178; and "MEMCON," December 20, 1960, ibid., doc. 180.

34. Quoted in Karpin, *Bomb in the Basement*, 161–62.

35. "DOS to Embassy in Israel," December 31, 1960, *FRUS*, 1958–1960, vol. XIII, doc. 181.

36. Embassy Tel Aviv telegram 625, January 4, 1961, as summarized in a "Chronology of Israel Assurances of Peaceful Use of Atomic Energy and Related Events," enclosed in "Read to Bundy, Israel's Assurances Concerning Uses of Atomic Energy," March 18, 1964, in Cohen and Burr, "The U.S. Discovery of Israel's Secret Nuclear Project," https://nsarchive2.gwu.edu/nukevault/ebb432/docs/3–18–64%20State%20Dept%20chronology.pdf.

37. Richelson, *Spying on the Bomb*, 254.

38. "MEMCON," January 9, 1961, *FRUS*, 1961–1963, vol. XVII, doc. 2.

39. "Rusk Memo to Kennedy," January 30, 1961, ibid., doc. 5.

40. Ibid.

41. "Memo to Rusk, President's Suggestions re Israeli Reactor," February 2, 1961, *Wilson Center Digital Archive*, https://digitalarchive.wilsoncenter.org/document/123812.

42. "Memorandum of Conversation," February 3, 1961, *FRUS*, 1961–1963, vol. XVII, doc. 7; "Memorandum of Conversation," February 16, 1961, *FRUS*, 1961–1963, vol. XVII, doc. 12; and "Jones Memo to Rusk, President's Suggestions re Israeli Reactor," February 2, 1961, *WCDA*, https://digitalarchive.wilsoncenter.org/document/123812; and "DOS MEMCON, Inspection of Israel's New Atomic Reactor," February 13, 1961, *WCDA*, https://digitalarchive.wilsoncenter .org/document/123815.

43. "MEMCON," February 3, 1961, *FRUS*, 1961–1963, vol. XVII, doc. 7.

44. Karpin, *Bomb in the Basement*, 187.

45. "DOS to Embassy in Israel, DEPTEL 819," March 21, 1964, *U.S. National Archives* [hereafter *USNA*], RG 59, Central Foreign Policy Files [hereafter CFPF], 1964–1966, Box 3068. Also see "Talking Paper: Israeli Foreign Minister Abba Eban," September 20, 1966, *USNA*, RG 59, CFPF, 1964–1966, Box 2356; and "Telegram from Department of State to Embassy in Tel Aviv, DEPTEL, 568," January 5, 1965, *USNA*, RG 59, CFPF, 1964–1966, Box 3068.

46. "MEMCON," April 10, 1961, FRUS, 1961–1963 Volume XVII, Document 31 and "Battle Memo to Bundy, 'American Scientists' Visit to Israel's Dimona Reactor,'" May 18, 1961, WCDA, https://digitalarchive.wilsoncenter.org/document/123835.pdf?v=10ea723e6bd1d31fb249b5011ed58755.

47. Cohen, *Israel and the Bomb*, 187.

48. Cohen, *Israel and the Bomb*, 106.

49. Karpin, *Bomb in the Basement*, 188.

50. Cohen, *Israel and the Bomb*, 106.

51. "Battle Memo to Bundy," May 26, 1961, *FRUS*, 1961–1963, vol. XVII, doc. 53.

52. Cohen, *Israel and the Bomb*, 107.
53. "MEMCON," May 30, 1961, *FRUS*, 1961–1963, vol. XVII, doc. 57.
54. This point didn't go unnoticed by US officials. See "Armin Meyer Memo to Phillips Talbot, Discussion on Ben-Gurion/Kennedy Meeting," June 09, 1961, *WCDA*, https://digitalarchive.wilsoncenter.org/document/123842.
55. "Farley and Gazit Meeting, Israeli Atomic Energy Program," May 16, 1961, *WCDA*, https://digitalarchive.wilsoncenter.org/document/123834.
56. CIA, "NIE 4–3–61: Nuclear Weapons and Delivery Capabilities of Free World Countries Other than the US and UK," September 21, 1961, *NSA*, https://nsarchive2.gwu.edu/NSAEBB /NSAEBB155/index.htm. Also see "McNarma Memo to Kennedy, The Diffusion of Nuclear Weapons With or Without a Test Ban Agreement," n.d. [circa July 26, 1962], *NSA*; and "McNamara Memo to Kennedy, The Diffusion of Nuclear Weapons With or Without a Test Ban Agreement," February 16, 1963, *NSA*.
57. Quoted in Graham Allison, "The Cuban Missile Crisis at 50," *Foreign Affairs* (July/August 2012).
58. "National Security Action Memorandum No. 231," March 26, 1963, *FRUS*, 1961–1963, vol. XVIII, doc. 199.
59. Quoted in Cohen, *Israel and the Bomb*, 118. Cohen's account comes from the Israeli notes from the meeting. The US notes say that "Peres had given an unequivocal assurance that Israel would not do anything in this field unless it finds that other countries in the area are involved in it." See "Memorandum of Telephone Conversation Between Talbot and Feldman," April 5, 1963, *FRUS*, 1961–1963, vol. XVIII, doc. 207.
60. "DOS to Embassy in Israel," May 10, 1963, *FRUS*, 1961–1963, vol. XVIII, doc. 243.
61. Quoted in Cohen, *Israel and the Bomb*, 119. For Ben-Gurion's reaction and possible mental state, as well as other Israeli officials', see ibid., 119–21; and Karpin, *Bomb in the Basement*, 210–11.
62. "Brubeck Memo to Bundy," April 27, 1963, *FRUS*, 1961–1963, vol. VIII, doc. 220.
63. "DOS to Embassy in Israel," May 4, 1963, *FRUS*, 1961–1963, vol. XVIII, doc. 236.
64. "Memorandum From the Board of National Estimates, Central Intelligence Agency, to Director of Central Intelligence McCone," March 6, 1963, *FRUS*, 1961–1963, vol. XVIII, doc. 179. Also see "Special National Intelligence Estimate 30–2–63," May 8, 1963, *FRUS*, 1961–1963, vol. XVIII, doc. 239.
65. "DOS Memo to Embassy in Tel Aviv, DEPTEL, 1085," June 11, 1966, *USNA*, RG 59, CFPF, 1964–1966, Box 3086.
66. This part of the letter is classified in the American version of the letter but not the Israeli one. See Cohen, *Israel and the Bomb*, 128.
67. Cohen, *Israel and the Bomb*, 129.
68. "Brubeck Memo to Bundy," May 29, 1963, *FRUS*, 1961–1963, vol. XVIII, doc. 258; and Cohen, *Israel and the Bomb*, 129–31.
69. "Brubeck Memo to Bundy," May 29, 1963, *FRUS*, 1961–1963, vol. XVIII, doc. 258

70. This part is once again classified in the American version. See Cohen, *Israel and the Bomb*, 154.

71. "DOS to Embassy in Israel," July 4, 1963, *FRUS*, 1961–1963, vol. XVIII, doc. 289.

72. Quoted in Karpin, *Bomb in the Basement*, 232.

73. "Letter from Levi Eshkol to President John F. Kennedy," August 19, 1963, *USNA*, RG 59, Presidential and Secretary of State Official Exchanges of Correspondence, 1961–1966, Box 10, Kennedy/Johnson-Israel, 1962–1965; and "Ball Memo to Kennedy," August 23, 1963, *FRUS*, 1961–1963, vol. XVIII, doc. 317. Also see Cohen, *Israel and the Bomb*, 162–64.

74. His interim reply is found in "Embassy in Israel to Secretary of State Dean Rusk," July 17, 1963, *USNA*, RG 59, Presidential and Secretary of State Official Exchanges of Correspondence, 1961–1966, Box 10, Kennedy/Johnson-Israel, 1962–1965.

75. "Ball Memo to Kennedy," August 23, 1963, *FRUS*, 1961–1963, vol. XVIII, doc. 317.

76. "Embassy in Israel to DOS, EMBTEL, 919," March 4, 1964, *USNA*, RG 59, CFPF, 1964–1966, Box 3068; and "Embassy in Israel to DOS, EMBTEL, 916," March 3, 1964, in ibid.

77. "Read Memo Bundy, Need to Reassure President Nasser on Peaceful Nature of the Dimona Reactor," February 11, 1964, *USNA*, RG59, CFPF, 1964–1966, Box 3068.

78. "MEMCON, Nuclear Proliferation," February 9, 1966, *USNA*, RG59, CFPF, 1964–1966, Box 2356.

79. "Eshkol Letter to President Johnson," April 15, 1964, *USNA*, RG 59, Presidential and Secretary of State Official Exchanges of Correspondence, 1961–1966, Box 10, Kennedy/Johnson-Israel, 1962–1965.

80. "Ball Memo to Kennedy," August 23, 1963, *FRUS*, 1961–1963, vol. XVIII, doc. 317.

81. "DOS to Embassy in Israel," August 26, 1963, *FRUS*, 1961–1963, vol. XVIII, doc. 319.

Chapter 8

The Bomb Which Shall Not Be Named (Israel, 1963–1979)

JFK's death made Israel's dash to the bomb considerably easier. Whereas, at least in 1963, Kennedy had generally seemed willing to confront Israel, Lyndon B. Johnson was not. Many of JFK's advisors stayed on under LBJ, and these officials continued to pressure Israel incessantly over its nuclear program. This pressure would always prove hollow, however, because the president was not willing to impose any real costs on Israel.

Ultimately, Israel assembled its first devices in the immediate run-up to the Six-Day War in 1967. For years, the United States and Israel struggled to deal with this new reality. The most contentious exchanges came near the end of the Johnson administration, when Israel was seeking to purchase F-4 Phantoms from the United States. It was during these negotiations that the two sides reached an understanding that was later formalized by Nixon and Golda Meir. This understanding was that neither side would acknowledge Israel's nuclear status and the United States would stop pressuring Israel over its nuclear program. That has continued until today.

All things considered, this understanding has served America's interests fairly well thus far. Given the reality of the Israeli bomb by 1967, it is difficult to imagine a policy that would be more effective. That doesn't mean it has been perfect, however. To keep Israel's bomb in the basement, America has had to ensure Israel's conventional power is unmatched in the region. This resulted in the United States providing Israel with increasingly large amounts of military assistance. Although far less than France and Pakistan, Israel contributed to the spread of nuclear weapons in the case of apartheid South Africa. Furthermore, Israel's opaque nuclear status has regularly made US arms control and nonproliferation initiatives more difficult. It has also forced America to stand steadfast by convenient fictions, even when they were blatantly false. The best example of this is when Israel tested nuclear weapons off the coast of South Africa. This chapter covers all these issues.

THE CAT AND MOUSE GAME

LBJ's more permissive attitude towards Israel's nuclear program is consistent with his extraordinarily friendly policy toward Israel overall. LBJ's friendliness toward Israel was consistent with the declining anti-Semitism in the United States and the growing strength of American Jews in US domestic politics, especially in the Democratic Party. But, as Karpin points out, an even more fundamental reason was LBJ's deep emotional attachment to the Jewish state. This was borne out of his strong Christian faith. The importance of the Jewish people had been impressed upon Johnson since his childhood—his grandfather had once inscribed on a photograph, "Take care of the Jews, God's chosen people. Consider them your friends and help them any way you can."[1]

While LBJ eschewed the confrontational stance of his predecessor, many of his aides—most of whom served under President Kennedy—attempted to keep it alive. In fact, US officials below the presidential level spoke in increasingly threatening terms about Israel's nuclear program. For instance, Robert Komer, an NSC official, told a senior Israeli military leader that nuclear proliferation was the one issue where the "vital interests [of] over 190 million Americans would simply have to override those of 2 1/2 million Israelis."[2] Secretary of State Rusk similarly told Israeli officials that their nuclear aspirations were the only issue that could have a "disastrous effect" on the relationship and warned that America would be "utterly harsh on the matter of non-proliferation."[3] Thus, a pattern developed during the Johnson administration where senior policymakers would press Israel hard over its nuclear program, only for President Johnson to overrule them.

Dimona inspections were one area where Israel immediately benefited from the transition of power in Washington. Before Kennedy's death, Eshkol had promised that US scientists would be allowed to visit the reactor before it was operational. As noted in the previous chapter, the US intelligence community believed this was necessary to get baseline estimates. The Israelis ultimately did not invite the scientists to visit until January 1964, and when they arrived, they found the reactor was already operating.[4] The semiannual visits Eshkol promised also never materialized. America's next inspection of the reactor didn't come until January 1965. After that, US scientists visited Dimona four more times. Each inspection was at least a year after the last one. Most of them were also far more rushed than the United States had wanted. All of this diminished America's confidence in its ability to be sure Israel wasn't hiding anything.[5] Ultimately, however, US officials concluded this was the best they could get from the Israelis. As Secretary Rusk wrote before the April 1966 visit, "Eshkol's delayed and apparently reluctant agreement

[to] permit [a] one-day visit [to] Dimona falls considerably short of what we would have hoped to have achieved with Israelis by now. . . . However, we have decided [to] pick up his offer as [the] best likely to be forthcoming for [the] present."[6]

Inspections were not the only reason US policymakers increasingly suspected Israel was pursuing nuclear weapons. In April 1963, Israel had signed an agreement with the French firm Dassault to purchase Jericho missiles. These missiles were wildly inaccurate but could carry a 750 kilogram payload five hundred kilometers.[7] Jerusalem initially tried to keep this agreement secret from the Americans, and in fact, continued to press Washington to sell it missiles.[8] The US knew about the deal almost immediately, and eventually confronted Israel about it. In general terms, Israeli leaders defended their need for missiles by pointing out that Egypt was acquiring its own. The Americans argued that Nasser's missiles were militarily useless and would not change the military balance. If anything, Israel spending exorbitant amounts of money purchasing French missiles might entice Nasser to seek better missiles from the Soviets.[9]

But there was a larger issue—Israel's missiles were also militarily useless when equipped with conventional warheads. They would only be effective if carrying a nuclear payload. When confronted with this inconvenient fact, Israeli leaders could not adequately explain why they would invest so much in a capability that was useless (beyond pointing to Egypt's program). In one memorable instance, after the US official Henry Rowen told Eshkol that the missiles weren't useful with conventional warheads, the Israeli prime minister responded "don't try to persuade us to put nuclear warheads on them."[10] This was not the only time Israel's rhetoric aroused US suspicion. On many occasions, mid to senior- level Israeli leaders, including some military officials, implied their country was pursuing nuclear weapons. To cite just one example, when Shimon Peres resigned as deputy defense minister in 1965, he listed Dimona and the nuclear program as one of his major achievements at the Ministry of Defense. It hardly made sense for a defense official to cite this as a major achievement if Dimona was only for scientific research.[11] All of these factors led at least some US policymakers to be "concerned that Israel may have succeeded in concealing a decision to develop nuclear weapons."[12]

ARMS SALES BEGIN

As Eshkol began linking the Dimona reactor to Israel's security environment, US policymakers began doing likewise. This became increasingly important as America began selling Israel major military systems during the LBJ administration. From Israel's inception through the Kennedy administration,

America didn't sell Israel advanced offensive weapons to avoid antagonizing the Arab states. At the tail end of the Kennedy presidency, Israel asked the United States to supply it with modern tanks to offset growing Arab capabilities. President Johnson's advisors persuaded him against doing so, and instead Washington arranged for West Germany to sell Israel the tanks. Unfortunately, when news of the sale became public, Bonn stopped delivering the tanks, causing Israel to panic. Much to the Johnson administration's dismay, Jordan was also requesting tanks from the United States, and Washington worried if it refused, the Jordanians would turn to Moscow. Facing what it called a "painful dilemma," the Johnson administration signed a memorandum of understanding (MOU) with Israel in March 1965 that pledged Washington to make up the shortfall in the West German tanks.[13]

This began what later became known as the qualitative military edge. Indeed, US aid to Israel soared during the Johnson administration. From 1949 to 1965, aid to Israel averaged $53 million per year (in historic dollars), with 95 percent of that coming in the form of economic assistance. Through 1965, Israel had received $248.6 million (in constant 2017 dollars) in military assistance from the United States. The following year, Israel received $535.6 million. In other words, in 1966 alone, Israel received more than twice as much military assistance from the United States than it had from the years 1948 to 1965 combined.[14]

The 1965 Memorandum of Understanding was thus a sea change in US-Israeli relations. And, while the LBJ administration was initially forced into this arrangement, some saw arms sales as possible leverage to rein in Israel's nuclear program. At first, US officials hoped the tanks would persuade Eshkol to forgo nuclear weapons and strategic missiles and to accept International Atomic Energy Agency (IAEA) safeguards on Dimona.[15] During the tense negotiations led by Robert Komer, the US dropped its demands for missiles and IAEA safeguards.[16] The final MOU simply stated that "The Government of Israel has reaffirmed that Israel will not be the first to introduce nuclear weapons into the Arab-Israel area." This was the first time the non-introduction pledge had been put into writing. After that, arms sales to Israel and nuclear weapons were increasingly linked, although the US rationale would change. Instead of using arms sales as leverage to extract concessions, some US officials argued that strengthening Israel's conventional forces would make nuclear weapons unnecessary. This began as soon as 1966, when Israel requested combat aircraft from the United States.[17] In a memo to President Johnson discussing the request, Komer, the NSC official, asked rhetorically: "[C]an we use planes as a lever to keep Israel from going nuclear?" He answered: "[D]esperation is what would most likely drive Israel to this choice, should it come to feel that the conventional balance was turning against it. So judicious US arms supply, aimed at maintaining a deterrent balance, is as good an inhibitor as we've got." Other US officials agreed.[18]

CROSSING THE THRESHOLD AND WAR

Although America ultimately sold Israel the aircraft, these and other conventional weapons failed to convince Israel to forgo nuclear weapons. The point became moot on the eve of the Six-Day War in June 1967, when Israel assembled its first nuclear devices. Incidentally, Israel's nuclear program contributed to the outbreak of the war. As tensions were mounting in the buildup to the war, Egyptian planes conducted an overflight of the Dimona reactor on May 17. "From that point on," Cohen writes, "concerns for Dimona's safety became a primary issue for Israeli military and political decision makers, as the crisis began to look as if Nasser were planning to carry out his threat of preventive war."[19] Michael Karpin agrees, writing "fear of an attack on Dimona was the main motive behind the IDF General Staff's demand that Israel take preemptive action."[20] This almost certainly overstates the case, as a number of factors precipitated the war. Nonetheless, Michael Oren, who wrote the definitive history of the conflict, agrees that Israeli policymakers had Dimona foremost in mind during the run-up to the war. Interestingly, as Oren points out, this wasn't the case for Nasser. There is little evidence that the Egyptian leader cared much about the reactor. Instead, Nasser seemed to believe—possibly because of US assurances[21]—that Israel was not close to producing a bomb. But because the Israelis knew they had acquired the technical capability—and possibly because US officials had warned them for years that Nasser would go to war before allowing Israel to go nuclear—they assumed the Egyptian leader was intent on destroying Dimona. Further overflights of the reactor near the end of May only heightened these concerns. In the end, Oren concludes, "Israel's fear for the reactor—rather than Egypt's of it—was the greater catalyst for war."[22]

In the weeks and months leading up to the war, the Central Intelligence Agency, US Joint Chiefs of Staff, and State Department all believed that Israel had a qualitative military edge over any combination of Arab states.[23] The Israelis themselves had become increasingly confident in the military balance in the region.[24] Yet even they were shocked by their success. Within minutes of the war beginning, Israeli aircraft had destroyed six air strips and 204 planes—roughly half the entire Egyptian Air Force. Only eight IAF aircraft were lost in the first wave of attacks, and one of those was from friendly fire. Roughly three hours after the attack began, an Israeli military official declared, "The Egyptian air force has ceased to exist."[25] Throughout the war, Israel's objectives expanded as a result of its surprising military successes.

After only six days of fighting, the Israeli state had tripled in size, conquering the Golan Heights from Syria, the West Bank and Jerusalem from Jordan, and Gaza and the Sinai Peninsula from Egypt.[26]

THE QUALITATIVE MILITARY EDGE

Israel had assembled its first nuclear devices on May 28, 1967, before these shocking successes.[27] This would eventually change the American rationale for continued arms sales to Israel. Instead of being used to get Israel to agree to safeguards, or to convince Israel it didn't need nuclear weapons at all, some US policymakers began viewing conventional arms sales as the only way to ensure Israel never used its nuclear arsenal. Robert Gallucci led the US side of the Joint Political Military Group with Israel when he was assistant secretary of state for Political-Military Affairs in the 1980s. This group is responsible for ensuring Israel's qualitative military edge. Gallucci explains that "qualitative military edge" is a "code word" for ensuring that Israel can defeat any combination of Arab states without relying on nuclear weapons. "We were very intent on making sure that Israel was not put in a position where it would have to fall back on nuclear weapons when conventional weapons would do," Gallucci said. "Although none of us wrote it down or said so," Gallucci added, "our enthusiasm for Israel having an overwhelming conventional capability is to make damn sure the nuclear issue never gets raised."[28]

William Quandt, a National Security Council staffer who worked on Middle East issues during the Nixon, Ford, and Carter administrations, concurs. "There has long been a sense among American policymakers that providing Israel with conventional weapons was justified, in part, by the concern that Israel would otherwise feel compelled to rely exclusively on a nuclear defense," Quandt has written. "This widespread view is rarely mentioned in policy deliberations, but I am convinced that it has had an impact on decisions."[29] This is reflected in US military assistance to Israel. As shown in the chart below, US military assistance to Israel went from just $2 million during the 1950s, to $1.4 billion in the 1960s, to over $41 billion in the 1970s. Although it would come down slightly in the decades ahead, it would never be less than over $28 billion during the 1980s, 1990s, and 2000s. To be sure, Israel's nuclear program is hardly the only reason America provides Israel with lavish military assistance. Nonetheless, it is an important and underappreciated one, which was especially influential in sparking the policy in the first place.

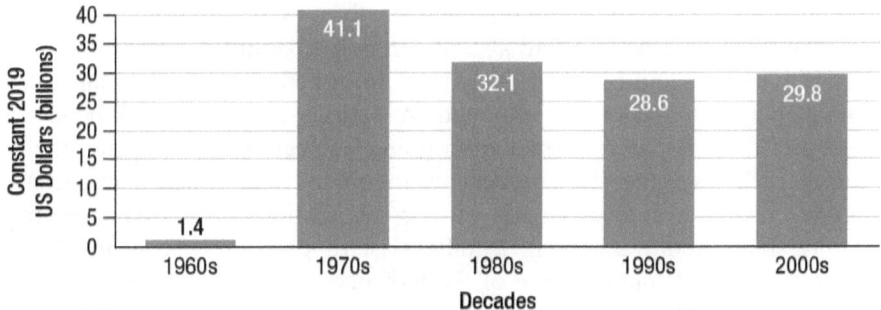

Figure 8.1. US Military Assistance to Israel by Decade (billions), USAID

THE 1968 F-4 NEGOTIATIONS

There is no clear time when US officials stopped viewing arms sales as a way to prevent Israel from acquiring nuclear weapons to a mechanism to prevent Israel from using them. For some officials, there was never a nexus between the qualitative military edge and Israel's nuclear arsenal at all. Even among those who recognized the linkage, the timing probably differed from person to person. For instance, it is possible LBJ always held this view to a greater or lesser extent even before Israel became a nuclear armed state. Other officials' views changed depending on when they discovered Israel had crossed the nuclear threshold, which differed widely because Israel didn't conduct an overt nuclear test.

The Central Intelligence Agency was the first to learn Israel had assembled nuclear weapons, thanks to the eminent scientist Edward Teller, a Jewish immigrant in America who is considered the father of the hydrogen bomb. Shortly after the Six-Day War, Teller was at a scientific conference with Yuval Ne'eman, a prominent Israeli military physicist. Teller told Ne'eman directly that he believed Israel had built the bomb. Ne'eman didn't deny this, thereby confirming Teller's suspicions. Teller proceeded to relay the information to Carl Duckett, the head of the CIA's Office of Science and Technology, who in turn told CIA Director Richard Helms. Still, it would take the CIA some time to confirm it through other sources.[30]

Many US officials learned of Israel's nuclear status in 1968 because of two developments. The first was the signing of the Nonproliferation Treaty, which Washington vigorously lobbied Israel to sign. Although Israeli leaders initially expressed openness to the treaty, they ultimately rejected it. This convinced some US officials Israel had the bomb. The more important development was the sale of F-4 Phantom aircraft to Israel. Eshkol first asked LBJ about acquiring the planes when the two men met in Texas in January 1968. Since Israel wanted the aircraft by 1970, President Johnson was told he'd have to decide by the end of 1968. Negotiations mostly took place in the fall of that year. By this time, the CIA had almost certainly concluded Israel possessed nuclear weapons, and LBJ had likely been informed. On the other hand, the State Department and DOD—although not entirely confident—still believed there was time to prevent Israel from going nuclear. Many viewed Israel's need for the F-4s as their last, best chance to rein in Israel's nuclear ambitions.

Other factors weighed heavily on the negotiations. The first were the ongoing talks about achieving Middle Eastern peace. These negotiations centered on Israel trading some of the territory it had acquired in the 1967 war in exchange for peace treaties with its neighbors. Some in the administration hoped Washington could use the Phantoms to persuade Israel to take a more accommodating stance. No less important were domestic politics in the United States. The discussions about the Phantom sale were taking place during a presidential election. The Israeli side, led by the new ambassador and former Chief of Staff of the IDF, Yitzhak Rabin, exploited this brilliantly, playing "the candidates against each other."[31] This included meeting with presidential candidate, Richard Nixon, who promised he'd sell Israel the Phantoms, if elected. The Israelis also lobbied Congress, and both houses passed a "sense of Congress" resolution urging the administration to sell Israel supersonic aircraft without naming the Phantoms specifically. This was later included in the Foreign Assistance Act of 1968 that LBJ signed into law in October.[32]

Despite these other considerations, State and Defense officials decided early on that they would use the sale of the Phantoms to force Israel to sign the NPT and end its missile program.[33] In preliminary discussions about the aircraft in October, Secretary Rusk "pressed [Israeli Foreign Minister] Eban hard about Israel's nuclear weapons and missile plans, stressing that this was [a] matter affecting our fundamental relationship."[34] President Johnson quickly undercut this effort. In his own meeting with the Israeli foreign minister, Johnson told Eban that he had decided in principle to supply the planes and "he was not making the question of the NPT a formal condition" for the sale.[35] Despite this, the Israelis were "up in arms" about Rusk's attempts to link the sale of the F-4s to Israel's willingness to sign the NPT, and believed that this pressure was a personal crusade by the secretary of state. Abe Feinberg appealed to the White House on Israel's behalf, asking Johnson to move the talks to the "technical" level where the American side would be led by the Department of Defense.[36] Johnson agreed.

This proved to be a mistake for the Israelis. Unbeknownst to them, Secretary of Defense Clark Clifford was just as intent on using the F-4s to press Israel on its nuclear program. The same was true of Paul Warnke, the assistant secretary of defense for International Security Affairs, who Clifford put in charge of negotiating with Rabin.[37] Rabin was also intensely disliked by DOD, primarily because he was the Israeli military's chief of staff during the 1967 war. On the third day of that conflict, Israeli planes attacked an American spy ship, the *USS Liberty*, that was loitering off the coast of Egypt. Thirty-four American sailors were killed. Israel claimed that the attack was a mistake during the fog of war, but many defense and military officials didn't believe them. Warnke, who was undersecretary of the navy in 1967, was among the skeptics, claiming, "I suspect that in the heat of the battle they figured that the presence of this American ship was inimical to their interests, and that somebody without authorization attacked it."[38]

All of these factors made for intense negotiations in what became the most authoritative discussion of Israel's nuclear program between the allies. Warnke wanted to use "every available means" to force Israel to accept four conditions: (1) forgo nuclear weapons, (2) not deploy strategic missiles, (3) sign and ratify the NPT, and (4) allow biannual inspections of all its nuclear and missile sites.[39] In the opening session with Rabin on November 4, Warnke made all four requests verbally. He added that America believed Israel was on the verge of acquiring nuclear weapons and missiles, a point Rabin did not dispute.[40] In the second session the following day, Warnke delivered America's proposed memorandum of understanding for the planes. Paragraph 3 included all four conditions. After reading the document, Rabin asked whether this was the official position of the United States, perhaps remembering that LBJ promised that signing the NPT would not be a precondition for the sale. Warnke was evasive, calling them his "recommendation." Rabin said his personal belief was the conditions would be rejected, but he had to check with his government. The meeting broke up before long.[41]

Although he kept his composure, Rabin was fuming inside. His anger was still palpable decades later. In his memoirs, he called the MOU a "shameful document" and claimed the United States was demanding Israel sign a document "the likes of which no sovereign nation had ever been asked to sign." Both during the negotiations and in his later recounting, Rabin focused his anger on the demand for twice-yearly inspections of Israel's nuclear and missile sites. Rabin also greatly embellished the demand, and his claims have led others to wildly misconstrue Warnke's position. For instance, based on Rabin's comments, Karpin writes that the United States was demanding "access to every place in Israel connected to the development of strategic weapons: air and sea ports, in order to examine imports; research and universities, to vet research projects; corporations and industrial plants, to check planning and production."[42] In reality, the MOU simply said that Israel "will permit semiannual inspection[s] by United States Government personnel of specified missile and nuclear sites in Israel and will provide full information on missile and nuclear programs."[43] This was what the United States had been asking for since 1963, albeit now Washington wanted access to Israel's missile facilities as well as its nuclear ones. America has asked other allies like South Korea for similar inspections. It's unclear why Rabin took such umbrage with this condition. One possibility is that he might have believed it had the support of President Johnson, unlike signing the NPT.

Warnke had to travel to Europe, so the next round of talks didn't take place until November 8. In the interim, Rabin confirmed Israel would not accept the four conditions. This set the tone for an extremely contentious meeting. Rabin began the talks by reading a written statement, which he warned "might not be diplomatic." That was an understatement. Rabin called the conditions "completely unacceptable," adding, "We have come here for the purpose of purchasing 50 Phantoms. We have not come here in order to mortgage the sovereignty of the State of Israel." At most, Jerusalem would reiterate its non-introduction pledge and promise not to equip the F-4s with nuclear weapons. Warnke tried to maintain a cordial discussion, but Rabin continued ranting. "You are only selling arms. How do you feel you have the right to ask all these things?" the Israeli ambassador wondered. "It is the national security of the United States that I am charged with protecting," Warnke countered. The talks soon adjourned.[44]

The truth was, Warnke had no authority to insist on these conditions, as he himself admitted.[45] The president had already approved the sale in principle, and Warnke had neither the president's approval nor knowledge in setting these conditions. Rabin and other Israelis did not realize this at the time. Instead, after the third negotiation session, Rabin began a ferocious lobbying effort to force the administration's hand. As he later wrote, he dropped "hints as heavy as elephants" to "Democratic friends of Israel" that if LBJ didn't approve the sale, president-elect Nixon would. Two of those friends were Abe Feinberg and Arthur Goldberg, America's ambassador to the UN, who alerted LBJ to what Warnke was doing.[46] Both Rusk and Clifford appealed to the president to reject the sale unless Israel agreed to the four conditions. As was often the case under LBJ, their pleas fell on deaf ears. In fact, LBJ said he wouldn't even insist on "the same assurances that we had previously received from the Israelis in connection with the A-4 negotiations," which were the non-introduction pledge and an agreement that Israel would not use the planes to deliver nuclear weapons.[47] Warnke, Rusk, and Clifford's play had been defeated.

Warnke continued to probe, however. When negotiations resumed on November 12, Warnke announced he would approve the deal if Israel agreed not to use the planes to deliver nuclear weapons and reaffirmed the non-introduction pledge. He then added, as if as an afterthought, that the United States had no record defining what Israel meant when it said it would not be the first to introduce nuclear weapons into the Middle East. "What specifically was meant by the word 'introduce,'" Warnke asked. Rabin pledged ignorance, but Warnke persisted: "There are two aspects to the question: the definition of what is and what is not a nuclear weapon, and what is and what is not introduction into the area." Warnke defined the first term as having all the components necessary to assemble a nuclear weapon, even if "part A may be in one room and part B in another room." But "introduction" was an Israeli term, so Warnke asked his counterpart to define it. Rabin was clearly caught off guard by this line of questioning, and he soon slipped up. When Warnke asked if the mere "physical presence" of a nuclear weapon would constitute introduction, Rabin replied "I suppose so."

Through the entire negotiations until that time, the official US memorandum of conversations only records Rabin and Warnke as having spoken. At this point, though, Mordechai Hod, the head of Israel's Air Force who had sat in on the previous negotiations, interjected to walk Rabin's comment back. Hod said that "throughout the world the experience was that introduction of a weapon could only mean after testing. You could not introduce a weapon until after it actually became a weapon." Rabin quickly recovered and began insisting that testing was required to introduce a weapon. Nonplussed, Warnke asked, if Egypt had nuclear warheads and missiles but hadn't tested them, would Israel consider Cairo as having not introduced nuclear weapons? The answer was obvious. All Rabin could weakly muster was that since Egypt was intent on destroying Israel, this would constitute introduction. Since Israel wasn't trying to destroy Egypt, the reverse was not true. The only value of nuclear weapons to Israel was deterrence, and they couldn't deter an adversary if no one knew they existed. "Then in your view," Warnke asked, "an unadvertised, untested nuclear device is not a nuclear weapon?" "Yes, that is correct," Rabin replied. What about an advertised but untested nuclear weapon? Warnke wondered. That indeed would constitute introduction, Rabin told him. The meeting ended with Warnke insisting that he defined the mere physical presence of a nuclear weapon as constituting introduction.[48]

The two sides could not agree on a definition of introduction, so it was papered over for the sale of the F-4s. Instead of signing a memorandum of understanding, each side issued separate letters. Rabin's letter reiterated the pledge Israel made in the 1965 MOU that it would not be the first to introduce nuclear weapons in the Middle East or use American planes to deliver nuclear weapons. Warnke's letter stated that it was "the position of the United States Government that the physical possession and control of nuclear arms by a Middle Eastern power would be deemed to constitute the introduction of nuclear weapons."[49]

Although he was dealt a bad hand, Warnke accorded himself well throughout the negotiations. Given that Johnson was fully intent on selling the Phantoms to Israel, Warnke was not in a position to use them as leverage on the nuclear issue. Nonetheless, he clearly made Rabin believe otherwise, as evidenced by the furious lobbying campaign the ambassador waged after the contentious third negotiation session. Even after that, Warnke was able to pin down the Israelis on the definition of introduction. In doing so, Israel revealed that it had nuclear weapons or, at least, was intent on acquiring them. These formal letters approving the sale of the Phantoms basically formed the basis of America's bargain with Israel over the latter's nuclear program that continues to this day.

THE NIXON AND MEIR UNDERSTANDING

This bargain was formalized the following year when the new Israeli prime minister, Golda Meir, met with President Richard Nixon in Washington, DC. Upon taking office, the Nixon administration considered trying to confront Israel over its nuclear program again, including potentially using the delivery of the F-4s as leverage. The Department of Defense was especially insistent on the need to pressure Israel to sign the NPT as well as renounce nuclear weapons and strategic missiles. Deputy Secretary of Defense David Packard warned that a failure to do so would "involve [the US] in a conspiracy with Israel which would leave matters dangerous to [US] security in their hands."[50] Others, including National Security Advisor Henry Kissinger, agreed that an overt Israeli nuclear arsenal would undermine US security. Kissinger, however, believed America could live with a secret arsenal. As he explained to Nixon, "While we might ideally like to halt actual Israeli possession, what we really want at a minimum may be just to keep Israeli possession from becoming an established international fact."[51]

In this sense, the Nixon administration had a willing partner in the new Israeli prime minister. Although she didn't become prime minister until 1969, Meir was a staunch veteran of Israeli politics who had been involved in the nuclear program since its inception. She began her public life as the minister of labor in 1949, just a year after the War of Independence. She spent a decade as the foreign minister between 1956 and 1966 and was one of the only officials Ben-Gurion read into the nuclear deal with France. From before the time the US discovered Dimona, Meir had been alone among Israeli leaders in believing that Israel should be honest with Washington about its nuclear intentions. As she explained her philosophy—"I was always of the opinion that we should tell them the truth and explain why"—that is, nuclear weapons were necessary to ensure Israel's national survival.[52] For nearly two decades, she had been overruled by her superiors—first Ben-Gurion and then Eshkol. Now in charge of Israel, she was finally able to put her stamp on Israel's nuclear doctrine.

There is no record of the crucial meeting between Nixon and Meir in September 1969. It is widely believed that an understanding was reached where Meir pledged that Israel would not announce it had nuclear weapons or test one.[53] In return, Nixon agreed to stop pressuring Israel about its nuclear program or signing the NPT. Although there is near consensus that such an understanding was reached, there is only circumstantial evidence to support it. For instance, in February 1970 Rabin told Kissinger: "in light of the conversation between the President and Golda Meir," Israel wouldn't sign the NPT.[54] Additionally, there were no US inspections of Dimona after the September 1969 meeting. Ultimately, whether there was an explicit agreement or not is of little importance. The United States and Israel had basically reached this understanding, if only implicitly, when they concluded the deal for the F-4s. The negotiations for the planes underscored that Israel believed it could build nuclear weapons. America's decision to sell Israel the Phantoms despite this made clear Washington was willing to live with a covert nuclear arsenal.

LIVING WITH A DIRTY LITTLE SECRET

To date, the nuclear understanding appears to have been a success, at least as measured by what concerned US policymakers most about Israel acquiring the bomb. As noted above, Israel's nuclear weapons did not prompt Nasser to wage a preventive war against Israel. Although Egyptian planes flying over Dimona in the run-up to the Six-Day War greatly concerned Jerusalem, there is no evidence that Cairo was interested in waging a war to prevent Israel from building the bomb.

America's greatest fear was that an Israeli bomb would substantially increase Soviet influence in the Middle East. In particular, US officials worried Arab states would turn to the Soviet Union to protect them from a nuclear-armed Israel. This could result in the Soviet Union deploying troops to the region, or perhaps even stationing nuclear weapons in friendly countries. In fact, Soviet influence in the Middle East declined drastically in the years after Israel went nuclear. This wasn't because of Israel's arsenal—it was because, especially after the Yom Kippur War in 1973, the Arab states realized only America had enough influence with Israel to force it to negotiate. Cairo therefore turned to America to help mediate negotiations that produced the Camp David Accords in 1978. The Camp David Accords established peace between Israel and Egypt in exchange for Israel returning Egyptian territory it had conquered in 1967. Jordan, which was always closer to America than Egypt, also signed a peace agreement with Israel in 1994. The Soviet Union continued to maintain relations with countries like Syria and Iraq, but its influence was significantly diminished.

US policymakers also feared that Israel acquiring nuclear weapons would prompt its neighbors to build their own bombs. Washington was especially concerned Egypt would go nuclear. This too never came to pass. Egypt's nuclear program was never very serious, and it petered out despite Israel building the bomb. There is some evidence that Saddam Hussein sought nuclear weapons in part because of Israel. Baathist documents captured after the 2003 invasion show that Saddam Hussein believed that an Arab bomb would deter Israel from using its own nuclear weapons in the event of conflict. Instead, Israel would be forced to fight a conventional war of attrition, which Saddam believed Israel would ultimately lose.[55] It's possible, however, that this was more of a convenient justification for investing significant resources into the Iraqi nuclear program. In any case, Saddam Hussein would later abandon his nuclear program, albeit not before Israel attacked it. Still, Iraq's progress toward acquiring a nuclear bomb at the time of the First Gulf War has been greatly exaggerated. As Jacques Hymans has explained, "when the Gulf War started, Iraq's bid for nuclear weapons was essentially a dead man walking."[56] There is also scant evidence that Israel's nuclear arsenal was a strong motivator for Iran's pursuit of nuclear weapons.

ISRAEL'S NUCLEAR OFFSPRING

As was the case with France—although to a much lesser degree—Israel's contribution to proliferation had more to do with its friends than its enemies. While France provided nuclear assistance to many countries, Israel's support was limited to apartheid South Africa. Especially in the 1970s, Israeli and South African leaders formed a close, mutually beneficial relationship that one scholar characterizes as a "marriage of interests and ideologies."[57] A significant part of this relationship was based on Israel's willingness to sell South Africa advanced military systems at a time when Pretoria was increasingly shunned by the Western world. This extended to the strategic realm. Declassified South African documents strongly suggest that in 1975, Israel offered to sell South Africa Jericho missiles with nuclear warheads. The offer was made by then-Israeli Defense Minister Shimon Peres to South Africa's Defense Minister P. W. Botha. The South African analysis of the offer stated: "In considering the merits of a weapon system such as the one being offered, certain assumptions have been made: a) That the missiles will be armed with nuclear warheads manufactured in RSA (Republic of South Africa) or acquired elsewhere." South Africa was not particularly close to building its own nuclear warheads at this time, suggesting it expected them to come from elsewhere. P. W. Botha and Peres met again a few months later to discuss the potential Jericho sale, which South Africa had code-named Chalet. According to South Africa's notes of this second meeting, "Botha expressed interest in a limited number of units of Chalet subject to the correct payload being available." Peres responded that three different payloads were available, likely referring to conventional, chemical, and nuclear warheads.[58] In the end, South Africa did not purchase off-the-shelf nuclear warheads from Israel and ended up building them itself. Israel did sell South Africa tritium, which can be used to produce higher explosive yields in fission weapons (or thermonuclear weapons).[59] Although Israel didn't sell the off-the-shelf Jericho missiles, it did provide Pretoria with the design and technology necessary to build its own Jericho-like, nuclear-capable missiles.[60]

NUCLEAR BLACKMAIL

Perhaps Israel's greatest contribution to South Africa's nuclear program was helping to inspire it in the first place. In the bipolar international system of the Cold War, Pretoria hitched its wagon to the US-led Western world. But as international opinion increasingly turned against them over their despicable apartheid policies, South African leaders worried that the United States would not come to their aid in the event of a conflict with Soviet-allied forces. This was especially problematic as more and more Communist-style regimes and insurgencies plagued their neighborhood. South African leaders concluded that building a small nuclear arsenal could help ensure America's protection. In their minds, by threatening to use nuclear weapons, apartheid leaders could blackmail the United States into intervening to save them.

The genesis of this theory was rooted in a persistent misbelief about why America agreed to resupply Israel during the 1973 Yom Kippur War. Unlike in 1967, it was Israel who was caught off guard in 1973 when Egyptian and Syrian forces launched a coordinated attack on Israel. Within days, Egyptian forces crossed the Suez Canal and quickly overran Israel's defensive positions. Israeli leaders feared the Egyptian army would soon invade the Sinai Desert and perhaps Israel proper. After assessing the frontlines on the second day of the war, Defense Minister Moshe Dayan, a hero of the Six-Day War, urged Prime Minister Meir to order a retreat to more defensible positions. Rejecting Dayan's advice, Meir ordered a counterattack on October 8 that failed spectacularly. The next day, Dayan was warning of the "destruction of the Third Commonwealth," a reference to Israel.[61] The deputy chief of staff of the Israeli military, Major General Yisrael Tal, would later say October 9 "was the blackest day of the war." After the counterattack failed, according to Tal, Israel believed it was fighting "a war for [their] very national and physical existence."[62] In the end, Israel's military, aided by America's military resupply, was able to beat back both invading powers and actually encircle the Egyptian Third Army. US shuttle diplomacy helped mediate an end to the war.

During the darkest days of the war, Israel is alleged to have armed aircraft or missiles with nuclear warheads in a way that would be seen by American and Soviet satellites.[63] In one version of events, Dayan—who had urged Meir to announce Israel had nuclear weapons or even test one to force the Arabs to halt their attacks—ordered that Israel's Jericho missiles be put on high alert and, perhaps, armed with nuclear warheads.[64] Another version came from Israel's president during the war, Ephraim Katzir, who said publicly a few years later that "Israel armed an aircraft with a nuclear bomb" during the conflict.[65] According to many accounts—most notably, Seymour Hersh's—Israel's nuclear signaling was done to "blackmail" the Nixon administration into ordering the military resupply of Israel.[66]

Hersh contends that either the Israeli ambassador told Henry Kissinger about the nuclear signaling in order to force him to order a military resupply, or the Soviets passed on the message to the United States. Kissinger's hand-picked ambassador to Egypt, Hermann F. Eilts, told Hersh Kissinger had mentioned the nuclear blackmail to him a few years after the fact.[67] Kissinger and most of the US and Israeli officials involved have vehemently denied that any nuclear signaling took place. The one exception is William Quandt, an NSC official working on the Middle East at the time. Quandt has maintained for decades that he saw intelligence reports early in the war saying Israel placed its Jericho missiles on high alert. The intelligence didn't specify whether they were armed with conventional or nuclear warheads, but the missile's poor accuracy would make it ineffective with conventional warheads.[68] But Quandt also rejects the notion that Israel had done this to blackmail the United States. The most comprehensive study on the subject was done by Elbridge Colby and four coauthors, who had access to most of the US officials, some Israeli officials, open- source material, and US classified documents. After their extensive review, they conclude that "Israel likely did take some steps associated with the readying of its nuclear weapons and/or nuclear weapons delivery forces in the very early stages of the Yom Kippur War." Furthermore, they find that the United States did pick up on this activity, but that it did not play a large role in US decision making. "Rather, US (and likely all nations') decision-makers were aware of the possibility of Israeli nuclear use as an implicit reality, but they judged that it was only plausible in *extremis*, and American leaders did not believe the situation, even in the dark hours of October 7, had reached those depths."[69] This is consistent with what Quandt told this author. According to him, while Israeli leaders panicked early in the war, US policymakers were always certain that Jerusalem would prevail militarily. Furthermore, Sadat was backchanneling with the United States throughout the war that his aims were limited—Cairo did not seek to destroy the Jewish state but rather to create the space for negotiations. All of this meant that the Nixon administration was not concerned that Israel would have to turn to nuclear weapons in a final act of desperation.[70] Thus, the notion that Israel used its nuclear arsenal to blackmail the United States doesn't hold water.

Although untrue, the blackmail narrative had real consequences, including influencing South Africa to build its own arsenal. Andre Buys, a nuclear weapons engineer who managed South Africa's bomb-making factory, has said that South Africa's nuclear strategists were aware of Israel's alleged nuclear blackmail. According to Buys, this event "influenced our thinking. We argued that if we cannot use a nuclear weapon on the battlefield . . . then the only possible way to use it would be to leverage intervention from the Western Powers by threatening to use it."[71] This is hardly unreasonable. The truth of the matter is that Israel couldn't blackmail the United States with nuclear weapons in 1973, because Washington knew Cairo's war aims were limited and Israel would win. Had circumstances been different, the threat of nuclear use might have led to American intervention. As Quandt puts it, "Without being told in so many words, we knew that a desperate Israel might activate its nuclear option. This situation, by itself, created a kind of blackmail potential."[72] South Africa was not the only country to take note of the blackmail narrative. During the Indo-Pakistani border crisis in 1990, Pakistani generals thought they could force America to engage in a massive resupply of their military because of their misperceptions about the events of 1973.[73]

THE NUCLEAR TEST

The nuclear partnership between Israel and South Africa was a two-way street, with Pretoria also aiding Jerusalem's nuclear arsenal. For starters, South Africa sold Israel fifty tons of uranium.[74] More significantly, South Africa almost certainly allowed Israel to violate its pledge not to test nuclear weapons, while still maintaining plausible deniability. This complicated the Jimmy Carter administration's ability to complete the Strategic Arms Limitation Talks Treaty (SALT II). In fact, Israel's nuclear arsenal has regularly made America's arms control efforts difficult.

On September 21, 1979, an aging US Vela satellite registered a double flash that was entirely consistent with a nuclear explosion. Vela 6911 covered an area three thousand miles in diameter from the southern tip of Africa through some of Antarctica, including parts of the southern Atlantic and Indian Oceans.[75] Nearby hydroacoustic signals also picked up signs of a nuclear explosion in the remote South African Prince Edward Islands in the

South Atlantic Ocean. These hydroacoustic signals were judged to be less conclusive than the satellite, however. Furthermore, since Vela 6911 was operating past its projected lifetime, it was possible the satellite had malfunctioned. The Carter administration wanted other intelligence to corroborate that a nuclear test had indeed taken place. Nonetheless, early assessments by the CIA and Defense Intelligence Agency (DIA) said there was at least a 90 percent chance the satellite had witnessed a nuclear explosion.[76] There were multiple other sources of technical intelligence that could confirm the Vela satellite's reading, including aircraft that could detect radiation. More traditional spy craft, such as human sources and intercepted communications, were also put on the task. Even unexpected sources could contribute, such as when the Institute of Nuclear Science in Gracefield, New Zealand, registered increased radioactive fallout in rainwater samples that were consistent with a small nuclear test. The institute was unable to replicate the tests, however.[77]

Although they lacked absolutely conclusive evidence, in October, the US intelligence community assessed with "high confidence . . . that a low yield atmospheric nuclear explosion occurred," and that South Africa was the most likely perpetrator. At the same time, the State Department noted the possibility of Israeli involvement.[78] Both South Africa and Israel had political and technical reasons to conduct a test. Some in the US government considered the possibility that Israel would want to test low-yield battlefield nuclear weapons or even a fission trigger for boosted nuclear or thermonuclear weapons. Another possibility was that South Africa tested an Israeli design in return for technical information.[79] The political ramifications of testing a nuclear device would be enormous for both countries. South Africa and Israel were signatories of the Partial Test Ban Treaty, which prohibited atmospheric tests. Furthermore, both countries had given the United States political commitments that they would not test a nuclear device.

Three major US government studies would be completed over the coming months regarding whether the Vela satellite had detected a nuclear explosion. The first two were done by scientists working at the Los Alamos and Sandia National Laboratories. They concluded that the double flash had most likely come from a nuclear blast. The other came from a presidential commission created by Frank Press, the president's science advisor. The Ruina panel, as it became known, was named after its chair, Jack Ruina, the former head of the Defense Advanced Research Projects Agency (DARPA), the Pentagon's premier advanced technology agency. The eight scientists on the Ruina panel were asked to consider whether the double flash had been caused by a nuclear detonation, a false alarm, or one or more natural phenomena. Among the natural phenomena some had proposed as the cause of the double flash was lightning or meteoroids. The latter phenomenon was judged to happen once every one billion years.[80]

The Ruina panel rejected some of the potential corroborating evidence of a test, such as the radio telescope and the acoustic readings, as being too weak to be considered. They also put strong weight on the fact that the two bhangmeters (light detectors) on the Vela satellite didn't register consistent signals, as they would if the satellite was working properly.[81] This evidence was used by the panel to conclude that the best explanation for the double flash was that it captured light reflected off a meteor that struck the Vela satellite. The panel didn't rule out the possibility of a nuclear test entirely, but believed a non-nuclear explanation was most probable. This conclusion was strongly challenged by scientists at the national laboratories, as well as officials at the Departments of Energy and State. One scientist at Sandia said that the Ruina panel's conclusion "strains credibility."[82] This was for good reason, as there was a clear explanation for the inconsistency between the two bhangmeters—the age of the satellite meant that one of them malfunctioned. In fact, the Vela satellite's bhangmeters had registered the same readings in all recent known nuclear tests. Los Alamos would cite the readings of the bhangmeters as confirming a test had occurred.[83] Even President Carter seemed to believe a test occurred. After the Ruina panel issued its preliminary conclusions, the president wrote in his diary, "We have a growing belief among our scientists that the Israelis did indeed conduct a nuclear test explosion in the ocean near the southern end of South Africa."[84]

Subsequent information has all but confirmed a nuclear test occurred. In June 1980, both the DIA and the Naval Research Laboratory (NRL) published reports about the Vela incident that concluded a nuclear explosion almost certainly occurred.[85] Meanwhile, the head of Israel's Jericho missile program in the 1970s, Dr. Anselm Yaron, later became a fellow at an MIT center founded by Ruina, the head of the presidential panel. Multiple sources say that while at MIT, Yaron admitted to a joint Israel–South Africa nuclear test.[86] Moreover, a recent study found evidence of radioactive debris. The Ruina panel had pointed to the lack of radioactive debris as a major reason it didn't believe a nuclear test had occurred.[87] It is, therefore, extremely likely a nuclear test took place, and logic would suggest Israeli involvement. As Leonard Weiss has pointed out, the five established nuclear powers would have had little reason to conduct a clandestine test, while India, Pakistan, and South Africa lacked the technical capability to do so at the time. Most likely, it conducted a few small nuclear tests, only the last of which was captured by the Vela satellite.[88]

Israel conducting a nuclear test was a major betrayal of the United States—given that Jerusalem had pledged not to conduct such a test. Of course, by 1979 Israel was well practiced in misleading the United States when it came to its nuclear program. It had kept Dimona secret from the United States until 1960 and then insisted it was for peaceful purposes. There was also the NUMEC affair, where three hundred kilograms of highly enriched uranium in the United States was likely secretly shipped to Israel.[89] Time and time again, US policymakers chose to go along with or at least acquiesce to Israel's actions.

The Vela incident was no different. President Carter and his administration were more than happy to accept the conclusions of the Ruina panel, even if they didn't fully believe them. If the Carter administration concluded Israel had conducted a nuclear test, it would have had to sanction Israel, especially considering it sanctioned Pakistan over its nascent nuclear program only months earlier. An Israeli nuclear test would also jeopardize one of Carter's crowning achievements: negotiating a peace agreement between Israel and Egypt. The Camp David Accords were signed at the White House almost exactly a year before the nuclear test in 1978. An Israeli nuclear test could unravel all that progress. A nuclear test by either South Africa or Israel would also cut against the Carter administration's claim of a strong nonproliferation record.

ISRAEL AND AMERICA'S NONPROLIFERATION AGENDA

There was a more specific arms control concern as well. The fact that US intelligence couldn't conclusively identify a nuclear test, much less the perpetrator, called into question its ability to monitor the Partial Test Ban Treaty. This came at a perilous time as the Carter administration had concluded SALT II with the Soviet Union in June 1979, and the treaty was still awaiting Senate confirmation. The US intelligence community's inability to confidently detect an atmospheric nuclear test would create doubts about its ability to monitor Soviet compliance with SALT II.[90]

Ultimately, SALT II unraveled when the Soviet Union invaded Afghanistan in December 1979. Still, this was not the first time that Israel's nuclear program became an issue for US arms control and nonproliferation treaties, nor would it be the last. As noted above, Israel signed onto the PTBT quickly, only to violate it in 1979. The battle over the NPT was more problematic and, ultimately, unsuccessful for Washington. US policymakers at the time worried immensely that Israel's failure to sign onto the NPT would impair America's ability to stop the proliferation of nuclear weapons. Even though he refused to use the F-4 sale as leverage, LBJ did tell Eshkol, "Israel's failure to sign the Non-Proliferation Treaty would be a severe blow to my Government's global efforts to halt the spread of nuclear weapons."[91] Similarly, acting Secretary of Defense Elliot Richardson told Israeli officials that their country's latent nuclear capability made it especially important that Jerusalem sign the NPT.[92]

Eventually, the NPT obtained widespread consensus, including from the Arab states, even though Israel refused to sign it. This state of affairs was briefly threatened, however, in 1995. The text of the NPT called for the parties of the treaty to decide on whether to extend it indefinitely—or for various periods of time—twenty-five years after it went into force. In 1995, the Clinton administration made it a major priority to secure the indefinite extension of the treaty. One of the major roadblocks was a coalition of Arab states, which sought to use the extension conference to pressure Israel to sign the NPT or at least close Dimona. For Israel, this was a nonstarter. The Clinton administration launched an extension-lobbying campaign to convince Egypt and other Arab states to agree to an indefinite extension without singling out Israel. Although progress was uneven, this effort was eventually successful.[93]

Israel's nuclear arsenal would quickly complicate another one of the Clinton administration's major nonproliferation goals. Since nearly the beginning of the atomic era, various proposals had been made to ban the production of highly enriched uranium or plutonium. Few went very far until the end of the Cold War—and especially during the Clinton administration. President Clinton first called for a fissile material cutoff in a speech to the UN General Assembly in 1993. Progress on it was slow, however, and it wasn't until 1998 that momentum began to ramp up. Israeli leaders were vehemently opposed to a fissile material cutoff treaty (FMCT), viewing it as a first step on a slippery slope that ended with a non-nuclear Israel. Then-Prime Minister Benjamin Netanyahu went so far as to reportedly warn President Clinton, "We will never sign the treaty, and do not delude yourselves—no pressure will help. We will not sign the treaty because we will not commit suicide."[94] Fearing that Israeli opposition could derail political support for the negotiations, President Clinton offered an extraordinary concession: a written statement promising that America's global arms control policies would never threaten Israel's nuclear arsenal. Clinton would send a similar letter to Netanyahu's successor, Ehud Barak, when he took over in the summer of 1999.[95] George W. Bush, Barack Obama, and Donald Trump would provide similar written statements to Israel soon after taking office. This has thus become the second pillar of the US and Israel's nuclear bargain.[96]

CONCLUSION

As noted in the introduction of the previous chapter, the Israel case is the hardest to draw definitive conclusions about. Still, a number of things are apparent. First, as with the French and British cases, geopolitical concerns were intertwined with America's views about Israel's nuclear program. America's greatest concern was that Israel acquiring nuclear weapons would increase the Soviet Union's influence in the Middle East. It's worth noting, however, that this turned out to be incorrect. After the 1973 Yom Kippur War, deft diplomacy by Henry Kissinger actually increased US influence in the region. In contrast to what proliferation optimists have predicted, nuclear proliferation did not allow America to reduce its commitment to Israel. To the contrary, the United States greatly expanded its military assistance to Jerusalem to ensure that Israel wasn't forced to use nuclear weapons to defend itself. Were US partners like Saudi Arabia to acquire nuclear weapons in the future, it is possible that Washington would feel similarly inclined to enhance security ties to Riyadh. At the very least, the United States would have an even greater interest in alleviating Saudi insecurity.

Perhaps the biggest lesson for future cases is the ways in which Israel's nuclear program complicated America's larger nonproliferation agenda. Whereas Great Britain and France were recognized nuclear weapon states under the NPT, Israel and Pakistan never joined the NPT. Any future allied proliferation cases will involve countries that withdraw from or violate the NPT. Although Israel's case is not directly analogous to these future cases, the lesson that partner nations acquiring nuclear weapons would hinder America's nonproliferation agenda is applicable. As mentioned in the introduction of this chapter, the nuclear bargain America struck with Israel was reasonably effective at securing America's interests. Some may see keeping the bomb in the basement as a key lesson for future cases of allied proliferation. While desirable, it seems unlikely that this can be replicated in the future. Since future allies and partners would have to withdraw from or violate the NPT, it would be difficult to hide the change in nuclear status. Even without the NPT complication, it is doubtful that the opaque status is repeatable. After all, the United States tried to strike a similar bargain with Pakistan, which also never joined the NPT, only to fail when Pakistan tested nuclear weapons in 1998. It is to that case we now turn.

NOTES

1. Quoted in Michael Karpin, *The Bomb in the Basement: How Israel Went Nuclear and What That Means for the World* (New York: Simon & Schuster, 2007), 243.

2. "Embassy in Israel to DOS, EMBTEL, 1119" March 5, 1965, *USNA*, RG 59, Records of Under Secretary of State George W. Ball, 1961–1966, Box 21, Folder 17.

3. "MEMCON, Nuclear Proliferation," February 9, 1966, *USNA*, RG 59, CFPF, 1964–1966, Box 2356, POL, ISR-US; and "DOS to Embassy in Israel, DEPTEL, 652," February 10, 1966, *USNA*, RG 59, CFPF, 1964–1966, Box 3068.

4. "Joint Chiefs of Staff Memo to McNamara," December 7, 1963, *FRUS*, 1961–1963, vol. XVIII, doc. 383.

5. "Read Memo to Bundy, Inspection and Need to Implement Initiative to Prevent Nuclear Proliferation in the Near East," February 5, 1965, *USNA*, RG 59, CFPF, 1964–1966, Box 3068.

6. "Telegram from Department of State to Embassy in Tel Aviv, DEPTEL, 761," March 19, 1966, *USNA*, RG 59, CFPF, 1964–1966, Box 3068. Also see "Telegram From the Department of State to the Embassy in Israel," December 14, 1964, *FRUS*, 1964–1968, vol. XVIII, doc. 113; and "Telegram from Department of State to Embassy in Tel Aviv, DEPTEL, 111019," December 30, 1966, *USNA*, RG59, CFPF, 1964–1966, Box 3068.

7. Karpin, *Bomb in the Basement*, 213–14.

8. Avner Cohen, *Israel and the Bomb* (New York: Columbia University, 1998), 172.

9. "Assessment Prepared by the Defense Intelligence Agency," January 24, 1963, *FRUS*, 1961–1963, vol. XVIII, doc. 140; "Memorandum for the Record," November 21, 1963, *FRUS*, 1961–1963, vol. XVIII, doc. 368; and "Special National Intelligence Estimate, 30–4–63," December 4, 1963, *FRUS*, 1961–1963, vol. XVIII, doc. 380.

10. "Read Memo, 'Israel's Assurances Concerning Use of Atomic Energy,'" March 18, 1964, *WCDA*, http://digitalarchive.wilsoncenter.org/document/117053.

11. "Embassy in Israel to DOS, A-955," June 15, 1965, RG 59, CFPF, 1964–1966, Box 3068.

12. "Read Memo to Bundy, Dimona Inspection and Need to Implement Initiative to Prevent Nuclear Proliferation in the Near East," February 5, 1965. Also see "Davis Memo to Talbot," March 5, 1965, *FRUS*, 1964–1968, vol. XVIII, doc. 178.

13. The painful dilemma line comes from "Komer Memo to Johnson," January 21, 1965, FRUS, 1964–1968, Volume XVIII, Document 124. The terms of the agreement are found in "Embassy in Israel to DOS," March 11, 1965, FRUS, 1964–1968, Volume XVIII, Document 185.

14. U.S. Agency for International Development, *U.S. Overseas Loans and Grants: Obligations and Loan Authorizations, July 1, 1945–September 30, 2017* (Washington, DC: USAID, 2018).

15. "Telegram from Department of State to Embassy in Amman, DEPTEL, 446," February 8, 1965, USNA, RG 59, Records of Under Secretary of State George W. Ball, 1961–1966, Box 21, Folder 17, Near East; "Telegram from Department of State (George W. Ball) to U.S. Embassy in Tel Aviv (W. Averell Harriman)," February 26, 1965, USNA, RG 59, Records of Under Secretary of State George W. Ball, 1961–1966, Box 21, Folder 17, Near East; and "Memorandum From Secretary of State Rusk to President Johnson," February 19, 1965, FRUS, 1964–1968, Volume XVIII, Document 155.

16. Interestingly, Rusk, typically a hardliner on Israeli nuclear matters, agreed with Israel that the missile prohibition was unfair. See "Memorandum for the Files," February 18, 1965, *FRUS*, 1964–1968, vol. XVIII, doc. 153. On Israel refusing IAEA safeguards, see "Telegram From the Embassy in Israel to the Department of State," February 25, 1965, *FRUS*, 1964–1968, vol. XVIII, doc. 158; "Telegram From the Embassy in Israel to the Department of State," February 26, 1965, *FRUS*, 1964–1968, vol. XVIII, doc. 161; and "Telegram From the Embassy in Israel to the Department of State," February 27, 1965, *FRUS*, 1964–1968, vol. XVIII, doc. 164. Somewhat

confusingly, Johnson told Komer before he left that he needed to get "a firm written reiteration of Israel's intentions not to develop nuclear weapons, and that Israel certify this by accepting IAEA safeguards on all of its nuclear facilities. So long as we receive the pledge, however, I do not insist on acceptance of IAEA controls now." See "Memorandum From President Johnson to the Under Secretary of State for Political Affairs (Harriman) and Robert W. Komer of the National Security Council Staff," February 21, 1965, *FRUS*, 1964–1968, vol. XVIII, doc. 157.

17. At first Israel asked for 210 planes for a complete modernization of the Israeli Air Force. See "Memorandum From Robert W. Komer of the National Security Council Staff to President Johnson," October 25, 1965, *FRUS*, 1964–1968, vol. XVIII, doc. 246.

18. "Memorandum From the President's Deputy Special Assistant for National Security Affairs (Komer) to President Johnson," February 8, 1966, *FRUS*, 1964–1968, vol. XVIII, doc. 267. Other officials like Ambassador Barbour agreed. See Cohen, *Israel and the Bomb*, 214.

19. Cohen, *Israel and the Bomb*, 270.

20. Karpin, *Bomb in the Basement*, 276. For an argument that the Soviet Union precipitated the war over concerns about Israel's nuclear program, see Isabella Ginor and Gideon Remez, *Foxbats Over Dimona: The Soviets' Nuclear Gamble in the Six-Day War* (New Haven, CT: Yale University Press, 2008).

21. In late 1966, Eshkol had finally allowed the US to brief Nasser on the Dimona inspections. "Telegram From the Embassy in Israel to the Department of State," November 29, 1966, *FRUS*, 1964–1968, vol. XVIII, doc. 351.

22. Michael Oren, *Six Days of War: June 1967 and the Making of the Middle East* (New York: Presidio Press, 2003), 75.

23. "Study Prepared in the Central Intelligence Agency," September 1, 1966, *FRUS*, 1964–1968, vol. XVIII, doc. 319; "Memorandum From Secretary of Defense McNamara to President Johnson," April 17, 1967, *FRUS*, 1964–1968, vol. XVIII, doc. 405; "Memorandum From the Under Secretary of State (Katzenbach) to President Johnson," May 1, 1967, *FRUS*, 1964–1968, vol. XVIII, doc. 415; and Central Intelligence Agency, "The President's Daily Brief," May 23, 1967, https://www.cia.gov/library/readingroom/docs/DOC_0005973816.pdf.

24. "Telegram From the Department of State to the Embassy in Israel," December 14, 1966, *FRUS*, vol. XVIII, doc. 366.

25. Oren, *Six Days of War,* 175–77.

26. Oren, *Six Days of War*, 307.

27. Karpin, *Bomb in the Basement,* 279–81.

28. Robert Gallucci, interview by phone with author Zachary Keck, July 16, 2018.

29. William Quandt, "How Far Will Israel Go?" *Washington Post*, November 29, 1991.

30. Karpin, *Bomb in the Basement,* 292–93; and John F. Fialka, "CIA Found Israel Could Make Bomb: Soil, Air Samples Disclosed Atomic Capability," *Washington Star*, December 8, 1977, https://www.cia.gov/library/readingroom/docs/CIA-RDP88-01315R000400060018-6.pdf.

31. Karpin, *Bomb in the Basement*, 268.

32. The relevant text as well as President Johnson's comments during the signing ceremony are included in "Telegram From the Department of State to Selected Posts," October 9, 1968, *FRUS*, 1964–1968, vol. XX, doc. 275. Also see Jeremy M. Sharp, *U.S. Foreign Aid to Israel* (Washington, DC: Congressional Research Service, December 4, 2009), 18; and Mitchell Geoffrey Bard, *The Water's Edge and Beyond: Defining the Limits to Domestic Influence on United States Middle East Policy* (New Brunswick, NJ: Transaction Publishers, 1991), 202. Also see "Notes on President Johnson's Meeting With Congressional Leaders," September 9, 1968, *FRUS*, 1964–1968, vol. XX, doc. 248.

33. "Memorandum From Harold H. Saunders of the National Security Council Staff to the President's Special Assistant (Rostow)," *FRUS*, 1964–1968, vol. XX, doc. 279; and "Memorandum of Conversation Between President Johnson and Foreign Minister Eban," *FRUS*, 1964–1968, vol. XX, doc. 284.

34. "Telegram From the Department of State to the Embassy in Israel," October 24, 1968, *FRUS*, 1964–1968, vol. XX, doc. 288.

35. "Memorandum of Conversation Between President Johnson and Foreign Minister Eban," October 22, 1968, *FRUS*, 1964–1968, vol. XX, doc. 284.

36. "Action Memorandum From the President's Special Assistant (Rostow) to President Johnson," October 25, 1968, *FRUS*, 1964–1968, vol. XX, doc. 290.

37. "Memorandum From the Assistant Secretary of Defense for International Security Affairs (Warnke) to Secretary of Defense Clifford," October 29, 1968, *FRUS*, 1964–1968, vol. XX, doc. 295.

38. Quoted in Karpin, *Bomb in the Basement*, 303.

39. "Memorandum From the Assistant Secretary of Defense for International Security Affairs (Warnke) to Secretary of Defense Clifford," October 29, 1968 *FRUS*, 1964–1968, vol. XX, doc. 295.

40. "Memorandum of Conversation," November 4, 1968, *FRUS*, 1964–1968, vol. XX, doc. 306.

41. "Memorandum of Conversation," November 5, 1968, *FRUS*, 1964–1968, vol. XX, doc. 308.

42. Karpin, *Bomb in the Basement*, 305.

43. "Memorandum of Agreement between the US and Israel in which the US Reaffirms its Concern for Israel's Security, Commits to the Independence and Integrity of Israel, and Agrees to Sell to Israel Fifty F-4 PHANTOM Aircraft," Undated, U.S. Declassified Documents Online, Gale Document Number: CK2349154612.

44. "Memorandum of Conversation," November 8, 1968, *FRUS*, 1964–1968, vol. XX, doc. 309.

45. Karpin, *Bomb in the Basement*, 305.

46. Karpin, *Bomb in the Basement*, 308; and "Draft Memorandum for the Record," November 9, 1968, *FRUS*, 1964–1968, vol. XX, doc. 311.

47. "Draft Memorandum for the Record," November 9, 1968, *FRUS*, 1964–1968, vol. XX, doc. 311.

48. "Memorandum of Conversation," November 12, 1968, *FRUS*, 1964–1968, vol. XX, doc. 317.

49. "Letter from the Assistant Secretary of Defense for International Security Affairs (Warnke) to the Israeli Ambassador (Rabin)," November 27, 1968, *FRUS, 1964–1968*, vol. XX, doc. 333.

50. "Deputy Secretary of Defense Memo, 'Subject Israeli Nuclear Program,'" July 14, 1969, *NSA*, https://nsarchive2.gwu.edu/nukevault/ebb485/.

51. "Kissinger to Nixon, 'Israeli Nuclear Program,'" n.d. with enclosures dated July 19, 1969, *NSA*. Also see "Memorandum for the Record," June 20, 1969, *FRUS, 1969–1976*, vol. XXIII, doc. 35.

52. Cohen, *Israel and the Bomb*, 132. Also see ibid., 72, 104, 142.

53. Avner Cohen and William Burr, "The Untold Story of Israel's Bomb," *Washington Post*, April 30, 2006; and Avner Cohen and William Burr, "Don't Like That Israel Has the Bomb? Blame Nixon," *Foreign Policy*, September 12, 2014.

54. "Memorandum of Conversation, Kissinger and Rabin," February 23, 1970, *NSA*.

55. Hal Brands and David Palkki, "Saddam, Israel, and the Bomb: Nuclear Alarmism Justified?" *International Security* 36, no. 1 (Summer 2011), pp. 133–66.

56. Jacques E. C. Hymans, *Achieving Nuclear Ambitions: Scientists, Politicians, and Proliferation* (New York: Cambridge University Press, 2012), 83. There has long been the contention that Saddam Hussein was six months away from the bomb at the time of the Gulf War. This premise, however, was based on the Iraqis breaking international safeguards and taking the highly enriched uranium France and Russia provided for research reactors, rather than Iraq being able to produce fissile material itself.

57. Sasha Polakow-Suransky, *The Unspoken Alliance: Israel's Secret Relationship with Apartheid South Africa* (New York: Pantheon, 2010), 6.

58. Chris McGreal, "Revealed: How Israel Offered to Sell South Africa Nuclear Weapons," *Guardian*, May 24, 2010; Peter Liberman, "Israel and the South African Bomb," *Nonproliferation Review* 11, no. 2 (Summer 2004), 46–80; and Polakow-Suransky, *Unspoken Alliance*.

59. Liberman, "Israel and the South African Bomb," 55.

60. Ibid., 56; and Nuclear Threat Initiative, "South Africa Missile Overview," April 2015.

61. Karpin, *Bomb in the Basement*, 326.

62. Karpin, *Bomb in the Basement*, 326.

63. The first public account of this was, "How Israel Got the Bomb," *Time* 107, no. 15 (April 12, 1976).

64. Avner Cohen, "The Last Nuclear Moment," *The New York Times*, October 6, 2003. Also see Adam Raz, "The Significance of the Reputed Yom Kippur War Nuclear Affair," *Strategic Assessment* 16, no. 4 (January 2014).

65. Quoted in Karpin, *Bomb in the Basement*, 327.

66. Seymour Hersh, *The Samson Option: Israel's Nuclear Arsenal and American Foreign Policy* (New York: Random House, 1991).

67. Hersh, *Samson Option*, 228–30.

68. William Quandt, interview by phone with author Zachary Keck, July 20, 2018; and Quandt, "How Far Will Israel Go?"

69. Elbridge Colby, Avner Cohen, William McCants, Bradley Morris, and William Rosenau, *The Israeli Nuclear Alert of 1973: Deterrence and Signaling in Crisis* (Washington, DC: CNA, April 2013), 2.

70. William Quandt, interview by phone with author Zachary Keck, July 20, 2018.

71. Peter Liberman, "The Rise and Fall of the South Africa Bomb," *International Security* 26, no. 2 (Fall 2001), 62. For more on South Africa's nuclear blackmail strategy, see Helen E. Purkitt and Stephen F. Burgess, "South Africa's Nuclear Strategy: Deterring 'Total Onslaught' and 'Nuclear Blackmail' in Three Stages," in *Strategy in the Second Nuclear Age: Power, Ambition and the Ultimate Weapon*, eds. Toshi Yoshihara and James R. Holmes (Washington, DC: Georgetown University Press, 2012), 43–46.

72. Quandt, "How Far Will Israel Go?" Colby and his coauthors agree, writing, "Because the situation never deteriorated to a level at which such [nuclear] use was seen as necessary or credible, the topic never arose in formal US government deliberations. But the possibility that a further deterioration of the situation could compel Israel to consider escalation, including to the nuclear level, was a significant but implicit factor in American deliberations." Colby et al., *Israeli Nuclear Alert of 1973*, 50.

73. Seymour M. Hersh, "On The Nuclear Edge," *New Yorker*, March 29, 1993.

74. Jeffrey T. Richelson, *Spying on the Bomb: American Nuclear Intelligence from Nazi Germany to Iran and North Korea* (New York: Norton, 2006), 283. The ensuing paragraphs on the nuclear test rely heavily on Richelson, *Spying on the Bomb*, chap. 7.

75. Richelson, *Spying on the Bomb*, 286.

76. Richelson, *Spying on the Bomb*, 286.

77. Richelson, *Spying on the Bomb*, 288–89.

78. Quoted in Richelson, *Spying on the Bomb*, 290 and 292.

79. Richelson, *Spying on the Bomb*, 294–95.

80. Richelson, *Spying on the Bomb*, 298–99.

81. As Leonard Weiss, a nuclear expert, explains: "Since the bhangmeters were designed to be identical except for sensitivity, the two signals would have been expected to be in synch chronologically (i.e., in phase) and consistent in terms of amplitude comparison. But it turned out that, although the two bhangmeter signals showed the classic shape of a nuclear double flash when graphed, there were anomalous phase differences that translated into inconsistent amplitudes between the two signals at certain times." See Weiss, "A Double-Flash from the Past and Israel's Nuclear Arsenal," *Bulletin of the Atomic Scientists*, August 3, 2018.

82. Quoted in Richelson, *Spying on the Bomb*, 304.

83. See Houston T. Hawkins's comments in Weiss, "Flash From the Past."

84. Quoted in William Burr and Avner Cohen, "New Evidence on the 22 September 1979 Velva Event," *National Security Archive*, Briefing Book no. 570, December 6, 2016.

85. Weiss, "Flash From the Past."

86. William Burr and Avner Cohen, "New Evidence on the 22 September 1979 Velva Event."

87. Lars-Erik De Geer and Christopher M. Wright, "The 22 September 1979 Vela Incident: Radionuclide and Hydroacoustic Evidence for a Nuclear Explosion," *Science & Global Security* 26, no. 1 (2018): 20–54.

88. Weiss, "Flash from the Past," *Bulletin of the Atomic Scientists*, August 3, 2018.

89. NUMEC stands for Nuclear Materials and Equipment Corporation, an American company that ran a nuclear fuel manufacturing plant in Pennsylvania in the 1950s–1970s. It was from this plant the highly enriched uranium (HEU) was stolen. On the NUMEC incident, see Victor Gilinsky and Roger J. Mattson, "Revisiting the NUMEC Affairs," *Bulletin of Atomic Scientists* 66, no. 2 (2010); and Roger J. Mattson, "The NUMEC Affair: Did Highly Enriched Uranium from the U.S. Aid Israel's Nuclear Weapons Program?" *National Security Archive*, Briefing Book no. 565, November 2, 2016.

90. Leonard Weiss, "Israel's 1979 Nuclear Test and the U.S. Cover-Up," *Middle East Policy* 18, November 4 (Winter 2011).

91. "Telegram From the Department of State to the Embassy in Israel," November 11, 1968, *FRUS*, 1964–1968, vol. XX, doc. 316.

92. "Memorandum of Conversation," July 29, 1969, *FRUS*, 1969–1976, vol. XXIII, doc. 41.

93. Gerald M. Steinberg, "Middle East Peace and the NPT Extension Decision," *Nonproliferation Review* 4, no. 1 (Fall 1996), 17–26.

94. Quoted in Zia Mian and A. H. Nayyar, "Playing the Nuclear Game: Pakistan and the Fissile Material Cutoff Treaty," *Arms Control Today* (April 2010), 19.

95. Aluf Benn, "Is Obama on the Way to Dimona?" *Haaretz*, December 18, 2008.

96. Adam Entous, "How Trump and Three Other US Presidents Protected Israel's Worst Kept Secret: It's Nuclear Arsenal," *The New Yorker*, June 18, 2018. It's unclear if President Biden has made a similar pledge.

Chapter 9

The Bomb from Hell
(Pakistan, 1973–1990)

The cover story of the December 2011 issue of *The Atlantic* was an article titled simply: "The Ally From Hell."[1] Coming roughly six months after the raid on Osama bin Laden's compound, which was located only miles from Pakistan's West Point, the headline didn't need to name the country for readers to know which one it is about. But the article wasn't simply about Islamabad's support for the worst terrorist groups in the world; it was also about Pakistan's nuclear arsenal. More precisely, it was really about the combination of the two: how the nuclear weapons in Pakistan's arsenal could end up in the hands of terrorist groups like al-Qaeda. This was a fear that kept many US leaders up at night.

Indeed, since its inception in the early 1970s, Pakistan's nuclear program has confounded generations of American officials. It has directly and indirectly strained the bilateral relationship more than any other issue. Since at least the end of the Cold War, nuclear crises have almost exclusively been on the Indian subcontinent. As this book was being written, Pakistan's support for terrorism once again precipitated a crisis with India that, once again, sparked fears about a nuclear war. While some may believe these concerns are overblown, all agree that such a conflict would be catastrophic. One often-cited study by three universities estimates a nuclear exchange between India and Pakistan involving just a hundred relatively small-yield warheads would kill twenty-one million people directly while also causing two billion others to starve.[2] Far more than any of the other countries explored in this book, Pakistan has truly been the nuclear state from hell.

Most of these issues are discussed in the following chapter. This chapter focuses on the beginning of Pakistan's nuclear program through October 1990, when then-President George H. W. Bush could no longer certify Islamabad didn't possess a nuclear bomb. Most of the existing accounts of this era argue that the United States failed to stop Pakistan from acquiring a nuclear weapon because Washington prioritized the proxy war with the Soviet Union in Afghanistan. As a result, Pakistan was given a free hand to pursue its nuclear program. There is certainly some truth to this viewpoint, but it is also too simplistic. The Carter and Reagan administrations did place more importance on turning Afghanistan into the Soviet Union's Vietnam than preventing Pakistan from becoming a nuclear power. But even before the Soviet invasion of Afghanistan, US policymakers were pessimistic about their chances of thwarting Pakistan's nuclear program. This was mostly because Pakistani leaders were absolutely certain that their country needed nuclear weapons to survive, and they were willing to do anything to obtain them. It was only with great difficulty that the United States blocked Islamabad's plutonium route to the bomb, and this was only accomplished by persuading European allies not to sell Pakistan the technology. No combination of US threats or inducements could persuade Pakistan not to purchase a reprocessing plant.

No sooner had Washington blocked the plutonium route to the bomb than it discovered that Islamabad was pursuing highly enriched uranium through the then-cutting-edge technology of centrifuges. At first, US policymakers were relieved because they doubted Islamabad's ability to master this technology. This relief quickly turned to dread when Washington discovered that A. Q. Khan, a Pakistani scientist previously employed by Europe's centrifuge consortium, had stolen the centrifuge designs and knew many of the primary suppliers for their components. Counterfactuals are always perilous to use and ultimately uncertain. Nonetheless, given A. Q. Khan's experience and networks—combined with Pakistan's willingness to "eat grass"—America probably would have failed to prevent a Pakistani bomb even if Moscow hadn't invaded Afghanistan. As it happened, the Soviet Union did invade Afghanistan and Pakistan did build nuclear weapons. This chapter tells that story.

DECIDING ON THE BOMB

Pakistan didn't pursue nuclear weapons in response to India's nuclear test in 1974, as some believe. In fact, Pakistan formally launched a nuclear weapons program in January 1972, two years before India's nuclear test. The seminal event that put Pakistan on the path to nuclear weapons was its traumatic defeat in the 1971 Indo-Pakistan War. And the man who chose that path was the newly installed prime minister, Zulfikar Ali Bhutto.

Z. A. Bhutto took power after the Pakistani military's disastrous showing in the 1971 war. The conflict had started after the Punjabi West Pakistani leaders refused to honor an election result that would have given control over the country to the Bengalis, the dominant ethnic group of East Pakistan. As unrest from the rebellion threatened to destabilize India, Delhi prepared to intervene militarily. Islamabad decided to launch a preemptive strike on western India. Everything went wrong for Pakistan. In just thirteen days in December 1971, Indian forces decisively defeated Pakistan forces on the eastern front, taking ninety-three thousand Pakistani troops prisoner. This secured East Pakistan's (Bangladesh's) independence from West Pakistan. Events were only slightly better on the western front. India quickly recovered from Pakistan's surprise attack, reversing all of Pakistan's territorial gains before pushing into Pakistan proper. By the time Pakistan surrendered on December 16, India had taken control of 5,500 square miles (14,000 km^2) of West Pakistan. It also destroyed about one-third of the Pakistani Navy. In the aftermath of this disastrous showing, much of the senior leadership in the country resigned, and Z. A. Bhutto was thrust into power.

This capped a meteoric rise for Bhutto. A charismatic figure born into a relatively wealthy Sindhi family, Bhutto had obtained college and law degrees in the West before returning to Pakistan to practice law in the mid-1950s. Despite his youth and the fact that he was a Sindhi in a Punjabi-dominated political system, Bhutto quickly rose in Pakistani politics, becoming a top advisor to then-President Ayub Khan by the late 1950s. Bhutto had a number of portfolios until 1966, when he resigned as foreign minister in protest over Khan's India policy, which Bhutto viewed as too conciliatory. Bhutto had always been a hardliner on India, as well as a relentless advocate of acquiring nuclear weapons. As foreign minister, Bhutto famously declared that if India built nuclear weapons, Pakistan would eat grass or even starve to acquire its own. His views on nuclear weapons were not supported by the senior leadership at the time. Through America's Atoms for Peace program, Pakistan did construct a modest civilian nuclear program, which included a 5-MW swimming pool–type reactor from the United States, as well as the Karachi Nuclear Power Plant (KANUPP), a Canadian Deuterium (CANDU)-type 137-megawatt electrical reactor from Canada.[3] But before the 1971 war and Bhutto's return to power, Pakistan's senior leadership, including the military, opposed building nuclear weapons.

Upon becoming president in December 1971, Bhutto wasted no time in launching the nuclear weapons program. On January 24, 1972, barely a month after taking office, Bhutto convened a meeting of the country's top scientists at Multan, a city in Punjab province. Appealing to their nationalism, Bhutto rallied the scientific community's support for the project. It wasn't a hard sell. Like most Pakistanis, the loss of East Pakistan and India's role in it was traumatic for Pakistani scientists. They saw the merit in acquiring nuclear weapons to safeguard the country's territorial integrity. At the meeting, Bhutto commanded the scientists to build a bomb within three years, the same amount of time it took the United States. He also made Munir Ahmad

Khan—who had studied in the United States—the new head of the Pakistan Atomic Energy Commission (PAEC) and had the nuclear agency report directly to him. This was in line with Bhutto's efforts to reduce the influence of the military and consolidate power himself.

HOW TO BUILD THE BOMB

Although the scientific, political, and military leadership now agreed on the necessity of acquiring nuclear weapons, there was no obvious path for doing so. One of Munir Khan's first major decisions at PAEC was to pursue a plutonium-based bomb. Recognizing the undeveloped nature of his country, Munir Khan turned to foreign suppliers to help. Specifically, he decided to acquire the necessary plants and facilities from abroad under international safeguards but to use the knowledge gained from these imports to build up parallel, unsafeguarded facilities. To that end, Pakistan signed a contract with Canada to purchase a fuel fabrication plant to produce fuel roads for KANUPP in 1973. Islamabad then entered into an agreement with West Germany to purchase a heavy water production plant.[4] The centerpiece of the program, however, was the purchase of a reprocessing plant from France. Pakistan first acquired a pilot reprocessing plant from the French corporation Saint-Gobain Techniques Nouvelles (SGN), the same company that built Israel's Dimona reprocessing plant. This facility would be used to train Pakistani scientists. Then, in March 1973, Pakistan and SGN inked a contract for a one-hundred-ton reprocessing plant. This would reprocess fuel from the KANUPP reactor.

Much to Pakistan's chagrin, India's actions would greatly complicate, and ultimately undermine, Pakistan's strategy for a plutonium-based bomb. In May 1974, India conducted what it called a "peaceful nuclear explosion." It had acquired the plutonium for the device from a reactor built by Canada and a reprocessing plant designed by an American company under the Atoms for Peace program. India had pledged to only use the technology for peaceful purposes, which it had blatantly violated. The fact that Western nuclear technology had been used to build nuclear devices resulted in a fundamental rethinking of US nuclear commerce. Instead of the generous Atoms for Peace philosophy, the Ford and, later, Carter administrations—with a strong push from Congress—would seek to limit the transfer of dangerous nuclear technology to non-nuclear powers.

Pakistan found itself in the crosshairs, with Washington suddenly focused on Pakistan's nuclear aspirations, and intent on forestalling the deals Pakistan had struck with Canada, West Germany, and especially France. The Indian nuclear test produced a nearly immediate transformation in America's and

Canada's nonproliferation policies. While not as dramatic, the Indian test did lead some French and West German officials to reconsider their own countries' policies. For instance, a French official stated that absent India's nuclear test, Paris's reprocessing plant sale would have gone through "like a letter through the post office. Piece of cake."[5] But once India conducted its test, French officials began raising questions about Pakistan's interest in such a large reprocessing facility. Still, France and West Germany were ultimately determined to reap the economic rewards of nuclear exports and pressed on with the sales. All France demanded was that Pakistan submit to IAEA safeguards, which Islamabad reluctantly did. The deal was approved by the IAEA Board of Governors in early 1976.[6]

These developments failed to alleviate America's concerns, and Washington undertook a two-pronged approach to end the sales. The first part was to try to use carrots—and occasionally sticks—to persuade Pakistan to abandon the sales. This included offering to sell Pakistan advanced America fighter jets and offering massive economic concessions if Islamabad canceled the reprocessing deal with France. This had zero success. As Teresita Schaffer, one of the State Department's top experts on Pakistan, explained, getting Pakistan to cancel the deal "was totally a lost cause . . . nobody had the slightest expectation that Pakistan would do that."[7]

The ultimately more successful route was to convince the European countries to not go through with the sales. This proved easier to do in some cases than in others. Canada canceled most of its nuclear commerce with Pakistan on its own. West Germany also abandoned plans to sell the heavy water plant in the face of strong US opposition. The French were the most difficult to persuade, and most accounts of Pakistan's nuclear program suggest the United States strong-armed France into canceling the sale of the reprocessing plant. The available documents and accounts by former US officials suggest that is not exactly true. Rather, US policymakers used intelligence about Pakistan's nuclear intentions to persuade French leaders it was not in their interest to complete the sale. As one Carter administration official put it, "[some] say that it was American pressure that changed the French view. I don't think that's right . . . basically it was provision of information that made the French realize that what they'd been saying was inconsistent with their long-term interest."[8] Joseph Nye, who chaired a National Security Council committee focused on nonproliferation, led this effort. In July 1977, he presented French officials with sanitized intelligence of some of the experiments Pakistan was doing related to weapons development.[9] France agreed to not go through with the sale, although it wouldn't be officially canceled until the following year.

Changes in French domestic politics enabled this success as well.[10] In August 1976, Prime Minister Jacques Chirac, one of the main proponents of the agreement in Paris, stepped down from office. This gave more power to

President Valéry Giscard d'Estaing, who had long been skeptical of exporting reprocessing plants. In discussing the Pakistani deal with President Ford in May 1976, Giscard stated, "I do not want France to be the cause of nuclear proliferation. I resisted the sale of a plant to South Korea."[11] The use of American intelligence, along with these changes in French domestic politics, not only blocked Pakistan's and South Korea's plutonium path to the bomb but also, in the words of a former Carter administration official, "had a long-term impact on changing France's entire non-proliferation policy from pro-proliferation to anti-proliferation."[12] Regardless of the reasons, blocking the sale of the reprocessing plant was a major success, setting Pakistan's reprocessing program back decades. The Carter administration did not have long to celebrate its victory, however, as it soon became clear that Pakistan was rapidly acquiring the ability to enrich uranium.

A. Q. KHAN AND THE URANIUM PROGRAM

In September 1974, a few months after India's nuclear test, Prime Minister Bhutto's office received an odd letter from a person claiming to be a Pakistani scientist working in Europe. The letter urged Bhutto to build an enrichment plant to acquire the fissile material necessary for a nuclear bomb. The writer claimed to have the know-how to build such a facility and offered to return to Pakistan to help. The letter appeared legitimate enough that Bhutto ordered his aides to investigate the author.

That person turned out to be Abdul Qadeer Khan. Khan had been born on the Indian side of the border in 1936 but moved to Pakistan a few years after partition. The injustices Muslims faced in India during this time instilled in Khan a deep, lifelong hatred of India. After going to university in Karachi, Khan moved to Europe to further his studies, first to West Berlin and the Netherlands before graduating with a PhD in metallurgy from Belgium in 1971. Like most Pakistanis, the loss of East Pakistan at the hands of India in the 1971 war infuriated A. Q. Khan. He resolved to never let it happen again. Unlike most Pakistanis, Khan soon found himself in a position to do something about it. After receiving his doctorate, Khan found a job working for a subcontractor to the Ultra-Centrifuge Nederland (UCN), the Dutch partner to URENCO, Europe's nascent enrichment consortium consisting of the UK, Germany, and the Netherlands.[13] As part of his work, Khan visited the Almelo enrichment plant near the Dutch-German border and was in contact with many of the European contractors that supplied URENCO with centrifuge parts and other valuable equipment. His fluency in both Dutch and German led his company to give him work translating documents his firm received from URENCO's German partners. This included a new centrifuge design

West Germany was developing. As a Pakistani national, Khan shouldn't have had the security clearance to view such sensitive information. But the security standards in URENCO at the time were extremely lax. In fact, Khan was able to walk around the facilities freely, copying documents he needed to help Pakistan build its own centrifuges.[14] During this time, Khan also forged relations with important European suppliers that proved crucial to his later work.

A few months after receiving the letter, Bhutto invited A. Q. Khan to Pakistan, and shortly thereafter, launched a secret gas centrifuge program, code-named Directorate of Industrial Liaison (DIL).[15] Although A. Q. Khan returned to the Netherlands, he later came under scrutiny by Dutch authorities and returned to Pakistan for good in December 1975.[16] At first, A. Q. Khan's centrifuge program was placed under the direction of PAEC and Munir Khan. The two Khans quickly butted heads, however, and A. Q. Khan urged Bhutto to give him autonomy. This was consistent with A. Q. Khan's enormous ego that would come into play repeatedly in the coming decades. Regardless, Bhutto decided to create competition within his nuclear program to help spur more progress. On July 31, 1976, he signed a secret order creating a new enrichment program, code-named Project 706. Khan was given complete control over the new project and reported directly to Bhutto.[17]

This project was daunting, as centrifuges were cutting-edge technology at the time, and Pakistan was hardly an industrialized powerhouse. A. Q. Khan, who was never one to underplay his accomplishments, would later reflect, "The task was gigantic, and there were no visible means to accomplish [it]. Not the slightest sign of any advanced scientific infrastructure was available from where one could kick off."[18] To overcome these obstacles, Khan turned to the European suppliers he had established relationships with during his time at FDO. This process was not without its challenges, as nuclear supplier nations had begun reversing the open export policies of the Atoms for Peace era. This included forming the Nuclear Suppliers Group (NSG) in 1975 to control the export of nuclear technology through the use of a triggers list. This list banned NSG members from selling significant nuclear technology to countries like Pakistan who were not parties to the NPT.

The NSG represented important progress, but it was hardly foolproof, as Khan would soon demonstrate. One ingenious strategy he used to great effect, particularly after Pakistan's centrifuge program was discovered, was purchasing the necessary components of the centrifuge program piecemeal and assembling them in Pakistan. This allowed him to bypass much of the triggers list, which at that time prohibited the sale of entire systems. Khan also benefited from the newness of the gas centrifuge technology, as it was not on the radar of many intelligence agencies. His cause was further aided by Western governments initially doubting that Pakistan could master centrifuge technology. As one former US official explained, "There was an initial reaction that it was great news that Pakistan was shifting its effort from reprocessing to enrichment because they would never succeed at enrichment."[19]

Western countries would quickly realize their error. In fact, before the United States even discovered his activities, Khan had made significant progress. Shortly after Project 706 was greenlit, construction began on a pilot enrichment plant in Sinhala. In late 1976, ground was broken on a full-scale centrifuge plant in the village of Kahuta, twenty miles outside Islamabad.[20] This location was prone to earthquakes but allowed Khan to stay close to the corridors of power in the capital, and Khan was highly attentive to building support for himself throughout the Pakistani elite. A. Q. Khan also found plenty of willing partners among European nuclear suppliers. This procurement program was run by S. A. Butt, a physicist-turned-diplomat operating out of the Pakistani embassy in Belgium.[21] But Khan also made some of the purchases himself during a trip to Europe in the fall of 1976, where he purchased a uranium conversion plant, vacuum tubes, valves, and specialized metal.[22]

THE CAT'S OUT OF THE BAG

Eventually, Khan's purchases attracted Western governments' attention. The centrifuge program appears to have first come on the US radar in early 1978. What initially triggered Western suspicion was a purchase of dozens of high-frequency inverters from the British subsidiary of the US-based Emerson Electrics. These inverters were used to power the centrifuges in a precise manner.[23] In March 1978, the UK approached a US State Department official to discuss the inverters. The British revealed that the Pakistanis first purchased the inverters in 1976 and admitted that there were "reasons at the time to suspect" the inverters would be used in an enrichment plant. The UK had allowed the sale to go through, however, because British laws didn't allow them to stop it. The UK official revealed Pakistan was now trying to buy additional inverters. Although there were still no UK laws available, the British decided to consult with the Americans about trying to block the sale. This appears to be the first time the United States had heard about any Pakistani centrifuges.[24]

This discovery did not produce immediate results, probably because initial US doubts about Pakistan's ability to master centrifuge technology also slowed progress. In fact, despite discovering Khan's activities, the Carter administration resumed aid to Pakistan in August 1978 after the French reprocessing sale fell through. By this time, Pakistan's enrichment program was advancing at a robust pace. A month before the UK launched its inquiry into the inverter sale, scientists at the Sihala pilot plant successfully enriched uranium for the first time.[25] By February 1979, a test-cascade of fifty-four machines was running successfully there.[26] Construction had begun on Kahuta, and this would be completed in early 1981. Much of the supplies Khan needed to enrich had already been secured.

Available documents suggest the United Kingdom was far ahead in understanding the seriousness of the centrifuge problem. By September 1978, a UK intelligence document had mapped out a significant portion of the program.[27] That same month, the administration was assuring Congress that "the technical problems in any centrifuge effort are enormous and we believe we can control this [Pakistan's enrichment program] through nuclear supplier consultations."[28] An October internal memo indicates the administration continued to be more concerned with reprocessing than enrichment, although by November, Washington was taking more forceful measures on the latter.[29] December 1978 was a turning point in the Washington's views on Pakistan's nuclear program. Early that month, the CIA warned that Pakistan's efforts to procure foreign centrifuge technology "have been more extensive and sophisticated than previously indicated." Already, the agency was doubting whether nuclear supplier states were capable of denying Pakistan the technology it needed to complete the Kahuta enrichment plant.[30] That same month, a French embassy official who had visited the Kahuta site over the course of months relayed the rapid pace of the site's expansion.[31] He also provided photos. In January 1979, the CIA concluded Pakistan had "probably" already acquired all the technology it needed to make the Kahuta plant and centrifuges operational, and that foreign suppliers cutting off sales could only "marginally complicate" Pakistan's efforts.[32] That same month, an interagency group warned: "Pakistan is moving rapidly and secretly toward the construction of facilities which could give it nuclear explosive capability within two to four years."[33] Near the end of the month, the State Department had its ambassador in Islamabad, Arthur Hummel, raise the issue with Pakistani President Muhammad Zia-ul-Haq, who had seized power from Bhutto in a coup. Zia dismissed the accusations as "outright lies."[34] By March, he was no longer denying these allegations.[35]

Many of the major accounts of Pakistan's nuclear program, especially the ones that came out after A. Q. Khan's foreign proliferation networks were exposed, argue that the United States failed to stop Pakistan from acquiring the bomb because it lacked the will. According to this view, once the Soviet Union invaded Afghanistan on Christmas Day 1979, the Carter and Reagan administrations turned a blind eye toward Pakistan's nuclear program to maintain Islamabad's cooperation in supporting the Afghan resistance. There is some truth to this argument. The day after the Soviet invasion, National Security Advisor Zbigniew Brzezinski wrote a long memo to President Carter outlining how the United States could turn Afghanistan into Moscow's

Vietnam. This strategy, Brzezinski noted, "will require a review of our policy toward Pakistan, more guarantees to it, more arms aid, and, alas, a decision that our security policy toward Pakistan cannot be dictated by our nonproliferation policy."[36] By January 2, 1980, Carter waived the sanctions that were imposed on Pakistan in early 1979 in response to Islamabad's enrichment program and Zia executing Bhutto. The Carter administration then offered Zia a two-year, $400 million aid package, but Zia rejected this as "peanuts."

Nonetheless, it is hardly the case that the United States could have stopped Pakistan's nuclear program, even if the Soviet Union hadn't invaded Afghanistan. For starters, Pakistan's nuclear program continued to be a concern during the 1980s. At the very least, the Carter and Reagan administrations tried to restrain the nuclear program enough to prevent Congress from cutting off aid to Pakistan.[37] As William Piekney, the CIA's station chief in Islamabad from 1984 to 1986, puts it, "I don't believe the Pakistanis ever got a pass on the nuclear program." As station chief, Piekney viewed arming the Afghan insurgents and collecting intelligence on Pakistan's nuclear program "as my chief responsibilities and I gave them equal attention." Still, Piekney admits that he knew that collecting intelligence on the nuclear program could not be allowed to undermine cooperation on Afghanistan.[38] What was true for Piekney was even more true for policymakers. Because of a number of laws passed by Congress, the executive branch could not continue to aid Pakistan unless it restrained its nuclear program to some degree. This was a constant challenge for both Carter and Reagan.

There is a bigger problem with the argument that America's preoccupation with Afghanistan allowed Pakistan to build the bomb. Namely, it ignores the critical period between when the US began to take Pakistan's enrichment program seriously in December 1978, and when the Soviets invaded Afghanistan a year later. During this time, the Carter administration was highly motivated to stop Pakistan's nuclear activities—but had little hope it could do so. In fact, many officials were already advocating that the United States should adopt some of the same, more limited objectives—such as preventing a Pakistani nuclear test—that Washington ultimately pursued in the 1980s.

Once it realized how far along Pakistan's enrichment program really was, the administration pursued a number of options. One of the first was pushing nuclear supplier countries to stop sensitive exports to Pakistan. President Carter personally wrote letters to the heads of state in Canada, England, France, and West Germany in April 1979, and between 1978 and 1981, lower-level officials sent three hundred demarches to foreign countries, warning them against sensitive nuclear exports to Pakistan.[39] As officials understood when discussing this option, these efforts could, at best, slow Pakistan's nuclear progress.[40] Even that was greatly complicated because many Western allies were more interested in profits than nonproliferation. One FRG official would confess that US warnings about nuclear sales to Pakistan "usually land in my wastepaper basket."[41]

The Carter administration simultaneously approached Pakistan to persuade it to abandon its enrichment program. As was the case with the reprocessing plant, Islamabad categorically refused. This didn't surprise US officials; Deputy Secretary of State Warren Christopher stated in one meeting "We certainly won't be able to stop their desire" to acquire nuclear weapons.[42] After Zia stopped even denying Pakistan was building an enrichment plant,[43] the Carter administration invoked the Symington Amendment in April 1979, reimposing sanctions on Pakistan. Before then, an interagency group decided to pursue a joint arms control approach toward India and Pakistan, but Delhi immediately rebuffed these efforts. This again wasn't a surprise. In discussing this approach, one official noted, "We probably all agree that this approach will fail but want to go ahead with it anyway." No one disputed this.[44] Offers to significantly raise economic and military assistance to Pakistan proved no more effective.[45]

In June 1979, Brzezinski warned the administration was at an "impasse."[46] In response, a new task force was established to consider the issue. Led by Gerard Smith, Carter's special envoy for nonproliferation and a hardliner on preventing the spread of nuclear weapons, the task force repeated earlier recommendations of offering larger arms sales or threatening more severe sanctions. It also proposed a third, more controversial option: military strikes on the Kahuta plant.[47] Secretary of State Cyrus Vance had actually previously asked Joseph Nye to write a private memorandum weighing the pros and cons of attacking Kahuta, but Nye had concluded that there were "too many unknowns and too many moving parts" to be a viable option.[48] In any case, the administration quickly dropped this option once the *New York Times* reported it was under consideration, provoking strong objections from Pakistan.

Pessimism quickly grew within the Carter administration. As already noted, in March 1979, the general consensus was US efforts could, at best, slow down a Pakistani program. By summer, Ambassador Hummel was telling colleagues that a Pakistani bomb was inevitable.[49] In September, Charles Van Doren, the assistant director of the Arms Control and Disarmament Agency, warned "this is a railroad train that is going down the track very fast, and I am not sure anything will turn it off."[50] Most revealing is a June 1979 memo by Secretary of State Vance, which began by arguing "the South Asian nuclear clock cannot be turned back." In light of this "unfortunate reality," Vance recommended pursuing the more limited objective of persuading India and Pakistan not to weaponize their nuclear capabilities. Vance wasn't even calling for a nuclear freeze; he admitted that "we may have to allow [Pakistan] to complete its enrichment program" to achieve parity with India.[51] Vance's position was by no means universally accepted at the time. Gerard

Smith, in particular, continued to push for a harder line.[52] Nonetheless, the Carter administration gradually resigned itself to the "unfortunate reality" Vance outlined in July.

In intense discussions in Washington over two days in October 1979, the United States asked for assurances that "Pakistan would not develop or explode any nuclear explosive device" or transfer any fissile material or technology to reprocess or enrich third countries. The Pakistani delegation was led by Foreign Minister Agha Shahi, who agreed to not sell or export any material or sensitive equipment. Confusingly, Shahi promised Pakistan wouldn't develop a nuclear explosive device but refused to rule out conducting a nuclear test. Instead, he said Pakistan "was not near the stage" where it could conduct a test and a future Pakistani government would have to decide whether to test once it acquired that capability. Puzzled, Secretary Vance noted that Shahi seemed to be saying that Pakistan would continue to develop a nuclear explosion capability, although he didn't explicitly point out this contradicted Shahi's earlier pledge. Shahi disputed that and simply stated, "The goal of Pakistan's nuclear program remains to be determined." Whether Pakistan would develop that capability is an "open question."[53] As we will see, the Reagan administration actually secured slightly more extensive pledges from Pakistan once it resumed assistance to Islamabad.

Thus, even before the Soviet invasion of Afghanistan, the Carter administration doubted that it could stop Pakistan's nuclear program, and many officials were already pushing for some of the same compromises Washington would make in the 1980s. As Deputy Secretary of State Christopher summed it up in the fall of 1979, "No set of incentives or disincentives (certainly nothing that it would be feasible for us to undertake) would be likely to cause Pakistan to dismantle, cut back or freeze construction of its sensitive facilities or to make a no-test pledge." Notably, the major European states—such as the UK, France, West Germany, and the Netherlands—had a similar viewpoint.[54] Even with years of hindsight, most US officials interviewed for this book agreed that Washington was not in a position to stop Pakistan's nuclear program before the Soviet invasion of Afghanistan. As Gary Samore, who worked on the Pakistan nuclear file from the Reagan administration through the Clinton presidency, puts it: "At the end of the day, Pakistan was going to produce nuclear weapons and there was nothing the US could do to stop it."[55]

ENTER REAGAN

Ronald Reagan came into office determined to increase pressure on the Soviet Union on many fronts, from risky military exercises in Soviet waters and airspace, to challenging the evil empire's ideology and legitimacy. In this effort, the new president found an eager partner in William Casey, his CIA director. Casey served in the CIA's predecessor agency during World War II before becoming a prominent lawyer and lifelong Republican operative. During the Nixon administration, he held a number of economic and diplomatic posts but had limited experience in intelligence. After advising Reagan's campaign, including helping mend fences between the candidate and his competitor turned running mate, George H. W. Bush, Casey angled for the secretary of state or defense positions. Instead, Reagan offered him the CIA. Casey was reluctant to accept the offer at first. Once he did, he dedicated himself to reviving the spy agency, which had been damaged by a number of scandals. Casey was especially enamored with reinvigorating the CIA's ability to conduct covert operations. Pakistan and Afghanistan were the perfect proving ground.[56]

Like the Carter administration, President Reagan believed it was necessary to improve the broader bilateral relationship to secure Islamabad's cooperation on Afghanistan. Early in the administration, the two countries agreed on an aid package of $3.2 billion (roughly $10.4 billion in 2022 dollars) over six years that would be split evenly between military and economic assistance. Much of the military assistance was used to purchase forty F-16 fighter jets.[57] The one obstacle the Reagan administration faced was securing congressional support. In the 1960s and 1970s, Congress passed two laws— the Symington and Glenn Amendments—that required the United States to cut off aid to countries pursuing unsafeguarded sensitive nuclear technology, such as enrichment facilities and reprocessing plants. The Reagan administration tried to get around this by arguing that arms sales would help restrain Pakistan's nuclear program. In a 1981 report to Congress, President Reagan wrote that "help from the United States in strengthening Pakistan's conventional military capabilities would offer the best available means for counteracting possible motivations toward acquiring nuclear weapons."[58] It's easy to dismiss this as merely a convenient justification for arming Pakistan, which to a large degree it was. But it wasn't entirely insincere. The administration made the same arguments in internal discussions. Moreover, the Reagan administration made strengthening the conventional military capabilities of allies a central plank of its broader nonproliferation policy. In one major strategy document, the Reagan administration argued "the threat of proliferation ... is largely (but not wholly) a product of political insecurity" and therefore "a basic component of a non-proliferation strategy, the most important one in the long term, must be to alleviate perceptions of insecurity."[59] In the end, Congress agreed to waive the Symington and Glenn Amendments for six years and approved the aid package to Pakistan.

PAKISTAN RACES TO THE BOMB

Whatever the Reagan administration's intentions, the bulk of Pakistan's nuclear progress took place on its watch. A few months after Reagan took office, Islamabad's main enrichment plant became operational. Amazed by the progress, President Zia renamed the Khatua complex Khan Research Laboratories (KRL) in honor of A. Q. Khan.[60] Massive earthquakes and faulty equipment temporarily slowed A. Q. Khan down, but he soon fixed these issues. Accounts differ as to when Pakistan acquired enough highly enriched uranium (HEU) for a nuclear bomb. Some sources put this as early as 1983, although this might be the first time Kahuta produced any HEU, as A. Q. Khan himself has claimed.[61] Most likely, Pakistan had produced enough HEU for a nuclear weapon in late 1984 or 1985.[62]

The other necessary component was building a nuclear bomb design. This effort began before Khan returned to Pakistan. In March 1974, PAEC established the Directorate of Technical Development (DTD), which coordinated the various aspects of Pakistan's bomb design and testing, and the Wah Group, which would do much of the work in designing the bomb.[63] Commensurate with his oversized ego, A. Q. Khan also tried to assert himself in the bomb design effort, although it's possible he was egged on by Zia.[64] As with the centrifuge program, A. Q. Khan ultimately turned to foreign sources to expedite the process. In this case, he was able to obtain China's CHIC-4 weapon design along with fifty kilograms of HEU from Beijing in 1981. In return, he probably provided China with modern centrifuge designs. This trade was a harbinger of things to come.[65] The search for a testing site had begun in the summer of 1974, when Z. A. Bhutto directed PAEC to find a suitable underground location, which wouldn't violate Pakistan's commitment to the Partial Test Ban Treaty. PAEC quickly selected a mountain in the Chagai Division of Balochistan. The Inspectorate General of Special Development Works (SDW), a subsidiary of PAEC, was created at this time to prepare the testing sites. The SDW, led by Brigadier Muhammad Sarfraz, began creating tunnels in the mountains in 1978. By 1980, the test sites were ready.[66]

The first cold test—a detonation of a nuclear design with natural uranium in its core so no actual fission takes place—was conducted on March 11, 1983. From 1983 to 1995, PAEC carried out twenty-four cold tests.[67] In September 1985, US intelligence suggested that Pakistan "probably" had a workable nuclear device.[68] Thus, near the end of the 1980s at the latest, and likely sooner, Pakistan was capable of conducting a nuclear test. Being capable of testing a nuclear device does not mean a country has a deliverable weapon, which is far more challenging. Pakistan chose the F-16s the Reagan administration had sold it as its first nuclear delivery system, even though

Pakistan had pledged not to arm the planes with nuclear weapons as a condition of the sale. According to some sources, Islamabad struggled to build a bomb that would fit inside the aircraft. For instance, Feroz Khan claims that PAEC and the Pakistani Air Force didn't successfully conduct an aerial cold test until May 1995.[69] Other sources suggest this took place earlier, possibly around 1990.[70]

Like other nuclear powers, Pakistan ultimately saw missiles as the best delivery vehicle. Pakistan first tested the Hatf-1 and Hatf-2 missiles—which were developed by PAEC perhaps using Chinese designs—in February 1989, although it probably didn't have a small enough nuclear warhead to mate with these missiles.[71] These missiles were both rather primitive. A year or so later, China began selling Pakistan more advanced M-11 missiles, which Islamabad christened Hatf-III/Ghaznavi. US pressure led Beijing to stop selling this missile to Pakistan, but China compensated by building Islamabad a factory to produce the missiles domestically.[72] China's missile sales were mostly with PAEC, which naturally didn't sit well with A. Q. Khan. As described in more detail in the next chapter, Khan would turn to North Korea for his own missiles.

DELICATE DANCE

The Reagan administration tried desperately to place strict limits on Pakistan's nuclear program; it had only limited success. As the two sides were finalizing the initial aid package in September 1981, Under Secretary of State James Buckley traveled to Pakistan to meet with President Zia. During those talks, Zia pledged that Pakistan would not manufacture nuclear weapons, transfer sensitive nuclear technology, or embarrass the Reagan administration with Pakistan's nuclear program. Washington took the last point to mean that Pakistan would not test a nuclear weapon.[73] By July 1982, Reagan was sending a personal emissary, Vernon Walters, to meet with Zia to show the Pakistani leader "incontrovertible" intelligence that Islamabad was not upholding these promises.[74] This intelligence was based at least in part on Pakistani agents trying to purchase materials for a nuclear bomb in Europe. Zia called these charges a "total fabrication," while reiterating his previous commitments.[75] Washington was not buying it. Only a few months later, Walters was sent back to Pakistan to confront Zia. This time, Zia promised not to develop nuclear weapons, a slightly more expansive pledge than his earlier one to not manufacture a device. But just a month later, Secretary of State George Shultz informed President Reagan that "there is overwhelming evidence that Zia has been breaking his assurances to us."[76] This pattern continued through the end of the 1980s. Pakistan would make various promises to the Reagan administration, and US intelligence would quickly find Islamabad was breaking them. For instance, in July 1984, Zia promised Pakistan would not enrich uranium beyond 5 percent, but the United States quickly determined Islamabad was exceeding this level.[77] The Reagan administration repeatedly threatened to cut off aid if Pakistan violated its pledges, but when the red lines were crossed, Washington backed down.

Still, Islamabad made matters difficult for the Reagan administration, especially in the latter's dealings with Congress. While Pakistan had long been buying nuclear technology from European countries, it began shopping in the United States. In June 1984, a Pakistani agent was arrested in Houston for trying to illegally export triggering devices for a nuclear bomb. The triggering devices, known as krytrons, have no known uses besides nuclear weapons. Moreover, at the time of his arrest, the agent had letters on him addressed to S. A. Butt, the former diplomat who ran Pakistan's foreign procurement operations.[78] This incident led Congress to pass the Solarz Amendment in 1985, which mandated all assistance be cut off to countries found to be trying to illegally export nuclear technology from the United States. At the same time, the legislative branch approved what became known as the Pressler Amendment. This legislation—which Pakistan had a role in writing—forced the president to annually certify that Pakistan did not possess a nuclear weapon as a condition of continuing aid.[79] None of this deterred the Pakistanis, however. Just two years after the Solarz Amendment passed, another Pakistani agent, Arshad Pervez, was arrested in the United States for trying to purchase maraging steel for centrifuges. The Pervez case could not have come at a worse time for the administration. Just a few months after his arrest, the six-year waiver of the Symington Amendment Congress had approved in 1981 was set to expire. In order to continue providing assistance to Pakistan, the Reagan administration needed Congress to agree to another waiver. Pervez's arrest made this exceedingly difficult. After intense lobbying from the administration—and after aid briefly lapsed—Congress approved a new two-and-a-half-year waiver at the end of 1987.

This provided a brief respite, but changing circumstances would upend the entire arrangement. The first major change was that the last Soviet soldier left Afghanistan in February 1989. This reduced America's interest in looking the other way on Pakistan's nuclear program. More importantly, however, was Islamabad's technical progress on the nuclear program. This is what ultimately made it impossible for George H. W. Bush to certify that Pakistan did not possess a nuclear warhead in October 1990. The Pressler Amendment required the president to certify to Congress before October 1 each year that "Pakistan does not possess a nuclear explosive" and that US assistance would significantly reduce the risk of it obtaining one. In the years leading up to the non-certification, Pakistan's technical progress made it increasingly difficult to make this certification. Inside the Reagan and then Bush administrations, there were intense debates about what constituted possession of a nuclear device. As one participant in these debates recalls, in 1989 it was "very, very hard" to make the case that Pakistan didn't have a nuclear device.[80] What finally caused a tipping point is that, as described in greater detail in the next chapter, Pakistan assembled nuclear devices during a border confrontation with India in the spring of 1990.

The Bush administration went to great lengths to warn Pakistan that it would not be able to certify Islamabad didn't have a nuclear device without a rollback of its program. As early as May 1990, Deputy National Security Advisor Robert Gates was dispatched to Islamabad to inform Pakistani leaders of this determination.[81] In September, President Bush wrote a letter to President Ghulam Ishaq Khan, warning him that "I must in all honesty advise you that under present circumstances, it is not possible for me to certify Pakistan's compliance" with the Pressler Amendment. This determination was made, Bush wrote, based on new information indicating "the status of your nuclear program has changed." President Bush also stated "I cannot overemphasize the seriousness of this situation or the urgency of efforts needed to address this problem," and warned "we are approaching a crisis in our relationship."[82] Around the same time, Secretary of State James Baker invited Pakistani Foreign Minister Sahabzada Yaqub Khan to Washington to discuss the issue. Khan did not deny that Islamabad had assembled a nuclear device, instead stressing that Pakistan had been "desperate." Before cutting off assistance, the Bush administration sent the top South Asian official at the State Department, Teresita Schaffer, to Capitol Hill to ask for a six-month waiver. Schaffer made the case that maintaining the aid might give Washington enough leverage to convince Pakistan to roll back its nuclear program. As she herself would admit, "it wasn't a convincing argument."[83] In fact, the administration didn't send Secretary of State Baker because they knew the lobbying wouldn't succeed. Not surprisingly, Congress refused to provide a waiver and the administration cut off assistance in October 1990.

CONCLUSION

This chapter traced Pakistan's nuclear program from its start through the time when the United States was unable to certify it no longer possessed the bomb. The United States was successful in blocking Pakistan's efforts to use foreign technology to acquire plutonium for the bomb. Washington proved far less effective at stopping A. Q. Khan's enrichment program, which was successful, in large part, by the ingenious procurement methods that stayed ahead of foreign export controls. Although the Soviet Union's invasion of Afghanistan made Islamabad's nuclear program a lower priority for US policymakers, it's difficult to imagine America being able to prevent a Pakistani bomb had the Soviet occupation not occurred.

Even before the Soviet invasion, US policymakers began lowering their objectives to limiting Pakistan's nuclear program. In this endeavor, they likely took inspiration from the Israeli nuclear program. That is, Washington wanted to keep Pakistan's bomb in the basement. By this measure, the United States succeeded until India conducted overt nuclear tests in 1998. One consequence of the Soviet invasion of Afghanistan was that US-Pakistani relations were relatively strong throughout the 1980s. Although there were still strong tensions over Islamabad's nuclear program, as well as aid levels, the two sides cooperated extensively in their proxy war in Afghanistan. These good relations ended when President Bush refused to certify that Pakistan didn't have a nuclear weapon, immediately triggering a cutoff of assistance. Despite the ample warning it had received from the Bush administration, Pakistan reacted with indignation when President Bush failed to make the certification. The decision put relations in a deep freeze that remained until after the 9/11 terrorist attacks on New York and Washington—and in some ways, to this very day. Long before then, however, there were numerous Indo-Pakistani crises that Washington intervened in to prevent a nuclear conflagration. Those crises are the subject of the following chapter.

NOTES

1. Jeffrey Goldberg and Marc Ambinder, "The Ally From Hell," *Atlantic* (December 2011).
2. O. B. Toon, "Atmospheric Effects and Societal Consequences of Regional Scale Nuclear Conflicts and Acts of Individual Nuclear Terrorism," *Atmospheric Chemistry and Physics* 7 (2007).
3. CADNU-type reactors use natural uranium as fuel. Feroz Khan, *Eating Grass: The Making of the Pakistani Bomb* (Stanford, CA: Stanford University Press), 54–55.
4. Khan, *Eating Grass*, 105.
5. Teresita Schaffer, interview by phone with author Zachary Keck, April 18, 2016.
6. Khan, *Eating Grass*, 130.
7. Schaffer, interview.
8. "War and Peace in the Nuclear Age; Visions of War and Peace; Interview with Joseph Nye, 1987," *WGBH*, May 28, 1987.
9. "War and Peace in the Nuclear Age"; and Robert Gallucci, interview by phone with author Zachary Keck, Washington, DC, April 20, 2016.
10. Some have also said that America's growing assistance to France's nuclear program also made it easier to convince Paris to abandon the sales. See Richard H. Ullman, "The Covert French Connection," *Foreign Policy*. 75 (Summer 1989), 19.

11. "Memorandum of Conversation," May 18, 1976, *FRUS*, 1969–1976, vol. E-15, part 2, doc. 339. Also see "Memorandum of Conversation," May 7, 1977, *FRUS*, 1977–1980, vol. XXVI, doc. 342.

12. Author correspondence with former Carter administration official.

13. URENCO was a joint Dutch-British-German company founded in 1971 to break America's monopoly over commercial gas centrifuge technology.

14. David Albright, *Peddling Peril: How the Secret Nuclear Trade Arms America's Enemies* (New York: Free Press, 2010), 15–19.

15. *Nuclear Black Markets: Pakistan, A.Q. Khan and the Rise of Proliferation Networks: A Net Assessment* (London: International Institute for Strategic Studies, 2007), 19.

16. Albright, *Peddling Peril*, 28.

17. Douglas Frantz and Catherine Collins, *The Nuclear Jihadist: The True Story of the Man Who Sold the World's Most Dangerous Secrets . . . And How We Could Have Stopped Him* (New York: Twelve, 2007), 76.

18. Quoted in Frantz and Collins, *Nuclear Jihadist*, 70.

19. Robert Gallucci, interview with author Zachary Keck, Washington, DC, April 20, 2016.

20. Frantz and Collins, *Nuclear Jihadist*, 68–71.

21. Carey Sublette, "Pakistan's Nuclear Weapons Program: The Beginning," *Nuclear Weapon Archive*, January 2, 2002, http://nuclearweaponarchive.org/Pakistan/PakOrigin.html.

22. Gordon Corera, *Shopping for Bombs: Nuclear Proliferation, Global Insecurity, and the Rise and Fall of the A.Q. Khan Network* (Oxford: Oxford University Press, 2006), 23; and Frantz and Collins, *Nuclear Jihadist*, 76.

23. Adrian Levy and Catherine Scott-Clark, *Deception: Pakistan, the United States, and the Secret Trade in Nuclear Weapons* (New York: Bloomsbury, 2010), 54.

24. "Allen Locke to Joseph Nye: UK Inquiry on Exports of Inverters to Pakistan," March 28, 1978, *NSA*. Locke says in his memo "we have no information that the Pakistanis are doing any work with centrifuge enrichment." The UK and US both weren't sure if the trigger list would be able to block this sale. The reason many of these items were not on export restrictions lists was that Western governments believed doing so would reveal secrets to potential proliferators. When they first began exploring the issue of centrifuges in the late 1950s and 1960s, they worried that export lists would provide a shopping list for countries seeking nuclear weapons. Instead, a "gentleman's agreement" was reached among Western governments to classify centrifuge R&D and its components in the hopes of forestalling the diffusion of this revolutionary technology. William Burr, "The Gas Centrifuge Secret: Origins of a U.S. Policy of Nuclear Denial, 1954–1960," *National Security Archive*, Electronic Briefing Book no. 518, June 29, 2015. The author thanks Thomas W. Graham for pointing this out.

25. Khan, *Eating Grass*, 154; Levy and Scott-Clark, *Deception*. 54. Elsewhere Khan has claimed that this happened on April 4, 1978. See Levy and Scott-Clark, *Deception*, 51.

26. Khan, *Eating Grass*, 156.

27. UK Defense Intelligence Staff Report, "Pakistan: Nuclear Weapons Intentions," September 29, 1978, *NSA*.

28. Khan, *Eating Grass*, 156.

29. "Christopher Memo to Carter," October 3, 1978, U.S. Declassified Documents Online, CK2349503863; and "DOS to Embassies in France and the United Kingdom," November 1, 1978, *FRUS*, 1977–1980, vol. XIX, doc. 310.

30. "Report Prepared in the Central Intelligence Agency," December 5, 1978, *FRUS*, 1977–1980, vol. XIX, doc. 316.

31. "Embassy in France to Secretary of State: Discussion with French Official on Nuclear Matters," December 19, 1978, *DNSA*.

32. "Report Prepared in the Central Intelligence Agency," January 18, 1979, *FRUS*, 1977–1980, vol. XIX, doc. 319.

33. "Harold Saunders and Mr. Pickering through Mrs. Benson to Mr. Newsom, 'Mini-PRC Meeting on the Pakistan Nuclear Program,'" January 20, 1979, *NSA*.

34. "DOS to Embassy in Pakistan," January 16, 1979, *FRUS*, 1977–1980, vol. XIX, doc. 318; and "Memo Prepared in the White House Situation Room," January 25, 1979, *FRUS*, 1977–1980, vol. XIX, doc. 322.

35. "Embassy in Pakistan to DOS," March 2, 1978, *FRUS*, 1977–1980, vol. XIX, doc. 325.

36. "Brzezinski to Carter, 'Reflections on Soviet Intervention in Afghanistan,'" December 26, 1979, *NSA*.

37. A number of Congressional statues prevented aid to countries that violated various nonproliferation rules.

38. William Piekney, interview with author Zachary Keck, Vienna, VA, April 18, 2016.

39. "Kreisberg to Newsom, 'Presidential Letter on Pakistan Nuclear Program to Western Leaders,'" March 30, 1979, *NSA*; and "Richard L. Williamson. 'Report on Diplomatic Actions Taken Concerning Foreign, Nuclear-Related Supplies to Pakistan,'" August 14, 1981, *NSA*.

40. "Minutes of a Policy Review Committee Meeting," March 9, 1979, *FRUS*, 1977–1989, vol. XIX, doc. 327. At the meeting, one official asks, "Does anybody really think we are going to stop the Pakistanis through this?" No one does. One State Department official suggests blocking foreign exports could double the time to when Pakistan gets a bomb to six to ten years. However, the Department of Energy representative suggests it won't even take three to five years for Pakistan to succeed.

41. Corera, *Shopping for Bombs*, 37.

42. "Minutes of a Policy Review Committee Meeting," March 9, 1979, *FRUS*, 1977–1989, vol. XIX, doc. 327. Also see the doubts in "Policy Review Committee Meeting," March 28, 1979, *FRUS*, 1977–1989, vol. XIX, doc. 333.

43. He returned to denying it by April. See "Embassy in Pakistan to DOS," April 10, 1979, *FRUS*, 1977–1980, vol. XIX, doc. 337.

44. "Policy Review Committee Meeting," March 28, 1979, *FRUS*, 1977–1989, vol. XIX, doc. 333.

45. "Anthony Lake et al. memo to Warren Christopher, 'Interagency Working Group Paper, South Asian Nuclear and Security Problems, Analysis of Possible

Elements in a U.S. Strategy,'" March 23, 1979, *NSA*; and "Embassy in India to DOS, India and the Pakistan Nuclear Program," June 7, 1979, *NSA*.

46. "Brzezinski to the Secretary of State, 'The South Asian Nuclear Problem,'" June 19, 1979, *NSA*.

47. Richard Burt, "U.S. Will Press Pakistan to Halt A-Arms Project," *New York Times*, August 12, 1979.

48. Quoted in Corera, *Shopping for Bombs*, 28. See also, Frantz and Collins, *Nuclear Jihadist*, 88.

49. Burt, "U.S. Will Press Pakistan to Halt A-Arms Project."

50. "Memcon, DOS General Advisory Committee on Arms Control and Disarmament," September 14, 1979 (morning session), *NSA*, http://nsarchive.gwu.edu/nukevault /ebb333/doc42.pdf.

51. "DOS to Embassy in India, Cable 145139," June 06, 1979, *WCDA*, https://digitalarchive.wilsoncenter.org/document/114198.pdf?v=33f09c486cf6dd1eddac462f381e6c6b.

52. In an October meeting with the Pakistani Foreign Minister Agha Shahi, Smith warned that Pakistan was "entering the valley of death" because India "can utterly destroy [them]." Dennis Kux, *Disenchanted Allies: The United States and Pakistan 1947–2000* (Washington, DC: Woodrow Wilson Center Press, 2001), 240–41.

53. "DOS to Embassy in Pakistan," October 20, 1979, *FRUS*, 1977–1980, vol. XIX, doc. 368. Earlier, Zia had already made a no test assurance, but walked it back in a letter to Carter. "DOS to Embassy in Pakistan," July 28, 1979, ibid., doc. 353; and "DOS to Embassy in Pakistan," September 4, 1979, ibid., doc. 360. Shahi had made essentially the same argument about testing the previous month in discussions with Secretary Vance. "DOS to Embassy in Pakistan," September 28, 1979, ibid., doc. 364.

54. "Christopher Memo to Thornton," September 25, 1979, ibid., doc. 362; and "Vance Memo to Carter," November 17, 1979, ibid., doc. 372.

55. Gary Samore, interview with author Zachary Keck, Cambridge, MA, May 9, 2016.

56. Bob Woodward, *Veil: The Secret Wars of the CIA 1981–1987* (New York: Simon & Schuster, 1987); and Steve Coll, *Ghost Wars: The Secret History of the CIA, Afghanistan, and Bin Laden, from the Soviet Invasion to September 10, 2001* (New York: Penguin Books, 2004).

57. Eleanor Clift, "Reagan Warns Pakistani: Build Nuclear Bomb and Lose U.S. Aid," *Los Angeles Times*, July 17, 1986.

58. James L. Buckley, "Why the U.S. Must Strengthen Pakistan," *New York Times*, August 5, 1981; and a statement by Deputy Assistant Secretary of State Jane Coon, quoted in Kux, *Disenchanted Alllies*, 260.

59. President of the United States, U.S. Arms Control and Disarmament Agency 1981 Annual Report (Washington, DC: Government Publishing Office, 1981). http://babel.hathitrust.org/cgi /pt?id=umn.31951p00679082u;view=1up;seq=47.

60. Khan, *Eating Grass*, 156; and Corera, *Shopping for Bombs*, 41.

61. Albright, *Peddling Peril*, 50; and Steven Aftergood, "A.Q. Khan Discusses Pakistan's Nuclear Program," *FAS Secrecy News*, September 8, 2009.

62. Albright, *Peddling Peril*, 50–51; Levy and Scott-Clark, *Deception*, 112; Franz and Collins, *Nuclear Jihadist*, 132; and Khan, *Eating Grass*, 159.

63. Khan, *Eating Grass*, 174–81.

64. Corera, *Shopping for Bombs*, 44; and Khan, *Eating Grass*, 187.

65. Khan, *Eating Grass*, 188; and Jeffrey T. Richelson, *Spying on the Bomb: American Nuclear Intelligence from Nazi Germany to Iran and North Korea* (New York: Norton, 2006), 342.

66. Khan, *Eating Grass*, 182.

67. Khan, *Eating Grass*, 185. The KRL, which briefly worked on a second bomb design based off of the CHIC-1 Chinese design that Beijing gave to Pakistan, also conducted its own cold tests.

68. *The Dynamics of Nuclear Proliferation: Balance of Power and Constraints*, National Intelligence Council, September 1985.

69. Khan, *Eating Grass*, 187.

70. Hersh, "On the Edge."

71. George Perkovich, *India's Nuclear Bomb: The Impact on Global Proliferation* (Berkeley: University of California Press, 1999), 300; and Levy and Scott-Clark, *Deception*, 198.

72. Levy and Scott-Clark, *Deception*, 257–58; and Khan, *Eating Grass*, 238–40.

73. "Shultz Memo to Reagan, 'How Do We Make Use of the Zia Visit,'" November 26, 1982, *NSA*, https://s3.documentcloud.org/documents/347090/doc-16-11-26-82.pdf; and "to Protect Our Strategic Interests in the Face of Pakistan's Nuclear Weapons Activities,'" November 26, 1982, *WCDA*. Obtained and contributed by William Burr and included in NPIHP Research Update no. 6; and "Ambassador Walters Memo to DOS, Cable 10239," July 05, 1982, *WCDA*, https://digitalarchive.wilsoncenter.org/document/114252.pdf?v=eebc65414611d33a0545aa5ea4db6800.

74. Ibid.

75. "Zia Letter to Reagan, Re Assurance of Their Commitment to a Peaceful Nuclear Program," July 5, 1982, CIA Public Reading Room [CREST].

76. "Shultz Memo to Reagan," November 26, 1982, *NSA*.

77. "Kanter and Murphy Memo to Armacost, Pakistan Nuclear Issue for the NSC," August 24, 1984, *NSA*, https://nsarchive2.gwu.edu/nukevault/ebb531-U.S.-Pakistan-Nuclear-Relations,-1984-1985/; and "Adelman Memo to Assistant to the President for National Security Affairs, 'Pakistan's Nuclear Weapons Programs and US Security Assistance,'" June 16, 1986, *WCDA*, https://digitalarchive.wilsoncenter.org/document/114316.

78. Seymour Hersh, "Pakistani in U.S. Sought to Ship A-Bomb Trigger," *New York Times*, February 25, 1985.

79. Pakistan's role in developing the Pressler Amendment comes from, Teresita Schaffer, interview with author Zachary Keck, Washington, DC, July 24, 2018.

80. Gary Samore, interview by phone with author Zachary Keck, July 13, 2018. Also, Teresita Schaffer, interview with author Zachary Keck, Washington, DC, July 24, 2018.

81. Kux, *Disenchanted Allies*, 307.

82. "Telegram from Department of State to Embassy in Islamabad, DEPTEL, 317456, Presidential Letter on Nuclear Certification," September 19, 1990, U.S. Declassified Documents Online, CK2349675698.

83. Schaffer, interview.

Chapter 10

Pandora's Box (Pakistan, 1990–Present)

Many of the concerns US officials had about Pakistan acquiring nuclear weapons came to pass. From an early date, Washington worried that Pakistan would proliferate nuclear technology to unstable, hostile countries. Indeed, Islamabad would go on to substantially aid the nuclear programs of America's greatest adversaries—from North Korea to Iran to Libya. There were also arguments—tinged, no doubt, with racism—that a Pakistani nuclear arsenal would be a "Muslim" bomb. These were mostly miscast. Nonetheless, the United States has spent considerable resources trying to prevent radical Islamist terrorists from acquiring nuclear weapons. Pakistan is the main concern in this regard. As Graham Allison, a Harvard professor who wrote a book on nuclear terrorism, put it, "When you map W.M.D. and terrorism, all roads intersect in Pakistan."[1]

Just as it did in the 1980s, Islamabad's nuclear program also complicated America's ability to operate in Afghanistan following 9/11. For starters, a crisis with India shortly after 9/11 helped al-Qaeda's top leadership to escape into the border regions in Pakistan. Furthermore, on the eve of the invasion of Afghanistan, members of George W. Bush's war cabinet, as well as the president himself, worried that the war in Afghanistan would spill over into Pakistan. Internally, the Bush administration referred to it as the "nightmare scenario," and it would also haunt the Obama administration.[2] Pakistan's nuclear arsenal also made the Bush administration wary of pressuring the government too much to crack down on the terrorist groups located in Pakistan.[3]

When Pakistan was pursuing nuclear weapons, US policymakers also worried about a destabilizing nuclear arms race on the subcontinent. This, too, has come to pass. Pakistan's nuclear arsenal has reportedly grown at a rapid clip. It has also built tactical nuclear weapons, which require the delegation of launch authority to commanders in the field. This has raised further concerns about whether Pakistan's nuclear arsenal is vulnerable to being stolen or used by terrorist groups or rogue commanders.

But perhaps the biggest concern US policymakers had was that nuclear weapons would make Indo-Pakistani tensions more dangerous. The nuclearization of the subcontinent has had a paradoxical effect on the rivalry between India and Pakistan. On the one hand, it has made the two countries far less likely to engage in a full-scale war. On the other hand, the presence of nuclear weapons has drastically increased the stakes of every crisis between Delhi and Islamabad. And, the protection of the nuclear shadow emboldened Pakistan to be more aggressive in supporting terrorist attacks inside India. The result is that the United States has been forced to take a more active role in mediating crises. America was hardly disinterested in prior Indo-Pakistani wars and crises. Still, starting in 1990, Washington was forced to treat every crisis as a major national security threat. During the border crisis in 1990, for instance, Washington sent its first high-level emissary to defuse tensions. This would become a regular feature of major Indo-Pakistani crises.[4] This points to a larger issue. Proliferation optimists argue that allies and partners acquiring nuclear weapons will reduce America's overseas commitments. This was not true of any case studies in the book. In fact, especially in the Pakistani case, the acquisition of nuclear weapons made the nuclear ally of far greater interest to Washington. This chapter is based, in part, on interviews with roughly twenty-five former US officials who worked on Pakistan for every administration from Gerald Ford to Barack Obama. Nearly all these officials agreed that Pakistan's nuclear arsenal made it far more important to the United States than it otherwise would be. When asked if this was the case, one former official said "100 percent." After a slight pause, she added, "One thousand percent. There's no way around it."[5]

This chapter examines four major crises between India and Pakistan after they got nuclear weapons: the 1990 border crisis mentioned in the last chapter, the Kargil Crisis in 1999, the Twin Peaks Crisis in 2001–2002, and the Mumbai attacks in 2008. It also explores how Pakistan's nuclear arsenal impacted the US war in Afghanistan following 9/11, as well as Pakistan's proliferation of nuclear technology to America's enemies. What is clear from this record is that Pakistan has truly been the bomb from hell.

1990 BORDER CRISIS

It's hard to point to one event as the catalyst for the first India-Pakistan nuclear crisis. Some would argue it was Operation Brass Tacks, a massive Indian military exercise held on the border with Pakistan in December 1986. Others would argue it was the increasingly heavy-handed manner in which

India governed Kashmir, a Muslim-majority region over which Pakistan claims sovereignty. Still others might argue that the crisis was precipitated by Pakistan being emboldened after driving the Soviet Union out of Afghanistan. To some extent, all these factors played a role.

The most immediate catalyst, however, was the kidnapping of the daughter of an Indian official by a Kashmiri insurgent group in early December 1989. The crackdown that followed set off a massive uprising in the province that led India to dissolve the state government and assert direct control over the region, including deploying tens of thousands of troops. Hundreds were killed in the skirmishes as India attempted to hunt down the militants and reassert control. Although the uprising was organic, Pakistan quickly exploited it, establishing camps for insurgents on its side of the border. Massive rallies were also held in Pakistan. At one such event in March 1990, Prime Minister Benazir Bhutto promised to support a "thousand-year war" to free Kashmir from Indian control. In response, Indian Prime Minister V. P. Singh warned that "those who talk about a thousand years of war should examine whether they will last a thousand hours of war."[6]

Following this, Pakistan's military chief, General Mirza Aslam Beg—an ideologue and hardliner—convened Islamabad's senior military commanders. In the meeting, Beg claimed India had one hundred thousand troops partially mobilized across the border. This likely referred to troops that were conducting regularly scheduled exercises fifty miles from the border. Nonetheless, the Pakistanis were worried that India would use these forces to attack the insurgent camps they had established in Pakistan. There were also fears that India would launch a preemptive attack on Islamabad's nuclear facilities, perhaps with Israeli support.[7] Meanwhile, since the crisis began in December 1989, Pakistan had been conducting the largest military exercise in its history. Modeled after Operation Brass Tacks, two hundred thousand soldiers, including an armored division, participated in the exercise, as did several air force squadrons. After the exercises were over, the forces remained in place, sparking fears that Islamabad was preparing to attack India.[8] Minor border skirmishes continued throughout the winter and spring, making the United States increasingly uncomfortable. By mid-April, one senior State Department official warned, "there is a growing risk of miscalculation which could lead events to spin dangerously out of control."[9] Richard Haass, who was on the National Security Council at the time and helped mediate the crisis, said he worried about a *"Guns of August* moment," referring to the view that World War I started because of miscalculation.[10]

Washington was especially worried that any conflict would quickly spiral into a nuclear war. Indeed, at some point during this crisis, US intelligence picked up signals that Pakistan was readying its nuclear forces in some fashion. It remains unclear exactly what the US intelligence picked up on.

A highly contested article by the investigative journalist Seymour Hersh claimed that satellites and other intelligence caught Pakistan conducting high-explosives testing at a nuclear storage site. Hersh also reported that convoys moved warheads to an air force base where nuclear-capable F-16s were located. The US ambassador to Pakistan at the time, Robert Oakley, disputed Hersh's account. According to Oakley, there was no "hard" evidence Pakistan had dispersed warheads to air force bases, although he allowed that one could guess that.[11] At the very least, US intelligence picked up incontrovertible evidence that Pakistan had turned its uranium metal into bomb cores and assembled nuclear devices. According to Paul Wolfowitz, who was serving as the undersecretary of defense for policy at the time, "We knew that Pakistan assembled a nuclear weapon."[12] This intelligence was likely what made it impossible for President Bush to certify that Pakistan didn't possess a nuclear weapon in October 1990.

With the two sides sliding toward war, President Bush dispatched Deputy National Security Advisor Robert Gates to the region in May, the first time a US president sent a personal envoy to de-escalate a South Asian crisis. Gates's delegation was surprised to find that it was received more warmly in India than in Pakistan given America's historically stronger ties to Islamabad.[13] Then again, Gates's message to Pakistani leaders was unnerving. As he later recounted, "I looked straight at Beg and said, 'General, our military has war-gamed every conceivable scenario between you and the Indians, and there isn't a single way you win.'"[14] Gates also told the Pakistanis the US would not assist them and demanded Islamabad stop supporting terrorism. At the same time, Gates promised both sides that if they mutually agreed to remove troops from the border region, Washington could verify each other's compliance. This US-mediated confidence-building measure is what allowed both sides to back down. A US military attaché in India went to the front lines and verified that Indian forces were winding down their exercises. Once this message was conveyed to Pakistan, the two sides began withdrawing their forces from the border. The crisis was over before July.

How close the two sides came to a nuclear conflict is hard to say, with reasonable people coming to vastly different conclusions. On the one extreme is Richard Kerr, the then-deputy director of the CIA. An intelligence officer since 1960 who is not known for hyperbole, Kerr called this the "the most dangerous nuclear situation" he'd ever seen, deeming it "far more frightening than the Cuban missile crisis." This is consistent with the intelligence community, which in this crisis and future ones would almost always believe war was more likely than the State Department.[15] Similarly, during a trip to India in June 1990, Rep. Stephen Solarz (D-NY) put the odds of war at 50 percent.[16] On the other hand, the State Department, including the Bureau of Intelligence and Research (INR), was far less pessimistic. INR judged war as "highly unlikely."[17] Still, Teresita Schaffer, the State Department's top South Asian official at the time, concedes that "diplomacy was taking place with a heightened sense of urgency because both countries had nuclear weapons. ... It was different from earlier crises because of it."[18]

Those closest to the situation were the least worried. This included Western diplomats in India and Pakistan. More importantly, it included the Indians and Pakistanis themselves, who scoffed at the notion that the crisis could spiral into nuclear war.[19] In fact, they believed—in this crisis and future ones—that America's fears about nuclear war were little more than thinly veiled racism. To their credit, in later years the Naval War College would host war games with Indian and Pakistani participants mapping out how a nuclear conflict on the subcontinent would unfold. During these games, Indian and Pakistani participants would always find moves short of using nuclear weapons. This frustrated the American hosts, who held the games to demonstrate how easily these border crises could get out of hand.[20] Still, Schaffer believes that Washington's concern was not due to racism but rather to America's own history. Many in Washington were cognizant of just how close the Soviet Union and America came to nuclear war during the Cuban Missile Crisis. As Schaffer points out, US and Soviet officials believed they had more control over the crisis than was actually the case, and US officials feared the same was true of India and Pakistan.[21] Other US officials argue that even a small chance of nuclear war justifies a significant diplomatic intervention.[22]

1999 KARGIL CRISIS

The 1990 border crisis shares many commonalities with future crises with one significant difference: Pakistan (and arguably India) was not an overt nuclear power at the time. That would change before the next crisis. In May 1998, Indian Prime Minister Atal Bihari Vajpayee ordered a series of nuclear tests. The Clinton administration lobbied Pakistani Prime Minister Nawaz Sharif furiously not to respond in kind, including dispatching Deputy Secretary of State Strobe Talbott to Islamabad. But, as one diplomat who accompanied Talbott on that trip admitted, "Most of us suspected that it was a lost cause."[23] By month's end, Pakistan conducted six nuclear tests, one more than India had.

A few months later in October 1998, Sharif successfully pushed out Chief of the Army Staff General Jehangir Karamat, replacing him with General Pervez Musharraf. Musharraf was a hardliner on Kashmir—when Benazir Bhutto was prime minister, Musharraf had urged her to approve a military plan to infiltrate the mountainous northern part of Kashmir near the city of Kargil. Because of the difficult terrain and weather—the mountains are roughly fifteen thousand feet above ground—each winter, Indian forces leave their strategic posts before returning in the spring. Musharraf's plan was for Pakistani soldiers dressed as Kashmiri militants to occupy the strategic mountain posts during these winter months. By the time the Indian forces discovered the infiltrations, the Pakistani forces would be dug in and difficult to dislodge. Kargil also sits astride the sole highway connecting the capital city of Kashmir, Srinagar, to the northern part of the state. Therefore, controlling the mountains could isolate northern India and leave the Indian military unable to resupply its forces on the disputed Siachen Glacier. Bhutto had rejected Musharraf's plan when he proposed it in the early 1990s. But Musharraf never gave up on it. Only weeks after becoming chief of the army staff, Musharraf and a couple of his deputies began implementing the Kargil infiltration. Prime Minister Sharif was at least briefed about the broad contours of the plan, but it's unclear how much he really knew.

On the surface, 1999 began with strong reasons for optimism about Indo-Pakistani relations. US-mediated diplomacy had been taking place since the nuclear tests, and the effort received a major boost when Indian Prime Minister Vajpayee made a historic visit to Lahore, Pakistan, in February 1999. Unbeknownst to Delhi and Washington, thousands of Pakistani troops had already seized 130 strategic outposts in the Kargil mountains up to five miles deep inside India.[24] The infiltrations were discovered in early May when Indian forces went to reoccupy their usual posts. By that point, the Pakistani troops were well entrenched. Indian officials knew it would be costly to remove them, but they didn't really have a choice. Besides the strategic implications, Delhi was humiliated that this operation occurred while Vajpayee was engaged in a diplomatic offensive. India quickly launched air and artillery strikes against the Pakistani forces. These were complemented by infantry assaults that led to substantial casualties on the Indian side.

In Washington, officials were once again staring at a border crisis with the potential to escalate into a nuclear war. "The nuclear scenario was obviously very much on our minds," said Bruce Riedel, the top South Asia official at the National Security Council.[25] The Clinton administration was especially nervous that, faced with mounting casualties in trying to retake difficult terrain, India would attack Pakistan where it was weaker along other parts of the Line of Control (LOC) that separated the two countries. These fears became especially pronounced in June, when India began firing on other parts of the LOC.[26] It was only years later that everyone learned Vajpayee gave his air force strict orders not to violate the LOC.

At first, the Clinton administration pushed both India and Pakistan to withdraw their troops. Before long, however, Washington began demanding that Pakistan unilaterally withdraw. This surprised both sides. India and Pakistan expected America to be neutral or lean toward Pakistan given their long-standing relationship.²⁷ In part, the Clinton administration's position reflected the changing geopolitical dynamics of the post–Cold War world. But it was also because the nuclearization of the rivalry had changed American priorities. Once nuclear weapons were involved, any sympathy Washington had for Pakistan's Kashmir position became almost irrelevant. Preventing nuclear war was all that mattered.²⁸

In pressuring Pakistan, US officials found it difficult to determine who was in charge. Was it Prime Minister Sharif or military chief Musharraf? With authority unclear, Washington pressed both men. Secretary of State Madeleine Albright called Sharif while the commander of US Central Command (CENTCOM), General Anthony Zinni—who had strong relationships with the Pakistani military leadership—reached out to Musharraf. Their message was the same: Pakistan had to withdraw before any talks about the future of Kashmir could occur. Sharif and Musharraf denied Pakistani troops were occupying the Kargil mountains. Throughout the crisis they maintained it was Kashmiri militants. By summer, the fighting intensified as India began shelling other parts of the LOC. With the situation deteriorating, Clinton sent Zinni to Pakistan, reprising the role Bob Gates played in the 1990 crisis. Zinni took separate meetings with both Sharif and Musharraf.²⁹ Still denying Pakistani troops were involved, the Pakistanis offered to try to contact the supposed Kashmiri guerillas to ask them to withdraw. US officials were cautiously optimistic but witnessed no progress in the days ahead.³⁰ Instead, Sharif flew to China in a desperate attempt to get Pakistan's old friend to find a face-saving way out for Islamabad. Sharif's calls fell on deaf ears in Beijing.

Out of options, Sharif prevailed upon President Clinton in a phone call on July 2, but the president refused to budge. Sharif again called the White House the next day. This time, he told Clinton he was flying to DC for an urgent meeting on July 4. Sharif brought his entire family with him on the trip, leaving US officials with the impression he might try to seek asylum in the United States. The Clinton administration prepared two letters for the meeting. The first praised Sharif for restoring the status quo; the second blamed the entire ordeal on Pakistan.³¹ The morning of the talks, the Clinton administration woke up to more distributing news: the CIA said Pakistan had begun preparing its nuclear weapons for deployment. As Riedel explained, "The intelligence was very compelling. The mood in the Oval Office was grim."³² This set the tone for the Blair House meeting with Sharif. As was the case in 1990, many US officials saw parallels to World War I and the Cuban Missile Crisis.³³

Despite Clinton's concerns over escalation, he continued to refuse to pressure India to negotiate over Kashmir. At one point, Sharif asked Clinton to get India to agree to a time-specific solution to Kashmir in return for Pakistan withdrawing its troops. Clinton shot down this idea, stating he couldn't agree to "nuclear blackmail." President Clinton promised to engage India on the Kashmir issue, but only after Pakistani troops had withdrawn. Even then, he warned Sharif that there could be no hint of a quid pro quo. America couldn't appear to be rewarding Pakistan's nuclear brinkmanship.[34] After trading proposals all day, Clinton presented Sharif with a joint statement for the press. The statement said Sharif had "agreed to take concrete and immediate steps" to withdraw from India. Once that was done, the statement called for restoring the diplomatic process that was interrupted by the infiltrations. The only real concession to Sharif was reaffirming President Clinton's intention to visit South Asia. Sharif reluctantly accepted, and Pakistani forces began withdrawing in the next few days. The Kargil conflict had killed around one thousand people, but a nuclear war had once again been averted. The political situation in Islamabad was untenable, however. Fearing his days were numbered, Sharif tried to oust Musharraf in October 1999. The military stood by Musharraf, and instead it was Sharif who ended up in jail. Musharraf assumed the presidency while maintaining control over the military. Naturally, with a hardliner like Musharraf in complete control, another, more worrisome Indo-Pakistani crisis was not long in coming.

THE TWIN PEAKS CRISIS (2001–2002)

In the fall of 2001, most Americans were focused on the 9/11 terrorist attacks and the ensuing invasion of Afghanistan. But US diplomats working on South Asia remember this period as the time India and Pakistan came closest to nuclear war. The crisis was certainly the longest of those covered in this chapter, stretching at least from October 2001 to June 2002. It was punctuated by two major flashpoints: an attack on the Indian Parliament in December 2001 and the slaughter of military families at an Indian Army barrack in April 2002. These flare-ups have given the crisis its name: the Twin Peak Crisis.

For America, the crisis was both similar to the previous ones and different. For one thing, it took place at a time when most of the US government was focused on the aftermath of 9/11. As a result, the National Security Council was not as involved as the previous crises, leaving the State Department to take the lead. Initially, the State Department disagreed with the Pentagon's and CIA's assessment that India and Pakistan were on the brink of war. By the second peak, however, even most of the State Department believed war was imminent. Still, US engagement—including sending a high-level emissary— allowed the crisis to pass without the worst occurring. As in earlier crises, the Pakistanis and Indians insisted Washington was hyping up the chances of war. Nonetheless, many in Washington believe that, like the Cuban Missile Crisis, the two sides simply got lucky.

Although it was only evident in hindsight, the Twin Peaks Crisis began when Pakistani militants attacked the Kashmir state assembly building in Srinagar on October 1. Thirty-eight people were killed in the assault.[35] India immediately blamed the attack on Jaish-e-Muhammad (JeM), and demanded Pakistan turn over its leader, Maulana Masood Azhar. With all that was going on after 9/11, this barely registered in Washington.[36] The crisis exploded on December 13, when five Pakistani militants sneaked into the complex housing the Indian Parliament, just as the legislature was adjourning for the day. Armed with AK-47s and explosives, the militants engaged in a nearly hour-long gunfight with the Indian security guards. The entire event was broadcast live on TV. Although only twelve people—including the militants, but no members of Parliament—were killed in the attack, India was outraged. The cabinet quickly vowed to "liquidate the terrorists and their sponsors wherever they are."[37] In a televised address, Prime Minister Vajpayee declared, "This was not just an attack on the building, it was a warning to the entire nation. We accept the challenge."[38]

India blamed JeM and Lashkar-e-Taiba, another militant group based in Pakistan. It arrested one person in the wake of the attack, who claimed that Pakistan's intelligence service, ISI, had supported the attack.[39] Indian leaders framed the Parliament assault and Pakistan-sponsored terrorism in general as part of America's Global War on Terrorism (GWoT). Secretary of Defense Donald Rumsfeld had already indicated that the Bush administration considered Kashmir to be part of the GWoT in November.[40] The day after the Parliament attack, Robert Blackwill, America's ambassador to India, declared "it was no different in its objective from the terror attacks in the US on Sept. 11."[41] Blackwill was close to National Security Advisor Condoleezza Rice and other top Bush officials, and, like many Bush officials, he came into office determined to establish a new strategic relationship with India. In the eyes of some State Department officials, though, Blackwill often acted as a free agent as ambassador. "He ran that embassy as his own fiefdom," said one State Department official.[42] Despite sympathizing with India's plight, US officials were worried events were rapidly spiraling out of control. India quickly launched Operation Parakram (Valor), mobilizing nearly eight hundred thousand troops along the border, including three strike corps.[43] Air force units were also put into place, with Islamabad claiming that 95 percent of India's air force was positioned for offensive strikes.[44] Pakistan responded by putting its own forces on high alert, including redeploying sixty thousand troops from its border with Afghanistan—where they were positioned at America's request to intercept al-Qaeda troops fleeing the US invasion.[45] Pakistan also reportedly deployed short-range ballistic missiles near the border, albeit without nuclear warheads.[46] Not to be outdone, India placed its own Prithvi missiles within range of Islamabad.[47] Artillery fire by both sides was common.

The conversations behind the scenes were not creating much optimism. America's defense attaché in Islamabad, Colonel David Smith, was a longtime South Asian hand with strong relationships with Pakistan's military and intelligence services. On January 21, ISI officials were telling Smith that the Parliament attack had been a false flag operation by India.[48] Meanwhile, conversations in Delhi indicated that India was preparing to conduct thrust attacks inside Pakistan to hit terrorist camps. Pakistani military officials were hearing the same thing, and told Col. Smith about it. Smith knew that Pakistan's war plans called for nuclear strikes if it was on the verge of losing. In an assessment on Christmas Day, the CIA concluded the same thing and warned that India could try to seize the city of Lahore.[49] According to two separate US diplomats who spoke to this author, the Pentagon was also circulating a "theory of plumology." These assessments sought to predict how prevailing winds would carry the radiological fallout following a nuclear exchange, and what US embassies would have to be evacuated as a result.[50] By New Year's Eve, the intelligence community was predicting a war would start within days.[51] At this point, though, the State Department—including INR—was not as pessimistic.[52]

Coordinating closely with the United Kingdom and other European allies, the United States decided on a strategy of persistent high-level engagement to delay and—hopefully—ultimately prevent a full-scale war. Specifically, the West ensured a senior foreign official was visiting the region at all times, with the belief that India would not attack when a foreign dignitary was there. In addition, Secretary of State Colin Powell, a former army general, hoped that after a few weeks of mobilization, both militaries would grow tired and run low on resources.[53] At the same time, US and British officials continued to press Musharraf to denounce the Parliament attack and distance himself from terrorism more generally. Eventually, the Pakistani leader agreed. In a long, rambling speech on January 12, 2002, Musharraf insisted that "Kashmir runs in our blood" and vowed to continue moral and political support for the separatists. At the same time, he condemned the attacks on India and "terrorism in all its forms," portraying the violence as a perversion of Islam. He also pledged that Pakistan would not allow its territory to be used by terrorists, even in "the name of Kashmir." Musharraf followed the speech by rounding up eight hundred suspected terrorists, giving India the political space to avoid attacking while the process played itself out. US and allied officials continued to pursue ardent diplomacy, but there was finally hope the crisis was winding down.[54]

It was not to be. Musharraf's speech had not been well received in Pakistan, and once the immediate crisis faded, the Pakistani president began backtracking. By March, US officials noticed that terrorists Pakistan had arrested were being released.⁵⁵ Groups that had been officially banned reemerged under new names. The Indian and Pakistani militaries had remained mobilized throughout. And, once the weather began improving, infiltrations into Kashmir resumed at the same pace as previous years. By mid-May, the *New York Times* reported that a senior Western diplomat in India "put the odds of a military conflict at even or better."⁵⁶

Then the unthinkable happened. On May 14, three militants disguised as Indian soldiers attacked an army garrison at Kaluchak near the city of Jammu. Their first target was the residential area, where they murdered twenty-two women and children. They then proceeded to engage in a gunfight with soldiers. Before all was said and done, the attackers had killed thirty-four people and injured scores of others.⁵⁷ American officials immediately grasped the gravity of the situation, with intelligence indicating Indian forces were ready to attack Pakistan at any moment.⁵⁸ Enraged at the attack on military families, Indian generals, despite their strong tradition of civilian control, were demanding retribution.⁵⁹ Intense firefights along the border occurred daily. On May 25, India told Pakistan that it had two weeks to stop infiltrations into Kashmir and dismantle all the terrorist camps on its soil. Pakistan responded by testing nuclear-capable missiles, while publicly reiterating its willingness to use nuclear weapons.

By this time, there was near universal agreement in the US government that war was imminent. Even the State Department's intelligence bureau, previously far more optimistic than the CIA and Pentagon, now agreed that conflict seemed likely. "The handwriting on the wall looked very much like both sides got themselves into a position where neither could back down," one INR official later reflected.⁶⁰ On May 31, the State Department published travel advisories for Pakistan and India, and issued voluntarily evacuation orders to nonessential personnel and dependents in India. A few days later on June 5, Ambassador Blackwill surprised the State Department by issuing mandatory evacuation orders for all nonessential personnel and warning American citizens to leave the country immediately.⁶¹ Other Western nations followed Blackwill's lead. Nearly all Indian officials—and many US ones—thought Blackwill was trying to coerce the Indian government into dialing down tensions. And, in hindsight, this move did help de-escalate the situation because Indian business leaders began lobbying their government to end the crisis lest it derail the country's economy. But Blackwill's deputy in the embassy, Ashley Tellis, says that this was not Blackwill's intention. There were genuine fears that a conflict was imminent, and it could quickly turn nuclear.⁶²

Indeed, at this time, Secretary of State Colin Powell and Deputy Secretary of State Richard Armitage were nearly alone in believing war could be avoided. Fortunately, they were in charge of preventing one. While closely monitoring the situation, Armitage had waited and waited for the perfect time to stage a visit, believing that timing was everything. At the prompting of Jack Straw, Britain's foreign secretary, Armitage now decided to make his move. Before leaving for the region, Armitage gathered six or seven aides in his office. Those in the room were some of the State Department's top experts on South Asia. Most had disagreed with the CIA and Pentagon in December and January that war was likely. Now Armitage asked them all a simple question: Did anyone believe he could prevent India and Pakistan from going to war? According to a person in the room, only one hand went up, "and it wasn't mine."[63] But Armitage, along with Powell, correctly perceived that Indian and Pakistani leaders did not want a war. In Armitage's mind, both sides had gotten themselves into an impossible position. It was his job to give them a way out.

Armitage first flew to Islamabad to meet with Musharraf on June 6. At the time, the crux of the impasse was that India would not end its mobilization and reduce troops from the border until Pakistan had stopped infiltrations and begun dismantling terrorist camps. Musharraf had once again publicly committed to do just that on May 27, 2002, but Delhi was not inclined to believe him. Armitage, an imposing figure, planned to tell both sides "I know you don't trust each other, but trust me and the United States."[64] In a two-hour-long meeting with Musharraf, Armitage presented the Pakistani president with concrete steps he could take to reassure India. Although at first denying that any infiltrations were occurring, Musharraf gradually offered up more and more assurances. It's unclear how strong these were, and Armitage probably exaggerated the assurances Musharraf offered with reporters immediately afterward.[65] Still, Armitage going public with the pledges allowed Indian leaders to take small, symbolic steps to ease tensions, including allowing civilian Pakistani airliners to use Indian airspace (which had been cut off in January), removing some naval vessels near Pakistan, and nominating a new ambassador for Islamabad (the previous one had been recalled following the Parliament attack). The situation remained tense for a number of months afterward, but the worst of the crisis had passed. All former officials agreed that Armitage's visit in June was crucial. "It was a masterful job of diplomacy," said Marvin Weinbaum, who was in the State Department's intelligence bureau at the time.[66]

AFGHANISTAN

One unique aspect of the Twin Peak Crisis is that it occurred roughly simultaneously with the initial US invasion of Afghanistan. Interestingly, most of the former US officials interviewed for this project did not discuss this connection until prompted. Even then, they didn't make much of it. This is probably because the State Department was primarily handling the Twin Peak Crisis, while other parts of the US government took the lead on Afghanistan. Still, the Twin Peak Crisis allowed more al-Qaeda leaders to escape into Pakistan. As one study noted, "In the last week of December, big roundups of al-Qaeda operatives took place along the border with Afghanistan. . . . These were to be the last such comprehensive dragnets for two years after the redeployment of Pakistani troops to counter the Indian military threat."[67]

Pakistan, and especially its nuclear weapons, was at the forefront of discussions about the best ways to respond to the 9/11 terrorist attacks. Top Bush administration officials, including the president himself, worried that the invasion of Afghanistan could destabilize the Pakistani government, resulting in terrorists gaining control over its nuclear weapons. After being presented with the CIA plan to topple the Taliban four days after 9/11, President Bush asked his top advisors what they believed the downside risks were. One of the biggest, his advisors told him, was that it would destabilize Pakistan and ultimately result in loose nuclear weapons. Vice President Dick Cheney and National Security Advisor Condoleezza Rice were especially concerned about this possibility. Rice's deputy, Stephen Hadley, called this the "nightmare scenario," a characterization that President Bush agreed with. The Pentagon also listed this scenario as a top risk of the campaign.[68] In the years ahead, America would spend around $100 million trying to increase the security of Pakistan's nuclear arsenal.[69]

A top Bush administration official with significant South Asia expertise agrees that destabilizing Pakistan was a major concern in the years after 9/11. But this official believes this "very common fear . . . was completely overblown. It was held mostly by policymakers who didn't understand the internal dynamics of Pakistan." In this person's view, Pakistan's military was firmly in control of the country, including its nuclear arsenal. Furthermore, Musharraf purposely stoked America's fears to shore up support for his regime. "He felt the only way to maintain the US commitment to his regime was to negotiate with a gun to his head. And this is what he did," the former official said. As a result, the Bush administration often acted with unwarranted restraint in dealing with Musharraf, especially when it came to pressuring the Pakistani president to shut down terrorist camps. Peter Bergen, a terrorism expert, agrees that Musharraf used the "fiction" that Pakistan was on the verge of collapsing to convince the Bush administration not to pressure him to do more to counter terrorism. Bergen claims that, at times, Washington even avoided carrying out attacks on known al-Qaeda operatives in Pakistan out of deference to Musharraf.[70] President Bush alluded to this in his memoirs, noting that a few months after the invasion of Afghanistan, he decided against attacking al-Qaeda forces in Pakistan, because Musharraf told Bush the Pakistani government "would probably fall" and extremists would take over Pakistan and its nuclear arsenal.[71]

This is all the more notable in light of how the Bush administration planned to approach the Indian subcontinent when taking office. During the 2000 presidential candidate, then-Governor Bush had promised to reorient American foreign policy back to great power competition, particularly with China. A major component of this strategy was to strengthen ties to India. At the National Security Council, Condoleeza Rice moved the India portfolio from the Near East Directorate to the Asia one, a harbinger of the Indo-Pacific concept.[72] The decision to make Robert Blackwill—who, as noted above, was close to senior Bush officials like Rice—the ambassador to India was also part of this effort to strengthen ties to India. The 9/11 terrorist attacks temporarily upended the administration's efforts to woo India. The need to maintain Pakistan's cooperation on Afghanistan, as well as fears of destabilizing a nuclear-armed country, limited the Bush administration's ability to pivot to India. And, in refusing to pressure Pakistan more to stop cross-border terrorism, Washington alienated Delhi. This began changing during Bush's second term, particularly with the civil nuclear cooperation agreement with India. By this point, the Bush administration was no longer as concerned about Pakistan's stability, or as wedded to the notion that only Musharraf could hold it together.

The 9/11 terrorist attacks also proved to be a financial boon for Pakistan. As noted in the last chapter, President George H. W. Bush was forced to cut off all assistance to Pakistan in 1990, when he was no longer able to certify it didn't have nuclear weapons. Military assistance remained cut off for the remainder of the 1990s. Despite Pakistan openly testing nuclear weapons in 1998, US military aid reached unprecedented levels after 9/11. America first provided Pakistan with military assistance in 1955. According to USAID's Greenbook, between then and 1979, when the Soviet Union invaded Afghanistan, military assistance averaged $191 million in constant 2017 dollars. During the 1980s, when the Soviets were in Afghanistan, military assistance to Pakistan totaled $390.4 million a year. In the first ten years after 9/11, from 2002 to 2011, US military assistance averaged $457.9 million each year. Of course, these funding levels had very little to do with Pakistan's nuclear program. The spikes in assistance in the 1980s and 2000s were due to events in Afghanistan. Still, these aid levels run counter to the proliferation optimists who argue that allies and partners acquiring nuclear weapons will allow the United States to reduce its commitments to those countries.

Some of the assistance cited above occurred during the Obama administration, which took office determined to refocus America's efforts away from Iraq and back on Afghanistan and Pakistan. This resulted in an AfPak review that consumed the better part of President Obama's first year in office. The main players in that AfPak review were Bruce Riedel, who was temporarily part of the National Security Council again; General David Petraeus for the military; Michèle Flournoy, the undersecretary of defense for policy; and Richard Holbrooke, who headed up the newly created position of special representative for Afghanistan and Pakistan at the State Department. A major outcome of this review was to more tightly integrate the administration's Pakistan and Afghanistan policies. The Taliban and other Afghan insurgent leadership lived in Pakistan, and the US relied on Pakistani territory to supply most of its troops in Afghanistan. Furthermore, Islamabad had enduring interests in Afghanistan and would be integral to any political settlement. For all these reasons, the administration decided it needed to improve ties with Pakistan if it wanted better results in Afghanistan. But more to the point, the Obama administration quickly determined that Pakistan was ultimately more important to America's future than Afghanistan. As Riedel would later put it, "If we were honest with ourselves, we would call this problem "'Pak/Af,' not 'Af/Pak.'"[73]

Still, interviews with General Petraeus, Flournoy, and members of Holbrooke's team reveal that Islamabad's nuclear arsenal was not a prominent factor in the decision-making process that led to the Afghan surge, when President Obama increased troop levels by thirty thousand. Everyone agreed that the Obama administration was worried about the prospect of loose nukes; indeed, Islamabad's nuclear arsenal was one of the reasons the administration believed Pakistan was more important than Afghanistan. But, when it came to Afghanistan, Washington had other priorities—most notably, getting Islamabad to crack down on the Haqqani Network and other Taliban factions. As General Petraeus told this author, "I don't think [Pakistan's nuclear arsenal] was ever an issue during the Afghan review."[74] For her part, Flournoy says the nuclear factor "wasn't absence, but it was not a driving factor" in the AfPak review. And Marc Grossman, who would later serve as the special representative for Afghanistan and Pakistan, said that the need to resupply US troops through Pakistani territory was a greater consideration than nuclear weapons.[75]

Unlike the Bush administration in the aftermath of 9/11, the Obama administration wasn't overly concerned that pressuring Pakistan could destabilize it. As Flournoy put it, "I don't remember a single instance where the nuclear shadow caused us to think we can't put that pressure on Pakistan."[76] This was partly due to the fact that—after nearly a decade of the US being deeply involved in the region—senior Obama administration officials had much greater knowledge of Pakistan than Bush administration officials did in the immediate aftermath of 9/11. But it also reflected a misalignment of interests and actions. Despite concluding that the much larger, nuclear-armed Pakistan was more important than Afghanistan, the administration's policies often gave preference to the latter. And with one hundred thousand US troops fighting in Afghanistan, it could hardly have been otherwise.

MUMBAI ATTACKS

Before the Obama administration took office, the outgoing Bush administration had to deal with one more major Indo-Pakistani crisis. After back-to-back crises in 1999 and 2001–2002, the next major India-Pakistan crisis didn't take place until November 2008. On the surface, the Mumbai attack was far more catastrophic than either the Parliament bombing or barracks attack in 2001 and 2002. Yet, all US officials agree that there was much less concern in Washington about a nuclear war in 2008. "Nobody thought it was going to rise to the point that there was a nuclear exchange," said Gerald Feierstein, who was involved in both of them.[77]

For roughly sixty hours between November 26 and November 29, 2008, ten young Pakistani men sent by Lashkar-e-Taiba (LeT) held the city of Mumbai hostage.[78] Heavily armed with AK-47-type guns, grenades, and improvised explosive devices (IEDs), the men conducted simultaneous attacks on soft targets in India's entertainment and financial capital, targeting prominent hotels, restaurants, and a Jewish community center. By the time the assault ended, at least 174 people had been killed, with hundreds of others wounded. Among the dead were a handful of Americans. To an even greater extent than the attack on the Parliament in 2001, the Mumbai assault was broadcast live on television around the world. Social media and bloggers were new variables in the latter crisis, creating a stream of misinformation in the early days. When Mumbai was still under siege, US officials were receiving most of their information from these sources.[79] It was difficult to tell what was real. For instance, on Friday, Pakistan's new president, Asif Ali Zardari, took a call from a person he thought was India's foreign minister, Pranab Mukherjee. The caller said India was planning to launch an attack on Pakistan the next day. It fell to the US to reach out to Mukherjee to confirm it was an imposter.[80] Further hindering America's response was that the attack began the day before Thanksgiving and senior US policymakers were spread around the country to celebrate the holiday. As one then mid-level official joked, these crises always seem to happen "when the kids are in charge." A final complicating factor for Washington was the presidential transition. Bush was still president, but Obama was the president-elect.

Nonetheless, the response was handed deftly, using many of the tactics honed from previous crises. Within hours, a task force to deal with the crisis was up and running at the State Department, with other task forces in the Pentagon, military commands, CIA, and other places to follow. The

National Security Council coordinated the various parts of the government bureaucracy. There was also high-level engagement from President Bush on down. The administration also made sure to brief President-elect Obama, who deferred to the current president (Obama did prove willing to help out when asked, including calling Indian Prime Minister Manmohan Singh.)

US officials agree that they were able to mediate the crisis better because of the Bush administration's efforts to strengthen the US-India relationship during its second term. This included the heads of state and lower-level officials. Of particular importance was the growing cooperation in the intelligence and law enforcement channels. In the months before the attack, Washington had passed to Delhi vague warnings that prominent landmarks in Mumbai could be targeted by terrorists. This intelligence cooperation significantly ramped up after the attack. Pakistan also agreed to share information with the Americans, who, in turn, passed it along to their Indian counterparts. Donald Camp, a veteran of many Indo-Pakistani crises, reflected, "I've never seen the resources of the US government exercised so comprehensively to gather intelligence that could then be shared with India."[81] Within a day of the start of the attack, the US was sending teams of FBI agents to help in the investigation. This level of law enforcement cooperation would have been unthinkable only a few years ago.

Simultaneously with this cooperation with India, the Bush administration pressed Pakistan to take steps to prosecute those responsible for the attacks and crack down on the terrorist camps inside its borders. Then Washington sought to reassure India that Pakistan was taking these steps. US officials said there was no Plan B, because they didn't feel they needed one. This proved correct. There were some concerns initially that India could launch surgical strikes into Pakistan, but these quickly dissipated. Pakistan's civilian leaders were quick to denounce the attacks and pledged to cooperate in the investigation. The United States tried to use these statements to persuade India that Pakistan was taking the problem seriously. Indian leaders were not buying this, arguing that the civilian government in Islamabad did not really run the country.

Still, in contrast to earlier crises, Delhi placed its faith in the United States. "In the Mumbai attacks, India . . . [almost] immediately turned to us and said 'you have to do something about this,'" said Richard Boucher, the assistant secretary of state for South and Central Asian Affairs. "'We expect you to perform.'"[82] The US embassy in Islamabad was doing its best to meet India's challenge. Gerald Feierstein, the number two at the embassy at the time, said they pushed Pakistan to, first, account for what happened, and then, take steps to eliminate the extremist threats. Islamabad never seriously addressed the problem but did enough that America was able to convince India not to retaliate.[83]

When I first began writing this chapter in 2018, two factors stood out when reviewing the nuclear crises between India and Pakistan. First, they had become much less frequent, with no major crises in a decade after there were three between 1990 and 2001. Second, the last major crisis in 2008 was much less intense than the ones that preceded it. This led one to wonder whether the nuclear dyad between Pakistan and India was stabilizing in the same way that US-Soviet relations did after the Cuban Missile Crisis. None of the former officials who were interviewed for this book believed that was the case. For instance, one official attributed India's restraint after Mumbai to the "exceptional leadership" of then-Indian Prime Minister Singh. "If Mumbai happened today, you'd have a war," this official said.[84] Another official agreed, stating "I think India now would respond under [Narendra] Modi."[85] Even those officials looking beyond Modi did not believe the relationship had stabilized. Rather, they felt the world had mostly been lucky. These views were partly validated by the aftermath of the terrorist attack in Pulwama in Jammu and Kashmir in February 2019. In this episode, an Indian Kashmiri conducted a suicide attack that killed forty Indian paramilitary forces. Although Pakistan's direct involvement in this attack was far less clear than the four crises discussed in this chapter, India responded by launching air strikes deep inside Pakistani territory, a redline Indian leaders did not cross in past crises. Islamabad responded with cursory air strikes of its own. This situation was a reminder that South Asia remains the most dangerous nuclear flashpoint in the world.

The Enemies of My Friend

In 2003, a merchant vessel left Malaysia with five forty-foot shipping containers full of centrifuge parts in its cargo. In August, the ship docked in Dubai, where it transferred its secret cargo to a German ship, the *BBC China,* which was bound for Tripoli. The Central Intelligence Agency and its British counterpart, the MI6, were tracking the ships the whole time. When the *BBC China* was traveling through the Suez Canal, its captain got a message from the boat's owner: Change course and sail to the port of Taranto in southern Italy. When it arrived there on October 4, British and US intelligence agents were waiting. They soon found the centrifuge parts among the legitimate cargo.[86]

Thus marked the end of a decade-and-a-half campaign that saw Pakistan arm some of America's biggest enemies with the world's most dangerous weapons. Like France, one of the most enduring legacies of the Pakistani nuclear program is the nuclear offspring it birthed. Whereas Paris had mostly sold or offered technology to US partners, Pakistan's and A. Q. Khan's programs were exclusively to hostile states: Iran, North Korea, Libya, and likely

Saddam Hussein's Iraq. Despite Pakistan's and America's official story, in nearly all these cases, A. Q. Khan was acting as an instrument of the Pakistani state. Much work has already been done on Pakistan's nuclear export network, so a full rehashing is not necessary. Still, it's worth providing a rough overview of these efforts.

Iran

Iran was the first customer for the Khan network. Despite some earlier meetings, the real sales appear to have begun in the very late 1980s. The timing is important here. In August 1988, President Zia died in a plane crash and was replaced as army chief by General Mirza Aslam Beg. Beg was a Shi'a Muslim, anti-Western, and determined to expand Pakistan's ties with the Muslim world, especially Iran. He was very open about this—in numerous meetings with US officials, Beg threatened to sell nuclear technology to Iran. At the same time, the Soviets were withdrawing from Afghanistan, leaving Islamabad concerned that US aid would stop. Pakistan's nuclear program was transitioning to using higher-quality P-2 centrifuges, leaving it with excess P-1s. Selling parts of these older centrifuges offered a windfall for the state. Iran found the components to be of inferior quality—likely because they were left over from Pakistan's program—and struggled to assemble the centrifuges. Despite Tehran's disappointment, in the mid-1990s, it purchased assembled P-1 centrifuges from Pakistan as well as blueprints for the more advanced P-2 designs. It's unclear how long this relationship continued. Iran later said it met with members of Khan's network thirteen times between 1994 and 1999.[87] Regardless, the assistance proved invaluable to Iran's nuclear development. As Gary Samore explained, "Without that infusion of Pakistani technology, Iran's nuclear program would be nowhere near as advanced as it is now."[88]

North Korea

North Korea is another nuclear threat for which Pakistan is partly to blame. Islamabad and Pyongyang have long-standing ties, with Prime Minister Zulfikar Ali Bhutto making a state visit to North Korea in 1976. In the early 1990s, North Korea developed the medium-range NoDong ballistic missile based on Russian technology. At this time, Pakistan was beginning to operationalize its nascent nuclear capability and wanted missiles to complement its F-16s. Most of the missile development was being done by A. Q. Khan's main rival, Munir Khan, and A. Q. Khan was determined to make his own mark. At the time, Z. A. Bhutto's daughter, Benazir Bhutto, was prime minister, and Khan asked her to make a state visit to Pyongyang. She agreed, and during this visit, North Korea passed blueprints for the NoDong to Pakistan.[89] Technical delegations between the two countries soon followed. Originally, Pakistan paid for the missiles with cash. But by 1996 and 1997, Pakistan's foreign exchanges were running perilously low. A new bargain was struck: in return for missiles, Pakistan would provide North Korea with centrifuges. North Korea's nuclear program had originally been centered around reprocessing plutonium. But in 1994, the US and North Korea signed the Agreed Framework, which mandated the closure of Pyongyang's nuclear reactor and reprocessing plant. North Korean leader Kim Jong-il thus set up a separate nuclear program outside of the Agreed Framework using Pakistani centrifuges. This was not unlike what Islamabad had done itself after France refused to sell a reprocessing plant to Pakistan in the 1970s. Many of the missile and centrifuge exchanges between Pakistan and North Korea were transported on military planes. The relationship was very intimate. North Korean officials were reportedly present at Pakistan's 1998 nuclear tests, and Korean scientists were a constant presence at A. Q. Khan's nuclear complex, KRL. In turn, Khan himself visited North Korea at least thirteen times to obtain technical experience with the NoDong missiles, which Khan renamed Ghauni. There is zero doubt that these nuclear exports were Pakistani state policy, and the relationship appears to have continued at least throughout the 1990s.[90]

Iraq

Then there is the peculiar case of Iraq. In 1995, international inspectors sent into the country after Desert Storm discovered documents related to Project A.B. These documents were memos by top Iraqi nuclear officials discussing an offer made by a Pakistani man, Zahid Malik, who was believed to be close to A. Q. Khan. According to the memos, Malik approached the Iraqis in October 1990 with an offer to sell the Iraqis the same items Islamabad had offered Iran: namely, a bomb design as well as blueprints and the components to build centrifuges. Iraq had invaded Kuwait only two months earlier, and an international coalition was gathering in Saudi Arabia to liberate Kuwait and possibly topple Saddam Hussein's regime. Baghdad had been pursuing nuclear weapons under the guise of a peaceful nuclear energy program. As a US-led coalition amassed to remove his forces from Kuwait, Saddam sought to divert highly enriched uranium under international safeguards to quickly construct rudimentary nuclear devices to deter the coming attack. Iraqi scientists were struggling with a bomb design—making that part of Malik's offer especially enticing. The Iraqi officials who met with Malik sent his offer to the highest levels of Iraq's nuclear establishment. The Iraqis discussed it intensely but decided to proceed with caution, because they feared it was a sting operation. Things didn't get very far before Desert Storm started and Saddam lost the war.

Libya

The most ambitious client for A. Q. Khan, and the one that ultimately unraveled his network, was Libya. Khan and his network offered Libya everything it would need to enrich uranium and design a nuclear bomb. This is also the one case where Khan might have been acting partly as a rogue agent instead of executing Pakistani policy. To be sure, Pakistan had long-standing ties to Libya and its eccentric leader, Muammar Gaddafi. Shortly after he came to power in the early 1970s, Gaddafi had provided some of the seed money for Pakistan's nuclear program. Khan also clearly had support from some elements within the Pakistani military to facilitate the sale. Unlike previous sales, however, Khan was not using leftover supplies from Pakistan's program. Instead, to execute the sale, Khan and his network set up operations throughout Europe, the Middle East, parts of Asia, and Africa. Khan's team also increasingly manufactured equipment itself. But these larger operations, along with the extensive travel that Khan and his top associates personally took to oversee them, caught the attention of Western intelligence services.[91]

The screws had begun tightening on Khan by the end of the 1990s. In early 1999, the Clinton administration began pushing Prime Minister Sharif to rein A. Q. Khan in, largely over his cooperation with North Korea.[92] Sharif doesn't appear to have done this, but Musharraf began targeting Khan as part of an anti-corruption campaign when he assumed power. This had little to do with American pressure—Pakistan was under sanctions because of its nuclear test, giving Washington very little leverage. Instead, Musharraf believed that Khan had outgrown his usefulness. Pakistan had tested nuclear devices and Khan's outsized ego and growing power made him a liability and a threat. Musharraf began having ISI agents secretly follow Khan, especially on his trips abroad.[93] On these trips, the ISI agents witnessed Khan's ongoing efforts to execute the Libya deal. In early 2001, Musharraf pushed Khan into retirement. Before then, in early 2000, the CIA was able to recruit a Swiss man, Urs Tinner, as a "reluctant" informer on Khan. Urs was the son of Friedrich Tinner, a Swiss nuclear scientist who Khan had known since the time he worked in Europe in the 1970s.

It wasn't until Urs Tinner began cooperating that the US, UK, and other Western intelligence agencies fully grasped the extent of Khan's nuclear exports. Some find this hard to believe, including many people who wrote sensational books charging Washington with complicity after Khan's activities became public. But it's actually quite understandable. After invoking the Pressler Amendment in 1990, America's intelligence on Pakistan's nuclear program significantly diminished as resources dried up and relationships were severed. Moreover, US intelligence was fully aware that Khan's proliferation network was active during the 1990s. The problem was that this network had been active for decades, and Washington assumed it was still focused primarily on supplying the Pakistani program. That being said, the US was not completely unaware of the exports—US intelligence correctly identified that Pakistan was trading centrifuges for North Korean missiles before Urs became an informant, and there were widespread suspicions about Iran. But North Korea was clearly Pakistani state policy. In the case of Iran, it was hard to determine what was coming from A. Q. Khan and Pakistan and what was the result of Iran's own proliferation networks, which operated in the same space as Khan's. Besides, in the 1990s, the United States was primarily focused on stopping Russian and Chinese assistance to Iran's nuclear program.

Urs's cooperation was invaluable for the CIA and MI6 but insufficient on its own. As one former National Security Council staffer put it, "The information was so sensitive it couldn't be used in any diplomatic initiative."[94] Urs Tinner did provide leads that the intelligence community used to piece together an entire picture of Khan's operations. Urs was particularly useful on Libya, as in 2002, he was sent to Malaysia to run a factory that was building the ten thousand centrifuges that Libya had ordered. This is what enabled the Western intelligence agencies to track the shipment that ended up on the *BBC China*.[95]

The question became when to take down the Khan network. There is almost always a tension between policymakers who want to act on intelligence and the intelligence community that wants to continue monitoring a target to get a fuller understanding. This was certainly true of the Khan case, when good arguments could be made by both sides. By waiting, the Western powers could gain a fuller understanding of the network, allowing them to wrap it up in one fell swoop. By acting too soon, they risked missing certain nodes that could continue to smuggle nuclear technology. The danger of waiting too long was that they could fail to stop a major nuclear sale, which could haunt the world for decades.[96]

As it turned out, outside events would largely force their hand. In August 2002, a former Iranian terrorist organization, possibly using intelligence provided by Israel's Mossad, exposed Iran's nuclear program to the world. In 2003, Iran began cooperating with the IAEA as part of Europe's diplomatic outreach. It was only a matter of time before the international nuclear agency discovered the Pakistan connection. Then, in October 2002, a US diplomat confronted North Korea with evidence of an enrichment program. To Washington's surprise, Pyongyang admitted the existence of the program.[97] Most importantly, after the US invasion of Iraq in March 2003, Libya reached out to London and Washington to explore surrendering its nuclear program in return for a rapprochement. Even as these talks were ramping up, the major components of Libya's deal with Khan were being prepared for shipment to Tripoli. In August 2003, the ship carrying the centrifuge parts left Malaysia. Accordingly, the Bush administration confronted Musharraf about A. Q. Khan during the UN General Assembly in New York in September. Specifically, CIA Director George Tenet presented Musharraf with overwhelming evidence that Khan was selling nuclear technology around the world. He also provided evidence of Khan's travels and bank account records, which proved the scientist was personally profiting from these sales. The evidence was undeniable; a Pakistani official later commented that "it seemed that the Americans had a tracker planted on Dr. Khan's body."[98] Still, US officials realized they had to frame it in the right way to convince Musharraf to act against A. Q. Khan, a nationally beloved figure in Pakistan. According to Tenet's later account, he said Khan was betraying his country by stealing its most valuable secrets and selling them to the highest bidder. This information was now in America's hands rather than a "vault in Pakistan."[99] Tenet's presentation was followed up by multiple trips to Islamabad by senior US and British officials.

As international pressure mounted, Musharraf began arresting members of KRL. Finally, in December 2003, the Pakistani leader ordered the arrest of A. Q. Khan himself. Two months later, Khan made a forced confession on national TV, taking sole responsibility for the sales. In return, Musharraf pardoned him. Khan was placed on house arrest, partly to keep him from talking to reporters (a favorite A. Q. Khan pastime). Nonetheless, before his death in October 2021, Khan occasionally popped up to retract his confession and, alternatively, to say he had acted at the behest of Pakistani civilian and military leaders. In truth, no one interviewed for this project believed Khan was a rogue actor. Most of the nuclear sales were Pakistani state policy. The Bush administration knew this but accepted Musharraf's story because they needed Islamabad's cooperation on other issues, like Afghanistan. As long as the nuclear sales stopped, what was the point in casting blame? Plus, in the end, what could Washington have really done to Pakistan anyway? It was a nuclear-armed power that couldn't be invaded and overthrown. Sure, severe economic sanctions could have been placed on the country, but if too effective, the sanctions could topple the very institutions that protected nuclear weapons from radical Islamist terrorist groups. Pakistan had built nuclear weapons to prevent India from being able to dismember the country. But for the United States, nuclear weapons had made Pakistan too big to fail.

CONCLUSION

Pakistan holds a number of important lessons for potential future partner nations that acquire nuclear weapons. This is especially true for Saudi Arabia, the most likely future nuclear weapon state that is a non-treaty ally partner of the United States. First, Pakistan's possession of nuclear weapons regularly made it more difficult for the United States to achieve its objectives next door in Afghanistan. The United States has been more actively engaged in the Middle East than any other region in the post–Cold War era. Despite the high level of engagement and resources spent, US policy in the Middle East has rarely been successful. A nuclear-armed Saudi Arabia would almost certainly make this problem worse. Every military engagement the United States undertook in the region would have to be weighed against how it could impact a nuclear Saudi Arabia. In addition, a number of factors—from the return of great power competition to America's reduced direct dependence on foreign oil—are pushing the United States to reduce its engagement in the Middle East. A nuclear-armed Saudi Arabia would make it more difficult for America to pivot away from the Middle East, just as pivoting to India proved more difficult because of Pakistan's nuclear arsenal.

Pakistan also presented US policymakers with the terrifying possibilities of loose nuclear weapons, insider threats, and nuclear terrorism. These problems would all be major concerns if Saudi Arabia acquired nuclear weapons. To be sure, Saudi Arabia isn't the safe haven for terrorist groups that Pakistan has proven to be. Nonetheless, the most dangerous Islamist terrorist groups profess ideologies eerily similar to Wahhabism, Saudi Arabia's official ideology. In fact, when the Islamic State first conquered territory in Syria and Iraq, schools under its control used old Saudi textbooks. While Saudi Arabia has generally controlled terrorism inside its own borders, Saudi nationals have been prolific terrorists abroad. Osama bin Laden was a Saudi national, as were fifteen of the nineteen hijackers who carried out the 9/11 attacks. More Saudi nationals carried out suicide bombings in Iraq than any other country, and only Tunisia had more foreign fighters in the Islamic State than Saudi Arabia.[100] Given the state ideology of Wahhabism, insider threats would be a scary possibility in a nuclear-armed Saudi Arabia. But perhaps the gravest danger would be the collapse of the Saudi royal family itself. The Gulf monarchies are increasingly archaic in the twenty-first century. Saudi Arabia's economic model does not seem sustainable over the long term, especially in the face of its citizens' vastly rising expectations. Saudi Arabia also faces an enormous youth bulge, with roughly 70 percent of its population thirty years old or younger.[101] It's difficult to imagine what kind of regime would replace the current Saudi royal family, but it is likely to be more extreme and less stable.

The most important lesson from the Pakistan case is how the nuclearization of its rivalry with India made that dispute far more important to the United States. As noted above, it is hard to dispute that the presence of nuclear weapons on the subcontinent has made it less likely that India and Pakistan will engage in a full-scale war. Still, for the United States at least, the stakes of every crisis have been infinitely higher. This is notable because Saudi Arabia is locked in its own vicious rivalry with Iran. These two countries do not border each other like India and Pakistan do, but they have been waging a proxy war across the Middle East for decades. This has grown more intense in recent years, with the conflict playing out in Lebanon, Syria, Yemen, and Iraq, among other places. At times, Tehran has targeted Riyadh directly, such as its missile and cyber attacks on Saudi oil facilities. As worrisome as this already is for the United States, it would become a much graver concern if Saudi Arabia and Iran acquired nuclear weapons. Imagine how different US policymakers would have treated Iran's missile and drone attack on Saudi Arabia's oil facilities in September 2019 if Riyadh could have responded with nuclear weapons. Moreover, the nuclearization of the Saudi-Iranian rivalry could make it more intense if either or both countries increase their aggressiveness as Pakistan has since becoming a nuclear state. Of course, a nuclear rivalry in the Middle East wouldn't be limited to Saudi Arabia and Iran, as Israel's own arsenal would also be a factor. It's unclear if this would be in the form of a true trilateral deterrence relationship or more like two separate dyads as is normally the case between India and Pakistan, as well as India and China.

Finally, one of the most consistent lessons across the cases examined in this book is that nuclear allies and partners generally help other countries acquire their own nuclear weapons. Countries like France and Pakistan were generous in sharing nuclear knowledge and equipment. Israel was much more restrained—though certainly not perfect—when it came to selling nuclear technology. Only the United Kingdom's record is relatively unscathed in this regard. It is impossible to know exactly how a country like Saudi Arabia would act when it comes to transferring nuclear technology to other countries. But the historical record suggests that it is more likely than not that Saudi Arabia would aid other countries' nuclear pursuits to some degree or another.

NOTES

1. David Sanger, "Obama's Worst Pakistan Nightmare," *New York Times Magazine*, January 8, 2009.

2. Bob Woodward, *Bush at War* (New York: Simon and Schuster, 2002); and Steve Coll, *Directorate S: The C.I.A. and America's Secret Wars in Afghanistan and Pakistan* (New York: Penguin Press, 2018).

3. Peter Bergen, *The Longest War: The Enduring Conflict Between America and Al-Qaeda* (New York: Free Press, 2011), 261.

4. Feroz Khan, *Eating Grass: The Making of the Pakistani Bomb* (Stanford, CA: Stanford University Press), 231.

5. Author phone interview, Shamila Chaudhary, July 25, 2018.

6. Quoted in P. R. Chari, Pervaiz Iqbal Cheema, and Stephen P. Cohen, *Four Crises and a Peace Process: American Engagement in South Asia* (Washington, DC: Brookings Institution Press, 2007), 91.

7. Chari et al., *Four Crises and a Peace Process*, 91–93; and Khan, *Eating Grass*, 231.

8. Chari et al., *Four Crises and a Peace Process*, 86 and 92.

9. Chari et al., *Four Crises and a Peace Process*, 97.

10. Richard Haass, interview by phone with author Zachary Keck, July 30, 2018.

11. Seymour M. Hersh, "On the Nuclear Edge," *New Yorker*, March 29, 1993.

12. Quoted in Mitchell Reiss, *Bridled Ambition: Why Countries Constrain Their Nuclear Capabilities* (Washington, DC: Woodrow Wilson Center Press, 1995), 188. Also see George Perkovich, *India's Nuclear Bomb: The Impact on Global Proliferation* (Berkeley: University of California Press, 1999), 308–09; Jeffrey T. Richelson, *Spying on the Bomb: American Nuclear Intelligence from Nazi Germany to Iran and North Korea* (New York: Norton, 2006), 345 and 429; and Dennis Kux, *Disenchanted Allies: The United States and Pakistan, 1947–2000* (Washington, DC: Woodrow Wilson Center Press) 306–07.

13. Richard Haass, interview by phone with author Zachary Keck, July 30, 2018; and Teresita Schaffer, interview with author Zachary Keck, Washington, DC, July 24, 2018.

14. Quoted in Hersh, "On the Nuclear Edge."

15. Quoted in Hersh, "On the Nuclear Edge."

16. Steve Coll, "100,000 Demonstrate in Kashmir; Slain Leader Mourned at Peaceful Service; Solarz in New Delhi," *Washington Post*, June 1, 1990.

17. Chari et al., *Four Crises and a Peace Process*, 96.

18. Teresita Schaffer, interview with author Zachary Keck, Washington, DC, July 24, 2018.

19. Chari et al., *Four Crises and a Peace Process*, 97–98.

20. Schaffer, interview.

21. Schaffer.

22. Richard Haass, interview by phone with author Zachary Keck, July 30, 2018.

23. Donald Camp, interview by phone with author Zachary Keck, August 5, 2018.

24. C. Christine Fair, *Fighting to the End: The Pakistan Army's Way of War* (New York: Oxford University Press, 2014), 151–52; and Khan, *Eating Grass*, 311.

25. Bruce Riedel, *American Diplomacy and the 1999 Kargil Summit at Blair House* (Philadelphia: Center for the Advanced Study of India, 2002), 3–4.

26. Strobe Talbott, *Engaging India: Diplomacy, Democracy, and the Bomb* (Washington, DC: Brookings University Press, 2004), 158–59.

27. Talbott, *Engaging India,* 158; and Riedel, *American Diplomacy*, 5.

28. Schaffer, interview.

29. Charles Stuart Kennedy, "Interview of Ambassador Edward Gibson Lanpher," The Association for Diplomatic Studies and Training Foreign Affairs Oral History Project, 2003, 107.

30. Kennedy, "Interview of Ambassador Edward Gibson Lanpher," 107.

31. Talbott, *Engaging India,* 161; and Riedel, *American Diplomacy*, 7.

32. Bruce Riedel, "Farewell, Sandy Berger, the Clinton Man Who Stopped Armageddon," *Daily Beast*, December 2, 2015.

33. According to Riedel, who was in the meetings, Clinton told Sharif that the "Kargil crisis seemed to be eerily like 1914, armies mobilizing and disaster looming." See Riedel, *American Diplomacy*, 10. Strobe Talbott, who was also in the meetings, claimed Clinton believed the world was closer to nuclear war than during the Cuban Missile Crisis. See Talbott, *Engaging India*, 167.

34. Riedel, *American Diplomacy*, 5.

35. Lars Eriksen, "Kashmir: History of a Flashpoint," *Guardian*, June 8, 2002.

36. Michael Krepon and Polly Nayak, *US Crisis Management in South Asia's Twin Peaks Crisis* (Washington, DC: Stimson Center, September 1, 2006), 50–51.

37. Celia W. Dugger, "Group in Pakistan is Blamed by India For Suicide Raid," *New York Times*, December 15, 2001.

38. "Indian Parliament Attack Kills 12," *BBC*, December 13, 2001.

39. Vanessa Gezari, "Indian Suspect Claims Pakistan Aided Parliament Attack," *Chicago Tribune*, December 21, 2001.

40. Krepon and Nayak, *US Crisis Management in South Asia's Twin Peaks Crisis*, 50.

41. Dugger, "Group in Pakistan is Blamed by India For Suicide Raid."

42. Author interview with former State Department official.

43. Praveen Swami, "Gen. Padmanabhan Mulls Over Lessons of Operation Parakram," *Hindu*, February 6, 2004.

44. P. R. Chari et al., *Four Crises and a Peace Process,* 153; and Krepon and Nayak, *US Crisis Management in South Asia's Twin Peaks Crisis*, 52.

45. Ahmed Rashid, *Descent Into Chaos: The United States and the Failure of Nation Building in Pakistan, Afghanistan, and Central Asia* (New York: Penguin Books, 2008), 117.

46. Atul Aneja and Sandeep Dikshit, "Pakistan Moves Missiles Closer to Border," *Hindu*, December 26, 2001.

47. Krepon and Nayak, *US Crisis Management in South Asia's Twin Peaks Crisis*, 52.

48. Steve Coll, "The Stand-Off," *New Yorker*, February 13, 2006.

49. Coll, "The Stand-Off."

50. Donald Camp, interview by phone with author Zachary Keck, August 5, 2018; Gerald Feierstein, interview with author Zachary Keck, Washington, DC, July 18, 2018.

51. Krepon and Nayak, *US Crisis Management in South Asia's Twin Peaks Crisis*, 52. This was perhaps driven by Indian Defense Minister George Fernandes saying that India's military deployments were finally in place.

52. Camp, interview; and Marvin Weinbaum, interview with author Zachary Keck, Washington, DC, July 18, 2018.

53. Richard Boucher, interview with author Zachary Keck, Washington, DC, August 3, 2018; and Weinbaum, interview. Although Indian officials denied it at the time, later writings by Indian strategists suggest that Delhi felt inhibited by the presence of large numbers of US troops in and around Pakistan for the Afghan War. See S. Kalyanaraman, "Operation Parakram: An Indian Exercise in Coercive Diplomacy," *Strategic Analysis* 26, no. 4, 484.

54. Krepon and Nayak, *US Crisis Management in South Asia's Twin Peaks Crisis*, 53.

55. Rashid, *Descent into Chaos*, 118.

56. Celia W. Dugger, "Minister Says India Won't Attack Pakistan," *New York Times*, May 14, 2002.

57. Coll, "The Stand-off."

58. Krepon and Nayak, *US Crisis Management in South Asia's Twin Peaks Crisis*, 33.

59. Coll, "The Stand-off."

60. Weinbaum, interview.

61. Donald Camp, interview by phone with author Zachary Keck, August 5, 2018.

62. Ashley Tellis, interview by phone with author Zachary Keck, July 31, 2018. In fact, the embassy had already explored whether a hardened bunker able to withstand a nuclear blast could be erected. See Steve Coll, "The Nuclear Stand-Off."

63. Weinbaum, interview.

64. Weinbaum, interview.

65. "US Assured Pakistan Will Not Begin War: Musharraf, Armitage Hold Talks," *Dawn*, June 7, 2002; and Krepon and Nayak, *US Crisis Management in South Asia's Twin Peaks Crisis*, 38.

66. Weinbaum, interview.

67. Krepon and Nayak, *US Crisis Management in South Asia's Twin Peaks Crisis*, 32.

68. Coll, *Directorate S*, 109–10; and George W. Bush, *Decision Points* (New York: Random House, 2010), 189.

69. David Sanger and William Broad, "U.S. Secretly Aids Pakistan in Guarding Nuclear Arms," *New York Times*, November 18, 2007.

70. Bergen, *Longest War*, 260–62.

71. Bush, *Decision Points*, 213.

72. Torkel Patterson, interview by phone with author Zachary Keck, July 18, 2018.

73. Quoted in David Sanger, *Confront and Conceal: Obama's Secret Wars and Surprising Use of American Power* (New York: Crown, 2012), 20.

74. David Petraeus, interview by phone with author Zachary Keck, August 21, 2018.

75. Marc Grossman, interview with author Zachary Keck, Washington, DC, July 18, 2018.

76. Michèle Flournoy, interview by phone with author Zachary Keck, August 1, 2018.

77. Gerald Feierstein, interview with author Zachary Keck, Washington, DC, July 18, 2018.

78. Among the best accounts of Mumbai are Angel Rabasa et al., *The Lessons of Mumbai* (Arlington, VA: RAND Corporation, 2009); and Cathy Scott-Clark and Adrian Levy, *The Siege: 68 Hours Inside the Taj Hotel* (New York: Penguin Books, 2013). On US crisis management, see Polly Nayak and Michael Krepon, *The Unfinished Crisis: US Crisis Management after the 2008 Mumbai Attacks* (Washington, DC: Stimson Center, 2012).

79. Nayak and Krepon, *The Unfinished Crisis*, 11.

80. Nayak and Krepon, *The Unfinished Crisis*, 12.

81. Donald Camp, interview by phone with author Zachary Keck, August 5, 2018.

82. Richard Boucher, interview with author Zachary Keck, Washington, DC, August 5, 2018.

83. Author interview, Gerald Feierstein, Washington, DC, July 18, 2018.

84. Author phone interview with former Obama administration official.

85. Torkel Patterson, interview by phone with author Zachary Keck, July 18, 2018.

86. David Albright, *Peddling Peril: How the Secret Nuclear Trade Arms America's Enemies* (New York: Free Press, 2010), 211–13; and William Tobey, "Cooperation in the Libya WMD Disarmament Case," *Studies in Intelligence* 61, no. 4 (December 2017).

87. Khan, *Eating Grass*, 368; and Albright, *Peddling Peril*, 98.

88. Gary Samore, interview by phone with author Zachary Keck, July 13, 2018.

89. Douglas Frantz and Catherine Collins, *The Nuclear Jihadist: The True Story of the Man Who Sold the World's Most Dangerous Secrets . . . And How We Could Have Stopped Him* (New York: Twelve, 2007), 207–08.

90. Gordon Corera, *Shopping for Bombs: Nuclear Proliferation, Global Insecurity, and the Rise and Fall of the A. Q. Khan Network* (Oxford: Oxford University Press, 2006), 90–95; and Michael Laufer, "A.Q. Khan Nuclear Chronology," Carnegie Endowment for International Peace, September 7, 2005.

91. Corera, *Shopping for Bombs*, 131–37.

92. Frantz and Collins, *Nuclear Jihadist*, 242.

93. Frantz and Collins, *Nuclear Jihadist*, 258–59.

94. Author phone interview with former National Security Council staffer.

95. Frantz and Collins, *Nuclear Jihadist*, 272.

96. George Tenet, *At the Center of the Storm: My Years at the CIA* (New York: HarperCollins, 2007), 281.

97. David E. Sanger, "North Korea Says It Has a Program on Nuclear Arms," *New York Times*, October 17, 2002.

98. Quoted in Corera, *Shopping for Bombs*, 202.

99. Tenet, *Center of the Storm*, 283.

100. Scott Shane, "Saudis and Extremism: 'Both the Arsonists and the Firefighters,'" *New York Times*, August 25, 2016.

101. Karen Elliott House, *Uneasy Lies the Head that Wears a Crown: The House of Saud Confronts its Challenges* (Cambridge, MA: Belfer Center for Science and International Affairs, March 2016), 3.

Chapter 11

Conclusion

This book has peered into the past to glean lessons for the future. But it also sought to use history to provide insight into the long-standing debate about how allied proliferation impacts US security. This conclusion chapter will review what the case studies have to say about the debate. The bulk of this chapter will be geared toward outlining lessons for future cases of allies and partners acquiring nuclear weapons. In doing so, it will apply the lessons of the past to concrete potential future cases like Japan, South Korea, and Saudi Arabia.

THE DEBATE

Throughout the nuclear era, countless analysts and policymakers have pontificated on how allies and partners acquiring nuclear weapons impacts US security. These debates have not been guided by history in any in-depth manner, however. In-depth case studies of Great Britain, France, Israel, and Pakistan's nuclear programs call into question many of the major arguments made by both sides of the debate. Additionally, the cases raise new issues that aren't typically discussed.

For instance, proliferation optimists argue that nuclear-armed allies and partners will be able to protect themselves, allowing America to reduce its overseas commitments. There was little evidence of that from any of the past cases of allied proliferation. Most frequently, US commitments to allies and partners were not impacted by those countries acquiring nuclear weapons. Thus, America maintained a large number of troops in Europe despite London and Paris acquiring nuclear weapons. Similarly, military assistance to Israel and Pakistan was actually higher after those countries acquired nuclear weapons than before. In the case of Israel, the increased military assistance was partly the result of Israel acquiring nuclear weapons.

Along with not reducing America's overseas commitments, allied proliferation often made it harder for Washington to achieve its objectives abroad. In the allied cases, this occurred when Britain and France reduced their conventional military spending as well as when de Gaulle removed France from NATO's military command. Launch control issues were also a problem. Pakistan's nuclear arsenal complicated America's ability to achieve its goals in Afghanistan during the 1980s and after 9/11. The nuclearization of the Indo-Pakistani dispute also made it a far greater concern to the United States than it had been previously, even if nuclear weapons made full-scale war less likely.

On the other hand, one of proliferation pessimists' major claims—the allied proliferation will cause a nuclear domino effect—is also not supported by the case studies in this book. The nuclear domino effect posits that if one country gets nuclear weapons, its enemies will get nuclear weapons followed by their enemies going nuclear. None of the case studies in this book caused a single country to acquire nuclear weapons in this fashion. But they did contribute to the proliferation of nuclear weapons in a different manner. Specifically, in the cases of France and Pakistan especially (but also to a lesser extent with Israel), allied proliferation caused the spread of nuclear weapons through the nuclear offspring effect. The nuclear offspring effect refers to countries selling the technology to build the bomb to other countries, thereby contributing to the spread of nuclear weapons. This tended to be countries the ally and partner was friendly with rather than enemies. In the case of Pakistan, though, the recipients of nuclear technology were enemies of the United States.

Proliferation pessimists are on stronger ground with other arguments they make. For instance, in every case, the ally's or partner's pursuit of nuclear weapons caused severe tensions in its alliance with the United States, although in certain cases that was caused by US opposition to the proliferation. This is consistent with those who argue that allied proliferation will weaken America's alliances, although the severe tensions haven't endured in most of the cases. Similarly, some proliferation pessimists claim that allies and partners who acquire nuclear weapons will be emboldened and act more independently of the United States. Although this is harder to prove with any certainty, on balance the evidence suggests this is the case. Great Britain became more adventurous temporarily around the time it acquired an operational nuclear arsenal. The best example of this was the Suez Crisis. Even before acquiring nuclear weapons, France under de Gaulle acted more independently of the US and NATO than Great Britain. Once Paris did possess an operational nuclear arsenal, however, de Gaulle acted even more boldly, especially by leaving NATO Command. Around the time it acquired nuclear weapons, Pakistan intensified its proxy war with India through the support of terrorist groups. Even Israel became more offensively focused after acquiring nuclear weapons, as best evidenced by its invasion of Lebanon. It is not clear whether these more audacious policies were motivated by nuclear weapons in all these cases. At least in the cases of France and Pakistan, nuclear weapons did play a major role. The same could be true of Great Britain in the middle of the 1950s. With Israel, the evidence is far more ambiguous. As noted in the introduction of the book, nuclear weapons have such a large presence in policymakers' minds that they don't even have to be discussed.

Between the proliferation optimists and pessimists are a group I have referred to as the relativists. These are people—more likely to be in policy positions than the proliferation optimists—who don't favor allied proliferation but are willing to accept it to advance broader objectives. For instance, proliferation relativists would argue that in some cases, Washington must prioritize geopolitics over nonproliferation. Certainly, the histories support the argument that America should not automatically terminate an alliance simply because an ally or partner acquires nuclear weapons. The United States has maintained extremely beneficial relationships with Great Britain, France, Israel, and arguably Pakistan despite those countries acquiring nuclear weapons. At the same time, the cases all show that proliferation and larger geopolitical issues cannot be completely compartmentalized. In fact, the two are usually linked. The nature of this linkage typically depends on the details of the case, but it is often hugely important for the United States. The nuclearization of the Indo-Pakistani rivalry made it of far greater concern to Washington and also inhibited America's ability to pivot toward India. The potential of a German nuclear weapon greatly increased tensions with the Soviet Union. Great Britain and France significantly cut the size of their conventional forces in Europe after acquiring nuclear weapons. This put more burden on the United States and made NATO more reliant on nuclear weapons to offset the Soviet Union's conventional superiority. In all these cases, proliferation impacted the biggest geopolitics of the day. The ways in which geopolitics were impacted were hard to foresee, making it difficult to judge the costs of failing to prevent allied proliferation.

LESSONS FOR THE FUTURE

Of course, this book wasn't written simply to illuminate academic debates; its main purpose is to better inform policymakers who are forced to grapple with allies and partners acquiring nuclear weapons. Accordingly, the remainder of this chapter explores the lessons the histories have for potential future cases of allied proliferation. As stated repeatedly, this doesn't mean that any two cases of allied proliferation are going to be identical. Rather, history can help illuminate the types of challenges and different outcomes future cases might present to US policymakers. There are some issues that stretched across all (or nearly all) the cases, including strong tensions within the bilateral alliance and the nuclear offspring phenomena. But one of the main takeaways from the cases is that proliferation impacts treaty alliances differently than strategic partners. Many of the challenges of the British case were present in the French one but not the Israeli or Pakistani cases. In general, the impact of the partner cases were more dependent on the nature of the countries and America's relationship with them. But even though the partner cases seem less generalizable, they have certain commonalities that aren't there with treaty allies.

As such, in reviewing the lessons, I am going to have a section focused on allies and another on strategic partners. To make the lessons less abstract, I will try to apply them to actual potential future cases. Specifically, the allies' section will apply the lessons from the British and French cases to South Korea and Japan. The partner section will focus on a potentially nuclear-armed Saudi Arabia. This doesn't necessarily mean South Korea, Japan, and Saudi Arabia are the allies and partners most likely to acquire nuclear weapons in the future. Certainly, with regards to allies, one could make a compelling case for Turkey. Partner cases besides Saudi Arabia would include Brazil and Egypt. And as one axiom puts it, predictions are difficult, especially about the future. It's certainly possible the next US ally and partner who acquires nuclear weapons isn't one we currently suspect. Regardless, South Korea, Japan, and Saudi Arabia are reasonable cases to use to illuminate the broader lessons from the cases.

ALLIED CASES

The twin developments of China's growing conventional power and North Korea's growing nuclear capabilities raise the possibility that South Korea and/or Japan could seek to acquire nuclear weapons in the future. Although Japan is said to have a nuclear allergy, Japanese society has regularly transformed itself nearly overnight in response to external stimuli. For over two hundred years, from the early seventeenth century to the middle of the nineteenth century, Japan lived in self-imposed extreme isolationism (*Sakoku*). Then in 1853, large American warships showed up on Japan's shores and forcibly opened the country. Realizing how far behind the West Japan had fallen, domestic reformers launched the Meiji Restoration. What followed was a rapid industrialization and modernization where the previously isolated Japan emulated Western societies with the zeal only found in a new convert. This eventually led to Imperial Japan, a hyper- militarized regime intent on ruling all of Asia. When Tokyo was defeated by the Allied Powers in World

War II, the militaristic government was replaced by a pacifist one that has continued to the present day. Given this backdrop, it's hardly unthinkable that if China seized the Senkaku Islands or other strategic real estate from Japan—and America either didn't intervene or was defeated—Tokyo's nuclear allergy would turn into an atomic craving. The same could be true if China conquers Taiwan. If so, Japan is well positioned to quickly build up a nuclear arsenal given its large stockpiles of plutonium and enrichment capability.

South Korea could also be impacted by the growing Chinese military threat. Indeed, the Air Defense Identification Zone (ADIZ) China announced in the East China Sea in 2013 included Socotra Rock, a submerged rock in the Yellow Sea claimed by Beijing and Seoul. In response, South Korea expanded its own ADIZ to include the rock. A reunified Korea would also border China, and Seoul and Beijing already both claim the Baekdu Mountain on the Chinese-North Korean border. Still, the more pressing issue for South Korea is that North Korea has acquired a nuclear weapons capability that it is unlikely to surrender. In fact, North Korea now has the capability to conduct nuclear strikes on the US homeland, raising the same concerns Europeans had during the Cold War about America's willingness to use nuclear weapons to defend their security if it meant losing US cities. Not surprisingly, there has been growing chatter in Seoul about the need for either forward deployed US tactical nuclear weapons or an independent nuclear arsenal. Another possibility is that South Korea ends up with an accidental nuclear arsenal. In this scenario, the North Korean regime could collapse and end up being absorbed by Seoul. Most people assume that South Korea would voluntarily give up the nuclear weapons it inherited, just as the former Soviet states did after the Cold War. This is certainly possible but not inevitable. One could imagine the leaders of a reunified Korea wanting to stoke Korean nationalism in order to unite the long-fractured nations. Furthermore, the only major contribution the former North Korea could bequeath to a unified Peninsula is a nuclear weapons arsenal.

If any of these scenarios came to pass, how would it impact the United States? The British and French cases offer several potential clues. To begin with, Japan or South Korea seeking nuclear weapons would undoubtedly put great strain on their relationships with America. Not only was this true in the cases of London and Paris, but also when Seoul itself pursued nuclear weapons in the 1970s. It's possible these tensions would eventually fizzle out years after Seoul or Tokyo acquired nuclear weapons, as happened with the UK and France. But before then, a few thorny issues would have to be addressed.

Launch Control

One of these is launch control, which created tensions in both the British and French cases. In the former, launch control was first addressed in the Quebec Agreement signed between FDR and Winston Churchill during World War II. That agreement prohibited either country from using the bomb without the other side's consent. This condition became an issue for the Truman administration when it became public after the war. Amidst Congressional outrage, the Truman administration pressured Britain to void this condition. London agreed to surrender its veto power but regretted that decision only a few years later, when the UK began hosting US bombers on its territory. British leaders belatedly realized that the US believed it could use these weapons without the United Kingdom's consent.

To their credit, some US officials anticipated that Great Britain acquiring nuclear weapons would create new launch control issues. Some US lawmakers worried that a nuclear-armed UK would entrap the US into conflict with the Soviet Union. Other American leaders worried it would allow London to stay neutral in a US-Soviet war. But anticipating the issues didn't make them any easier to solve. Instead, the problem festered into the John F. Kennedy administration. Shortly after taking office, the JFK administration talked about putting Great Britain out of the nuclear business. But launch control really became an issue when the Kennedy administration tried to implement its Flexible Response doctrine, including the gradual escalation/ no cities nuclear targeting. The concern was that even if the US pursued a deliberately slow nuclear escalation toward the Soviet Union, London or Paris could launch their own nuclear weapons at Soviet cities. Thus, Defense Secretary McNamara began pushing for centralized nuclear decision making. Unsurprisingly, neither Great Britain nor France was interested in surrendering its ability to use nuclear weapons independently of the United States. Charles de Gaulle rejected the Kennedy administration's overtures out of hand; the British tried to placate the United States while ultimately retaining its ability to use nuclear weapons independently. Ultimately, the Kennedy administration realized the controlled nuclear escalation/no cities targeting system was unrealistic on several grounds and abandoned it. But the question of who decided when and how to use nuclear weapons created tensions within NATO for decades.

These operational challenges are inherent in any military alliance that features two or more independent nuclear arsenals. As such, launch control issues would also be a problem if either Japan or South Korea acquired nuclear weapons (assuming the US maintained its current military alliances with them). Of course, launch control disputes are issues in military alliances when only one country or no countries have nuclear weapons. When

President Trump was ratcheting up tensions with Kim Jong-un in 2017, South Korean President Moon Jae-in publicly argued that Washington needed Seoul's permission to attack North Korea. With South Korea building up its own independent strike capabilities, the United States is likely to want some say over their use.[1] Still, these issues are magnified when nuclear weapons are involved given the higher stakes. Furthermore, in the case of Flexible Response, allied nuclear arsenals were one of the factors that prevented the United States from adopting the military strategy its leaders felt was best able to deal with the Soviet threat. Even if one disagrees with Flexible Response, as the Kennedy/LBJ administrations themselves eventually did, there's nothing to prevent a strategy one does favor from being similarly hindered by South Korea or Japan having nuclear weapons.

Conventional Cuts

South Korea and Japan going nuclear could also lead to conventional military cuts that undermine America's defense posture in the Asia-Pacific. Once they had an operational nuclear deterrent, both Great Britain and France pursued a nuclear substitute defense policy. Under this policy, they based their security primarily on their nuclear arsenals, reducing defense spending and the size of their conventional forces accordingly. This proved problematic for the United States because allied arsenals added very little to the overall strategic balance. At the same time, Washington wanted its European NATO forces to shoulder a larger share of the conventional burden.

As a percentage of GDP, Great Britain's defense spending went from 11% in 1953 to 7% in 1960. A decade after that, London was spending only 5.2% of its GDP on defense. Similarly, in 1952 the UK had 871,700 service members on active duty. That declined to 521,100 in 1960 and 373,000 in 1970. The largest cuts came after the British published its 1957 Defense White Paper, which laid out the rationale for a smaller, nuclearized force. For instance, the UK cut its air force squadrons deployed in Germany by two-thirds after 1957 and the size of the British army in Europe by 33%.[2] French military forces were never as large a part of NATO as Great Britain in the 1950s. Still, French defense spending and the size of its military forces also declined by similar numbers. From 1961 to 1966, the size of the French armed forces declined by 50%, from 1,000,000 to 522,000 men under arms. During that time, the French Army declined from 804,000 to 338,000 men.[3] Defense spending declined from 5.4% in 1960 to 3.1% of GDP by 1973. While some of the cuts in the British and French armed services were inevitable, they were more drastic because of how nuclear weapons changed London's and Paris's defense doctrines. Of the major European powers,

French and British defense spending as a percentage of GDP declined the furthest between 1960 and 1980.

If a nuclear-armed Japan or South Korea followed the European allies' example, it would be a major blow to America's defense posture in the Asia-Pacific. In 2020, Japan and South Korea had the ninth and tenth largest defense budgets in the world.[4] The South Korean armed services have 555,000 active-duty personnel (along with a reserve force of 2.75 million) and an increasingly powerful missile arsenal. Seoul's navy has seen impressive modernization, and its submarine fleet is particularly powerful, especially the three- thousand-ton *Dosan Ahn Chang-ho*-class, which will be able to launch ballistic missiles.[5]

By number of personnel, Japan's forces are significantly smaller, with only 261,000 active-duty members. But most observers consider the Japanese Self Defense Forces to be even more powerful than their larger South Korean counterparts. Tokyo is especially proficient in certain capabilities like submarines and undersea warfare. These are likely to be essential to any denial strategy toward China. Japan is also building more force projection capabilities, including missiles and turning its largest amphibious assault ships into smaller aircraft carriers. More importantly, recent years have seen Tokyo increasingly vocal about not allowing Beijing to conquer Taiwan. According to news reports, the US and Japan are devising joint contingency plans to prevent any invasion from being successful.[6] Put simply, the United States is counting on Japan's military forces to check China's ambitions in the Indo-Pacific, just as Tokyo helped check the Soviet Union in Asia during the Cold War.[7] They are extremely important to US forces, especially as China builds up its military forces. Were Japan to devote less money to capabilities like submarines in favor of nuclear weapons, it would greatly weaken America's defense posture in the Asia-Pacific.

Losing a Base

Perhaps nothing could impact America's defense posture in the Asia-Pacific more than losing US bases in Japan or South Korea. After France acquired an operational nuclear arsenal, de Gaulle withdrew Paris from NATO's military command and ordered all US and NATO forces and bases off of French territory. Acquiring nuclear weapons does not inevitably lead to this outcome. Rather, de Gaulle's decision was rooted in his views about French sovereignty and alliances. These views long predated Paris going nuclear. Still, once France did have the bomb, de Gaulle felt liberated to act on his views in a way he probably otherwise would not. In fact, de Gaulle claimed that France's nuclear arsenal made integration in NATO's military command impossible.

In one sense, the fact that France leaving NATO's military command was rooted in de Gaulle's peculiar viewpoints is reassuring. After all, a future nuclear-armed Japan or South Korea will not be led by Charles de Gaulle. This notion is misguided, however. For starters, de Gaulle merely acquired a French nuclear program that was already in full swing by the time he returned to power in 1958. It was the Fourth Republic leaders who put France on the path to acquiring nuclear weapons. These men did not view the *force de frappe* as a way to liberate France from the constraints of a military alliance. In fact, they thought that the *force de frappe* would enhance France's position within NATO. Then de Gaulle returned to power and used the nuclear arsenal in ways that the leaders who initiated the nuclear program would have strongly opposed.

Therefore, the best lesson to take away from the French case is that America cannot control which leaders will govern its allies in the future. Even if a strongly pro-American leader starts a nuclear program, there is nothing to prevent a future, more anti-American leader from using the arsenal to disrupt the bilateral alliance. Moreover, de Gaulle's nationalistic ideology is not wholly unique. In Europe today, one can point to clear parallels between de Gaulle and Turkish President Recep Tayyip Erdogan, especially with regard to their views of the United States and NATO. Northeast Asia is still a hotbed of nationalism, much like de Gaulle. In Japan, this currently manifests itself in pro-US sentiment. The same is not true in South Korea. There is arguably latent anti-Americanism in South Korea's left wing, dating back to Washington's support of ROK dictators Park Chung-hee and Chun Doo-hwan. South Korea's left also has strong nationalist tendencies, which extends to its more favorable view of North Korea and priority on building up indigenous military capabilities. Absent a threat from North Korea, it's hardly unthinkable that South Korea would veer closer to China than a US-Japanese bloc. In this environment, the best way to safeguard US interests is to prevent allies from acquiring weapons that can be used to severely undermine the relationship.

It is beyond dispute that losing access to Japan or South Korea would harm America more than France's withdrawal from NATO command. This is due to the nature of the US alliance systems in the two respective regions. In Europe, America has a multilateral alliance system that allowed Washington to relocate the bases it lost in France to other countries. By contrast, in Asia, the United States has a hub-and-spoke system where Washington maintains ties with each ally on a bilateral basis. US forces in the Asia-Pacific are highly concentrated in Japan and South Korea, leaving Washington more reliant on these countries than it was on any European nation in the Cold War. For all these reasons, if South Korea or Japan ordered US forces to vacate their country, it is highly unlikely these forces could be relocated to a third country.

Even if a country like the Philippines or Australia did agree to a sizable US presence, the huge distances of the Asia-Pacific would not make this a seamless trade- off. Moreover, we currently live in an era where precision-guided missiles make static, concentrated forces extremely vulnerable. The United States is looking to better distribute its forces to reduce their vulnerability. Accordingly, it needs to be expanding its bases in the region, not losing them.

Emboldened Allies?

Although less definitive, Britain and France both acted with greater assertiveness and autonomy after acquiring nuclear weapons. Mark Bell's careful examination of Britain's willingness to use force to defend its interests in the Middle East immediately prior to and after acquiring an operational nuclear deterrent is instructive in this regard. After reviewing six crises, Bell concludes that before it had an operational nuclear force in 1955, "Britain was extremely wary of responding to challenges with force without the support of the United States, and British responses were characterized by compromise and deference to US preferences." Once London had an operational nuclear deterrent, it "[was] more willing to use force unilaterally, paid less attention to American preferences, and was less inclined to compromise." Certainly, de Gaulle always acted more independently from the United States than British leaders. Still, he became more audacious following France's first nuclear test in 1960 and, again, when it acquired an operational deterrent around 1965. This was best exemplified by his decision to leave NATO command and pursue stronger ties with the Soviet Union. In both the British and French cases, however, it's worth noting that the greater autonomy, to the extent it was motivated by their nuclear arsenals, did not last long. It's hard to extrapolate from these cases how or if this tendency would impact a nuclear-armed Japan or South Korea. Neither Japan nor South Korea has far-flung interests in other regions as Great Britain did in the 1950s. France's experience was colored by its leader at the time. It's possible acquiring nuclear weapons would make South Korea more likely to cut a separate peace with North Korea. On the other hand, Seoul could become more aggressive in challenging Pyongyang. A nuclear Japan could also more aggressively push back against China. On the other hand, a nuclear-armed Japan or South Korea could be more reluctant to assist the United States in combating Chinese assertiveness. As these scenarios suggest, it is very hard to predict how nuclear weapons would change Japan's and South Korea's aggressiveness and autonomy.

Nuclear Offspring

The nuclear offspring phenomenon was present to a greater or lesser degree in all the cases except Great Britain. France has more than compensated among the allies. Most notably, France sold Israel nearly everything it needed to build nuclear weapons. Paris also made significant efforts to sell reprocessing plants to South Korea, Taiwan, and Pakistan. France did sell Japan reprocessing plants that Tokyo has so far not used to build nuclear weapons. France is also considering selling China a massive reprocessing plant, despite growing tensions between Washington and Beijing. It seems exceedingly unlikely that Japan or South Korea would ever agree to a deal similar to what France sold Israel. That took place in a different era, and Seoul and Tokyo are both responsible members of the international community. Indeed, both Japan and South Korea already have highly developed nuclear industries, which export nuclear technology abroad. Acquiring nuclear weapons would probably not have a substantial impact on either country's nuclear export policies. Still, it's worth noting that although both states are generally responsible, there are already disagreements about nuclear exports. For instance, the United States has insisted that Saudi Arabia forgo enriching uranium as part of any nuclear program it establishes. This has not stopped South Korea from signing a nuclear cooperation agreement that would allow Saudi Arabia to enrich uranium to 20 percent levels. Although it has mostly occurred behind the scenes, Washington and Seoul have disagreed about South Korea's ability to sell Saudi Arabia nuclear reactors if the kingdom doesn't sign a nuclear cooperation agreement with the United States. Thus, while the nuclear offspring phenomenon would probably not be appreciably worse if Tokyo or Seoul got nuclear weapons, disagreements over nuclear exports are already taking place in the case of Saudi Arabia. It is to the Saudi case we now turn.

PARTNERS

Under the definition used in this book—a major non-NATO ally—Saudi Arabia doesn't technically qualify as a partner nation. Nonetheless, the United States and Saudi Arabia have maintained strong political and military ties since World War II. The two countries signed a Mutual Defense Assistance Agreement in 1951. When Saddam Hussein invaded Kuwait in 1990, the George H. W. Bush administration deployed roughly half a million US troops to protect Saudi Arabia. Even after defeating the Iraqi military, thousands of US troops remained in the kingdom throughout the 1990s and early 2000s. In 2003, US troops were relocated elsewhere in the Gulf because of domestic opposition within the kingdom. Yet, some troops remained in the kingdom, and during the Trump administration, thousands of US troops were deployed in Saudi Arabia in response to tensions with Iran. Furthermore, Saudi Arabia is the largest purchaser of US arms. By any reasonable definition, Saudi Arabia is a major security partner of the United States.

Saudi Arabia has also made clear its intention to acquire at least a latent nuclear capability. To begin with, the kingdom announced plans to purchase two power reactors from abroad. Despite the modest nature of the program, Saudi Arabia has repeatedly insisted on enriching uranium domestically. Given the price of uranium on international markets, domestic enrichment cannot be justified on economic grounds. This capability would be necessary to acquire fissile material for nuclear weapons. According to numerous reports, Riyadh has also continuously refused to sign an Additional Protocol with the IAEA, which would give international inspectors greater access to Saudi Arabia's future nuclear program. All of this makes sense only when one considers that Saudi officials have repeatedly stated that if Iran acquires nuclear weapons, the kingdom will follow suit. Most notably, Mohammed bin Salman (MBS), the crown prince and de facto leader of Saudi Arabia, told *60 Minutes* that Saudi Arabia would acquire nuclear weapons "without a doubt" if Iran built its own.

What lessons do the Israeli and Pakistani cases have for a potentially nuclear-armed Saudi Arabia? In general, partner cases seem much less generalizable than the allied cases. Many of the top lessons from the British and French cases—such as launch control—are inherent to the nature of military alliances. By contrast, the lessons from the partner cases seem to depend more on the countries themselves, as well as their relationship with the United States. As such, the Pakistani case is likely to offer more lessons for a potential nuclear-armed Saudi Arabia than the Israeli one. But there are a couple of lessons that apply to both cases.

US Engagement

As noted above, proliferation optimists believe that allies and partners acquiring nuclear weapons will enable those countries to protect themselves, allowing the United States to reduce its commitments. The Israeli and Pakistani cases saw the opposite happen: as these countries pursued and acquired nuclear weapons, US military assistance to them increased. When both countries were pursuing nuclear weapons, Washington argued it needed to increase arms sales to Israel and Pakistan to persuade them they didn't need the bomb. As the NSC official Robert Komer told President Johnson, Israel was most likely to build the bomb out of "desperation" that the "conventional balance was turning against it." Komer concluded from this that larger US arms sales could be the best tool to prevent an Israeli nuclear weapon. The

Reagan administration used a similar logic to justify maintaining arms sales to Pakistan in the 1980s. Once Israel acquired nuclear weapons, arms sales became essential to ensure Israel wasn't forced to use nuclear weapons to defend itself. Military assistance to Pakistan reached its highest levels in the 2000s, albeit this was a result of the Afghan war. Although Saudi Arabia is already the largest purchaser of US arms, American policymakers would likely seek to increase arms sales to the kingdom as it got closer to nuclear weapons. This pressure would be more acute if the United States was trying to convince Saudi Arabia not to test a nuclear weapon it already developed.

Alternative Facts

In both partner cases, but especially the Israeli one, US policymakers were forced to present alternative facts to Congress, the American public, and the rest of the world. These alternative facts sought to downplay Israel's and Pakistan's nuclear status. In the Israeli case, US policymakers pretended that cursory inspections made Washington confident Israel wasn't building a nuclear weapon. In internal communications, US officials recognized the severe shortcomings in these inspections. To this day, the US government doesn't officially acknowledge Israel's nuclear status. During the 1980s, the Reagan administration similarly sought to downplay Pakistan's nuclear progress in order to continue arms sales to Islamabad. The administration also denied that Pakistan had rewired the F-16s it purchased from the United States in order to carry nuclear weapons. And it swept Pakistani nuclear smuggling operations under the rug. It's hard to quantify the costs of these alternative facts, but it would be naive to assume there are none.

The United States would surely pursue a similar approach toward Saudi Arabia if it were seriously seeking nuclear weapons. After all, the United States has downplayed Riyadh's involvement in spreading Jihadist ideology and international terrorism, including the Saudi links to 9/11. Both the Obama and Trump administrations backed Saudi Arabia's increasingly brutal conduct in the war in Yemen. President Trump similarly downplayed MBS's role in the assassination of Jamal Khashoggi. Even revelations that Riyadh helped Saudi nationals flee the United States after being charged with violent crimes has provoked surprisingly little outrage among US policymakers. Given this past, it seems inevitable that the United States would downplay Saudi Arabia's nuclear status.

Nuclear Targets

One lesson that the Israeli case does have for a future Saudi one is the potential vulnerability of a Saudi reactor or enrichment program. As noted in the

Israeli case study, there was a major nuclear element to the 1967 War. At the very least, Israeli leaders were greatly concerned when Egyptian MiGs flew over Dimona twice in the run-up to the war.

For the purposes of this book, the exact details are less important than the fact that Israel's nuclear reactor played an important role in the conflict. This is crucial because a Saudi nuclear program would also be extremely vulnerable to attacks by Iran or other adversaries. Indeed, nuclear reactors in the Middle East have rarely fared well. Beyond the Dimona example, Iranian, Iraqi, and Syrian nuclear reactors have come under attack at some point. Future Saudi reactors would be especially vulnerable given the proliferation of highly accurate missiles and drones in the region. Iran's attack on Saudi oil facilities in September 2019 was especially instructive in this regard. This attack targeted the custom-built "stabilization towers" at Saudi Arabia's most important oil facility. As previous analyses noted, these towers were the biggest bottleneck in the Saudi oil production process, suggesting the missiles and drones hit exactly where they were aimed. Needless to say, a nuclear reactor is a much larger target to hit. In any case, as the 1967 example demonstrates, a reactor doesn't even have to be targeted for it to create insecurity that leads to armed conflict.

Complicating US Foreign Policy

Pakistan's nuclear weapons made it significantly more difficult for the United States to achieve its objectives in the region. This first occurred in the 1980s, when the Reagan administration had to walk a tightrope in downplaying Pakistan's nuclear progress to continue cooperation with Islamabad in Afghanistan. Islamabad's nuclear arsenal also complicated America's response to the 9/11 attacks. As the George W. Bush administration planned an invasion of Afghanistan, US officials worried how this action could destabilize Pakistan and its nuclear weapons. This concern was so great that President Bush passed up opportunities to take out al-Qaeda terrorists located in Pakistan. Moreover, Bush came into office determined to pivot to India as part of a larger effort to focus on China's rise. The 9/11 terrorist attacks and America's subsequent war in Afghanistan greatly hampered this effort. Nonetheless, Pakistan's nuclear arsenal also complicated the shift to India. Despite Islamabad's long-standing and close ties to China, Washington cannot fully abandon Pakistan, because of the risk of loose nuclear weapons and its bitter rivalry with India.

It's easy to see how these lessons could apply to a nuclear-armed Saudi Arabia. Since the First Gulf War, US foreign policy has been dominated by the Middle East. This deep engagement has rarely resulted in major successes. With the notable exception of Desert Storm, the United States has largely failed in the Middle East. For instance, despite the extensive attention the issue has received from US diplomats, there has been no peace agreement between the Israelis and Palestinians. America's invasion of Iraq was a failure on many fronts and became even worse with the rise of the Islamic State. Meanwhile, America's greatest foe in the region, Iran, has significantly expanded its influence during this time.

The United States' ability to achieve its objectives in the Middle East would be more difficult if Saudi Arabia acquired nuclear weapons. On top of the current challenges, the United States would have to navigate a Saudi nuclear arsenal. Before making major decisions in the region, US policymakers would have to consider its impact on Saudi Arabia's stability. Moreover, under both Presidents Obama and Trump, the United States has identified that it needs to pivot to Asia and away from the Middle East. This makes sense given the growing importance of Asia, as well as the Persian Gulf's reduced importance to America. Already, shifting US resources away from the Middle East has proven difficult. Saudi Arabia acquiring nuclear weapons would probably end the Asia pivot.

Nuclearized Proxy Wars

Reducing US commitments in the Middle East would be especially difficult because of the nuclearized proxy war. As noted in the previous chapter, the nuclearization of the Indo-Pakistani rivalry greatly increased its importance to the United States. Mutually assured destruction has made it far less likely that India and Pakistan will engage in a full-scale shooting war. Still, the three wars India and Pakistan fought before acquiring nuclear weapons were of only secondary importance to the United States. Once both sides had nuclear weapons, America had to treat every crisis on the subcontinent as an urgent priority. The fact that none of the myriad Indo-Pakistani crises have escalated into nuclear war is due to Indian and Pakistani leaders, deft US diplomacy, and probably a certain degree of luck. There's no guarantee this formula is sustainable.

It's difficult to imagine a scenario where Iran doesn't acquire nuclear weapons but Saudi Arabia does. Tehran already possesses significant latent nuclear capabilities, including an enrichment program and ballistic missiles. As such, Saudi Arabia acquiring nuclear weapons would likely lead to a nuclearized rivalry between Riyadh and Tehran. This would not be identical to the situation between India and Pakistan. India and Pakistan share a large land border and fought three major wars before acquiring the bomb. By contrast, Saudi Arabia and Iran have mostly engaged in a proxy war across the greater Middle East. Still, this proxy war already greatly worries US policymakers, and the stakes would be infinitely higher were nuclear weapons to enter the equation. Furthermore, there has been at least one instance—Iran's missile and drone attack on Saudi oil facilities in September 2019—when the two engaged in direct, kinetic fire. Tehran has also engaged in cyber attacks against Saudi Arabia. Trying to contain the fallout from this proxy war would take on much greater importance for the United States if both sides had nuclear weapons. Pivoting away from the Middle East would be a pipedream. Given the presence of a nuclear-armed Israel, there would actually be a trilateral or two nuclear dyads. This could be somewhat akin to the Indo-Pakistani-Chinese nuclear triangle in Asia.

Terrorism, Loose Nukes, and Insider Threats

America's greatest concerns with Pakistan's nuclear arsenal have arguably been the potential threats of terrorism, loose nuclear weapons, and insider threats. Pakistani leaders have cultivated Jihadist terrorist groups since the 1980s, and as a result, Pakistan is home to a combustible mix of various terrorist groups. US policymakers have long worried that one of these terrorist groups might steal some of Islamabad's nuclear weapons or fissile material. Another possibility is that a sympathetic insider in Pakistan's scientific or military establishment could provide a terrorist group with a nuclear weapon. Terrorism isn't the only worry: given the unknown level of radicalization within Pakistan's military, Washington is concerned about an unauthorized launch from a Pakistani field commander. Of course, perhaps the biggest worry is about the stability of the Pakistani state itself. Were the Pakistani government to collapse, it's difficult to know who'd end up with its nuclear arsenal.

To some degree, all of these concerns would be present with a nuclear Saudi Arabia. To be sure, the kingdom doesn't host countless terrorist groups like Pakistan. In fact, the Saudi regime has been fairly successful at stamping out domestic terrorist groups. Nonetheless, there have been numerous high-profile terrorist incidents in the kingdom, including the Grand Mosque seizure in 1979, the Khobar Towers bombings in 1996, and al-Qaeda's campaign inside the kingdom in the 2000s. Saudi nationals have also played a prominent role in global Jihadist groups. Osama bin Laden and fourteen of the nineteen 9/11 hijackers were Saudi nationals. It is difficult to conduct public opinion polls inside a country like Saudi Arabia. Nonetheless, surveys have shown that Saudi citizens have generally more favorable opinions of Islamist terrorist groups than the Muslim world at large. Along with the Saudi regime promoting Wahhabism, this suggests that insider threats and rogue commanders would be a major concern for a nuclear Saudi Arabia. While predicting the collapse of the Saudi regime is a fool's errand, its indefinite stability can't be taken for granted. The growing strife within the royal family, an unsustainable economic model, and a youth bulge are all daunting challenges. Whether the archaic governing system can handle these challenges remains to be seen. Were Saudi Arabia to acquire nuclear weapons, however, the regime's potential collapse would take on even more importance to the United States.

Nuclear Offspring

Compared with South Korea or Japan, a nuclear Saudi Arabia is more likely to contribute to the spread of nuclear technology through nuclear sales or transfers. This doesn't mean that it would be another Pakistan. As noted in the previous chapter, there were a lot of factors motivating Pakistan's nuclear sales, including A. Q. Khan's desire to get into the missile business (in the case of North Korea) and Islamabad's need for extra hard currency. Still, unlike South Korea or Japan, Riyadh is not a member of the Nuclear Suppliers' Group. The kingdom's limited experience in the nuclear business thus far has not been encouraging. MBS has threatened to build nuclear weapons even as the kingdom has dragged its feet on international safeguards agreements. Although a limited sample size, this suggests Saudi Arabia may be willing to buck the global nuclear order.

More generally, Riyadh has not adhered to international norms to the same degree as Seoul or Tokyo. For instance, human rights groups have accused Saudi Arabia of violating myriad international norms in its brutal fight in Yemen. Although nuclear technology and ideology are not completely analogous, Saudi Arabia has been proliferating its radical Wahhabi ideology across the Muslim world for decades, even as this has helped spur radicalization. This has continued despite some pressure from the United States and Western groups. It is certainly possible that the kingdom would come to see nuclear exports as another avenue to enhance its influence in the Islamic world.

In short, then, the consequences of partners acquiring nuclear weapons are less likely generalizable than with allies. This unpredictability alone should be a cause for concern. The impact of a partner nation acquiring nuclear weapons will depend heavily on the nature of the country in question as well as its relationship with Washington. In that sense, Israel and Pakistan are interesting contrasts. Israel is likely to be on the best-case side of the spectrum, whereas Pakistan would fall closer to the worst-case scenario. Saudi Arabia would almost certainly be closer to the Pakistani case than the Israeli one. Nonetheless, the unpredictability of the partner cases makes it difficult to predict just how bad it will be.

NONPROLIFERATION TREATY

In terms of illuminating the impact of future cases of allied proliferation, one of the major weaknesses of the case studies is the absence of the Nonproliferation Treaty. Britain and France acquired nuclear weapons before the NPT came into effect and joined the treaty as nuclear-weapon states. Israel and Pakistan never joined the NPT at all. In all future cases, the ally or partner will probably have to leave the treaty to build the bomb. Another possibility is that the friendly state will secretly acquire nuclear weapons without exiting the treaty. Regardless, this will be a new dynamic that wasn't present in the histories reviewed in this book. How this changes the issue for US policymakers is hard to say with any sort of confidence. But US policymakers will definitely have to worry about how the allied proliferation erodes the credibility of the NPT and nonproliferation more generally.

These disclaimers aside, there are some useful clues from the case studies. For one thing, in all the cases, US policymakers worried that the allied proliferation would lead to a cascade of other proliferation. This was most prominent in the case of France, where Washington worried that Paris acquiring nuclear weapons would force West Germany to pursue the bomb. US policymakers also believed that if Israel acquired nuclear weapons, its Arab enemies would follow suit. As discussed earlier in this chapter, the nuclear domino effect never occurred. This should give US policymakers some confidence they could prevent the collapse of the NPT.

The other interesting parallel is how Israel's nuclear program interacted with America's nonproliferation and arms control efforts. Washington put strong pressure on Israel to sign the NPT because American officials believed Jerusalem's failure to do so would make it impossible to get countries like West Germany and Japan to sign the treaty. Unbeknown to most US policymakers at the time, Israel had acquired nuclear weapons by 1967. Jerusalem therefore refused to join the NPT. This did not prevent the nearly universal adoption of the NPT. Israel's nuclear program became a complication again when the NPT was up for extension in 1995. Once again, US diplomacy was able to overcome these challenges, and the NPT was indefinitely extended. This too suggests that the NPT could endure a US ally or partner acquiring nuclear weapons, although this is by no means certain. At the very least, it would require robust US diplomacy, which is another cost Washington would have to endure.

CONCLUSION

In the end, costs are what allied proliferation is all about. There were real costs in every single case in this book. The costs were greater in some of the cases, such as France and Pakistan, and lesser in others, such as Great Britain and Israel. In none of the cases, however, did the United States benefit from allied proliferation. There are some generalizable costs that are likely to occur in all the allied cases—most notably, launch control issues. The costs of the partners cases are likely to depend more on the nature of the friendly state and its relationship with the United States. This makes them more unpredictable. As de Gaulle's leadership demonstrates, the allied cases will also have their own unpredictable consequences.

Of course, trying to prevent a determined ally or partner from acquiring nuclear weapons comes with its own costs. The best policies are those that convince US allies and partners early on that their security is safe without nuclear weapons. Short of that, keeping allies and partners as technologically far from the bomb as possible will help US policymakers minimize the costs. After all, the more resources allies and partners devote to a nuclear program, and the closer they come to crossing the threshold, the harder it will be to dissuade them from acquiring the bomb. Thus, Washington would ideally pursue policies early on to fend off a crisis. For instance, it should hold the line on South Korea's efforts to acquire an enrichment or pyroprocessing capability and push Saudi Arabia not to pursue nuclear energy. If Riyadh insists on pursuing a nuclear energy program, the United States should take a hard line on the so-called Gold Standard, where countries pledge not to reprocess or enrich domestically. America's pressure must go beyond not agreeing to a civilian nuclear cooperation agreement with the kingdom, as Saudi Arabia can acquire nuclear technology elsewhere. Rather, Washington should threaten broader consequences to the relationship. The United States could also pressure other nuclear suppliers—especially allies like South Korea and France—to insist on the same conditions as Washington does in its own dealings with Saudi Arabia.

The hardest cases will be those where the costs of stopping the ally or partner from acquiring the bomb are formidable. Whether it is worth paying those costs will be hard decisions for US policymakers to make. The purpose of this book was to illuminate the costs of failing to stop allied proliferation better than the current literature. If readers find it has some utility for that purpose, it will have been a success.

NOTES

1. Zachary Keck and Henry Sokolski, "How to Handle South Korea's Missile Ambitions," *Foreign Affairs*, November 6, 2017.

2. G. Wyn Rees, *Anglo-American Approaches to Alliance Security, 1955–60* (New York: Palgrave Macmillan (1996), 55; Mark Bell, "Nuclear Weapons and Foreign Policy" (MIT Doctoral diss., September 2016), 113; and Bill Taylor, "Historical Background," The RAF in Germany 1945–1993 (Brighton, UK: Royal Air Force History Society, 1998), 14.

3. IISS Military Balance, 1961 and 1966.

4. Diego Lopes Da Silva et al., "Trends in World Military Expenditure," SIPRI Fact Sheet, April 2021.

5. Yosuke Onchi, "South Korea becomes 8th country to fire ballistic missile from sub," *Nikkei Asia Review*, September 8, 2021.

6. "Japan, U.S. Draft Operation Plan for Taiwan contingency: Sources," *Kyodo News*, December 23, 2021; Demetri Sevastopulo and Kahtrin Hille, "US and Japan conduct war Games Amid Rising China-Taiwan Tensions," *Financial Times*, June 30, 2021; and David Axe, "It's Getting More Likely the Japanese Would Fight For Taiwan," *Forbes*, July 2, 2021.

7. On Japan's role in contemporary times, see Jeffrey W. Hornung, *Japan's Potential Contributions in an East China Sea Contingency* (Santa Monica, CA: RAND Corporation, 2020); Ken Moriyasu, "US Eyes Using Japan's Submarines to 'Choke' Chinese Navy," *Nikkei Asia Review*, May 5, 2021. On its role during the Cold War, see Narushige Michishita, Peter M. Swartz, and David Winkler, *Lessons of the Cold War in the Pacific: U.S. Maritime Strategy, Crisis Prevention, and Japan's Role* (Washington, DC: Wilson Center, 2016); and Alessio Patalano, "'The Silent Fight': Submarine Rearmament and the Origins of Japan's Military Engagement with the Cold War, 1955–76," *Cold War History* 21, no. 1 (2021).

Bibliography

A note on archival documents:
DNSA = The Digital National Security Archive, the subscription service of the National Security Archive at George Washington University.
FRUS = The Foreign Relations of the United States series put out by the US State Department.
JFKL = The John F. Kennedy Presidential Library.
NSA = The National Security Archive at George Washington University.
US Declassified Documents Online = The GALE subscription service that used to be called Declassified Documents Reference System (DDRS).
USNA = The United States National Archive at College Park, Maryland.

Aftergood, Steven. "A.Q. Khan Discusses Pakistan's Nuclear Program." *FAS Secrecy News,* September 8, 2009. https://sgp.fas.org/news/secrecy/2009/09/090809.html.
Albright, David. *Peddling Peril: How the Secret Nuclear Trade Arms America's Enemies.* New York: Free Press, 2010.
Allison, Graham T. "The Cuban Missile Crisis at 50." *Foreign Affairs,* July/August 2012. https://www.foreignaffairs.com/articles/cuba/2012-07-01/cuban-missile-crisis-50.
"America's top brass responds to the threat of China in the Pacific." *The Economist,* March 13, 2021. https://www.economist.com/asia/2021/03/11/americas-top-brass-responds-to-the-threat-of-china-in-the-pacific.
"Army cuts: How have UK armed forces personnel numbers changed over time?" *Guardian,* September 1, 2011. https://www.theguardian.com/news/datablog/2011/sep/01/military-service-personnel-total.
Aneja Atul, Aneja, and Sandeep Dikshit. "Pakistan Moves Missiles Closer to Border." *The Hindu,*. December 26, 2001.
Axe, David. "It's Getting More Likely the Japanese Would Fight For Taiwan." *Forbes,* July 2, 2021. https://www.forbes.com/sites/davidaxe/2021/07/02/its-getting-more-and-more-likely-japanese-troops-would-fight-for-taiwan/?sh=4ea7e5c3a4c3.
Bandow, Doug. "Let Them Make Nukes." *Foreign Affairs,* July 26, 2016.

Bard, Mitchell Geoffrey. *The Water's Edge and Beyond: Defining the Limits to Domestic Influence on United States Middle East Policy.* New Brunswick, NJ: Transaction Publishers, 1991.

Baylis, John. "American Bases in Britain: The 'Truman-Attlee Understandings.'" *World Today* 42, no. 8/9 (August–September, 1986).

———. "Exchanging Nuclear Secrets: Laying the Foundations of the Anglo-American Nuclear Relationship," *Diplomatic History* 25, no. 1 (Winter 2001).

———. "The 1958 Anglo-American Mutual Defence Agreement: The Search for Nuclear Interdependence." *Journal of Strategic Studies* 41, no. 3 (June 2008).

———. *Ambiguity and Deterrence: British Nuclear Strategy, 1945–1964.* New York: Oxford University Press, 1995.

———. *Ambiguity and Deterrence: British Nuclear Strategy, 1945–1964.* New York: Clarendon Press, 1996.

Beauchamp, Zack. "Trump's Comments on Japanese Nukes Are Worrisome—Even By Trump Standards." *Vox,* March 31, 2016. https://www.vox.com/2016/3/31/11339040/trump-nukes-japan-south-korea.

Bell, Mark. "Nuclear Weapons and Foreign Policy." PhD diss., Massachusetts Institute of Technology, September 2016.

Benn, Aluf. "Is Obama on the Way to Dimona?" *Haaretz,* December 18, 2008.

Beres, Louis Rene. "Nuclear Weapons and the War Between Iran and Iraq," *Chicago Tribune.* October 14, 1987.

Bergen, Peter. *The Longest War: The Enduring Conflict Between America and Al-Qaeda.* New York: Free Press, 2011.

Billaud, Pierre, and Venance Journe. "The Real Story Behind the Making of the French Hydrogen Bomb: Chaotic, Unsupported, but Successful." *Nonproliferation Review* 15, no. 2 (2008).

Blair, Bruce G. *The Logic of Accidental Nuclear War.* Washington, DC: Brookings, 1993.

Bleek, Philipp C. "Does Proliferation Beget Proliferation? Why Nuclear Dominos Rarely Fall." PhD diss., Georgetown University, 2010.

Bleek, Philipp C., and Eric Lorber. "Security Guarantees and Allied Proliferation." *Journal of Conflict Resolution* 58, no. 3 (2014).

Botti, Timothy J. *The Long Wait: The Forging of the Anglo-American Nuclear Alliance, 1945–1948.* New York: Greenwood Press, 1987.

Bracken, Paul. *The Second Nuclear Age: Strategy, Danger, and the New Power Politics.* New York: Times Books, 2012.

Brands, Hal. "Non-Proliferation and the Dynamics of the Middle Cold War: The Superpowers, the MLF, and the NPT." *Cold War History* 7, no. 3 (2007).

Brands, Hal, and David Palkki. "Saddam, Israel, and the Bomb: Nuclear Alarmism Justified?" *International Security* 36, no. 1 (Summer 2011).

Brauer, Jurgen, and Hubert van Tuyll. *Castles, Battles, and Bombs: How Economics Explains Military History.* Chicago: University of Chicago Press, 2008.

Brewer, Eric. "The Nuclear Proliferation Landscape: Is Past Prologue?" *Washington Quarterly* 44, no. 2 (2021).

Buckley, James L. "Why the U.S. Must Strengthen Pakistan." *New York Times,* August 5, 1981. https://www.nytimes.com/1981/08/05/opinion/l-why-the-us-must-strengthen-pakistan-220569.html.

Burr, William. "The Gas Centrifuge Secret: Origins of a U.S. Policy of Nuclear Denial, 1954–1960." *National Security Archive.* Electronic Briefing Book no. 518, June 29, 2015.

Burr, William, and Avner Cohen. "New Evidence on the 22 September 1979 Velva Event." *National Security Archive.* Briefing Book no. 570, December 6, 2016.

Burt, Richard. "U.S. Will Press Pakistan to Halt A-Arms Project." *New York Times,* August 12, 1979.

Bush, George W. *Decision Points.* New York: Random House, 2010.

Chari, P. R., Pervaiz Iqbal Cheema, and Stephen P. Cohen. *Four Crises and a Peace Process: American Engagement in South Asia.* Washington, DC: Brookings Institution Press, 2007.

Clausewitz, Carl Von. *On War.* Translated by Michael Howard and Peter Parat. Princeton, NJ: Princeton University Press, 1976.

Clift, Eleanor. "Reagan Warns Pakistani: Build Nuclear Bomb and Lose U.S. Aid." *Los Angeles Times,* July 17, 1986. https://www.latimes.com/archives/la-xpm-1986-07-17-mn-21668-story.html.

Cohen, Avner. "The Last Nuclear Moment." *New York Times,* October 6, 2003. https://www.nytimes.com/2003/10/06/opinion/the-last-nuclear-moment.html.

Cohen, Avner, and William Burr. "Don't Like That Israel Has the Bomb? Blame Nixon." *Foreign Policy,* September 12, 2014. https://foreignpolicy.com/2014/09/12/dont-like-that-israel-has-the-bomb-blame-nixon/.

———. "The Untold Story of Israel's Bomb." *Washington Post,* April 30, 2006. https://www.washingtonpost.com/archive/opinions/2006/04/30/the-untold-story-of-israels-bomb/8351206c-e6da-493e-897d-447a350824eb/.

Colby, Elbridge. "Choose Geopolitics Over Nonproliferation." *National Interest,* February 28, 2014. https://nationalinterest.org/commentary/choose-geopolitics-over-nonproliferation-9969.

Colby, Elbridge, Avner Cohen, William McCants, Bradley Morris, and William Rosenau. *The Israeli "Nuclear Alert" of 1973: Deterrence and Signaling in Crisis.* Washington, DC: CNA, April 2013.

Coll, Steve. "100,000 Demonstrate in Kashmir; Slain Leader Mourned at Peaceful Service; Solarz in New Delhi," *Washington Post.* June 1, 1990.

———. "The Stand-Off." *New Yorker,* February 13, 2006. https://www.newyorker.com/magazine/2006/02/13/the-stand-off.

———. *Directorate S: The C.I.A. and America's Secret Wars in Afghanistan and Pakistan.* New York: Penguin Press, 2018.

———. *Ghost Wars: The Secret History of the CIA, Afghanistan, and Bin Laden, from the Soviet Invasion to September 10, 2001.* New York: Penguin Books, 2004.

Corera, Gordon. *Shopping for Bombs: Nuclear Proliferation, Global Insecurity, and the Rise and Fall of the A.Q. Khan Network.* Oxford: Oxford University Press, 2006.

Correll, John T. "Churchill's Southern Strategy. *Air Force Magazine,* January 2013. https://www.airforcemag.com/article/0113churchill/.
Corrs, Andres. "Japan: Go Nuclear Now." *Forbes,* January 31, 2017. https://www.forbes.com/sites/anderscorr/2017/01/31/japan-go-nuclear-now/?sh=594023a57745.
Costigliola, Frank. *France and the United States: The Cold Alliance Since World War II.* New York: Twayne Publishers, 1992.
David, Stephen R. "Risky Business: Let Us Not Take a Chance on Proliferation." *Security Studies* 4, no. 4 (Summer 1995).
Davis, Ian. *The British Bomb and NATO: Six Decades of Contributing to NATO's Strategic Nuclear Deterrent.* Solna, Sweden: Stockholm International Peace Research Institute, November 2015.
De Geer, Lars-Erik, and Christopher M. Wright. "The 22 September 1979 Vela Incident: Radionuclide and Hydroacoustic Evidence for a Nuclear Explosion." *Science & Global Security* 26, no. 1 (2018).
de Mesquita, Bruce Bueno, and William H. Riker. "An Assessment of the Merits of Selective Nuclear Proliferation." *Journal of Conflict Resolution* 26, no. 2 (June 1982).
Dombey, Norman, and Eric Grove. "Britain's Thermonuclear Bluff." *London Review of Books* 14, no. 20 (October 1992).
Doty, Robert C. "U.S.-French Strain Laid to Paris Plan for Nuclear Force." *New York Times,* February 27, 1962. https://www.nytimes.com/1962/02/27/archives/usfrench-strain-laid-to-paris-plan-for-nuclear-force-usfrench-rift.html.
Dugger, Celia W. "Group in Pakistan is Blamed by India For Suicide Raid." *New York Times,* December 15, 2001. https://www.nytimes.com/2001/12/15/world/group-in-pakistan-is-blamed-by-india-for-suicide-raid.html.
———. "Minister Says India Won't Attack Pakistan." *New York Times,* May 14, 2002. https://www.nytimes.com/2002/05/14/world/minister-says-india-won-t-attack-pakistan.html.
Eckstein, Harry. "Case Studies and Theory in Political Science." In *Handbook of Political Science*, Vol. 7, edited by Fred Greenstein and Nelson Polsby. Reading, MA: Addison-Wesley, 1975.
Elleman, Michael. "North Korea's Newest Ballistic Missile: A Preliminary Assessment." *38 North,* May 8, 2019. https://www.38north.org/2019/05/melleman050819/.
Ellis, Sylvia. "A Foreign Policy Success? LBJ and Transatlantic Relations." *Journal of Transatlantic Studies,* 8, no. 3 (2010).
Entous, Adam. "How Trump and Three Other U.S. Presidents Protected Israel's Worst Kept Secret: Its Nuclear Arsenal." *New Yorker,* June 18, 2018. https://www.newyorker.com/news/news-desk/how-trump-and-three-other-us-presidents-protected-israels-worst-kept-secret-its-nuclear-arsenal.
Fair, C. Christine. *Fighting to the End: The Pakistan Army's Way of War.* New York: Oxford University Press, 2014.
Farmelo, Graham. *Churchill's Bomb: How the United States Overtook Britain in the First Nuclear Arms Race.* New York: Basic Books, 2013.

Feaver, Peter D. "Command and Control in Emerging Nuclear Nations." *International Security* 17, no. 3 (Winter 1992/93).

———. "Optimists, Pessimists, and Theories of Nuclear Proliferation Management: A Debate." *Security Studies*, 4 (1995).

Fialka, John F. "CIA Found Israel Could Make Bomb: Soil, Air Samples Disclosed Atomic Capability." *Washington Star*, December 8, 1977. https://www.cia.gov/library/readingroom/docs/CIA-RDP88-01315R000400060018-6.pdf.

"France's Nuclear Weapons: French Nuclear Facilities." *Nuclear Weapons Archive*, May 1, 2001. https://nuclearweaponarchive.org/France/FranceFacility.html.

Frantz, Douglas, and Catherine Collins. *The Nuclear Jihadist: The True Story of the Man Who Sold the World's Most Dangerous Secrets . . . And How We Could Have Stopped Him*. New York: Twelve, 2007.

Freedman, Lawrence. *The Evolution of Nuclear Strategy*. 3rd ed. New York: Palgrave Macmillan, 2003.

"Full Rush Transcript: Donald Trump, CNN Milwaukee Republican Presidential Town Hall." *CNN*, March 29, 2016. https://cnnpressroom.blogs.cnn.com/2016/03/29/full-rush-transcript-donald-trump-cnn-milwaukee-republican-presidential-town-hall/.

Gavin, Francis J. "Strategies of Inhibition: U.S. Grand Strategy, the Nuclear Revolution, and Nonproliferation." *International Security* 40, no. 1 (Summer 2015).

———. *Nuclear Statecraft: History and Strategy in America's Atomic Age*. Ithaca, NY: Cornell University Press, 2012.

Gerzhoy, Gene. "Alliance Coercion and Nuclear Restraint: How the United States Thwarted West Germany's Nuclear Ambitions." *International Security* 39, no. 4 (Spring 2015).

———. "Coercive Nonproliferation: Security, Leverage, and Nuclear Reversals." PhD diss., University of Chicago, 2014.

Gerzhoy, Gene, and Nick Miller. "Donald Trump Thinks More Countries Should Have Nuclear Weapons. Here's What the Research Says." *Washington Post*, April 6, 2016. https://www.washingtonpost.com/news/monkey-cage/wp/2016/04/06/should-more-countries-have-nuclear-weapons-donald-trump-thinks-so/.

Gezari, Vanessa. "Indian Suspect Claims Pakistan Aided Parliament Attack." *Chicago Tribune*, December 21, 2001.

Gilinsky, Victor, and Roger J. Mattson. "Revisiting the NUMEC Affairs." *Bulletin of Atomic Scientists* 66, no. 2 (2010).

Ginor, Isabella, and Gideon Remez. *Foxbats Over Dimona: The Soviets' Nuclear Gamble in the Six-Day War*. New Haven, CT: Yale University Press, 2008.

Goldberg, Jeffrey, and Marc Ambinder. "The Ally From Hell." *Atlantic*, December 2011. https://www.theatlantic.com/magazine/archive/2011/12/the-ally-from-hell/308730/.

Goldstein, Avery. *Deterrence and Security in the 21st Century: China, Britain, France, and the Enduring Legacy of the Nuclear Revolution*. Stanford, CA: Stanford University Press, 2000.

Gordon, Michael R., and Felicity Barringer. "Nuclear Standoff: North Korea Wants Arms and More Aid from U.S." *New York Times*, February 13, 2003. https://www

.nytimes.com/2003/02/13/world/threats-responses-nuclear-standoff-north-korea-wants-arms-more-aid-us-chief-cia.html.

Gordon, Phillip H. *A Certain Idea of France: French Security Policy and Gaullist Legacy,* Princeton, NJ: Princeton University Press, 1993.

Haberman, Maggie, and David Sanger. "Transcript: Donald Trump Expounds on His Foreign Policy Views." *New York Times,* March 26, 2016. https://www.nytimes.com/2016/03/27/us/politics/donald-trump-transcript.html.

Hacke, Christian. "Why Germany Should Get the Bomb." *National Interest,* August 12, 2018. https://nationalinterest.org/feature/why-germany-should-get-bomb-28377.

Hagel, Chuck, Malcolm Rifkind, Kevin Rudd, and Ivo Daalder. "When Allies Go Nuclear." *Foreign Affairs,* February 12, 2021. https://www.foreignaffairs.com/articles/asia/2021-02-12/when-allies-go-nuclear.

Harrison, Hope M. "New Evidence on the Building of the Berlin Wall." Cold War International History Project, e-Dossier no. 23, undated.

Heginbotham, Eric, and Richard J. Samuels. "Vulnerable US Alliances in Northeast Asia: The Nuclear Implications." *Washington Quarterly* 44, no. 1 (2021).

Hersh, Seymour. "Pakistani in U.S. Sought to Ship A-Bomb Trigger." *New York Times,* February 25, 1985. https://www.nytimes.com/1985/02/25/world/pakistani-in-us-sought-to-ship-a-bomb-trigger.html.

———. *The Samson Option: Israel's Nuclear Arsenal and American Foreign Policy.* New York: Random House, 1991.

Hershberg, James G. *James B. Conant: Harvard to Hiroshima and the Making of the Nuclear Age.* Stanford, CA: Stanford University Press, 1995.

Hewlett, Richard G., and Oscar E. Anderson, Jr. *Volume I: A History of the United States Atomic Energy Commission, The New World, 1939/1946.* University Park: The Pennsylvania State University Press, 1962.

Hornung, Jeffrey W. *Japan's Potential Contributions in an East China Sea Contingency.* Santa Monica, CA: RAND Corporation, 2020.

House, Karen Elliot. *On Saudi Arabia: Its People, Past, Religion, Fault Lines–and Future.* New York: Vintage, 2012.

———. *Uneasy Lies the Head that Wears a Crown: The House of Saud Confronts its Challenges.* Cambridge, MA: Belfer Center for Science and International Affairs, March 2016.

"How Israel Got the Bomb." *Time* 107, no. 15, April 12, 1976.

Hymans, Jacques E. C. *Achieving Nuclear Ambitions: Scientists, Politicians, and Proliferation.* New York: Cambridge University Press, 2012.

———. *The Psychology of Nuclear Proliferation: Identity, Emotions and Foreign Policy.* Cambridge, UK: Cambridge University Press, 2006.

"Indian Parliament Attack Kills 12." *BBC News,* December 13, 2001. http://news.bbc.co.uk/2/hi/south_asia/1707865.stm.

Jackson, Galen. "The United States, the Israeli Nuclear Program, and Nonproliferation, 1961–1969." *Security Studies* 28, no. 2 (2019).

"Japan, U.S. Draft Operation Plan for Taiwan Contingency: Sources." *Kyodo News*, December 23, 2021. https://english.kyodonews.net/news/2021/12/f5ed60ab6502-japan-us-draft-operation-plan-for-taiwan-contingency-sources.html.

Jones, Matthew. *The Official History of the UK Strategic Nuclear Deterrent, Volume I: From the V-Bomber Era to the Arrival of Polaris, 1945–1964*. New York: Routledge, 2017.

Kalyanaraman, S. "Operation Parakram: An Indian Exercise in Coercive Diplomacy," *Strategic Analysis* 26, no. 4 (2002).

Kane, Tim. "Global U.S. Troop Deployment, 1950–2003." Heritage Foundation, October 27, 2004. https://www.heritage.org/defense/report/global-us-troop-deployment-1950-2003.

Kaplan, Edward. *To Kill Nations: American Strategy in the Air-Atomic Age and the Rise of Mutually Assured Destruction*. Ithaca, NY: Cornell University Press, 2015.

Kaplan, Lawrence. *NATO Divided, NATO United: The Evolution of an Alliance*. Westport, CT: Praeger, 2004.

Karpin, Michael. *The Bomb in the Basement: How Israel Went Nuclear and What That Means for the World*. New York: Simon & Schuster, 2006.

Keck, Zachary. "4 Reasons America Shouldn't Send Nuclear Weapons to South Korea or Japan." *National Interest*, September 15, 2017. https://nationalinterest.org/blog/the-buzz/4-reasons-america-shouldnt-sent-nuclear-weapons-south-korea-22339.

Keck, Zachary, and Henry Sokolski. "How to Handle South Korea's Missile Ambitions." *Foreign Affairs*, November 6, 2017. https://www.foreignaffairs.com/articles/north-korea/2017-11-06/how-handle-south-koreas-missile-ambitions.

Khan, Feroz. *Eating Grass: The Making of the Pakistani Bomb*. Stanford, CA: Stanford University Press, 2012.

Kissinger, Henry. "Henry Kissinger on Nuclear Proliferation." *Newsweek*, February 6, 2009.

———. *The Troubled Partnership: A Re-Appraisal of the Atlantic Alliance*. New York: McGraw-Hill, 1965.

———. *White House Years*. Boston: Little, Brown, 1979.

Knopf, Jeffrey W., ed. *Security Assurances and Nuclear Proliferation*. Stanford, CA: Stanford University Press, 2012.

Kohl, Wilfred L. *French Nuclear Diplomacy*. Princeton, NJ, Princeton University Press, 1971.

Krauthammer, Charles. "Cold War Relic, Present Day Threat." *Washington Post*, January 5, 2017. https://www.washingtonpost.com/opinions/global-opinions/cold-war-relic-present-day-threat/2017/01/05/623c720e-d384-11e6-9cb0-54ab630851e8_story.html.

Krepinevich, Andrew, and Jacob Cohn. "Rethinking the Apocalypse: Time for Bold Thinking About the Second Nuclear Age." *War on the Rocks*, March 1, 2016. https://warontherocks.com/2016/03/rethinking-the-apocalypse-time-for-bold-thinking-about-the-second-nuclear-age/.

Krepon, Michael, and Polly Nayak. *US Crisis Management in South Asia's Twin Peaks Crisis*. Washington, DC: Stimson Center, 2006.

Kroenig, Matthew. "Exporting the Bomb: Why States Provide Sensitive Nuclear Assistance." *American Political Science Review* 103, no. 1 (2009).

———. *Exporting the Bomb: Technology Transfer and the Spread of Nuclear Weapons.* Ithaca, NY: Cornell University Press, 2010.

Kux, Dennis. *Disenchanted Allies: The United States and Pakistan, 1947–2000.* Washington, DC: Woodrow Wilson Center Press, 2001.

Lavoy, Peter R. "The Strategic Consequences of Nuclear Proliferation: A Review Essay." *Security Studies* 4, no. 4 (1995).

Layne, Christopher. "Hillary Clinton and Nuclear Weapons: More Dangerous Than Trump?" *National Interest,* October 31, 2016. https://nationalinterest.org/feature/hillary-clinton-nuclear-weapons-more-dangerous-trump-18241.

Levy, Adrian, and Catherine Scott-Clark. *Deception: Pakistan, the United States, and the Secret Trade in Nuclear Weapons.* New York: Bloomsbury, 2010.

Liberman, Peter. "Israel and the South African Bomb." *Nonproliferation Review* 11, no. 2 (Summer 2004).

———. "The Rise and Fall of the South Africa Bomb." *International Security* 26, no. 2 (Fall 2001).

Lieber, Robert J. "The French Nuclear Force: A Strategic and Political Evaluation." *International Affairs* 42, no. 3 (July 1966).

Lind, Jennifer, and Daryl G. Press. "Should South Korea Build its Own Nuclear Bomb?" *Washington Post,* October 7, 2021. https://www.washingtonpost.com/outlook/should-south-korea-go-nuclear/2021/10/07/a40bb400-2628-11ec-8d53-67cfb452aa60_story.html.

Ludi, Jeremy. "The Rising American Chorus for a Nuclear Japan." *Asia Times,* August 29, 2017.

M.A.U.D. Committee. *Report by M.A.U.D. Committee on the Use of Uranium for a Bomb.* London: Ministry of Aircraft Production, July 1941.

Macmillan, Harold. *Riding the Storm, 1956–1959.* London: Macmillan, 1971.

Mahan, Erin. *Kennedy, De Gaulle, and Western Europe.* New York: Palgrave Macmillian, 2002.

Mahoney, James, and P. Larkin Terrie. "Comparative-historical Analysis in Contemporary Political Science." In *Oxford Handbook of Political Methodology,* edited by Janet M. Box-Steffensmeier, Henry E. Brady, and David Collier. New York: Oxford University Press, 2008.

Mann, Richard. "Eduardo Bolsonaro Defends Possession of Nuclear Weapons." *Rio Times,* May 15, 2019.

Mattison, Roger J. "The NUMEC Affair: Did Highly Enriched Uranium from the U.S. Aid Israel's Nuclear Weapons Program?" *National Security Archive.* Briefing Book no. 565, November 2, 2016.

McDermott, Rose. *Risk-Taking in International Politics: Prospect Theory in American Foreign Policy.* Ann Arbor: University of Michigan Press, 2001.

McGreal, Chris. "Revealed: How Israel Offered to Sell South Africa Nuclear Weapons." *Guardian,* May 24, 2010. https://www.theguardian.com/world/2010/may/23/israel-south-africa-nuclear-weapons.

Mearsheimer, John J. "Back to the Future: Instability in Europe After the Cold War." *International Security* 15, no. 1 (Summer 1990).

———. "The Case for a Ukrainian Nuclear Deterrent." *Foreign Affairs*. (Summer 1993). https://www.foreignaffairs.com/articles/ukraine/1993-06-01/case-ukrainian-nuclear-deterrent.

Mian, Zia, and A. H. Nayyar. "Playing the Nuclear Game: Pakistan and the Fissile Material Cutoff Treaty." *Arms Control Today,* (April 2010).

Michishita, Narushige, Peter M. Swartz, and David Winkler. *Lessons of the Cold War in the Pacific: U.S. Maritime Strategy, Crisis Prevention, and Japan's Role.* Washington, DC: Wilson Center, 2016.

Miller, Nicholas L. *Stopping the Bomb: The Sources and Effectiveness of U.S. Nonproliferation Policy.* Ithaca, NY: Cornell University Press, 2018.

———. "Nuclear Dominoes: A Self-Defeating Prophecy?" *Security Studies*, 23, no. 1 (2014).

Moriyasu, Ken. "US Eyes Using Japan's Submarines to 'Choke' Chinese Navy." *Nikkei Asia Review,* May 5, 2021. https://asia.nikkei.com/Politics/International-relations/Indo-Pacific/US-eyes-using-Japan-s-submarines-to-choke-Chinese-navy.

Murdock, Clark, and Thomas Karako. *Thinking about the Unthinkable in a Highly Proliferated World.* Washington, DC: Center for Strategic and International Studies, July 2016.

Nayak, Polly, and Michael Krepon. *The Unfinished Crisis: US Crisis Management after the 2008 Mumbai Attacks.* Washington, DC: Stimson Center, 2012.

Neustadt, Richard E., and Ernest R. May. *Thinking in Time: The Uses of History for Decision Makers.* New York: Free Press, 1986.

Neustadt, Richard E. *Report to JFK: The Skybolt Crisis in Perspective.* Ithaca, NY: Cornell University Press, 1999.

Nuclear Black Markets: Pakistan, A.Q. Khan and the Rise of Proliferation Networks: A Net Assessment. London: International Institute for Strategic Studies, 2007.

Olsenspecial, Arthur J. "NATO Shield Units Lag in Building Up." *New York Times,* January 2, 1960. https://www.nytimes.com/1960/01/02/archives/nato-shield-units-lag-in-building-up-brightest-spot-in-defense.html.

Onchi, Yosuke. "South Korea Becomes 8th Country to Fire Ballistic Missile from sub." *Nikkei Asia Review,* September 8, 2021. https://asia.nikkei.com/Politics/International-relations/South-Korea-becomes-8th-country-to-fire-ballistic-missile-from-sub.

Oren, Michael. *Six Days of War: June 1967 and the Making of the Middle East.* New York: Presidio Press, 2003.

Ota, Masakatsu. "U.S. Weighed Giving Japan Nuclear Weapons in 1950s." *Kyodo,* January 23, 2015. https://www.japantimes.co.jp/news/2015/01/23/national/history/u-s-weighed-giving-japan-nuclear-weapons-in-1950s/.

Patalano, Alessio. "'The Silent Fight': Submarine Rearmament and the Origins of Japan's Military Engagement with the Cold War, 1955–76." *Cold War History* 21, no. 1 (2021).

Paul, Septimus H. *Nuclear Rivals: Anglo-American Atomic Relations, 1941–1942.* Columbus: Ohio State University Press, 2000.

Perkovich, George. *India's Nuclear Bomb: The Impact on Global Proliferation.* Berkeley: University of California Press, 1999.

Petersen, Tore T. *The Middle East Between the Great Powers: Anglo-American Conflict and Cooperation, 1952–7.* New York: Palgrave Macmillan, 2000.

Pierre, Andrew J. *Nuclear Politics: British Experience with an Independent Strategic Force, 1939–70.* Oxford, UK: Oxford University Press, 1972.

Pitman, Paul M. "'A General Named Eisenhower': Atlantic Crisis and the Origins of the European Economic Community." In *Between Empire and Alliance: America and Europe During the Cold War*, edited by Marc Trachtenberg. Oxford, UK: Rowman & Littlefield Publishers, 2003.

Polakow-Suransky, Sasha. *The Unspoken Alliance: Israel's Secret Relationship with Apartheid South Africa.* New York: Pantheon, 2010.

Purkitt, Helen E., and Stephen F. Burgess. "South Africa's Nuclear Strategy: Deterring 'Total Onslaught' and 'Nuclear Blackmail' in Three Stages." In *Strategy in the Second Nuclear Age: Power, Ambition and the Ultimate Weapon*, edited by Toshi Yoshihara and James R. Holmes. Washington, DC: Georgetown University Press, 2012.

Quandt, William. "How Far Will Israel Go?" *Washington Post*, November 24, 1991. https://www.washingtonpost.com/archive/entertainment/books/1991/11/24/how-far-will-israel-go/e3dd4707-9f6b-469f-a966-308524865b3e/.

Rabasa, Angel, Robert D. Blackwill, Peter Chalk, Kim Cragin, C. Christine Fair, Brian A. Jackson, Brian Michael Jenkins, Seth G. Jones, Nathaniel Shestak, and Ashley J. Tellis. *The Lessons of Mumbai.* Arlington, VA: RAND Corporation, 2009.

Rashid, Ahmed. *Descent Into Chaos: The United States and the Failure of Nation Building in Pakistan, Afghanistan, and Central Asia.* New York: Penguin Books, 2008.

Raz, Adam. "The Significance of the Reputed Yom Kippur War Nuclear Affair." *Strategic Assessment* 16, no. 4 (January 2014).

Reiss, Mitchell. *Bridled Ambition: Why Countries Constrain Their Nuclear Capabilities.* Washington, DC: Woodrow Wilson Center Press, 1995.

Rhodes, Richard. *The Making of the Atomic Bomb, 25th Anniversary Edition.* New York: Simon & Shuster, 2012.

Richelson, Jeffrey T. *Spying on the Bomb: American Nuclear Intelligence from Nazi Germany to Iran and North Korea.* New York: Norton, 2006.

Riedel, Bruce. "Farewell, Sandy Berger, the Clinton Man Who Stopped Armageddon." *Daily Beast,* December 2, 2015.

———. *American Diplomacy and the 1999 Kargil Summit at Blair House.* Philadelphia: Center for the Advanced Study of India, 2002.

Rosenberg, David Alan. "The Origins of Overkill: Nuclear Weapons and American Strategy, 1945–1960." *International Security* 7, no. 4 (Spring 1983).

Royal Air Force Historical Society. *Royal Air Force in Germany, 1945–1993.* Brighton, UK: Royal Air Force Historical Society, 1999.

Rusk, Dean. "Toward a New Dimension in the Atlantic Partnership." October 27, 1963, in *Department of State Bulletin* 39, no. 1271 (November 11, 1963).
Sachs, Jeffrey D. *To Move the World: JFK's Quest for Peace*. New York: Random House, 2014.
Sagan, Scott D. "More Will Be Worse." In *The Spread of Nuclear Weapons: A Debate Renewed*, edited by Scott D. Sagan and Kenneth N. Waltz. New York: Norton, 2003.
———. "Two Renaissances in Nuclear Security Studies." H-Diplo/ISSF Forum 2 (2014). https://issforum.org/ISSF/PDF/ISSF-Forum-2.pdf.
Sagan, Scott D., and Kenneth N. Waltz. *The Spread of Nuclear Weapons: A Debate Renewed*. New York: Norton, 2003.
Sandler, Todd, and Justin George. "Military Expenditure Trends for 1960–2014 and What They Reveal." *Global Policy* (March 2016).
Sanger, David E. "North Korea Says It Has a Program on Nuclear Arms." *The New York Times*. October 17, 2002. https://www.nytimes.com/2002/10/17/world/north-korea-says-it-has-a-program-on-nuclear-arms.html.
———. "Obama's Worst Pakistan Nightmare." *New York Times Magazine,* January 8, 2009. https://www.nytimes.com/2009/01/11/magazine/11pakistan-t.html.
Sanger, David E. *Confront and Conceal: Obama's Secret Wars and Surprising Use of American Power.* New York: Crown, 2012.
Sanger, David E., and William Broad. "U.S. Secretly Aids Pakistan in Guarding Nuclear Arms." *New York Times*, November 18, 2007. https://www.nytimes.com/2007/11/18/washington/18nuke.html.
Santoro, David. "Will America's Asian Allies Go Nuclear?" *National Interest*, January 30, 2014. https://nationalinterest.org/commentary/will-americas-asian-allies-go-nuclear-9794.
Sapolsky, Harvey M., and Christine Leah. "Let Asia Go Nuclear." *National Interest,* April 14, 2014. https://nationalinterest.org/feature/let-asia-go-nuclear-10259.
Scheinman, Lawrence. *Atomic Energy Policy in France Under the Fourth Republic.* Princeton, NJ: Princeton University Press, 1983.
Schnabel, James F. *History of the Joint Chiefs of Staff, Volume 1: The Joint Chiefs of Staff and National Policy, 1945–1947.* Washington, DC: Office of Joint History, 1996.
Scott-Clark, Cathy, and Adrian Levy. *The Siege: 68 Hours Inside the Taj Hotel.* New York: Penguin Books, 2013.
Sevastopulo, Demetri, and Kahtrin Hille. "US and Japan conduct War Games Amid Rising China-Taiwan Tensions." *Financial Times,* June 30, 2021. https://www.ft.com/content/54b0db59-a403-493e-b715-7b63c9c39093.
Shane, Scott. "Saudis and Extremism: 'Both the Arsonists and the Firefighters.'" *New York Times,* August 25, 2016. https://www.nytimes.com/2016/08/26/world/middleeast/saudi-arabia-islam.html.
Sharp, Jeremy M. *U.S. Foreign Aid to Israel*. Washington, DC: Congressional Research Service, December 4, 2009.
Sherwin, Martin J. *A World Destroyed: Hiroshima and Its Legacies*, 3rd ed. Stanford, CA: Stanford University Press, 2003.

Simons, Jake Wallis. "How Washington Owns the UK's Nukes." *Politico,* April 30, 2015. https://www.politico.eu/article/uk-trident-nuclear-program/.
Snyder, Glenn H. "The Security Dilemma in Alliance Politics." *World Politics* 36, no. 4 (July 1984).
Sokolski, Henry, and Zachary Keck. "Kim Jong Un Is Going Ballistic In More Ways Than One." *Wall Street Journal,* July 30, 2017. https://www.wsj.com/articles/kim-jong-un-is-going-ballistic-in-more-ways-than-one-1501446238.
Speiser, Peter. *The British Army of the Rhine: Turning Nazi Enemies into Cold War Partners.* Champaign: University of Illinois Press, 2016.
Steinberg, Gerald M. "Middle East Peace and the NPT Extension Decision." *Nonproliferation Review* 4, no. 1 (Fall 1996).
Swami, Praveen. "Gen. Padmanabhan Mulls Over Lessons of Operation Parakram." *Hindu,* February 6, 2004.
Szasz, Ferenc Morton. *British Scientists and the Manhattan Project: The Los Alamos Years.* New York: Macmillan, 1992.
Talbott, Strobe. *Engaging India: Diplomacy, Democracy, and the Bomb.* Washington, DC: Brookings University Press, 2004.
Taylor, Bill. "Historical Background." In *The RAF in Germany 1945–1993.* Brighton, UK: Royal Air Force History Society, 1998.
Tenet, George. *At the Center of the Storm: My Years at the CIA.* New York: HarperCollins, 2007.
Tertrais, Bruno. "*Destruction Assurèe*: The Origins and Development of French Nuclear Strategy, 1945–81." In *Getting MAD: Nuclear Mutual Assured Destruction, Its Origins and Practice,* edited by Henry D. Sokolski. Washington, DC: Strategic Studies Institute, 2004.
Tobey, William. "Cooperation in the Libya WMD Disarmament Case." *Studies in Intelligence* 61 no. 4, (December 2017).
Toon, O. B. "Atmospheric Effects and Societal Consequences of Regional Scale Nuclear Conflicts and Acts of Individual Nuclear Terrorism." *Atmospheric Chemistry and Physics* 7 (2007).
Trachtenberg, Marc. *A Constructed Peace: The Making of the European Settlement, 1945–1963.* Princeton, NJ: Princeton University Press, 1999.
———. "The French Factor in U.S. Foreign Policy during the Nixon-Pompidou Period, 1969–1974." *Journal of Cold War Studies* 13 (2011).
Tucker, Robert W. "What This Country Needs Is a Touch of New Isolationism." *New York Times,* June 21, 1972. https://www.nytimes.com/1972/06/21/archives/what-this-country-needs-is-a-touch-of-new-isolationism.html.
Ullman, Richard H. "The Covert French Connection." *Foreign Policy* 75 (Summer 1989).
"US Assured Pakistan Will Not Begin War: Musharraf, Armitage Hold Talks." *Dawn,* June 7, 2002, https://www.dawn.com/news/41166/us-assured-pakistan-will-not-begin-war-musharraf-armitage-hold-talks.
Van de Velde, James. "Go Ahead. Let Japan and South Korea Go Nuclear." *National Interest,* October 1, 2016. https://nationalinterest.org/feature/go-ahead-let-japan-south-korea-go-nuclear-17897.

Van Evera, Stephen. "Primed for Peace: Europe after the Cold War." *International Security* 15, no. 3 (Winter 1990/91).
Volpe, Tristan, and Ulrich Kühn. "Germany's Nuclear Education: Why a Few Elites Are Testing a Taboo." *Washington Quarterly* 40 (2017).
Walt, Stephen. "It's Time to Fold America's Nuclear Umbrella." *Foreign Policy*, March 23, 2021. https://foreignpolicy.com/2021/03/23/its-time-to-fold-americas-nuclear-umbrella/.
"War and Peace in the Nuclear Age; Visions of War and Peace; Interview with Joseph Nye, 1987." *WGBH*, May 28, 1987, http://openvault.wgbh.org/catalog/V_908DE510DE294060AC9A37A69E7B670D.
Ward, Alex. "The President of South Korea Has a Strong Message for Trump." *Vox*, August 17, 2017. https://www.vox.com/world/2017/8/16/16152774/south-korea-north-korea-trump-military-liberation-day-speech.
Weiss, Leonard. "A Double-Flash from the Past and Israel's Nuclear Arsenal." *Bulletin of the Atomic Scientists,* August 3, 2018. https://thebulletin.org/2018/08/a-double-flash-from-the-past-and-israels-nuclear-arsenal/.
———. "Israel's 1979 Nuclear Test and the U.S. Cover-Up." *Middle East Policy* 18 (Winter 2011).
Wetterqvist, Fredrik. *French Security and Defence Policy: Current Developments and Future Prospects.* Stockholm: National Defence Research Institute, 1990.
Wheeler, N. J. "British Nuclear Weapons and Anglo-American Relations 1945–1954." *International Affairs* 62, no. 1 (Winter, 1985–1986).
Wohlstetter, Albert. *Swords from Plowshares: The Military Potential of Civilian Nuclear Energy.* Chicago: University of Chicago Press, 1979.
———. "Nuclear Sharing: NATO and the N+1 Country." *Foreign Affairs* (April 1961). https://www.foreignaffairs.com/articles/1961-04-01/nuclear-sharing-nato-and-n1-country.
Woodward, Bob. *Bush at War.* New York: Simon and Schuster, 2002.
———. *Veil: The Secret Wars of the CIA 1981–1987.* New York: Simon & Schuster, 1987.
Young, Ken. "The Skybolt Crisis of 1962: Muddle or Mischief?" *Journal of Strategic Studies* 27, no. 4 (2004).
Zarate, Robert. "America's Allies and Nuclear Arms: Assessing the Geopolitics of Nonproliferation in Asia." *Project 2049 Institute,* May 6, 2014. https://project2049.net/wp-content/uploads/2018/06/Zarate_America_Allies_and_Nuclear_Arms_Geopolitics_Nonproliferation.pdf.

Index

Page locators in italics indicate figures and tables.

9/11 attacks, 19, 205, 212, 217, 250
60 Minutes, 246

Abe, Shinzo, 27
Acheson, Dean, 49, 56, 59, 60, 77, 102
Adenauer, Konrad, 86, 104, 109
Afghanistan, 193; and Pakistan, 12, 19, 182, 216–20; Soviet invasion of, 10, 24, 30, 172, 189–90, 197–98; US war in, 206, 216–17, 232n53
AfPak review (Obama administration), 218–19
Agreed Framework (North Korea and US), 224
Agreement and Declaration of Trust (Britain and US, 1944), 44
Ailleret, Charles, 86, 114–15
Air Defense Identification Zone (ADIZ, China), 239
Algeria: France's nuclear test in (1957), 88, 244; independence movement, 114, 136–37
allied proliferation, 1–6; Britain as gold standard of, 37–38; contributions to additional proliferation, 20–21; costs of, 253; by France, 115–16; and geopolitics, 21–23, 38, 42, 237; lessons for future cases, 25–29, 235, 237–51; and lessons of history, 9–25; and role of history, 6–8; and US overseas objectives with allies, 12–17. *See also* allied proliferation; Britain; nonproliferation; specific allies and partner nations
Allison, Graham, 6–7, 205
Almelo enrichment plant (Dutch-German border), 186
Alphand, Hervé, 95
al-Qaeda, 19, 181, 205, 213, 217–18
Anderson, John, 41, 46–47
Arab Federation Proclamation, 144
Arab Spring, 28
Arab states, 147–48; and Dimona inspection requests, 152, 155; effect of Israel's nuclear program on, 144–45; and NPT, 18, 173; US fear of alienating, 11, 135, 165
Armitage, Richard, 215–16
Arms Control and Disarmament Agency, 191
Asia, US hub-and-spoke alliance system, 113, 122. *See also* China; Japan; North Korea; South Korea
Atlantic magazine, 181

Atomic Energy Act. *See* McMahon Act (Atomic Energy Act)
Atomic Energy Act of 1954, 63
Atomic Energy Commission (AEC), 56, 58, 141
Atoms for Peace program (US), 183, 184, 187
Attlee, Clement, 13, 45–49, 55, 58, 62
Australia, 5
Azhar, Maulana Masood, 213

Baekdu Mountain, 239
Baker, James, 197
Ball, George, 77, 107, 108–9, 125n37
Barak, Ehud, 173
Barbour, Walworth, 144, 146
bases, US, 12–13, 242–44; need for dispersal of, 27, 69, 122, 244
Bay of Pigs fiasco, 102
BBC China (German ship), 222, 226
Beg, Mirza Aslam, 207, 208, 223
Belgian Congo mines, 49, 56, 59
Belgium, 112, 113
Bell, Mark, 24, 34n56, 244
Ben-Gurion, David, 133, 136–37, 140–42, 164; resignation of, 145–46
Bergen, Peter, 217
Bergmann, David, 136, 139, 148n28
Berlin blockade (1949), 13
Berlin Crisis (1948), 60
Berlin Crisis (1958–1962), 84, 93, 102, 103–4, 109
Bermuda Conference (1957), 70
bhangmeters (light detectors), 170, 179n81
Bhutto, Benazir, 207, 209–10, 223–24
Bhutto, Z. A. (Zulfikar Ali), 182–84, 189, 194, 223; and A. Q. Kahn, 186, 187
"Big Three" proposal (United States, UK, and France), 90
bilateral alliances, 9, 27–28, 30, 243–44
Blackwill, Robert, 213, 215
Boeing, 93
Bohlen, Charles, 111, 125nn37,38

Botha, P. W., 166
Boucher, Richard, 221
Bourgès-Maunoury, Maurice, 88–89, 137, 138
Bracken, Paul, 5
Brandt, Willy, 118
Brazil, 2
Brezhnev, Leonid, 113
Britain, 7, 8, 9; active military personnel, 8, *16*; as best-case scenario for allied proliferation, 37–38; conventional forces, reduction in, 73–74; defense spending, *17*, 33n46; defense spending as % GDP, *17*, 17–18, 241–42; freedom of action, 24–25, 244; launch control, 38, 50n2, 60–61, 71, 76–78; as possible target for Soviet Union, 13–14, 59, 60, 79; raw materials agreements with US, 46, 49–50, 57, 70–71, 78; white paper (1952), 16. *See also* Britain
Britain, US-British atomic collaboration (1939–1946), 37–53; early lead in nuclear development, 39–41; MAUD Committee report, 39–40, 50; Roosevelt and full exchange of information, 43–45; Roosevelt's secret agreement, 37–38; tables turned, 41–43; Tube Alloys as code name for, 39, 42, 43; ultimate betrayal, 45–50; Washington Summit, 43. *See also* World War II
Britain, US-British atomic collaboration (1947–1955), 55–67; bilateral agreement of 1955, 63–64; British plutonium production plant, 58; Calder Hall reactor, 64–65; and Eisenhower administration, 61–65; exchange of information request (1948), 58–59; Global Strategy Paper (1952), 73; launch control, 60–61; leaks to Soviet Union, US concerns about, 55, 59; Modus Vivendi (1948), 55–58, 60, 76; nuclear tests

(1952), 55, 62, 69, 73; Princeton University conference (1949), 59; spy scandals (1950), 55, 59; stuck in the mud (1948–1952), 58–60
Britain, US-British atomic collaboration (1956–1962), 69–82; and amendments to McMahon Act, 71–73; bilateral agreement (1958), 73; British defense white paper (1957), 73–75; hydrogen bomb program (1957), 64, 72, 73, 81n14; launch control, 76–79; new type of military, 73–76; Skybolt air-launched ballistic missile program, 73, 76–77; Sputnik Moment, 69, 71–72; Suez as British opportunity, 70–71; US-UK Mutual Defense Agreement (1958), 70; Washington Summit (1957), 71–72

Brownell, Herbert, 64
Brzezinski, Zbigniew, 189–90, 191
Buchalet, General, 90
Buckley, James, 195
Bueno de Mesquita, Bruce, 3
Bundy, McGeorge, 15, 141
Bureau of General Studies (France), 87
Bureau of Intelligence and Research (INR), 208–9, 214
Bush, George H.W., administration, 19, 20, 181, 193, 227; impossibility of proving Pakistan's nuclear status, 12, 181, 196–98, 208, 218; tactical nuclear weapons removed from Korean Peninsula, 79
Bush, George W., administration, 205, 217–18
Bush, Vannevar, 40–44
Butt, S. A., 188, 196
Buys, Andre, 169
Byrnes, James F., 47, 48

Caccia, Harold, 64, 71
Calder Hall reactor (Britain), 64–65
Camp, Donald, 221

Camp David Accords (1978), 165, 172
Canada: and atomic bomb development, 45–48; Pakistan, nuclear assistance to, 184–86; World War II alliance with Britain and US, 38
Carter, Jimmy, administration, 120; explanation of South Africa nuclear test, 135; Pakistan, aid to, 185, 188–89, 189–90; Pakistan, demarches about, 190–91; SALT II talks, 169, 172
Casey, William, 193
Center for Strategic and International Studies, 5
Central Intelligence Agency (CIA), 139, 159–60; and *BBC China* cargo, 222, 226; and Pakistan, 189, 193, 211, 214
centralized nuclear decision making, 5, 15, 105–6, 240
Chatillon, EL-1 (Zoe) (French nuclear reactor), 85
Cheney, Dick, 19, 217
CHIC-4 weapon design (China), 194
China, 1, 2, 122n6; Air Defense Identification Zone (ADIZ), 239; counterweights to, 26, 79–80, 121; French nuclear assistance to, 245; and international communist movement, 103; and Pakistan, 194, 195, 211; and South Korea, 239
Chirac, Jacques, 185
Christopher, Warren, 191, 192
Churchill, Winston, 22, 40–45, 240; feasibility study for building bomb without US, 42–43; first world leader to initiate nuclear weapons development, 41; and Hyde Park Aide Memoire, 45; and Quebec Agreement, 43–44; return to power (1951), 62
city-avoidance nuclear doctrine, 105–6
Clausewitz, Carl von, 26, 105, 123n14
Clifford, Clark, 160–61, 162

Clinton, Bill, 231n33; on "nuclear blackmail," 211–12
Clinton, Bill, administration, 18–19, 21; and NPT, 173; and Pakistan, 209–12, 225
Cohen, Avner, 142, 145, 148n17
Cohn, Jacob, 5
Colby, Elbridge, 4, 6, 21–22, 168, 179n72
Cold War, 1, 10, 23, 29
Combined Development Trust (Britain and US), 44–45, 46
Combined Policy Committee (CPC, Britain and US), 44–49
Commissariat a l'Energie Atomique (CEA), 85
communist movement, international, 103
Communist Party, French, 90
Conant, James, 40, 42–43, 44
Congress, 12, 19, 33n34, 140, 184, 190; alternative facts presented to, 247; Israel's lobbying of, 160; Joint Committee on Atomic Energy (JCAE), 3, 56, 58, 64–65, 66n28; kept in dark, 45, 48–49, 76; and McMahon Act, 48–49, 70, 72–73, 89, 93–94, 135; Military Liaison Committee, 59; Pressler Amendment, 196–97, 225–26; and Quebec Agreement, 61; Symington Amendment, 191, 193, 196
conventional military forces, 73–75, 80, 84, 97n26, 104–7, 237, 241–42; Flexible Response doctrine, 14, 26, 105–6, 112, 240, 241; France, 88, 101, 114–15, 121; Israel, 156–57; NATO, 14, 73–74, 86, 123n12
conventional military spending, 8, 15–17, *17*; change in as % GDP, *17*, 241–42
counterforce and decapitation strikes, 5–6
Croach, Jesse, 141–42

Cuban Missile Crisis, 77, 108, 117, 136, 142, 143; Indo-Pakistan conflicts compared with, 208, 209, 211, 212
Cyrnes, James, 46

Darwin, Charles (British scientific liaison), 40
Dayan, Moshe, 167–68
Defense Advanced Research Projects Agency (DARPA), 170
Defense Intelligence Agency (DIA), 170
de Gaulle, Charles, 14, 15, 17, 23, 29–30; accused of wanting to kick US out of Europe, 107; and French assistance to Israel, 138; and NATO, 25, 27; nuclear interests of, 83, 90–92; resignation (1969), 117; return to power (1958), 27, 29, 83, 90–93; Soviet Union, overtures to, 113; speech to military officials, 94; three strands of thought, 92–93; tripartite body proposals, 91–92, 93, 95, 114; withdrawal of forces and independence from NATO, 83–84, 92, 110–13, 242–44. *See also* France
Department of Defense (DOD), 4–5, 59, 64, 106, 160–61, 164
Desert Storm, 224, 225, 248
deterrent-by-punishment military doctrines, 17
Dimona reactor (Israel), 134–39, 164–65, 173, 184; as catalyst for Six-Day War, 157, 165; Egyptian overflight of, 157, 248; and inspections, 141–47, 154–65; underground reprocessing plant, 141. *See also* Israel
Dinstein, Zvi, 146
Directorate of Industrial Liaison (DIL, Pakistan), 187
domino effect, 2, 3, 5, 9, 20–21, 115, 134, 236, 252
Duckett, Carl, 159
Dulles, Allen, 140

Dulles, John Foster, 63, 74–76, 88–91, 94, 104

East-West crisis (1958), 93
Eban, Abba, 160
Eden, Anthony, 64, 70, 73–74, 75
Egypt, 2, 18, 147, 165–66; and Camp David Accords, 165; France's nuclear assistance to, 116; overflight of Dimona reactor, 157, 248; Suez Canal, nationalization of, 70, 137; Suez Crisis (1956), 24, 38, 69, 70–71, 87; and Yom Kippur War, 167–69
Eilts, Hermann F., 168
Eisenhower, Dwight, 38; background, 101–2; on de Gaulle, 83; and dual key system proposal, 89, 97n31; elected president (1952), 55; France, support of, 95; Germany, view of, 84; and McMahon Act, 71–72, 89, 94; multilateral deterrent preferred by, 85, 107; and Suez crisis, 70, 87; as Supreme Allied Commander Europe (SACEUR), 62, 72
Eisenhower, Dwight, administration, 14, 38, 61–65, 121; New Look strategy, 63, 73, 79
Elbrick, Charles Burke, 122n2
Ely, Paul, 88
Emerson Electrics, 188
entrapment issue, 13–14
Erdoğan, Recep Tayyip, 2, 121, 243
Escalate to De-Escalate, 14–15, 26, 105–6, 240
Eshkol, Levi, 146–47, 154–55, 156; F-4 Phantom request, 159–60, 172
Euromissile crisis (1980s), 13
Europe: "fair burden" called for by US, 74; geopolitics, 29–30; independence of important to US, 22–23, 63, 74, 85, 89, 118, 128n91; reduced US commitments in, 9–10, *10*; as "third force," Eisenhower's goal of, 62

European Atomic Energy Community (EURATOM), 87
European Defense Community (EDC), 86, 96n9
European Economic Community, 107

F-4 Phantoms (US), 153, 159–64, 172
F-16s (US), 194–95, 208, 223, 247
Farley, Philip J., 143
fatalism, 5
Federal Bureau of Investigation (FBI), 221
Feierstein, Gerald, 220, 221
Feinberg, Abe, 133–34, 141, 160, 162
Feldman, Myers, 141
Ferguson, Niall, 6–7
Fernandes, George, 232n51
finite deterrence proponents, 3
First Gulf War, 21
fissile material cut-off treaty (FMCT), 18–19, 173
Flexible Response doctrine, 14, 26, 105–6, 112, 240, 241
Flournoy, Michèle, 219
force de frappe (France), 15, 22, 83–84, 114, 121
Ford, Gerald, 119–20, 186
Foreign Assistance Act of 1968, 160
Forrestal, James, 58
France, 7–9, 22–23, 38; and Algerian independence movement, 114, 136–37; change from pro-proliferation to anti-proliferation, 186; China, nuclear assistance to, 245; conventional forces reduced by nuclear arsenal, 74, 84, 101, 121; defense spending, *17,* 17–18, 114–15, 241–42; *force de frappe,* 15, 22, 83–84, 114, 121; Fourth Republic, 27, 29–30, 83, 87, 138; freedom of action, 24–25, 244; Germany, bilateral overtures to, 107; Germany, concerns about, 86, 128n92; Israel, conventional weapons sales to, 137, 155; Israel, nuclear assistance to,

21, 115, 116, 133–34, 138, 245; JFK administration hard line on, 15, 101; military's view of NATO withdrawal, 113; Mirage IV aircraft, 25, 87, 94, 110, 125n39, 126n55; and multilateral nuclear force, 84, 94, 107–8, 125n37; National Assembly, 86; and NATO, 24–25, 27, 83–86, 110; nuclear assistance to other countries, 21; Pakistan, nuclear assistance to, 184–85; Sevres summit with Israel, 137, 138. *See also* de Gaulle, Charles

France (1945–1960), 83–99; de Gaulle's return to power, 90–93; early nuclear weapons program, 85–86; Germany, contradictory policies on, 92–93; nuclear program advances, 93–95; nuclear reactors built by, 86–87, 93–94; nuclear test (1957), 88, 244; preparing groundwork for nuclear weapons program, 87–90; Sahara Desert nuclear test (1960), 88, 90, 94–95; SEREB consortium, 93; and Suez Crisis, 87, 88; tripartite body proposal, 91–92, 94, 95, 114; US forces expelled from, 83, 84

France (1961–1975), 101–30; and atomic assistance, 106–7; and Berlin Crisis, 102, 103–4; conventional military cuts, 114–15; Germany, forces kept in, 113; joint atomic research with Italy and Germany, 104; launch control and flexible response, 105–6, 112, 120–21; long freeze in relations with US, 101–3; and multilateral nuclear force proposals, 107–9, 111–12, 125n33; NATO, military withdrawal and independence from, 83–84, 92, 110–13, 121, 236, 242–43; negative guidance policy, 119; Nixon's assistance to, 117; nuclear offspring, 21, 115–16, 122; US improvement in relations with, 117–20; US Polaris missile proposal, 108–9

freedom of action, 24–25, 244
Frisch, Otto, 39–40
Frisch-Peierls Memorandum, 39–40
Fuchs, Klaus, 59
Fulbright, William, 140

Gaddafi, Muammar, 225
Gaillard, Félix, 89, 90
Gallucci, Robert, 11
Gates, Robert, 197, 208, 211
Gazit, Mordechai, 143
geopolitics, 21–23, 29–30, 118; allied proliferation separated from, 38, 42, 237; link with nuclear weapons, 84–85, 120, 134
German Democratic Republic (GDR, East Germany), 93, 109
Germany, Nazi, 22, 41, 43, 136
Germany, West (Federal Republic of Germany, FRG), 1, 29, 134; allied fears about nuclear weapons, 102–3; conventional forces, 74; defense spending as % GDP, *17*; French forces kept in, 113; and French nuclear weapons, 84; NPT signed by, 112, 117–18; Ostpolitik policy, 118; Pakistan, nuclear assistance to, 184–85, 190–91; rearmament, 23, 63, 74, 86, 96n9; tank sales to Israel, 156; US assistance with nuclear weaponry, 104; US military presence in on permanent basis, 109
Giscard d'Estaing, Valéry, 119, 185–86
Global War on Terrorism (GWoT), 213
Goldberg, Arthur, 162
Gold Standard, 253
Gomberg, Henry, 139
Gordon, Phillip, 115
Greece, *17*
Grossman, Marc, 219
Groves, Leslie, 42, 44, 46–47, 49, 78
Gulf War, 166, 178n56

Haass, Richard, 207
Harman, Avraham, 140–41
Harmel, Pierre, 112
Harmel Doctrine, 112
Hatf-1 and Hatf-2 missiles (Pakistan), 195
Healey, Denis, 78
Helms, Richard, 159
Hersh, Seymour, 168, 208
Herter, Christian, 95, 140
Hickenlooper, Bourke, 58, 61
highly enriched uranium (HEU), 116, 173, 194, 224
history, 2–3; applied history, 6–7; lessons of, 9–25; role of, 6–8
Hod, Mordechai, 162
Holbrooke, Richard, 219
Holifield Report, 97n31
Holocaust, 133, 136
Hopkins, Harry, 43
Hummel, Arthur, 189, 191
Hussein, Saddam, 21, 116, 166, 178n56, 224–25
Hyde Park Aide Memoire, 45, 56
Hymans, Jacques, 86, 166

Imperial Chemical Industries (ICI), 39, 42
India: and arms control proposals, 191; nuclear test (1974), 184–85; nuclear tests (1998), 209; Operation Brass Tacks, 206–7; Operation Parakram (Valor), 213
Indian subcontinent, nuclear arms race on, 205–6
Indo-Pakistani-Chinese nuclear triangle, 250
Indo-Pakistani crises, 30; Kargil Crisis (1998–1999), 25, 206, 209–12, 231n33; Kashmir border crisis (1990), 25, 206–9; Line of Control (LOC), 210; Mumbai attacks (2008), 206, 220–22; nuclearization of, 8, 20, 25, 28–29, 198, 206, 236–37, 249; treated as major national security threats, 206; Twin Peaks Crisis (2001–2002), 206, 212–18
Indo-Pakistani crisis (1971), 183
Indo-Pakistani crisis (1990), 169, 197, 206–9
insider threats, 28, 228, 250–51
Institute of Nuclear Science (New Zealand), 170
intercontinental ballistic missiles (ICBMs), 93
intermediate-range ballistic missiles (IRBMs), 13, 71, 72, 79; Blue Streak, 76; and France, 88, 89–90
International Atomic Energy Agency (IAEA), 140, 156, 176n16, 185, 226; Additional Protocol, 246
International Security Affairs (US), 160
Iran, 116, 166; Pakistan's nuclear assistance to, 21, 223, 226; and Saudi Arabia, 28–29, 229, 249–50
Iraq, 166; France's reactor sale to, 116; Kuwait, invasion of, 116, 224, 245; Pakistan's nuclear assistance to, 224–25; Project A.B., 224; US invasion of (2003), 226–27
ISI (Pakistan's intelligence service), 213, 214, 225
Islamic State, 228
Ismay, Hastings Lionel (Lord Ismay), 85
Israel, 7, 9, 29; and Algeria, 136–37; and Camp David Accords, 165; Division of Research and Infrastructure (EMET), 136; and domino effect, 20–21; and FMCT, 19, 173; France's nuclear assistance to, 21, 115, 116, 133–34, 138, 245; HEMED (Machon 4) science division, 136; Ministry of Defense, 136; and NPT, 18–19, 28; nuclear signaling by, 167–69; and PTBT, 18; qualitative military edge (QME), 11, 134–35, 156–58; reduced US commitments in, 10–11, *11*; refusal to acknowledge nuclear weapons, 18, 134–35, 141, 153, 247; South Africa,

nuclear assistance to, 134, 166–67; and Suez crisis, 70; US military assistance to, *11,* 11–12, 153, 155–57, 246–47; US presidential pledges to, 19, 173. *See also* Dimona reactor (Israel)

Israel (1950s-1963), 133–51; Dimona reactor, 134, 135, 136d; early nuclear program, 136–38; Kennedy's involvement, 140–43; LBJ's attitude toward, 154; Sevres summit with France, 137, 138; South Africa offered nuclear missiles by, 134; US conventional weapons sales to, 135; US response to reactor, 138–40

Israel (1963–1979), 153–80; betrayal of US, 171–72; F-4 Phantom negotiations, 153, 159–64, 172; inspections requested by US, 156, 161–62; memorandum of understanding (MOU) with US, 156, 161–62; Nixon and Meir understanding, 164–65; non-introduction pledge, 156, 162–64; nonproliferation agenda, 172–73; nuclear offspring, 166–67; NUMEC affair, 171–72, 180n89; qualitative military edge (QME), 156–58; Six-Day War (1967), 153, 157–58, 160, 165, 248; South Africa, nuclear test off coast of, 135, 153, 169–72, 179n81; success of secret, 165–66; US arms sales to, 155–57; Yom Kippur War (1973), 119, 165, 167–69, 174

Israel Atomic Energy Commission (IAEC), 136

Israeli Air Force, 139

Israeli Defense Forces (IDF), 137

Italy, *17*

Jackson, Galen, 148n6

Jaish-e-Muhammad (JeM) (militant group), 213

Japan, 1, 4, 22; as counterweight to China, 26, 79–80, 121; defense budget, 242; France's nuclear assistance to, 21, 115; future scenarios, 239–45; isolationism (Sakoku), 238; Meiji Restoration, 238; nuclear reactors as potential target, 79; surrender, World War II, 37, 45; US troops in, 27–28; and World War II, 238–39

Japanese Self-Defense Forces (SDF), 26, 242

Jericho missiles (Israel), 21, 155, 167, 168

Johnson, Lyndon B.: and Feinberg, 134; and France's withdrawal from multilateral agreements, 111; handling of de Gaulle, 113; Israel, attitude toward, 153, 154–55, 161–62, 175–76n16

Johnson, Lyndon B., administration, 18, 26, 246; Flexible Response policy, 14, 26, 241; multilateral nuclear force (MLF) proposal, 84, 94

Joint Atomic Energy Intelligence Committee (JAEIC), 139

Joint Chiefs of Staff, British, 73

Joint Chiefs of Staff, US, 55–56

Joint Committee on Atomic Energy (JCAE), 3, 56, 58, 64–65, 66n28

Jones, G. Lewis, 141

Jordan, 156, 165

Jurgensen, Jean Daniel, 112

Kahuta (Sinhala) enrichment plant, 188–89, 191, 194

KANUPP reactor (Pakistan), 184

Karamat, Jehangir, 209

Kargil Crisis (1998–1999), 25, 206, 209–12, 231n33. *See also* Kashmir border crisis (1990)

Karpin, Michael, 133, 138, 157, 161

Kashmir border crisis (1990), 25, 206–9. *See also* Kargil Crisis (1998–1999)

Katzir, Ephraim, 168

Kennedy, John F., 1, 5, 15, 102, 120; assassination of, 147, 153; background, 101–2; and Cuban Missile Crisis, 77, 108, 117, 136, 142; and Feinberg, 134; Germany, view of, 23, 85; last year spent on reducing nuclear dangers, 143–47; national security action memorandum (NSAM), 144, 145; opposition to proliferation, 102; Polaris missile proposal, 108–9; stabilizing of German question, 109–10

Kennedy, John F., administration, 26, 38; Bay of Pigs fiasco, 102; and Berlin Crisis of 1958–1962, 84; Flexible Response policy, 14, 26, 105, 240, 241; France, hard line on, 15, 101, 107; multilateral nuclear force (MLF) proposal, 84, 94, 107–9, 112, 125n33; and Skybolt program, 73, 76–77

Kerr, Richard, 208

Khan, A. Q. (Abdul Qadeer), 30, 182, 186–95, 197; forced confession on television, 227; and nuclear assistance to US enemies, 222–27; and PAEC, 194–95

Khan, Ayub, 183

Khan, Feroz, 195

Khan, Ghulam Ishaq, 197

Khan, Munir Ahmad, 183–84, 223

Khan, Sahabzada Yaqub, 197

Khan Research Laboratories (KRL), 194, 202n67, 224, 227. *See also* Kahuta (Sinhala) enrichment plant

Khashoggi, Jamal, 247

Khrushchev, Nikita, 93, 103–4, 109, 122n6

Kill Chain doctrine, 26

Kim Jong-il, 224

Kim Jong-Un, 26, 241

King, Mackenzie, 46

Kissinger, Henry, 7, 14, 23; and France, 117–18; France's nuclear cooperation sought by, 85; independent arsenals, view of, 117, 128n90; on Israel's nuclear program and US security, 164

Kohl, Wilfred L., 83

Komer, Robert, 156–57, 176n16, 246

Korean War, 8, 10, 13, 60, 61

Krepinevich, Andrew, 5

Kroenig, Matthew, 115

Kuwait, Iraq's invasion of, 116, 224, 245

bin Laden, Osama, 181, 228, 250

Lashkar-e-Taiba (LeT), 25, 220–22

Lashkar-e-Taiba (militant group), 213

launch control, 12–15, 236, 240–41; and Britain, 38, 50n2, 60–61, 71, 76–79; and France, 105–6, 120–21; launch on warning, 5. *See also* Quebec Agreement (1943)

Lavoy, Peter, 3

Lawrence, Ernest, 40

lessons for future cases, 25–29, 235, 237–51; allies, 25–27, 238–45; partner nations, 27–29, 245–51

LeT and JeM (Pakistani proxy groups), 25

Libya, Pakistan's nuclear assistance to, 225–27

Lilienthal, David, 56, 58

Limited Test Ban Treaty (LTBT), 109–10, 143, 146

Lind, Jennifer, 4–5

Lindemann, Frederick (Lord Cherwell), 41, 51n15

Locke, Allen, 199n24

London Conference (1954), 86

Lovett, Robert A., 57

M-11 missiles (China), 195

Maclean, Donald, 59

Macmillan, Harold, 70, 71, 77–78, 102

Malaysia, centrifuge factory, 226, 227

Malik, Zahid, 224

Manhattan Project, 37, 44, 45, 59

Mao Zedong, 110

MAUD Committee report (Britain), 39–40, 50
May, Ernest R., 6, 7
McCone, John, 106
McMahon, Brien, 48–49, 66n28
McMahon Act (Atomic Energy Act of 1946), 38, 48–49; amendments to, 71–73, 91, 95; Eisenhower's attempt to seek changes, 62–63, 94; restrictions in, 62–63, 89, 94, 119
McNamara, Robert, 14, 26, 77, 105–6, 122n15, 240
Meir, Golda, 138, 142, 153; Nixon, understanding with, 164–65; and Yom Kippur War, 167–68
Memorandum of Intention (Britain and US), 5658
Mendès France, Pierre, 85–88
Middle East, 29; Britain's foreign policy in, 24; European opposition to US policy, 119; lack of US success in, 228, 248–49. *See also* Egypt; Iran; Iraq; Israel; Saudi Arabia
MiG planes (Egypt), 248
Military Liaison Committee, 59
Mirage IV aircraft (France), 25, 87, 94, 110, 125n39, 126n55
Mirage planes (France), 25
Modi, Narendra, 222
Modus Vivendi (1948), 55–58, 60, 76
Mollet, Guy, 87, 88, 97n26, 137, 138
Monnet, Jean, 87
Moon Jae-in, 26, 121, 241
Morrison, Herbert, 61
Mossad (Israel), 226
Mukherjee, Pranab, 220
multilateral nuclear force (MLF), 84, 85, 87, 94, 107–9, 112, 125n33, 125n37
multiple independently targetable reentry vehicles (MIRVs), 120
Mumbai attacks (2008), 206, 220–22
Musharraf, Pervez, 209–12, 214–15; and A. Q. Khan, 225, 227; and Twin Peaks crisis, 216–18

Mutual Defense Assistance Agreement (US-Saudi Arabia), 245
mutually assured destruction, 74, 249
Mystère fighter jets (France), 137

Nassau Agreement (1962), 15, 29, 77, 108
Nassau Conference (1962), 78
Nasser, Gamal Abdel, 24, 70, 136–37, 147, 155, 157
National Academy of Sciences, 40
National Intelligence Estimate (NIE) (US), 88, 140
National Security Council, 59, 63; and Mumbai attacks, 221; and Pakistan, 207, 210, 212, 219, 226
Naval Research Laboratory (NRL), 170
Naval War College, 209
Ne'eman, Yuval, 159
Negev (location of Dimona reactor), 136, 138–39
Netanyahu, Benjamin, 19, 173
Netherlands, 186–87
Neustadt, Richard E., 6, 7
New Look strategy, 63, 73, 74, 79
New York Times, 191, 215
New Zealand, 170
Nitze, Paul, 106
Nixon, Richard, 14, 23; and F-4 Phantom request, 160; France's nuclear cooperation sought by, 85; Meir, understanding with, 164–65; resignation, 119
Nixon, Richard, administration: and French nuclear program, 85, 101, 117–19; and nuclear signaling by Israel, 168–69
NoDong ballistic missile (Ghauni, North Korea), 223–24
nonproliferation: and Israel, 18–19, 28; trumped by geopolitics, 21–23; and West Germany, 109–10. *See also* allied proliferation; Nuclear Non-Proliferation Treaty (NPT)

North Atlantic Treaty Organization
  (NATO), 13–14, 23, 32–33n32; and
  British arsenal, 77–78; conventional
  forces reduced, 74–76; dual key
  system proposal, 89, 97n31;
  first heads of state summit, 89;
  and France, 24–25, 27, 83–86;
  France's military withdrawal and
  independence from, 83–84, 92,
  110–13, 121, 236, 242–44; MC
  48 strategy, 89; Mediterranean
  Command, 110; nuclearization
  of, 87–88, 104; Nuclear Planning
  Group, 112; Supreme Allied
  Commander Europe (SACEUR),
  62, 72, 89–90, 91, 114; and US-UK
  atomic cooperation, 72; and "Year of
  Europe" (1973), 119
North Korea, 4, 79, 226, 239; Pakistan's
  nuclear assistance to, 223–24;
  Trump's threats to attack, 25–26
Nuclear Materials and Equipment
  Corporation (NUMEC) affair, 171–
  72, 180n89
Nuclear Non-Proliferation Treaty
  (NPT), 7, 78, 112; future scenarios,
  252; and Germany, 112, 117–18;
  Israel's refusal to sign, 18–19, 135,
  159, 165, 172–73, 252; and partner
  nations, 27–28
nuclear offspring, 236, 245, 251;
  France, 21, 115–16, 122; Israel,
  166–67; Pakistan, 222–27
Nuclear Suppliers Group (NSG), 187,
  199n24, 251
Nye, Joseph, 191

Oakley, Robert, 208
Obama, Barack, administration, 21,
  205, 249; AfPak review, 218–19; and
  Mumbai attacks, 221
Office of Scientific Research and
  Development (US), 40
Oliphant, Mark, 39, 40
Oppenheimer, Robert, 40

optimists, 2, 4–5, 12, 20, 30n6, 84, 206,
  218, 235, 237, 246
Oren, Michael, 157
organizational theory, 3–4
Osiris reactor (France), 116

Packard, David, 164
Pakistan, 7, 9, 29–30, 135, 236; and
  Afghanistan, 12, 19, 182; East
  Pakistan, loss of, 186; enrichment
  facilities, 23; France's nuclear
  assistance to, 21, 115; freedom of
  action, 25; future scenarios, 246;
  India, current situation with, 181;
  ISI (intelligence service), 213, 214,
  225; as partner nation, 19–20; refusal
  to sign NPT, 174; Saudi Arabia,
  similarities with, 28–29; as terrorist
  safe haven, 28, 30, 181, 208, 213,
  214–15, 228, 250; US impossibility
  of proving nuclear status, 12, 181,
  196–98, 208, 218; US military
  assistance to, 11–12, *13*, 185, 189–
  90, 193–95, 218, 246–47. *See also*
  Indo-Pakistani crises
Pakistan (1973–1990), 181–213;
  Canadian nuclear assistance to, 184–
  86; cold tests, 194–95; decision on
  the bomb, 182–84; denial of nuclear
  capabilities, 195–96; German nuclear
  assistance to, 184–85, 190–91;
  Kahuta (Sinhala) enrichment plant,
  188–89, 191, 194; plutonium route
  to the bomb, 182; Project 706, 188;
  Punjabi-Bengali conflict, 182–83;
  race to the bomb, 194–95; and
  Reagan, 192–93; Western discovery
  of nuclear program, 188–92
Pakistan (1990-present), 205–34; and
  Afghanistan, 216–20; insurgent
  camps at border, 207; Kargil Crisis
  (1998–1999), 25, 206, 209–12,
  231n33; Kashmir border crisis
  (1990), 25, 206–9; military exercises,
  207; and Mumbai attacks (2008),

206, 220–22; nuclear offspring, 222–27, 251; nuclear tests, 209, 215, 225; proliferation of nuclear technology to US enemies, 205, 206, 222–27, 236; short-range ballistic missiles, 213–14; Twin Peaks Crisis (2001–2002), 206, 212–18; US withdrawal of support, 208
Pakistan Atomic Energy Commission (PAEC), 184, 187; Directorate of Technical Development (DTD), 194; Inspectorate General of Special Development Works (SDW), 194
Palestine, 133, 144
Paris Conference (1954), 86
Partial Test Ban Treaty (PTBT), 18, 170, 172, 194
partner nations, 7, 12, 30; achieving overseas objectives with, 18–20; lessons for future cases, 27–29, 245–51. *See also* Israel; Pakistan
Peierls, Rudolf, 39–40
Peres, Shimon, 136–38, 144, 150n59, 155
Perrin, Michael, 39, 41
pessimists, 2–3, 5, 20–21, 24, 30n6, 236–37
Petraeus, David, 219
Piekney, William, 190
Pineau, Christian, 88–89
Polaris submarine-launched ballistic missile (US), 77–79, 94, 108–9
Pompidou, Georges, 117, 118, 119, 126n55
Pontecorvo, Bruno, 59
Powell, Colin, 214, 215–16
Prat, Mannes, 142, 143
precision-guided missiles, 79, 122
Press, Daryl, 4–5
Press, Frank, 170
Pressler Amendment (US), 196–97, 225–26
Prince Edward Islands, 168–70
Prithvi missiles (India), 213–14
Project A.B. (Iraq), 224

proxy wars, 28–29, 182, 198, 229, 236, 249–50
Pulwama terrorist attack (2019), 222

qualitative military edge (QME), 11, 134–35, 156–58
Quandt, William, 168
Quebec Agreement (1943), 43–49; veto clause, 46, 50n2, 56–57, 240
Quebec Conference (1943), 43, 76

Rabin, Yitzhak, 160–64
Radford, Arthur W., 88
radicalization, concerns about, 28, 205, 227, 250, 251
Reagan, Ronald, administration, 10, 19, 192–93; and Pakistan, 189, 190, 192, 195–97, 247
Reid, Ogden, 140
relativists, 2–5, 9, 21, 237
"restricted data," 48
Rice, Condoleezza, 19, 213, 217
Richardson, Elliot, 172
Riedel, Bruce, 210, 211, 219, 231n33
Riker, William. H., 3
Roosevelt, Franklin D., 40, 240; Britain, secret agreement with, 37–38; death of, 45; and full exchange of information, 43–45; and Hyde Park Aide Memoire, 45
Rose, Francois de, 95, 114
Rowen, Henry, 155
Ruina, Jack, 170, 171
Ruina panel, 170–71
Rumsfeld, Donald, 213
Rusk, Dean, 24–25, 56, 102, 107, 125nn37,38, 147; and France's withdrawal from multilateral agreements, 111; on inspection of Israel's reactors, 154–55; Israel, concern about, 141, 175n16; and Polaris missile proposal, 108–9

Saclay Nuclear Research Center (France), 85

Sadat, Anwar, 168–69
Sagan, Scott, 3–4
Saint-Gobain Nuclear Company, 85
Saint-Gobain Techniques Nouvelles (SGN), 184
bin Salman, Mohammed (MBS), 246
Samore, Gary, 21, 192, 223
Sandia, 170
Sandys, Duncan, 73, 75
Sarfraz, Muhammad, 194
Saudi Arabia, 2, 174, 224; Buraimi, occupation of, 24; future scenarios, 245–51; internal security, concerns about, 28–29; and Iran, 28–29, 229, 249–50; as major non-NATO ally, 7, 245; Mutual Defense Assistance Agreement with US, 245; oil facility, 248; Pakistan, similarities with, 28–29; royal family, 228–29, 250–51; US conventional weapons sales to, 246; US troops in, 245–46; Wahhabism, 228, 250; Yemen, war in, 247
Schaffer, Teresita, 12, 185, 197, 209
Scheel, Walter, 119
second-strike nuclear capability, 3, 105
Senkaku Islands, 239
sensitive nuclear assistance, 115–16
Shahi, Agha, 192, 201n52
Sharif, Nawaz, 209–12, 235
Shavitt II rocket (Israel), 143
Shultz, George, 195
Sinai Peninsula, 137
Singh, Manmohan, 221, 222
Singh, V. P., 207
Six-Day War (1967), 153, 157–58, 160, 165, 248; *USS Liberty* attacked, 161
Skybolt air-launched ballistic missile program, 73, 76–77
Slessor, John, 60–61
Smith, Cyril, 58
Smith, David, 214
Smith, Gerard, 191–92, 201n52
Socotra Rock, 239
Solarz, Stephen, 208

Solarz Amendment (1985, US), 196
Sonneborn Institute, 133
South Africa, 32n25; Israel's nuclear assistance to, 21, 134, 166–67; Israel's nuclear test off coast of, 135, 153, 169–72, 179n81; raw materials from, 57; uranium sales to Israel, 169
South Asia, 12; as most dangerous nuclear flashpoint, 222. *See also* India; Pakistan
South Korea, 1, 4–5, 116; defense budget, 242; future scenarios, 239–45; ground forces, 27, 121; Kill Chain doctrine, 26; launch control, 240; nuclear offspring, 245, 251; nuclear reactors as potential target, 79; and Trump presidency, 25–26, 241
Soviet Union, 23–25; Afghanistan, invasion of, 10, 24, 30, 172, 182, 189–90, 197–98; Afghanistan, withdrawal from, 196, 223; after Camp David Accords, 165; anti-ballistic missile systems, 119; and Berlin Crisis of 1958–1962, 84, 93, 102–4, 109; Britain as possible target for, 13–14, 59; conventional superiority, 63; de Gaulle's visit to, 113; and France, 25; Germany, plans to separate from West, 104; independent arsenals thought to be deterrent to, 117; and international communist movement, 103; and Israel's nuclear program, 134, 141; multilateral alliance, views of, 108, 122n23; multiple independently targetable reentry vehicles (MIRVs), 120; nuclear parity, 117; nuclear test (1949), 62; and Reagan, 192–93; SALT II talks, 169, 172; Sputnik Moment, 38, 69, 71–72, 89; and Suez crisis, 70
Special Weapons Command (French Army), 86
Sputnik Moment, 38, 69, 71–72, 89

spy scandals (1950), 55, 59–60
Staebler, Ulysses M., 141–42
State Department: and France, 90–91, 93–94, 102–3, 111–12, 126n52; and Israel, 140, 143–44, 157, 160, 170; and MLF, 108; and Mumbai attacks, 220; and Pakistan, 189, 200n40, 207–9, 212–17, 215
Stimson, Henry, 42, 44
Strategic Arms Limitation Talks Treaty (SALT II), 169, 172
Strauss, Franz Josef, 104
Strauss, Lewis, 58, 64, 70, 73
Straw, Jack, 216
submarines: anti-submarine warfare (ASW), 80; nuclear propulsion technology, 64, 65; South Korean, 242; submarine-launched ballistic missiles, 77, 110
Suez Crisis (1956), 24, 38, 69, 70–71, 87–88; France, Britain, and Israel's operation, 70, 116, 133, 137–38; Suez Canal, Nasser's nationalization of, 70, 137; US kept in dark about, 137–38
Supreme Allied Commander Europe (SACEUR), 62, 72, 89–90, 91, 114
Supreme Headquarters Allied Powers Europe (SHAPE), 113
Symington Amendment (US), 191, 193, 196
Syria, 248

Taiwan, 1, 115, 116, 239, 242, 245
Tal, Yisrael, 167
Talbott, Strobe, 209, 231n33
technology transfers, 9, 115–16
Teller, Edward, 159
Tellis, Ashley, 215
Tenet, George, 5, 227
terrorism, 6, 250–51; Pakistan as terrorist safe haven, 28, 30, 181, 208, 213, 214–15, 228, 250
Tertrais, Bruno, 113
Thomas, Abel, 136, 137

thorium, 44
Thor missiles (US), 71, 72
Tillerson, Rex, 5
Tinner, Friedrich, 225
Tinner, Urs, 225–26
Tolkowsky, Dan, 139
Trachtenberg, Marc, 92, 99n70, 103, 108
treaty allies, 9, 12, 121, 238
triggers list, 187, 199n24
tritium, 21
Truman, Harry, 13, 78; and Feinberg, 134; Korean War nuclear weapons statement, 60, 61; reelection, (1948), 59
Truman, Harry, administration, 38, 45–50; hydrogen bomb program (1950), 62
Trump, Donald, 4, 5, 25–26, 241, 249
Trump, Donald, administration, 246
Tube Alloys (British atomic weapons program code name), 39
Tucker, Robert W., 31n14
Turkey, 2, *17*, 18, 34n59, 79, 121
Twin Peaks Crisis (2001–2002), 206, 212–18

Ulbricht, Walter, 103
Ullman, Richard H., 120
Ultra-Centrifuge Nederland (UCN), 186
United Nations, 227; Charter, Article 102, 47; and Suez crisis, 70
United States: access to allied countries, 27–28; achieving overseas objectives: allies, 12–17; achieving overseas objectives: partners, 18–20; Afghanistan, war in, 206, 216–17, 232n53; atomic program (1942), 39; Atoms for Peace program, 183, 184, 187; basing, 12–13, 242–44; conventional forces reduced in 1960s, 105; conventional military spending, 15–17, *17*; enemies of, nuclear technology proliferated to, 205, 206, 222–27,

236; France, withdrawal of troops from, 25, 83, 110–11, 113; Glenn Amendment, 193; Global War on Terrorism (GWoT), 213; increased commitments, 10–11, 84, 246–47; Indo-Pacific forces, 28; intelligence community (IC), 138–39, 144–45; Israel, military assistance to, *11*, 11–12, 153, 155–57; nonproliferation agenda, 172–74; Pakistan, military assistance to, 11–12, *13*, 185, 189–90, 193–95, 218; plans to control all design and construction information, 42, 51n16; possibility of being asked to withdraw troops, 27, 34n59, 83, 243; presidential elections, effect on foreign policy, 160; Pressler Amendment (US), 196–97; racism as factor in worries of, 208–9; raw materials, demand for, 46, 49–50, 56, 70–71, 78; reducing commitments of, 9–12, *10, 11,* 246–47; refusal to acknowledge Israel's nuclear weapons, 18, 134–35, 141, 153, 247; Solarz Amendment (1985), 196; Symington Amendment, 191, 193, 196; uranium in, 62; US-UK atomic relations, 22, 29

uranium: Combined Development Trust designed to secure, 44–45; highly enriched uranium (HEU), 116, 173, 194, 224; and Memorandum of Intention, 46, 49; in United States, 62

URENCO (European enrichment consortium), 186–87, 199n13

USAID Greenbook, 218

US Central Command (CENTCOM), 211

US-Israel Joint Political Military Group, 11

USS Liberty, Israeli attack on, 161

US–UK Mutual Defense Agreement (1958), 70

Vajpayee, Atal Bih209ari, 210, 213
Valluy, Jean Etienne, 88
Vance, Cyrus, 191–92
Vandenberg, Arthur, 58
Van Doren, Charles, 191
Vanunu, Mordechai, 142
V bombers (British), 34n56, 73, 76
Vela satellite (US), 169–72, 179n81
Vietnam War, 23, 128n91
Wah Group (Pakistan), 194
Wahhabism, 228, 250
Walt, Stephen, 4, 23, 31n14
Walters, Vernon, 195
Waltz, Kenneth, 3
Warnke, Paul, 160–64
War of Independence (Israel and Palestine, 1947–1949), 133
Warsaw Pact, 112
Webster, William, 59
Weinbaum, Marvin, 216
Weiss, Leonard, 170, 179n81
Wohlstetter, Albert, 3
Wolfowitz, Paul, 208
World War II, 13, 22, 29; Japan in, 238–39; US-British cooperation during, 37–45, *39. See also* Britain, US-British atomic collaboration (1939–1946)

Yaron, Anselm, 170
"Year of Europe" (1973), 119
yellowcake, 2
Yemen, 247
Yom Kippur War (1973), 119, 165, 167–69, 174
Young, Ken, 77

Zardari, Asif Ali, 220
Zia-ul-Haq, Muhammad, 189, 191, 194, 195, 201n53, 223
Zinni, Anthony, 211

About the Author

Zachary Keck has worked on nuclear weapons and national security issues in the US government, think tanks, and media. He has been a professional staff member on the House Foreign Affairs Committee in the US Congress, including on the Subcommittee for Nonproliferation. Before that, Zach was a research fellow at the Nonproliferation Policy Education Center and a researcher at the Belfer Center for Science and International Affairs in the Harvard Kennedy School. Zach began his career in the media industry, working as the Managing Editor of *The Diplomat* and, later, in the same role at *The National Interest*.

Zach has published around a thousand articles on US foreign policy and defense issues for numerous outlets, including *The Wall Street Journal*, *The Atlantic*, CNN.com, *Foreign Affairs*, *Foreign Policy*, *The Hill*, and *The Bulletin of Atomic Scientists*. He has been widely quoted and cited in the media, including by *The New York Times, Washington Post, Reuters, The Financial Times, USA Today, The Wall Street Journal*, BBC, Vox, Yahoo!

News, and *Bloomberg News*. He has written four Pentagon-commissioned studies on nuclear weapons.

Zach has done fellowships with the Atlantic Council, the Wilson Center, the Center for Strategic and Budgetary Assessments, and the East-West Center. He is a member of Foreign Policy 4 America's Next Gen Program. Zach has a BA in political science from SUNY New Paltz and an MA in political science from George Mason University. He lives in Washington, DC, and can be found on Twitter: @ZacharyKeck.

The views in this book are his own and do not necessarily represent the views of any company or any organization in the US government.

www.ingramcontent.com/pod-product-compliance
Lightning Source LLC
Chambersburg PA
CBHW031546300426
44111CB00006BA/198